FROMMER'S
EasyGuide
TO
WASHINGTON, D.C.

By
Elise Hartman Ford

EasyGuides are ✦ Quick To Read ✦ Light To Carry
✦ For Expert Advice ✦ In All Price Ranges

FrommerMedia LLC

Published by
FROMMERMEDIA LLC

ISBN 978-1-62887-016-9 (paper),978-1-62887-045-9 (ebk)

Editorial Director: Pauline Frommer
Editor: Pauline Frommer
Production Editor: Lindsay Conner
Cartographer: Roberta Stockwell
Cover Design: Howard Grossman
Editorial Interns: Christiana Mecca and H. Eki Ramadhan

For information on our other products or services, see www.frommers.com.

FrommerMedia LLC also publishes its books in a variety of electronic formats. Some content that appears in print may not be available in electronic formats.

Manufactured in the United States of America

5 4 3 2 1

CONTENTS

ABOUT THE AUTHOR

Washington, D.C.-based freelance writer **Elise Hartman Ford** has written for *The Washington Post*, *Washingtonian* magazine, *Ladies Home Journal*, *National Parks* magazine, the travel website Home & Abroad, and countless other national, regional, trade, and online publications. Ford is the author of several other guidebooks in addition to this one, and the author as well of the bestselling travel app, Washington, DC ★ A to Z, published by Sutro Media.

ABOUT THE FROMMER TRAVEL GUIDES

For most of the past 50 years, Frommer's has been the leading series of travel guides in North America, accounting for as many as 24% of all guidebooks sold. I think I know why.

Though we hope our books are entertaining, we nevertheless deal with travel in a serious fashion. Our guidebooks have never looked on such journeys as a mere recreation, but as a far more important human function, a time of learning and introspection, an essential part of a civilized life. We stress the culture, lifestyle, history and beliefs of the destinations we cover, and urge our readers to seek out people and new ideas as the chief rewards of travel.

We have never shied from controversy. We have, from the beginning, encouraged our authors to be intensely judgmental, critical—both pro and con—in their comments, and wholly independent. Our only clients are our readers, and we have triggered the ire of countless prominent sorts, from a tourist newspaper we called "practically worthless" (it unsuccessfully sued us) to the many rip-offs we've condemned.

And because we believe that travel should be available to everyone regardless of their incomes, we have always been cost-conscious at every level of expenditure. Though we have broadened our recommendations beyond the budget category, we insist that every lodging we include be sensibly priced. We use every form of media to assist our readers, and are particularly proud of our feisty daily website, the award-winning Frommers.com.

I have high hopes for the future of Frommer's. May these guidebooks, in all the years ahead, continue to reflect the joy of travel and the freedom that travel represents. May they always pursue a cost-conscious path, so that people of all incomes can enjoy the rewards of travel. And may they create, for both the traveler and the persons among whom we travel, a community of friends, where all human beings live in harmony and peace.

Arthur Frommer

THE BEST OF WASHINGTON, D.C.

The sun has come up, dappling the surface of the Potomac. It warms the front plaza of the Supreme Court Building, where visitors stand in line awaiting their chance to attend an oral argument. Sunlight splays across the National Mall and pours through the south-facing windows of the Oval Office, where the President works away at the problems of the day. Commuters of all sorts, from diplomats to nonprofit wonks to corporate execs to shopkeepers, spill from cars and buses and Metro stations onto sunlit downtown streets armed with briefcases, coffee cups, PDAs, and newspapers. They rub elbows from sunup to sundown, in the halls of Congress, in Penn Quarter restaurants, in Georgetown shops, in bars along 14th Street. The city bustles. Bustle with it. It's a beautiful day.

Each day dawns anew in this "city of magnificent intentions," as Charles Dickens once called it. Maybe this will be the day that Republican and Democratic legislators hammer out a deal on the debt ceiling or that President Obama welcomes world leaders to the White House for a Middle East summit. Or maybe today's the day that you fulfill your own intentions, sublime or otherwise, of setting eyes on the original Declaration of Independence, perhaps, or tasting something called a "half-smoke," or listening to a jazz concert in the same place where Duke Ellington once performed. Things happen here that can happen nowhere else on earth. You're in America's capital, and this city and this day belong to you. Best get crackin'!

THE most unforgettable WASHINGTON, D.C., EXPERIENCES

- **Watching the Supreme Court in Action:** Behind the stately marble facade of the Supreme Court Building, the nation's nine black-gowned justices reveal their intellectual brilliance and individual personalities as they listen to and question both sides of an argument. Will the famously silent Justice Thomas talk today? Is the notably aggressive Justice Scalia really so blunt? Only one way to find out: Wait in line for entry and a coveted seat inside the Courtroom. See p. 97.

o **Viewing Washington Landmarks by Moonlight:** There is nothing as spectacular as the Lincoln Memorial illuminated at night, unless it's the sight of the White House, the Capitol, or the Washington Monument lit up after dark. Go by Old Town Trolley, by bike via a Bike and Roll excursion, or by boat aboard a Potomac Riverboat Co. cruise; all three operations offer narrated day- and nighttime tours. See p. 242.

o **Visiting Your Senator or House Representative:** If you're a U.S. citizen, take advantage of your constituent status and stop by your senator's and/or representative's office on Capitol Hill to offer your two cents on current issues. Pick up passes to the Capitol's Senate and House chambers and attend a session to observe your elected politicians at work. Make sure you've reserved Capitol tour passes online and tour the Capitol. See p. 91.

o **Bicycling Past the Potomac River and Around the Tidal Basin:** Rent a bike and cycle the paved bike/pedestrian path that extends 11 miles from the Lincoln Memorial to the Maryland border (through Rock Creek Park). Or head the other direction, following the combination of street, sidewalk, and pathway that encircles the Tidal Basin. You'll enjoy a view of the Potomac River, Rock Creek, and spectacular Washington sites on either side of you as you make your way. For a really epic ride, follow the pathway past the Lincoln Memorial, cross the Arlington Memorial Bridge to the trail on the other side, and pedal the 19 miles to Mount Vernon. See p. 241.

o **Participating in a Protest:** What causes do you believe in? I mean this sincerely. Find out if there's a gathering on the National Mall, a protest at an embassy, or some other public event that reflects your point of view, and join in! This is the capital of the United States, the world's most successful democracy, imperfect though it may be. Countless such protests take place here annually. It can be thrilling and inspiring, or really, just plain fun, to meet up with other citizens of the world and make your presence known.

THE best FAMILY EXPERIENCES

o **Hanging out at the National Zoo:** Make faces at the cute giant pandas; listen to the mighty lion's roar; laugh at the playful monkeys; watch an elephant exercise; ride the new, solar-powered carousel. The National Zoo is essentially one big (163 acres!), family-friendly park, offering the chance to observe some 2,000 animals at play (or snoozing or eating). See p. 145.

o **Ice Skating at the National Gallery:** The pool in the National Gallery of Art Sculpture Garden turns into an ice-skating rink in winter. Rent some skates and twirl around on the ice, admiring sculptures as you go. Treat yourself to hot chocolate and sandwiches at the Pavilion Café in the garden. See p. 157.

o **Paddling Your Way Around the Tidal Basin:** Rent a paddleboat for four people and skim the surface of the Tidal Basin for an hour. You'll still be sightseeing as you pedal away, in full view of the Washington Monument on the Mall, the Jefferson and the Martin Luther King, Jr. memorials bordering the Basin, and, should you be here during cherry blossom season, the blooming cherry trees encircling the Tidal Basin. See chapter 6.

○ **Riding a Roller Coaster or Piloting a Jet:** Two Smithsonian museums offer amusement-park-like rides in their simulator machines. At the National Air and Space Museum, these machines allow children to experience the feeling of being airborne in a jet or in the pilot's seat of a World War II fighter airplane. At the National Museum of American History, your simulated adventures feel real in racecar and roller coaster machines. *Note:* Height requirements and fees apply. See p. 107 and 113.

THE best FOOD

○ **Best for a Splurge:** I've got two suggestions for you, as different as night and day. Dupont Circle's **Komi** (p. 78) is a sparely appointed town-house dining room with just 12 tables. The young genius chef, Johnny Monis, sends out 15 or so little gastronomic masterpieces that often hint of Greek tastes, like the mascarpone-stuffed dates; the cost is $135 per person. The Penn Quarter's **Fiola** (p. 70) is as splashy as Komi is serene. The fare is sophisticated Italian, the décor and clientele headturning.

○ **Best for Romance:** If a trendy, sexy scene and exotic tastes appeal, consider the Penn Quarter's softly lit **Rasika** (p. 73), whose hot Indian food spices up the night

○ **Best for Families:** Beyond the usual burger (Five Guys; p. 74) and pizza (Pizzeria Paradiso; p. 79) why not introduce your kids to international cuisine at the Lebanese Taverna (see p. 85).

○ **Best for Regional Cuisine: Johnny's Half Shell** (p. 64) is the place to go for superb Eastern Shore delicacies: crab cakes, crab imperial, and soft-shell crab. While Washington doesn't have its own cuisine per se, its central location within the Mid-Atlantic/Chesapeake Bay region gives it license to lay claim to these local favorite foods. And nobody does 'em better than Johnny's.

○ **Best All-Around for Fun and Food:** Unstoppable José Andrés is behind the always-crowded **Oyamel** (p. 72), where everyone's slurping foam-topped margaritas and savoring small plates of authentic Mexican food. A few blocks away, **Central Michel Richard** (p. 69) makes everybody happy with its convivial atmosphere and chef Richard's take on French bistro and American classics, from mussels in white wine to fried chicken.

○ **Best for a "Taste of Washington" Experience:** Eat lunch at the **Monocle** (p. 65) and you're bound to see a Supreme Court justice, congressman, or senator dining here, too. For some down-home fare, sit at the counter at **Ben's Chili Bowl** (p. 76), and chat with the owners and your neighbor over a chili dog or a plate of blueberry pancakes. The place is an institution, and you can stop by anytime—it's open for breakfast, lunch, and dinner.

○ **Best for Vegetarians: Amsterdam Falafelshop** (p. 78) draws lovers of its mashed chickpea falafels and 21 possible toppings, plus the twice-cooked Dutch-style fried potatoes; **Zaytinya** (p. 73) offers a most diverse selection of sweet and savory veggie tapas, including a Brussels sprouts dish that vegetarians and carnivores alike go crazy for.

THE best THINGS TO DO FOR FREE IN WASHINGTON, D.C.

○ **Peruse the Constitution:** Only in Washington and only at the National Archives will you be able to read the original documents that grounded this nation in liberty.

Here you'll find the Declaration of Independence, the Constitution of the United States, and the Bill of Rights—all on display behind glass. See p. 109.

○ **People-Watch at Dupont Circle:** This traffic circle is also a park—an all-weather hangout for mondo-bizarre biker-couriers, chess players, street musicians, and lovers. Sit on a bench and watch scenes of Washington life unfold around you. See p. 221.

○ **Attend a Millennium Stage Performance at the Kennedy Center:** Every evening at 6pm, the Kennedy Center presents a free 1-hour concert performed by local, up-and-coming, national, or international musicians. After the performance, head through the glass doors to the terrace for a view of the Potomac River. See p. 179.

○ **Groove to the Sounds of Live Jazz in the Sculpture Garden:** On summery Friday evenings at the National Gallery of Art Sculpture Garden, you can dip your toes in the fountain pool and chill out to live jazz from 5 to 8pm. The jazz is free; the tapas, wine, and beer served in the garden's Pavilion Café are not. See p. 111.

○ **Pick a Museum, (Just About) Any Museum:** Because this is the U.S. capital, many of the museums are federal institutions, meaning admission is free. The National Gallery of Art, the U.S. Botanic Garden, and the Smithsonian's 17 Washington museums, from the National Air and Space Museum to the Freer Gallery, are among many excellent choices. See chapter 4.

○ **Attend an Event on the Mall:** Think of the National Mall as the nation's public square, where something is always going on. There's the National Book Festival in the fall, the splendid Independence Day celebration every Fourth of July, and soccer, baseball, and even cricket games year-round. See p. 35 for a calendar of annual events.

THE best NEIGHBORHOODS
FOR GETTING LOST

○ **Georgetown:** The truth is, you *want* to get lost in Georgetown because it's the neighborhood's side streets that hold the history and centuries-old houses of this one-time Colonial tobacco port. And not to worry—Georgetown is so compact that you're never very far from its main thoroughfares, M Street and Wisconsin Avenue. For a back-streets tour of Georgetown, see p. 214.

○ **Old Town Alexandria:** Just a short distance from the District (by Metro, car, boat, or bike) is George Washington's Virginia hometown. On and off the beaten track are quaint cobblestone streets, charming boutiques and antiques stores, 18th-century houses and other historic attractions, and fine restaurants. See p. 195.

○ **Dupont Circle:** Explore Dupont Circle's lovely side streets extending off Connecticut and Massachusetts avenues. You'll discover picturesque 19th-century town houses serving as homes to small art galleries, historic museums, and actual residences. Stroll Embassy Row (northward on Massachusetts Ave.) to view Beaux Arts mansions, many built by wealthy magnates during the Gilded Age.

○ **Foggy Bottom:** Take the White House walking tour (p. 207) if you like, then continue westward to mingle with George Washington University's students on its urban campus and with international employees of the World Bank and the International Monetary Fund, both headquartered here. Foggy Bottom is one of the oldest parts of the city, so you'll come across rows of 19th-century town houses; historic sites, like the building at 2017 I St. NW, where James Monroe briefly lived; and old churches, like St. Mary's Episcopal, at 728 23rd St. NW, designed by James Renwick (see the Renwick Gallery, p. 126).

THE best WAYS TO SEE WASHINGTON, D.C., LIKE A LOCAL

o **Shop at Eastern Market:** Capitol Hill is home to more than government buildings; it's a community of old town houses, antiques shops, and the venerable institution, the Eastern Market. Here locals shop and barter every Saturday and Sunday for fresh produce, baked goods, and flea-market bargains as they've done for well over a century. Trying the blueberry pancakes at the Market Lunch counter is an absolute must. See p. 169.

o **Pub and Club It in D.C.'s Hot Spots:** Join Washington's footloose and fancy-free any night of the week (but especially Thurs–Sat) along 14th Street, in Adams Morgan, and in the Penn Quarter.

o **Go for a Jog on the National Mall:** Lace up your running shoes and race down the Mall at your own pace, admiring famous sites as you go. Your fellow runners will be buff military staff from the Pentagon, speed-walking members of Congress, and downtown workers doing their best to stave off the telltale pencil pusher's paunch. It's about 2 miles from the foot of the Capitol to the Lincoln Memorial. See p. 23.

o **Attend a Hometown Game:** Depending on the season, you can take yourself out to a Washington Nationals baseball game at Nationals Ballpark, drive to FedEx Field to root for the Washington Redskins, stay in town to catch a Washington Wizards or Mystics basketball game at the Verizon Center, or take the Metro to RFK Stadium for a D.C. United soccer match. To experience the true soul of the city, attend a Washington Capitals ice hockey match at the Verizon Center; at the moment, there's no more loyal fan than a Caps fan. Wear red. See p. 189.

o **Sit at an Outdoor Cafe and Watch the Washington World Go By:** Locals watching locals. What better way to keep tabs on each other? The capital is full of seats offering front-row views of D.C. on parade. Here's a bunch: **Johnny's Half Shell** (p. 64), **Le Bon Café** (p. 68), **Montmartre** (p. 65), **Paul** (p. 80), **Central** (p. 69), **Zaytinya** (p. 73), **Cork** (p. 75), and **Martin's Tavern** (p. 82).

THE best PLACES TO STAY

o **Best Historic Hotel:** The **Willard InterContinental** celebrated its 100th anniversary in 2006 as the "new" 12-story Willard, replacing the original, smaller "City Hotel" that existed here between 1816 and 1906. Whether known as the City or the Willard, the hotel has hosted nearly every U.S. president since Franklin Pierce in 1853. President Ulysses S. Grant liked to unwind with cigar and brandy in the Willard lobby after a hard day in the Oval Office, and such literary luminaries as Mark Twain and Charles Dickens used to hang out in the Round Robin bar. See p. 47.

o **Best for Romance:** Its discreet service, intimate size, exquisitely decorated guest rooms, and the fact that you need never leave the hotel for pampering or dining makes **The Jefferson** (p. 53) perfect for romantic rendezvous. Its bar, **Quill,** has pull-the-curtain niches, perfect for private canoodling. A Spa Suite combines a guest bedroom and adjoining spa treatment room. There's fine dining in restaurant Plume and cozy spots for reading in the Book Room, where a fire crackles in the hearth.

o **Best When You Have Business on Capitol Hill:** The **George, a Kimpton Hotel** (p. 43), lies a short walk from the Capitol and offers free Wi-Fi and an excellent in-house power dining spot, **Bistro Bis**, among other business-friendly amenities.

o **Best Bang for Your Buck:** Its great Georgetown location, spacious studio and one-bedroom suites with kitchens, free Wi-Fi, and reasonable rates recommend **Georgetown Suites** (p. 59) as one of the best values in town.

o **Best Views:** The **Hay-Adams** (p. 50) has such a great, unobstructed view of the White House that the Secret Service comes over regularly to do security sweeps of the place. Ask for a room on the H Street side of the hotel, on floors six through eight.

o **Best for Families:** The **Omni Shoreham Hotel** (p. 60) is adjacent to Rock Creek Park and within walking distance of the National Zoo and Metro, and it has a large outdoor pool and kiddie pool. The neighborhood has plenty of kid-friendly eateries, including fast-food choices like McDonald's and local favorites like **Lebanese Taverna** (p. 85). Children receive a backpack upon check-in, and the concierge can provide board games and books (at no charge; just remember to return them). Parents appreciate receiving the first aid/safety kit holding outlet covers, nightlights, and a list of emergency numbers.

THE best OFF-BEAT EXPERIENCES

o **Listen to "Fiscal Shades of Gray" and "Help Me Fake It to the Right" tunes:** The Capitol Steps, a musical political satire troupe, performs these and other irreverent original tunes in skits that skewer politicians on both sides of the aisle. You can see them every weekend at the Ronald Reagan Building. See p. 188.

o **Dare to Dine at a Drag Brunch:** Sassy drag queens dressed to the hilt sashay around the room, lip-synching to the DJ's tunes and entertaining all who've turned up for the all-you-can-eat $23.95 buffet at **Perry's Drag Brunch,** 1811 Columbia Rd. NW (www.perrysadamsmorgan.com; ℂ **202/234-6218**), held every Sunday 10am to 3pm. The brunch is a Washington institution: Everyone comes to this Adams Morgan hot spot at some point, so expect to see partiers burning the candle at both ends and straight-laced types likely heading to the office after the show, even though it's Sunday.

o **Explore Washington from an Unconventional Angle:** Yes, it's a graveyard, but Oak Hill Cemetery is also a beautiful wooded and landscaped garden with a grand view of the city from its hillside perch. Here lie monuments and resting places for some of Washington's most illustrious residents, from the city's early days as well as recent years. See p. 219.

o **Play Street Hockey in Front of the White House:** Pennsylvania Avenue in front of the White House is closed to traffic, which makes it a perfect place for street hockey fanatics to show up Saturdays and Sundays at noon for pickup games. All you need are skates and a stick.

SUGGESTED ITINERARIES & NEIGHBORHOODS

Ask 10 Washingtonians for their sightseeing hit lists and you'll get 10 different answers. There's so much to see here, and everyone has her own way of seeing it. But we can make some suggestions. This chapter lays out a key itinerary for a 3-day tour of the capital's iconic sites, plus two themed itineraries: one devoted to family activities, the other to exploring women's history. Follow them to the letter or adapt them for your own purposes—it's up to you.

If you're the type of traveler who doesn't like surprises, call ahead and make sure all of the attractions on your desired itinerary are open. Be calm and flexible: Lines to enter public buildings are longer than ever, thanks to security clearance procedures and the capital's continuing popularity as a tourist destination. Reserve spots on tours to avoid some of those waits, and book advance reservations at recommended restaurants to make sure you get a table. Most importantly, don't be afraid to ask questions. The police on Capitol Hill, the National Park Service rangers on duty at the memorials, and the staff at all the museums know an awful lot; take advantage of their expertise.

Following the itineraries is an overview of D.C.'s neighborhoods. Among the most enjoyable activities in D.C. is exploring its neighborhoods on foot, so if you tire of crowded museums and of following a structured itinerary, choose a neighborhood that appeals to you and simply stroll. See chapter 10 for walking tours of a few standout neighborhoods.

ICONIC WASHINGTON, D.C.

If you have limited time in Washington, D.C., and would like to have a full-fun experience of several landmark attractions (rather than a rushed experience of many), then this is the itinerary for you. *Start: Metro on the Blue Line to the Smithsonian stop on the National Mall.*

1 Washington Monument ★★★

People often ask: Which is taller, the Washington Monument or the Capitol? The answer is the Washington Monument. Panoramic views stretch for miles (60 miles on a clear day!) from inside the Monument's observation tower. Order free tickets in advance or be prepared to stand in line for admission. And if the monument isn't open? Then stand back and consider the fact that this 555⅛-foot-

Iconic Washington, D.C.

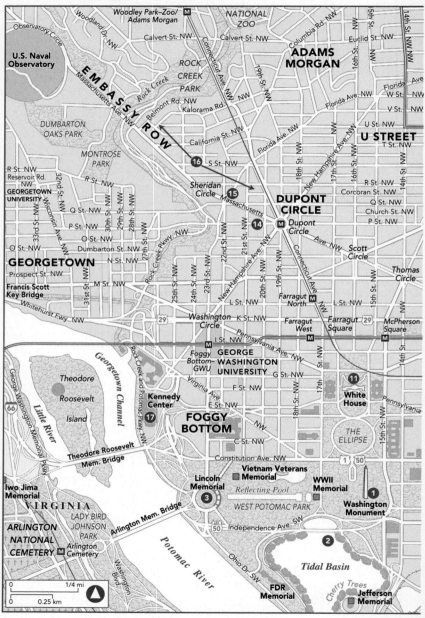

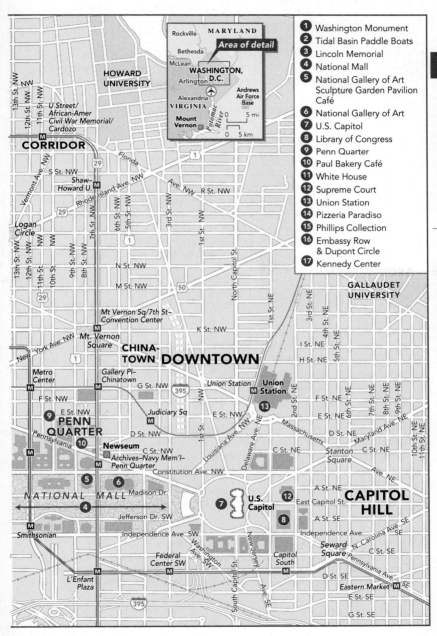

① Washington Monument
② Tidal Basin Paddle Boats
③ Lincoln Memorial
④ National Mall
⑤ National Gallery of Art Sculpture Garden Pavilion Café
⑥ National Gallery of Art
⑦ U.S. Capitol
⑧ Library of Congress
⑨ Penn Quarter
⑩ Paul Bakery Café
⑪ White House
⑫ Supreme Court
⑬ Union Station
⑭ Pizzeria Paradiso
⑮ Phillips Collection
⑯ Embassy Row & Dupont Circle
⑰ Kennedy Center

high obelisk, D.C.'s version of a skyscraper, is one of the world's tallest free-standing works of masonry. See p. 120.

Walk up 15th St. and cross Independence Avenue to get to the:

2 Tidal Basin Paddle Boats ★

Rent a paddle boat for an hour and skim the surface of the Tidal Basin, sightseeing as you go: Jefferson looks on from his memorial at one end, Martin Luther King presides from the other side of the basin, and the Washington Monument stands tall over all. See p. 159. If the weather isn't permitting or boat season (mid-March to mid-October) is over, continue on to your next stop.

Return to and cross Independence Avenue and follow it west until you reach the:

3 Lincoln Memorial ★★★

There is joy to be had in visiting this templelike memorial to contemplate the inspiring life and spirit of the nation's 16th president. Citizens of the world surround you, reading aloud the words inscribed on its walls: "Four score and seven years ago our fathers brought forth on this continent, a new nation, conceived in liberty and dedicated to the proposition that all men are created equal…" Stand at the top of the memorial's steps and face away from Lincoln to take in the sweeping view, from the Reflecting Pool below you, all the way to the Capitol nearly 2 miles away. In the middle distance is the National Mall and that's where you're headed next. See p. 106.

Follow the path that parallels the Reflecting Pool, continuing past the National World War II Memorial and the Washington Monument, until you cross 15th Street to reach the:

4 National Mall ★★★

Stroll the green promenade or sit upon a bench and watch the Washington world go by: fitness buffs with buzz cuts sprinting back to the Pentagon, office workers playing hooky, and tourists like yourself, enjoying the view. Keep your eyes peeled for your senator or representative trotting past you; a number of congressional members are known to take their daily constitutional along this stretch. See p. 99. Once you've had a chance to catch your breath, it's time to hit the museums. What interests you? Native American culture? Aviation? African art? Avant garde art? The natural world? The Smithsonians flanking the Mall cover these and other subjects. If you have time or energy for only one Mall museum, the one I'd recommend isn't a Smithsonian at all. But wait, aren't you starving?

Proceed eastward down the Mall in the direction of the Capitol until you reach 7th Street and the:

5 Pavilion Café at the National Gallery Sculpture Garden ☕

Order an Italian hoagie or a Mediterranean salad and maybe some sangria, and try to snag a seat at one of the outside tables, in pleasant weather, so you can take in the sights. Be sure to wander through the entire garden to admire all 18 sculptures. (☏ 202/289-3360. See p. 111.

Now cross 7th Street to enter the:

6 National Gallery of Art ★★★

Yes, I do believe this to be the capital's best museum, despite the fact that it is not part of the Smithsonian family. The East Wing is closed for renovations, which means you can focus on the West Wing's galleries of European paintings and sculptures spanning the 13th to 19th centuries. Don't leave without checking out the gallery's special exhibits, which are always amazing, like the Degas/Cassatt show, on view May 11 to Oct. 5, 2014. See p. 110. If you're here on a Friday night in summer, return to the Sculpture Garden to enjoy a jazz concert and tasty café items. If you're here in winter, return to the Sculpture Garden to go ice skating. And if you're here on a Sunday evening October through June, attend a classical music concert in the Gallery's Garden Court.

ICONIC WASHINGTON, D.C., IN 2 DAYS

With a second day added on, you can get to Capitol Hill's capital attractions, tour the Penn Quarter neighborhood, and cap off the day with a presidential flourish. *Start: Metro on the Blue Line to Capitol South, or on the Red Line to Union Station.*

7 The Capitol

This is Congress's "House," whose cornerstone was laid in 1793 by President George Washington. Seventy years later, the Capitol was completed when the 19-foot, 6-inch *Statue of Freedom* was placed atop the dome in December 1863, at the height of the Civil War—the same year that Abraham Lincoln issued his Emancipation Proclamation. Head inside the Capitol Visitor Center to take the hour-long guided Capitol tour (highly recommended), armed with the timed passes you've ordered in advance online. If you've neglected to order these you may still be in luck: Go to the "public walk up" line to see if any same-day passes are available. The Visitor Center is itself worth checking out. See. p. 88.

Not everyone knows it, but there's a tunnel that runs between the Capitol Visitor Center and the Library of Congress. If you're inside the Capitol Visitor Center, find it and follow it to the:

8 Library of Congress ★★

The world's largest library is not only a keeper of books: Ongoing exhibits show off other precious objects, such as an "original Rough Draught" of Thomas Jefferson's much marked-up Declaration of Independence and a 1797 manuscript in George Washington's hand, outlining a plan of government for Virginia. See p. 93.

Exit and head south on First Street to hop the Metro at the Capitol South station, catching a Blue Line train for the Archives/Navy Memorial/Penn Quarter, to reach:

9 Penn Quarter

This lively neighborhood just off the National Mall is full of restaurants, bars, and assorted sightseeing attractions, all within a short walk of each other. Wander up 7th Street, the main artery, and explore side streets and you're sure to come upon something that strikes your fancy. Some suggestions: Sign up for a

Ford's Theatre (p. 133) "History on Foot" walking tour that brings Civil War Washington to life. Go on a self-guided scavenger hunt at the **Smithsonian American Art Museum and National Portrait Gallery** (p. 140). (Good to know: The American Art Museum and Portrait Gallery stay open until 7pm nightly, which is later than other museums.) Test your sleuthing skills during the **International Spy Museum's** (p. 135) hour-long Operation Spy experience. But first, fortify yourself at one of the Quarter's excellent eateries. Here's one that comes with a view:

10 Paul Bakery Café ☕

Sit at a sidewalk table overlooking the Navy Memorial and Pennsylvania Avenue, or inside the charming French café (✆ 202/524-4500), and treat yourself to a delicious smoked salmon and lemon cream sandwich, or an almond croissant, or a baguette layered with thinly sliced ham and brie, or a chocolate éclair, or…all of the above. See p. 80.

Whether you finish your Penn Quarter activities before dinner or aft, hop on the Metro and take a Red Line train to Metro Center, or walk or cab it, to reach the:

11 White House ★★★

Whether or not you're able to tour the interior of the executive mansion, you can admire its exterior view and consider the facts: Its cornerstone was laid in 1792, making the White House the capital's oldest federal building. It's been the residence of every president but George Washington (although the nation's second president, John Adams, only lived here four months.). The British torched the mansion in 1814, so what you see is the house rebuilt in 1817, using the original sandstone walls and interior brickwork. Be sure to walk past the house before 11pm, when the White House dims its exterior lights ("This is a residence, remember," notes a National Park Service ranger.) See p. 128.

ICONIC WASHINGTON, D.C., IN 3 DAYS

Last but not least comes the Supreme Court on your third day, and then you're off to a different part of town altogether. **Start:** *Metro on the Blue Line to the Capitol South stop to reach Capitol Hill.*

12 Supreme Court ★★★

You may be shocked to know that the U.S. Constitution specifies neither an age nor an education level nor even a citizenship requirement for a person to become a Supreme Court justice. No, all that is required is that the president nominates the person and that the Senate confirms the nomination. Attend a Supreme Court argument, or at the very least, a docent lecture, and be further amazed! See p. 97.

Continue north to the end of the block to find Constitution Avenue. Turn left and follow the street to the:

13 Union Station ★

Notable for its Beaux Arts architecture, Union Station is also a historic landmark, having hosted inaugural balls and presidential receptions for all sorts of royalty. And it's a shopping mall, let's not forget, so if you want to pick up some corny mementoes (Commander in Chief aprons?) from **America!,** this would be the place. Washingtonians mostly look on Union Station as a transportation hub, however, since subway and commuter trains, buses, taxis, rental cars, and bike rental companies all operate here. And that's why you're here, too, to be transported. See p. 98.

Catch Metro's Red Line going in the direction of Shady Grove or Grosvenor and exit at Dupont Circle, on the 19th Street, or north side, of the Circle, to find this favorite pizzeria:

14 Pizzeria Paradiso ☕
These pies are a cut above, cooked in an oak-burning oven and topped with your choice of nearly 50 toppings. See p. 79.

Walk across Massachusetts Avenue to reach the:

15 Phillips Collection ★★
Tour this charming museum to view French, American, and post-Impressionist art, as well as modernist art, housed in an 1897 mansion and its modern wings. Always keep an eye out for favorites, like Renoir's *Luncheon of the Boating Party*, numerous Bonnards, the gallery devoted to Mark Rothko's bold artworks, and on display from time to time, *Night Baseball*, a painting executed by founder Duncan Phillips's wife, Marjorie Phillips.

16 Embassy Row & Dupont Circle
Stop in shops along Connecticut Avenue, and then follow side streets to discover boutiques, little art galleries, and quaint century-old town houses. If you look carefully, you'll start to notice that some of these buildings are actually embassies or historic homes. The most awesome embassies lie on Massachusetts Avenue, west of Dupont Circle. Flags and plaques clearly identify them. Turn onto S Street NW and look for no. 2340 to see where President Woodrow Wilson lived after he left the White House. The **Woodrow Wilson House** is worth touring if you have time. Embassies are rarely open to the public. See p. 22 and 143.

Walk, if you feel up to it, or take a taxi to the Kennedy Center.

17 Kennedy Center ★★★
Head to the Kennedy Center for the 6pm nightly free concert in the Grand Foyer (part of the center's Millennium Stage program). At concert's end, proceed through the glass doors to the terrace overlooking Rock Creek Parkway and the Potomac River, and enjoy the view. See p. 179.

WASHINGTON, D.C., FOR FAMILIES

The good thing about the capital, parents, is that history is in plain view. The National Mall, with its green sweep of landmarks from the Capitol to the Lincoln Memorial, offers plenty of opportunities for educational moments. This itinerary leans more toward fun, though as you'll see, there's a lot of learning going on, too. *Start: The National Museum of American History.*

1 National Museum of American History ★★★
Like all of the Smithsonians, this one has tons of kid-friendly activities and exhibits. Check out the exhibit on snowboarding; "interactive carts" of objects that children can pick up and experiment with, like a stereoscope; artifacts on

2

Washington, D.C., for Families

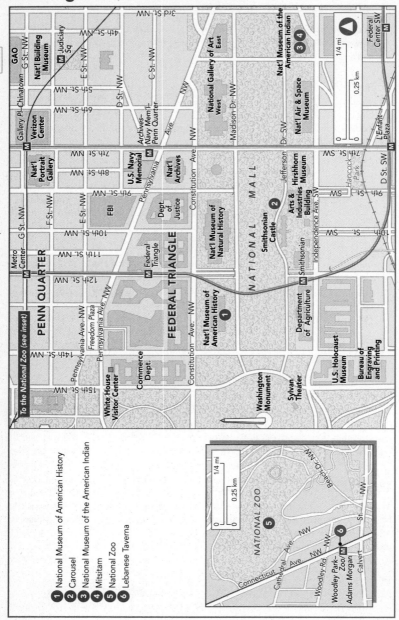

1 National Museum of American History
2 Carousel
3 National Museum of the American Indian
4 Mitsitam
5 National Zoo
6 Lebanese Taverna

display such as Kermit the Frog; sightings of historical figures in your midst (is that Mary Pickersgill? Yes); and the simulator rides that make you feel like you're on a roller coaster or driving a race car. See p. 113.

Exit to the National Mall and walk diagonally across it to reach the part of the Mall between the Smithsonian Castle and the Arts and Industries Building, where you'll find the:

2 Carousel

For little and not-so-little children, the carousel is a treat, operating year-round, weather permitting. It's not free, though: $3.50 per child per ride. See p. 100. Good to know: Another carousel awaits at your final destination, the National Zoo, where a solar-powered custom-designed carousel with 58 animal figures operates daily, for $3 a ride.

Continue down the Mall toward the Capitol until you reach the:

3 National Museum of the American Indian ★

Inside the museum's imagiNATIONS Activity Center, children can traipse through Amazonian stilt houses, test their balance while learning about kayaks, weave a giant basket, and learn to make beautiful music using traditional instruments. See p. 114.

Follow up that experience with a traditional Indian meal right inside the museum at:

4 Mitsitam 🍴

It's easy to learn about Native American culture when learning involves delicious bites of it: fry bread with cinnamon and honey, huckleberry fritters, "totopos," and more. ✆ 202/633-7039. See p. 115.

Exit to the Independence Avenue side of the museum, walk to 3rd Street, cross Independence Avenue, and follow 3rd Street to the Federal Center SW Metro station, where you should board either a Blue or Orange line train headed in the direction of Franconia/Springfield. Debark the train at the Metro Center stop, but stay in the station and switch to the Red Line, boarding a train going in the direction of either Shady Grove or Grosvenor. Debark at the Woodley Park–Zoo station and walk up Connecticut Avenue to reach the:

5 National Zoo ★★

Certain children's exhibits (the Kids Farm, the pizza sculpture) lie at the very bottom of this large zoo, situated on a hill. Keep that part in mind as you explore the zoo, since it'll be all uphill—and quite a long hill it is—back to Connecticut Avenue. But you need not go all the way to the bottom of the hill, as pandas, a solar-powered carousel, a new elephant exhibit, and nearly 2,000 other animals that young ones will love to see are on view elsewhere in the zoo. See p. 145.

6 Lebanese Taverna 🍴

If you're longing for a pick-me-up, head down Connecticut Avenue to the family-friendly establishment. The menu has something for everyone, including gluten-free items, if your child has that allergy. The restaurant stays open straight through from noon until closing. ✆ 202/265-8681. You might also be happy to know that there's a McDonalds right across the street from the taverna. See p. 85.

A Women's History Tour of Washington, D.C.

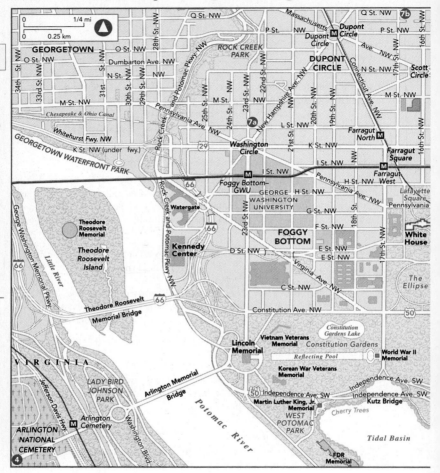

A WOMEN'S HISTORY TOUR OF WASHINGTON, D.C.

"Remember the ladies," Abigail Adams famously advised her husband, John Adams, in 1776, when he was attending the Continental Congress and busy formulating his ideas about the new government. John Adams, who went on to become the second president of the United States in 1797, did his best. But that was a long time ago, and women have long acted as their own advocates. Perhaps one day soon a First Man might feel compelled to urge Madame President to "remember the men." In the mean-

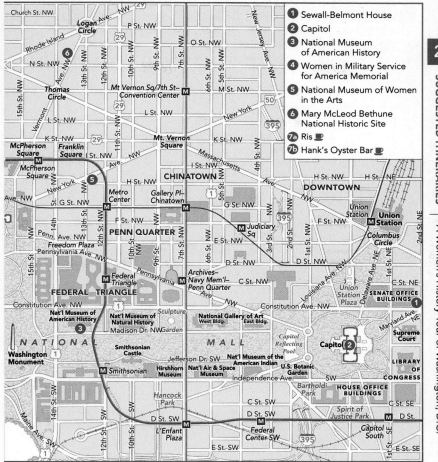

2

SUGGESTED ITINERARIES | A Women's History Tour of Washington, D.C.

1 Sewall-Belmont House
2 Capitol
3 National Museum of American History
4 Women in Military Service for America Memorial
5 National Museum of Women in the Arts
6 Mary McLeod Bethune National Historic Site
7a Ris 🍽
7b Hank's Oyster Bar 🍽

time, let us now celebrate the achievements of women in many realms. *Start: The Sewall-Belmont House on Capitol Hill.*

1 Sewall-Belmont House

The Equal Rights Amendment is just three states' votes short of ratification in Congress. Here is the proposition in its entirety: "Equality of rights under the law shall not be denied or abridged in the United States because of sex." Nineteen words. Is it so controversial? Alice Paul, founder of the National Woman's Party, headquartered here, penned the amendment in 1923. See p. 96.

From the house, head up to 1st Street and turn left. Give a nod to the Supreme Court, where three of the nine justices are women, then cross the street to reach the:

2 U.S. Capitol ★★★

The 113th Congress has 81 women representatives out of a total of 435, and 20 women senators out of a total of 50. Montana Rep. Jeannette Rankin, in 1917, was the first woman elected to Congress. Look for her statue in the Capitol Visitor Center. And for in-depth information about women in Congress, consult the excellent website http://womenincongress.house.gov. See p. 88.

Return to Constitution Avenue and either flag a taxi (easy to do in this part of town) or make your way on foot (about 1½ miles) to the:

3 National Museum of American History ★★★

As has been noted, the First Ladies exhibit is the most popular one in the museum and gives First Ladies their due as strong and interesting people in their own right. But don't miss Julia Child's Kitchen (within the "Food: Transforming America's Table" exhibit), a tribute to a different kind of icon. And the Star-Spangled Banner? The handiwork of a woman, or rather, several women: Mary Pickersgill and daughter, nieces, and a maid. See p. 113.

You could walk it, but you'll have to navigate a terrifying traffic circle; it will be safer to hop on the Metro at the Smithsonian station on the Mall, directly across from the American History Museum. Board a Blue Line train headed in the direction of Franconia/Springfield and get of at the Arlington Cemetery stop. Or: take one of the National Park Service shuttles that goes to Arlington Cemetery (p. 150). Hop off and walk to the memorial to:

4 Women in Military Service for America ★

This is the only major national memorial honoring all servicewomen, from the American Revolution onward. Its archives include information about two nurses aboard Commodore Stephen Decatur's ship *United States* during the War of 1812, and the more recent development in 2008 when, for the first time in military history, a woman was promoted to the rank of four-star general in the U.S. Army. See p. 151.

The best thing to do from here is to hop on the Metro, take the Blue or Orange line headed into D.C., and get off at Metro Center, exiting at 13th and G streets and walking a block north to the:

5 National Museum of Women in the Arts ★

From Renaissance paintings to contemporary sculptures to silver pieces created by 18th- and 19th-century Irish and British female silversmiths, this museum is full of masterpieces by women. See p. 138.

If it's a nice day, consider walking to your last stop, just about half a mile away. Walk to 14th Street and head north, going around Scott Circle at Massachusetts Avenue to pick up Vermont Avenue on the other side. Proceed about a block to the:

6 Mary McLeod Bethune National Historic Site

Mary McLeod Bethune bought this house not as a residence, but to serve as headquarters for the National Council for Negro Women. So while she did live here from 1943 to 1949, it is the sense of her professional rather than personal life that you absorb from the exhibits. They speak volumes. Look for a black-and-white photo of FDR's cabinet in the 1930s, and there you will see a panel of white men and, in their midst, this black woman. When you consider that Bethune was born poor, the 15th of 17 children of former slaves, you start to truly appreciate her accomplishments. See p. 144.

The Neighborhoods in Brief

ADAMS MORGAN This ever-trendy, multiethnic neighborhood is crammed with boutiques, bars, clubs, and restaurants. Everything is located on either 18th Street NW or Columbia Road NW. In 2015, Adams Morgan expects to welcome the first hotel to be located within its actual boundaries; until then, the nearest hotel options remain in the nearby Dupont Circle and Woodley Park neighborhoods (see below). Parking is manageable during the day but difficult at night, especially on weekends (a parking garage on Champlain St., just off 18th St., helps a little). Luckily, you can easily walk to Adams Morgan from the Dupont Circle or Woodley Park Metro stops, or take the bus or a taxi there. (Be alert in Adams Morgan at night and try to stick to the main streets, 18th St. and Columbia Rd.) The weekend begins Thursday nights in the nightlife-centric world of Adams Morgan.

ANACOSTIA When people talk about the Washington, D.C. that tourists never see, they're talking about neighborhoods like this; in fact, they're usually talking about Anacostia, specifically. Named for the river that separates it from "mainland" D.C., it's an old part of town, with little commercial development and mostly modest, often low-income housing. Anacostia does have two attractions: the Smithsonian's **Anacostia Community Museum** and the **Frederick Douglass National Historic Site** (see "Museums in Anacostia," p. 150).

ATLAS DISTRICT The Atlas District, no more than a section of H Street NE to the northeast of Union Station, stretches between 4th and 14th streets, but centers on the 12th to 14th streets segment. The Atlas District is increasingly known as a nightlife and live music destination, with a couple of recommendable restaurants thrown in. A hardscrabble part of town by day, the Atlas District turns into a playground at night, especially Thursday through Saturday, as the city's thirsty scenemakers hit the street. There are no hotels, for now. A much-talked-about streetcar was on track to begin service in the fall of 2013, finally providing the neighborhood with easier access to and from other parts of town and the nearest Metro stop (Union Station).

BARRACKS ROW Barracks Row refers mainly to a single stretch of 8th Street SE, south of Pennsylvania Avenue SE, but also to side streets occupied by Marine Corps barracks since 1801 (hence the name). This southeastern subsection of Capitol Hill is known for its lineup of shops, casual bistros, and pubs. Its attractions continue to grow as a result of the 2008 opening of the Nationals baseball team's stadium, Nationals Park, half a mile away. In fact, the ballpark has spawned its own neighborhood, dubbed the Capitol Riverfront (see below). The closest hotels are the **Capitol Hill Hotel** (p. 46), 6 blocks away, at C and 2nd St. SE, close to the Capitol, and those in Capitol Riverfront.

CAPITOL HILL Everyone's heard of "the Hill," the area crowned by the Capitol building. The term, in fact, refers to a large section of town, extending from the western side of the Capitol to the D.C. Armory going east, bounded by H Street to the north and the Southwest Freeway to the south. It contains not only this chief symbol of the nation's capital, but also the **Supreme Court Building,** the **Library of Congress,** the **Folger Shakespeare Library, Union Station,** and **Eastern Market.** Much of it is a quiet residential neighborhood of tree-lined streets, rows of Federal and Victorian town houses, and old churches. Restaurants keep increasing their numbers, with most located along Pennsylvania Avenue SE on the south side of the Capitol and near North Capitol Street NW on the north side of the Capitol—the north side, near Union Station, is where most of the hotels are, too. Keep to the well-lit, well-traveled streets at night, and don't walk alone—crime occurs more frequently in this neighborhood than in some other parts of town.

Washington, D.C., at a Glance

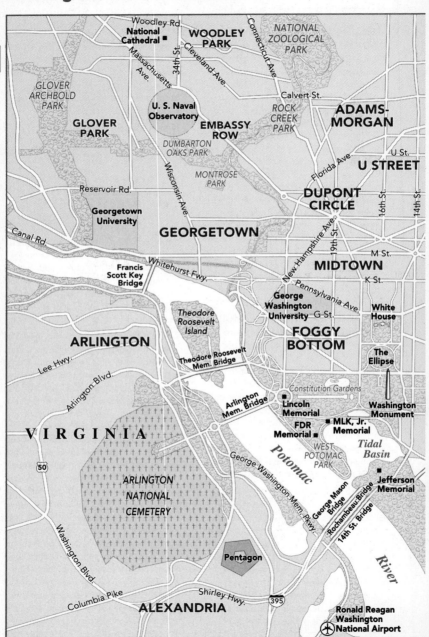

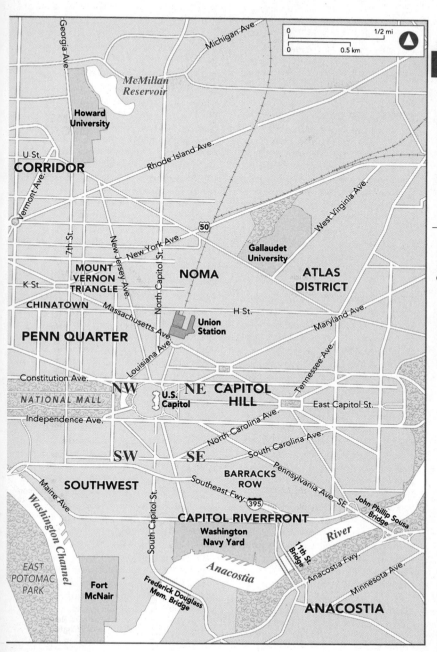

CAPITOL RIVERFRONT The opening of **Nationals Park** in 2008 has led the way in the development of this old and worn part of town. The revitalized 500-acre neighborhood abuts 1½ miles of the Anacostia River and, besides the ballpark, has a relatively new Courtyard by Marriott hotel (other hotels are due to open in 2015 and beyond), several restaurants, and public parks, trails, and docks. More to come.

CLEVELAND PARK Cleveland Park, just north of Woodley Park, is an enclave of beautiful old houses with wraparound porches, found on picturesque streets extending off the main artery, Connecticut Avenue. With its own stop on the Red Line Metro system and a respectable number of excellent restaurants, Cleveland Park is worth visiting when you're near the zoo (just up the street) or in the mood for some fine cuisine and a sense of affluent D.C. neighborliness. Most hotels lie a short walk away in Woodley Park, and farther south in the city.

DOWNTOWN The area bounded roughly by 6th and 21st streets NW to the east and west, and M Street and Pennsylvania Avenue to the north and south, is a mix of the Federal Triangle's government office buildings; K Street, ground zero for the city's countless law and lobbying firms; Connecticut Avenue restaurants and shopping; historic hotels; the city's poshest small hotels; **Chinatown;** the huge Walter E. Washington Convention Center; and the White House. You'll also find the historic **Penn Quarter,** one of D.C.'s hottest locales, which has continued to flourish since the 1997 opening of the Verizon Center (the venue for Wizards and Mystics basketball games, Capitals hockey games, and rock concerts). A number of off-the-Mall museums, like the mammoth **Newseum,** the **International Spy Museum,** and the **Smithsonian's National Portrait Gallery and American Art Museum,** are here. This is also where you'll find hip restaurants, boutique hotels, and nightclubs. The total downtown area encompasses so many blocks and attractions that I've divided discussions of attractions, restaurants, and hotels in this area into two sections: **"Midtown,"** referring to the area from 15th Street west to 21st Street, and from Pennsylvania Avenue north to M Street; and **"Penn Quarter,"** from 15th Street east to 6th Street, and Pennsylvania Avenue north to New York Avenue.

DUPONT CIRCLE One of my favorite parts of town, Dupont Circle provides easy fun, day or night. It takes its name from the traffic circle minipark, where Massachusetts, New Hampshire, and Connecticut avenues converge. Washington's famous **Embassy Row** centers on Dupont Circle and refers to the parade of grand embassy mansions lining Massachusetts Avenue and its side streets. The streets extending out from the circle are lively, with all-night bookstores, good restaurants, wonderful art galleries and art museums, nightspots, and Washingtonians at their loosest. It is also the hub of D.C.'s gay community. There are plenty of hotel choices in this neighborhood, and most of them are moderately priced.

FOGGY BOTTOM/WEST END The area west of the White House, south of Dupont Circle, and east of Georgetown encompasses both Foggy Bottom and the West End. Foggy Bottom, located below, or south, of Pennsylvania Avenue, was Washington's early industrial center. Its name comes from the foul fumes emitted in those days by a coal depot and gasworks, but its original name, Funkstown (for owner Jacob Funk), is perhaps even worse. There's nothing foul nor funky about the area today. The West End edges north of Pennsylvania Avenue, booming with the latest big-name restaurants and new office buildings. Together the overlapping Foggy Bottom and West End neighborhoods present a mix: the **Kennedy Center,** town-house residences, George Washington University campus buildings, offices for the World Bank and the International Monetary Fund, State Department headquarters, small- and medium-size hotels, student bars, and several fine eateries, lining either side of Pennsylvania Avenue and its side streets.

GEORGETOWN This historic community dates from Colonial times. It was a thriving tobacco port long before the District of Columbia was formed, and one of its attractions, the **Old Stone House,** dates from pre-Revolutionary days. Georgetown action centers on M Street and Wisconsin Avenue NW, where you'll find numerous boutiques, chic restaurants, and popular pubs. Expect lots of nightlife here. Two new hotels opened in Georgetown in 2013, including the ultra-luxurious **Capella Hotel** (p. 58). Fortunately, less pricey options are available, as well (see chapter 4). Detour from the main drags to relish the quiet, tree-lined streets of restored Colonial row houses, stroll the beautiful gardens of **Dumbarton Oaks,** and check out the **C&O Canal.** Georgetown is also home to **Georgetown University.** (See chapter 10 for a walking tour of Georgetown.) *Note:* Not surprisingly, the neighborhood gets pretty raucous on weekends.

GLOVER PARK Mostly a residential neighborhood, this section of town just above Georgetown and just south of the **Washington National Cathedral** is worth mentioning because of several good restaurants and bars located along its main stretch, Wisconsin Avenue NW. Glover Park sits between the campuses of Georgetown and American universities, so there's a large student presence here.

THE NATIONAL MALL This lovely, tree-lined stretch of open space between Constitution and Independence avenues, extending for nearly 2 miles from the foot of the Capitol to the steps of the Lincoln Memorial, is the hub of tourist attractions. It includes most of the Smithsonian Institution museums and several other notable sites. Tourists as well as natives—joggers, food vendors, kite flyers, and picnickers among them—traipse the 700-acre Mall. Most hotels and restaurants are located beyond the Mall to the north, with a few located south of the Mall, across Independence Avenue. The proper name for the entire parkland area that encompasses the National Mall, as well as the Jefferson, FDR,

and Martin Luther King, Jr. memorials, and other sites, is actually **National Mall and Memorial Parks,** which is how I refer to it in chapter 6.

MIDTOWN This refers roughly to the part of downtown from 15th Street west to 21st Street, and from Pennsylvania Avenue north to M Street. See "Downtown," above.

MOUNT VERNON TRIANGLE Yet another old neighborhood experiencing renewal, Mount Vernon lies east of the convention center, its boundary streets of New Jersey, Massachusetts, and New York avenues defining a perfectly shaped triangle. Within that triangle, attractions, like the hot restaurant Kushi, are starting to multiply. Talk of hotel developments has come to naught, for now.

NORTHERN VIRGINIA Across the Potomac River from the capital lies Northern Virginia and its close-in city/towns of Arlington and Old Town Alexandria. The Arlington Memorial Bridge leads directly from the **Lincoln Memorial** to **Arlington National Cemetery,** and beyond to Arlington and Old Town (see chapter 9, "Day Trips from Washington, D.C."). Commuters travel back and forth between the District and Virginia all day using the Arlington Memorial Bridge and others, including the Key Bridge, which leads to and from Georgetown; the Theodore Roosevelt Memorial Bridge, whose roadways connect Rte. 50 and I-66; and the 14th Street Bridge, whose I-395 roadway connects downtown D.C. and Northern Virginia's access to I-95 and points south.

PENN QUARTER This refers roughly to the part of downtown from 15th Street east to 6th Street, and Pennsylvania Avenue north to New York Avenue. See "Downtown," above.

SOUTHWEST/WATERFRONT This stretch of waterfront is a working marina, with fishing boats docked the length of the Washington Channel and vendors selling fresh crabs and fish from stalls up and down the promenade. This is where locals and restaurateurs come to buy fresh seafood. The neighborhood is also home to **Arena Stage**

(p. 179), whose October 2010 reopening after a massive expansion and renovation is bringing more people back to this out-of-the-way part of town. Southwest does have its own Metro station (Southwest-Waterfront, on the Green Line), and change is in the air.

U STREET CORRIDOR U Street NW and 14th Street NW form the crux of D.C.'s most diverse neighborhood, where people of varied race, color, nationality, and age mix more comfortably than anywhere else in the city. The quarter continues to rise from the ashes of the nightclubs and theaters located here decades ago, when the performances of jazz and blues legends Duke Ellington, Louis Armstrong, and Cab Calloway gave the area the name "Black Broadway." Today clubs like the renovated Howard Theatre and the smaller Twins Jazz honor that legacy, drawing jazz lovers, while the Corridor's many bar hangouts fill nightly with the city's young and restless. New restaurants (see chapter 5) and little shops are proliferate, including offshoots of successful startups in other neighborhoods. The Penn Quarter may be hot and high energy, but the U Street Corridor is officially now the hippest part of town. **The Helix** (p. 54) is one of the few hotels within U Street's near reach. FYI: My presentation of the U Street Corridor neighborhood in this book encompasses the greater Shaw neighborhood as well as smaller areas, like Logan Circle.

WOODLEY PARK Home to Washington's largest hotel (the Washington Marriott Wardman Park), Woodley Park boasts the **National Zoo,** many good restaurants, and some antiques stores. Washingtonians are used to seeing conventioneers wandering the neighborhood's pretty residential streets with their name tags still on.

WASHINGTON, D.C., IN CONTEXT

E verybody knows at least a little something about Washington, D.C. It's the nation's capital, after all; what goes on here on a daily basis is top-of-the-news stuff. Images such as the Capitol, the Washington Monument, the Potomac River, the National Mall, the White House, and Pennsylvania Avenue are called immediately to mind by the mention of this city's name.

There are others I'd like to introduce to you: cherry blossoms, Black Broadway, the Verizon Center, Eleanor Holmes Norton, Embassy Row, the U Street Corridor, Rock Creek Park. These images illustrate just a fraction of the rich history and diverse cultural experiences this city has to offer.

That's what this book is about. This chapter, specifically, aims to provide you with a context for understanding Washington, D.C.'s story and personality beyond the headlines, as well as practical information that will be useful to you while planning your trip and upon your arrival.

WASHINGTON, D.C., TODAY

Washington, D.C. is both the capital of the United States and a city unto itself; therein lie its charms, but also a host of complications. Control of the city is the main issue. The District is a free-standing jurisdiction, but because it is a city with a federal rather than a state overseer, it has never been entitled to the same governmental powers as the states. Congress supervises the District's budget and legislation. Originally, Congress granted the city the authority to elect its own governance, but it rescinded that right when the District overspent its budget in its attempts to improve its services and appearance after the Civil War. The White House then appointed three commissioners, who ran D.C.'s affairs for nearly 100 years.

In 1972 the city regained the right to elect its own mayor and city council, but Congress retains control of the budget and the courts, and can veto municipal legislation. District residents can vote in presidential primaries and elections and can elect a delegate to Congress who introduces legislation and votes in committees, but this delegate cannot vote on the House floor. This unique situation, in which residents of the District pay federal income taxes but don't have a vote in Congress, is a matter of great local concern. D.C. residents publicly protest the situation by displaying license plates bearing the inscription TAXATION WITHOUT REPRESENTATION.

Another wrinkle in this uncommon relationship is the fact that Washington's economy relies heavily upon the presence of the federal government, which employs about 18.8% of D.C. residents (according to a 2012 Gallup Poll), making it the city's single largest employer, and upon the tourism business that Washington, as the capital, attracts. The city struggles toward political independence, although it recognizes the economic benefits of its position as the seat of the nation's capital.

Will any of this affect you as you tour the city this year? Yes.

You will find Washington, D.C. to be a remarkably vibrant city. The economic hard times that the rest of the country is experiencing are muted here. Take the federal budget cuts known as "sequestration": as dependent as the District's economy is upon federal dollars, it has not truly suffered. The White House has cancelled tours, the National Park Service has fewer rangers in the National Mall and Memorial Parks, and some of the Smithsonian museums have cut back on staff hours, but that's it.

Income remains higher than the national average, unemployment is lower, at least one-third of the population is between the ages of 20 and 35, residents are better educated than elsewhere, and the people are remarkably diverse: 50.1% African American, 9.9% Latino, 13.3% foreign-born, and 14.5% speaking a language other than English at home. The presence of embassies and the diplomatic community intensifies the international flavor.

In other words, Washington, D.C. is thriving. Restaurants and bars dominate most neighborhoods. In fact, eating out is a way of life here, whether simply for the pleasure of it or for business—the city's movers and shakers meet over breakfast, lunch, and dinner. Washington's restaurant scene offers an immense variety of international cuisines, from Ethiopian to Peruvian, as well as soul food and regional specialties like Chesapeake Bay crabs served in soft-shell, hard-shell, soup, or cake form.

Theaters, music venues, hotels, and brand-name stores abound. Because of the abundance of jobs thanks to tourism and the presence of the federal government, many Washingtonians can afford to go to the theater, attend cultural events, shop, and dine out. But whatever it is, play, concert, or restaurant meal, it better be good. As well-traveled, well-educated, and, let's face it, pretty demanding types, capital dwellers have high standards and big appetites. They expect the best, and they get it.

But it wasn't always this way. About 20 years ago, Washington wasn't so attractive. Tourists came to visit federal buildings like the Capitol, the White House, and the city's memorials but stayed away from the dingy downtown and other off-the-Mall neighborhoods. The city had the potential for being so much more, and certain people—heroes, in my book—helped inspire action and brought about change themselves: Delegate Eleanor Holmes Norton, who fought steadfastly for states' rights and economic revival for the District; former Mayor Anthony Williams, who rescued the District's budget when his predecessor, the notoriously mismanaging Mayor Marion Barry, brought the city to the brink of financial ruin; and the community-minded developers Abe and Irene Pollin, who used their own funds to finance the $200-million MCI sports center, now called the Verizon Center, in the heart of town (today the wildly successful arena anchors the utterly transformed Penn Quarter neighborhood, now one of the liveliest city centers in the country).

The city's resident population has grown by more than 5% in the past 10 years and now stands at approximately 632,323, a size not seen in more than 50 years. The growth spurt is especially significant given that the District's population reached a relative low point in 2002, when the U.S. Census counted 572,000 D.C. residents. Revitalization continues to take root throughout the city—from Southeast D.C., where a grand baseball stadium, Nationals Ballpark, opened in March 2008, to the Columbia Heights enclave in upper northwest D.C., now a mélange of Latino culture, loft condominiums, and ethnic eateries. The city's evergreens—the memorials and monuments, the historic neighborhoods, and the Smithsonian museums—remain unflaggingly popular.

But D.C. has its share of problems, starting with its Metro transportation system, which is in the midst of a much-needed overhaul. (See "Getting Around," in chapter 11, for details.) Other problems relate to the city's gentrification efforts, such as the displacement of residents from homes they can no longer afford in revitalized but increasingly expensive neighborhoods. Mayor Vincent Gray has had his work cut out for him in a municipality that struggles to provide health care, good schools, safe neighborhoods, adequate housing, and basic social services to all citizens.

Diverse in demographics, residents are alike in loving their city, despite the issues it faces. Visitors seem to share this love, as statistics bear out: D.C. welcomes 18.9 million visitors a year, 1.8 million of whom are international tourists.

THE MAKING OF WASHINGTON, D.C.

As with many cities, Washington, D.C.'s past is written in its landscape. Behold the lustrous Potomac River, whose discovery by Captain John Smith in 1608 led to European settlement of this area. Take note of the city's layout: the 160-foot-wide avenues radiating from squares and circles, the sweeping vistas, the abundant parkland, all very much as Pierre Charles L'Enfant intended when he envisioned the "Federal District" in 1791. Look around and you will see the Washington Monument, the U.S. Capitol, the Lincoln Memorial, the White House, and other landmarks, their very prominence in the flat, central cityscape attesting to their significance in the formation of the nation's capital.

But Washington's history is very much a tale of two cities. Beyond the National Mall, the memorials, and the federal government buildings lies "D.C.," the municipality. Righteous politicians and others speak critically of "Washington"—shorthand, we understand, for all that is wrong with government. They should be more precise. With that snide dismissal, critics dismiss, as well, the particular locale in which the capital resides. It is a place of vibrant neighborhoods and vivid personalities, a vaunted arts-and-culture scene, international diversity, rich African-American heritage, uniquely Washingtonian attractions and people—the very citizens who built the capital in the first place and have kept it running ever since.

Early Days

The settlers who arrived in 1608 weren't the region's first inhabitants, of course. Captain John Smith may have been the first European to discover this waterfront property of lush greenery and woodlands, but the Nacotchtank and Piscataway tribes were way ahead of him. As Smith and company settled the area, they disrupted the Indians' way of life and introduced European diseases. The Indians gradually were driven away.

By 1751, Irish and Scottish immigrants had founded "George Town," named for the king of England and soon established as an important tobacco-shipping port. Several houses from those days still exist in modern-day Georgetown: The Old Stone House (on M St. NW), a woodworker's home built around the 1760s, is now operated by the National Park Service and open to the public, and a few magnificent ship merchants' mansions still stand on N and Prospect streets, though these are privately owned and not open to the public. (Their properties once directly overlooked the Potomac River, but no longer: The Potomac River has receded quite a bit, as you'll see.) For a walking tour of Georgetown, see p. 214.

On This Spot

3

WASHINGTON, D.C., IN CONTEXT | The Making of Washington, D.C.

① Built in 1912, directly two miles west of the Capitol, the **Lincoln Memorial ①ₐ** honors our most inspiring president. Among the inspired was the Rev. Dr. Martin Luther King. Find the marked spot, 18 steps down from the chamber, and you will be standing exactly where King stood on Aug. 28, 1963, when he delivered his remarkable "I Have a Dream" speech to the crowd of 200,000 people who had gathered here after "Marching on Washington" with King to pressure Congress to pass the Civil Rights Act. Forty-eight years later, on October 16, 2011, the country honored King with his own memorial; the **Washington, D.C. Martin Luther King, Jr. National Memorial ①ᵦ** lies across Independence Ave., on the lip of the Tidal Basin.

The Lincoln Memorial was the site of another significant moment in civil rights history, on Easter Sunday, 1939, when contralto Marian Anderson sang to a crowd of 75,000 people on the memorial steps, after the Daughters of the American Revolution refused to allow the African American to perform at their **Constitution Hall ①꜀**. First Lady Eleanor Roosevelt resigned her DAR membership over the incident. Eventually, Anderson did sing at Constitution Hall (in 1943 and again in 1952), and at the Lincoln Memorial a second time, in 1952.

② **The Watergate Building** looks harmless enough these days, despite the fact that the very word "Watergate" calls up its scandalous history. In June 1972, members of President Nixon's re-election staff broke into the Democratic National Committee's offices here, an act that eventually forced Nixon to resign. Two decades later, Pres. Clinton carried on an affair at the White House with a 20-something intern, who just happened to live at the Watergate.

③ **The Washington Hilton** was the scene of the attempted assassination of Pres. Reagan on March 30, 1981, when John Hinckley, Jr. shot Pres. Reagan, his press secretary James Brady, a DC police officer, and a Secret Service agent. All survived.

④ President Lincoln was not so lucky. On April 14, 1865, John Wilkes Booth fatally shot Abraham Lincoln as the president sat in the President's Box in **Ford's Theatre** watching a performance of "Our American Cousin." Visitors can view Lincoln's seat, but not sit there.

⑤ In the early to mid-20th century, U Street was known as Black Broadway, and the general area between 7th and 15th streets was the epicenter of a black cultural renaissance. At places like the **Howard Theatre ⑤ₐ** and the **Club Caverns ⑤ᵦ** (now Bohemian Caverns), African Americans came to hear the music of Ella Fitzgerald, Cab Calloway, and most of all, DC native son Duke Ellington. Visit the reborn neighborhood today and you can follow in their footsteps, as you walk by the houses at **1805 and 1816 13th St. NW ⑤꜀**, where the Duke grew up, or take in a show at the restored Howard Theatre or at smaller venues, like Twins Jazz, always ending the night with a half-smoke at the decades-old Ben's Chili Bowl.

⑥ Since its beginnings in 1850, and continuing on through its current incarnation (built on the site of the original in 1901), **The Willard Hotel** has always played a special role in the life of the capital. At least six presidents, from Zachary Taylor to Abraham Lincoln, lived at the Willard for a while. Julia Ward Howe composed "The Battle Hymn of the Republic" at the hotel in 1861, and the Rev. Dr. Martin Luther King completed his "I Have a Dream" speech here in 1963. Stop in at the hotel to admire the ornate lobby and exquisite architecture, but don't leave without visiting the bar, the city's historic center of activity. Sip a mint julep, introduced here by statesman Henry Clay in 1850, and consider the tradition you're upholding: It was here that Washington Irving brought Charles Dickens for a brandy, Samuel Clemens (Mark Twain) imbibed bourbon with his pal, Nevada Sen. Stewart, and Nathaniel Hawthorne set up his base for covering the Civil War for the Atlantic Monthly magazine, writing "…for the conviviality of Washington sets in at an early hour, and, so far as I have had the opportunity to observe, never terminates at any hour."

3

WASHINGTON, D.C., IN CONTEXT | The Making of Washington, D.C.

Birth of the Capital

After colonists in George Town and elsewhere in America rebelled against British rule, defeating the British in the American Revolution (1775–83), Congress, in quick succession, unanimously elected General George Washington as the first president of the United States, ratified a U.S. Constitution, and proposed that a city be designed and built to house the seat of government for the new nation and to function fully in commercial and cultural capacities. Much squabbling ensued. The North wanted the capital; the South wanted the capital. President Washington huddled with his Secretary of State, Thomas Jefferson, and devised a solution that Congress approved in 1790: The nation's capital would be "a site not exceeding 10 miles square" located on the Potomac. The South was happy, for this area was nominally in their region; Northern states were appeased by the stipulation that the South pay off the North's Revolutionary War debt, and by the city's location on the North–South border. Washington, District of Columbia, made her debut.

The only problem was that she was not exactly presentable. The brave new country's capital proved to be a tract of undeveloped wilderness, where pigs, goats, and cows roamed free, and habitable houses were few and far between. Thankfully, the city was granted the masterful 1791 plan of the gifted but temperamental French-born engineer, Pierre Charles L'Enfant. Slaves, free blacks, and immigrants from Ireland, Scotland, and other countries worked to fulfill L'Enfant's remarkable vision, erecting first the White House (the city's oldest federal structure), then the Capitol and other buildings. (Read *The Great Decision: Jefferson, Adams, Marshall and the Battle for the Supreme Court,* by Cliff Sloan and David McKean, for excellent descriptions of the early days of the capital, its institutions, and the strong personalities that helped forge them.) Gradually, the nation's capital began to take shape, though too slowly perhaps for some. The writer Anthony Trollope, visiting in 1860, declared Washington "as melancholy and miserable a town as the mind of man can conceive."

The Civil War & Reconstruction

During the Civil War, the capital became an armed camp and headquarters for the Union Army, overflowing with thousands of followers. Parks became campgrounds; churches, schools, and federal buildings, including the Capitol and the Patent Office (now the National Portrait Gallery), became hospitals; and forts ringed the town. The population grew from 60,000 to 200,000, as soldiers, former slaves, merchants, and laborers converged on the scene. The streets were filled with the wounded, nursed by the likes of Walt Whitman, one of many making the rounds to aid ailing soldiers. In spite of everything, President Lincoln insisted that work on the Capitol continue. "If people see the Capitol going on, it is a sign we intend the Union shall go on," he said.

Lincoln himself kept on, sustained perhaps by his visits to St. John's Church, across Lafayette Square from the White House. Lincoln attended evening services when he could, arriving alone after other churchgoers had entered and slipping out before the service was over. And then on the night of April 14, 1865, just as the days of war were dwindling down and Lincoln's vision for unity was being realized, the president was fatally shot at Ford's Theatre (p. 133) while attending a play.

In the wake of the Civil War and President Lincoln's assassination, Congress took stock of the capital and saw a town worn out by years of war—awash with people but still lacking the most fundamental facilities. Indeed, the city was a mess. There was talk of moving the capital city elsewhere, perhaps to St. Louis or some other more centrally located city. A rescue of sorts arrived in the person of public works leader

Alexander "Boss" Shepherd, who initiated a "comprehensive plan of improvement" that at last incorporated the infrastructure so necessary to a functioning metropolis, including a streetcar system that allowed the District's overflowing population to move beyond city limits. Shepherd also established parks, constructed streets and bridges, and installed water and sewer systems and gas lighting, gradually nudging the nation's capital closer to showplace design. Notable accomplishments included the completion of the Washington Monument in 1884 (after 36 years) and the opening of the first Smithsonian museum, in 1881.

Washington Blossoms

With the streets paved and illuminated, the water running, streetcars and rail transportation operating, and other practical matters well in place, Washington, D.C. was ready to address its appearance. In 1900, as if on cue, a senator from Michigan, James McMillan, persuaded his colleagues to appoint an advisory committee to develop designs for a more beautiful and graceful city. This retired railroad mogul was determined to use his architectural and engineering knowledge to complete the job that L'Enfant had started a century earlier. With his own money, McMillan sent a committee that included landscapist Frederick Law Olmsted (designer of New York's Central Park), sculptor Augustus Saint-Gaudens, and noted architects Daniel Burnham and Charles McKim to Europe for 7 weeks to study the landscaping and architecture of that continent's great capitals.

"Make no little plans," Burnham counseled fellow members. "They have no magic to stir men's blood, and probably themselves will not be realized. Make big plans, aim high in hope and work, remembering that a noble and logical diagram once recorded will never die, but long after we are gone will be a living thing, asserting itself with ever growing insistency."

The committee implemented a beautification program that continued well into the 20th century. Other projects added further enhancements: A presidential Commission of Fine Arts, established in 1910, positioned monuments and fountains throughout the city; FDR's Works Progress Administration erected public buildings embellished by artists. The legacy of these programs is on view today, in the cherry trees along the Tidal Basin, the Lincoln Memorial at the west end of the Mall, the Arlington Memorial Bridge, the Library of Congress, Union Station, the Corcoran Gallery, and many other sights, each situated in its perfect spot in the city.

The American capital was coming into its own on the world stage, as well, emerging from the Great Depression, two world wars, and technological advancements in air and automobile travel as a strong, respected, global power. More and more countries established embassies here, and the city's international population increased exponentially.

Black Broadway Sets the Stage

As the capital city blossomed, so did African-American culture. The many blacks who had arrived in the city as slaves to help build the Capitol, the White House, and other fundamental structures of America's capital stayed on, later joined by those who came to fight during the Civil War, or to begin new lives after the war. (See p. 144 for a description of the African American Civil War Memorial and Museum, which commemorates the lives of the 209,145 black Civil War soldiers.)

From 1900 to 1960, Washington, D.C. became known as a hub of black culture, education, and identity, centered on a stretch of U Street NW, called "Black Broadway," where Cab Calloway, Duke Ellington, and Pearl Bailey often performed in

3

WASHINGTON, D.C., IN CONTEXT | The Making of Washington, D.C.

speakeasies and theaters. Many of these stars performed at the Howard Theatre (p. 186), which was the first full-size theater devoted to black audiences and entertainers when it opened in 1910. Nearby Howard University, created in 1867, distinguished itself as the nation's most comprehensive center for higher education for blacks. (The reincarnated "U Street Corridor," or "New U," is now a diverse neighborhood of blacks, whites, Asians, and Latinos, and a major restaurant and nightlife destination.)

The Civil Rights Era Ushers in a New Age

By 1950 blacks made up 60% of Washington's total population of 802,000, a record number that would then steadily decrease throughout the rest of the 20th century. Nearly a century after the passage of the 13th Amendment (abolishing slavery) and the 15th Amendment (outlawing the denial of voting rights based on race or color), blacks generally remained unequal members of society. Despite the best efforts and contributions of individuals—from abolitionist Frederick Douglass (p. 150), a major force in the human rights movement in the 19th century, to educator and civil rights leader Mary McLeod Bethune (p. 144), who served as an advisor to President Franklin Delano Roosevelt in the 1930s—the country, and this city, had a long way to go in terms of equal rights. (Consider reading works by Edward P. Jones, the Pulitzer Prize–winning author whose short-story collections, *Lost in the City* and *All Aunt Hagar's Children,* will take you beyond D.C.'s political and tourist attractions into the neighborhoods and everyday lives of African Americans during the mid-20th century.)

The tipping point may have come in 1954, when Thurgood Marshall (appointed the country's first black Supreme Court justice in 1967) argued and won the Supreme Court case *Brown v. Board of Education of Topeka,* which denied the legality of segregation in America. This decision, amid a groundswell of frustration and anger over racial discrimination, helped spark the civil rights movement of the 1960s. On August 28, 1963, black and white Washingtonians were among the 200,000 who marched on Washington and listened to an impassioned Rev. Dr. Martin Luther King, Jr. deliver his stirring "I Have a Dream" speech on the steps of the Lincoln Memorial, where 41 years earlier, during the memorial's dedication ceremony, black officials were required to stand and watch from across the road.

The assassination of President John F. Kennedy on November 22, 1963, added to a general sense of despair and tumult. On the day before his funeral, hundreds of thousands of mourners stood in line for blocks outside the Capitol all day and night to pay their respects to the president, who lay in state inside the Rotunda of the Capitol.

Then Martin Luther King, Jr. was assassinated on April 4, 1968, and all hell broke loose. The corner of 14th and U streets served as the flashpoint for the riots that followed. Ben's Chili Bowl (p. 76) was ground zero and remained open throughout the riots to provide food and shelter to activists, firefighters, and public servants.

As the 20th century progressed, civil rights demonstrations led to Vietnam War protests led to revelations about scandals, from President Nixon's Watergate political debacle (ever seen *All the President's Men*? You have to), to D.C. Mayor Marion Barry's drug and corruption problems, to President Clinton's sexual shenanigans. It was an era of speaking out to expose corruption and scandal. A president who authorizes illegal activity? Not acceptable. A mayor with a drug problem? Not acceptable. A president who dallies with a White House intern his daughter's age, then lies about it? Nope, not acceptable.

And still the city flourished. A world-class subway system opened, the Verizon Center sports and concert arena debuted and transformed its aged downtown neighborhood into

LITTLE-KNOWN facts

○ Many people—including Washington, District of Columbia residents themselves—wonder how the city wound up with such an unwieldy name. Here's how: President Washington referred to the newly created capital as "the Federal City." City commissioners then chose the names "Washington" to honor the president and "Territory of Columbia" to designate the federal nature of the area. Columbia was the feminine form of Columbus, synonymous in those days with "America" and all she stood for—namely, liberty. The capital was incorporated in 1871, when it officially became known as Washington, District of Columbia.

○ The distance between the base of the Capitol, at one end of the National Mall, and the Lincoln Memorial, at the other, is nearly 2 miles. The circumference of the White House property, from Pennsylvania Avenue to Constitution Avenue and 15th Street to 17th Street, is about 1½ miles.

○ More than 27 percent of Washington, D.C. is national parkland, which makes the capital one of the "greenest" cities in the country. The biggest chunk is the 2,000-acre Rock Creek Park, the National Park Service's oldest natural urban park, founded in 1890.

○ Every country that maintains diplomatic relations with the United States has an embassy in the nation's capital. Currently, the number of embassies comes to 176, mostly located along Massachusetts Avenue, known as Embassy Row, and other streets in the Dupont Circle neighborhood.

3

WASHINGTON, D.C., IN CONTEXT | The Making of Washington, D.C.

the immensely popular Penn Quarter, and the city's Kennedy Center, Shakespeare theaters, and other arts-and-culture venues came to world attention, receiving much acclaim.

Twenty-First-Century Times

Having begun the 20th century a backwater town, Washington finished the century a sophisticated city, profoundly shaken but not paralyzed by the September 11, 2001, terrorist attacks. The first decade of the 21st century was marked by the Afghanistan and Iraq wars and by a precipitous economic decline. Here in Washington, these situations continue to foment rancorous relations in Congress and between Capitol Hill and the White House, as Democrats and Republicans disagree over how best to resolve these issues. Barack Obama's landmark win as the first African-American president, in 2008, temporarily restored some hope and an "all things are possible" perspective. Six years later, however, even as the U.S. has slowly extricated itself from Iraq and is working to do the same in Afghanistan, and even as the economy seems to be showing signs of a steady improvement, the outlook is not entirely certain. Peace and prosperity? One can hope. Certainly President Obama is working to achieve that, halfway through his second term. Meanwhile, in the District, Congresswoman Eleanor Holmes Norton, halfway through her twelfth term, continues to work for the good of her constituents. For D.C. Mayor Vincent Gray, success has been hard to come by. The people will measure his progress in the next mayoral election, takes place at the end of 2014.

History informs one's outlook, but so does the present. Look again at the Potomac River and think of Captain John Smith, but observe the Georgetown University crew teams rowing in unison across the surface of the water, and tour boats traveling between Georgetown and Old Town Alexandria. As you traverse the city, admire L'Enfant's inspired design, but also enjoy the sight of office workers, artists and students, and people of every possible ethnic and national background making their way around town. Tour the impressive landmarks and remember their namesakes, but make time for D.C.'s homegrown attractions, whether a meal at a sidewalk cafe in Dupont Circle, jazz along U Street, a walking tour past Capitol Hill's old town houses, or a visit to a church where slaves or those original immigrants once worshiped.

WHEN TO GO

The city's peak seasons generally coincide with two activities: the sessions of Congress, and springtime—beginning with the appearance of the cherry blossoms.

Specifically, from about the second week in September until Thanksgiving, and again from about mid-January to June (when Congress is "in"), hotels are full of guests whose business takes them to Capitol Hill or to conferences. Mid-March through June is traditionally the most frenzied season, when families and school groups descend upon the city to see the cherry blossoms and enjoy Washington's sensational spring. Hotel rooms are at a premium, and airfares tend to be higher. This is also a popular season for protest marches.

If crowds turn you off, consider visiting Washington at the end of August or in early September, when Congress is still "out" and families have returned home to get their children back to school, or between Thanksgiving and mid-January, when Congress leaves again and many people are busy with their own at-home holiday celebrations. Hotel rates are cheapest at this time, too, and many hotels offer attractive packages.

If you're thinking of visiting in July and August, be forewarned: The weather is very hot and humid. Despite the heat, Independence Day (July 4th) in the capital is a spectacular celebration. Summer is also the season for outdoor concerts, festivals, parades, and other events (see chapter 8 for details about performing arts schedules). If you can deal with the weather, this is a good time to visit: Locals often go elsewhere on vacation, so the streets and attractions are somewhat less crowded. In addition, hotels tend to offer their best rates in July and August.

Weather

Season by season, here's what you can expect of the weather in Washington:

Fall: This is my favorite season. The weather is often warm during the day—in fact, if you're here in early fall, it may seem entirely *too* warm. But it cools off, and even gets a bit crisp, at night. By late October, Washington has traded its famous greenery for the brilliant colors of fall foliage.

Winter: People like to say that Washington winters are mild—and sure, if you're from Minnesota, you'll find Washington warmer, no doubt. But D.C. winters can be unpredictable: bitter cold one day, an ice storm the next, followed by a couple of days of sun and higher temperatures. The winters of 2010 and 2011 were especially severe, bringing record snows; 2012's was very mild; and winter 2013 was a mix! Pack with all possibilities in mind.

Spring: Early spring weather tends to be colder than most people expect. Cherry blossom season, late March to early April, can be iffy—and very often rainy and windy. As April slips into May, the weather usually mellows, and people's moods with it. Late spring is especially lovely, with mild temperatures and intermittent days of sunshine, flowers, and trees colorfully erupting in gardens and parks all over town. Washingtonians sweep outdoors to stroll the National Mall, relax on park benches, or laze away the afternoon at outdoor cafes.

Summer: Anyone who has ever spent July and August in D.C. will tell you how hot and steamy it can be. Though the buildings are air-conditioned, many of Washington's attractions, like the memorials and organized tours, are outdoors and unshaded, and the heat can quickly get to you. Make sure you stop frequently for drinks (vendors are plentiful), and wear a hat, sunglasses, and sunscreen.

Average Temperatures & Rainfall in Washington, D.C.

	JAN	FEB	MAR	APR	MAY	JUNE	JULY	AUG	SEPT	OCT	NOV	DEC
Temp (°F)	43/24	47/26	55/33	66/42	76/52	84/62	89/67	87/65	80/57	69/44	58/36	48/28
Rainfall (in.)	3.57	2.84	3.92	3.26	4.29	3.63	4.21	3.90	4.08	3.43	3.32	3.25

Holidays

Banks, government offices, post offices, and many stores, restaurants, and museums are closed on the following legal national holidays: January 1 (New Year's Day), the third Monday in January (Martin Luther King, Jr. Day), the third Monday in February (Presidents' Day), the last Monday in May (Memorial Day), July 4 (Independence Day), the first Monday in September (Labor Day), the second Monday in October (Columbus Day), November 11 (Veterans Day/Armistice Day), the fourth Thursday in November (Thanksgiving Day), and December 25 (Christmas).

Washington, D.C., Calendar of Events

Washington's 2013 will start off with a bang, with the presidential inauguration in January. Otherwise the city's most popular events are the annual Cherry Blossom Festival in spring, the Fourth of July celebration in summer, and the lighting of the National Christmas Tree in winter. But some sort of special event occurs almost daily. For the latest schedules, check **www.washington.org**, **www.culturaltourismdc.org**, **www.dc.gov**, and **www. washingtonpost.com**.

The phone numbers in the calendar below were accurate at press time, but these numbers change often. If the number you try doesn't get you the details you need, call **Destination D.C.** at ✆ **202/789-7000**.

When you're in town, grab a copy of the *Washington Post* (or read it online), especially the Friday "Weekend" section.

JANUARY

Martin Luther King, Jr.'s Birthday. Events include speeches by prominent leaders and politicians, readings, dance, theater, concerts and choral performances, and prayer vigils at the National Martin Luther King, Jr. Memorial, on the national holiday (third Mon in Jan). Call the National Park Service at ✆ **202/619-7222**.

FEBRUARY

Black History Month. Numerous events, museum exhibits, and cultural programs celebrate the contributions of African Americans to American life, including a celebration of abolitionist Frederick Douglass's birthday. For details check the *Washington Post* or call the National Park Service at ✆ **202/619-7222**.

Chinese New Year Celebration. A Friendship Archway, topped by 300 painted dragons and lighted at night, marks the entrance to Chinatown at 7th and H streets NW. The celebration begins the day of the Chinese New Year and continues for 10 or more days, with traditional firecrackers, dragon dancers, and colorful street parades. Some area restaurants offer special menus. For details call Destination D.C. at ℂ **202/789-7000.** Early February.

Abraham Lincoln's Birthday. Expect great fanfare at Ford's Theatre and its Center for Education and Leadership, an exploration of Lincoln's legacy in the time since his assassination (p. 133). As always, a wreath-laying and reading of the Gettysburg Address will take place at noon at the Lincoln Memorial. Call Ford's Theatre at ℂ **202/426-6924,** or the National Park Service at ℂ **202/619-7222.** February 12.

George Washington's Birthday/Presidents' Day. The city celebrates Washington's birthday in two ways: on the actual day, February 22, with a ceremony that takes place at the Washington Monument; and on the federal holiday, the third Monday in February, when schools and federal offices have the day off. Call the National Park Service at ℂ **202/619-7222** for details. The occasion also brings with it great sales at stores citywide. (See chapter 10, "Side Trips from Washington, D.C.," for information about the bigger celebrations held at Mount Vernon and in Old Town Alexandria on the third Mon in Feb.)

D.C. Fashion Week. This biannual event features designers from around the world. The weeklong extravaganza stages parties, runway shows, and trunk shows at citywide venues, always culminating in an international couture fashion show at the French Embassy. Most events are open to the public but may require a ticket. Call ℂ **202/600-9274** or visit www.dcfashionweek.org. Mid-February and mid-September.

MARCH

Women's History Month. Count on the Smithsonian to cover the subject to a fare-thee-well. For a schedule of Smithsonian events, call ℂ **202/633-1000** or visit www.si.edu; for other events, check the websites listed in the intro to this section.

St. Patrick's Day Parade. This big parade on Constitution Avenue NW, from 7th to 17th streets, is complete with floats, bagpipes, marching bands, and the wearin' o' the green. For parade information, call Destination D.C. at ℂ **202/789-7000** or visit www.dcstpatsparade.com. The Sunday before March 17.

APRIL

National Cherry Blossom Festival. Strike up the band! This year, 2014, marks the 102nd anniversary of the city of Tokyo's gift of cherry trees to the city of Washington. This event is celebrated annually; if all goes well, the festival coincides with the blossoming of the more than 3,700 Japanese cherry trees by the Tidal Basin, on Hains Point, and on the grounds of the Washington Monument. Events take place all over town and include the Blossom Kite Festival on the grounds of the Washington Monument, fireworks, concerts, special art exhibits, park-ranger-guided talks and tours past the trees, and sports competitions. A Japanese Street Festival takes place on one of the final days of the celebration, and a grand parade caps the festival, complete with floats, marching bands, dancers, celebrity guests, and more. All events are free except for the Japanese Street Fair, which costs $5, and grandstand seating at the parade, which costs $17 (otherwise the parade is free). For information call ℂ **877/44BLOOM** (442-5666) or go to www.nationalcherryblossomfestival.org. March 20 to April 13, 2014.

White House Easter Egg Roll. A biggie for kids 12 and under, the annual White House Easter Egg Roll continues a practice begun in 1878. Entertainment on the White House South Lawn and the Ellipse traditionally includes appearances by costumed cartoon characters, clowns, musical groups (Fergie and the Jonas Brothers are among those who have performed in the past), egg-decorating exhibitions, puppet and magic shows, an Easter egg hunt, and an egg-rolling contest. To obtain tickets, you must use the online lottery system, up and running about 6 weeks before Easter Monday. For details all ℂ **202/208-1631** or visit www. whitehouse.gov/eastereggroll. Easter Monday between 8am and 5pm.

African-American Family Day at the National Zoo. This tradition extends back to

1889, when the zoo opened. The National Zoo, 3001 Connecticut Ave. NW, celebrates African-American families on the day after Easter with music, dance, Easter egg rolls, and other activities. Free. Call ☏ **202/633-1000** for details. Easter Monday.

Earth Day. This year marks the 44th anniversary of Earth Day. Official Earth Day is April 22; D.C. often marks the event on a Sunday close to that date. The National Mall is ground zero for green-themed volunteer activities, campaigning, and live music performed by big names—Los Lobos and the Flaming Lips have played in the past. Call ☏ **202/518-0044** or visit www.earthday.org. April 22.

Smithsonian Craft Show. Held in the National Building Museum, 401 F St. NW, this juried show features one-of-a-kind limited-edition crafts by more than 120 noted artists from all over the country. There's an entrance fee of about $15 per adult each day; it's free for children 12 and under. No strollers. For details call ☏ **888/832-9554** or 202/633-5006, or visit www.smithsoniancraftshow.org. Four days in mid- to late April.

MAY

Washington National Cathedral Annual Flower Mart. Now in its 75th year, the flower mart takes place on cathedral grounds, featuring displays of flowering plants and herbs, decorating demonstrations, ethnic food booths, children's rides and activities (including an antique carousel), costumed characters, puppet shows, and other entertainment. Admission is free. For details call ☏ **202/387-2979** or visit www.allhallowsguild.org. First Friday and Saturday in May, rain or shine.

Memorial Day. Ceremonies take place at the Tomb of the Unknowns in Arlington National Cemetery (☏ **703/607-8000**), at the National World War II and Vietnam Veterans memorials (☏ **202/619-7222**), and at the U.S. Navy Memorial (☏ **202/737-2300**). A National Memorial Day Parade marches down Constitution Avenue from the Capitol to the White House. On the Sunday before

Memorial Day, the National Symphony Orchestra performs a free concert at 8pm on the West Lawn of the Capitol to honor the sacrifices of American servicemen and servicewomen (☏ **202/619-7222**). And one other thing: Hundreds of thousands of bikers from around the country roll into town in an annual event called "Rolling Thunder," to pay tribute to America's war veterans, prisoners of war, and those missing in action (www.rollingthunder1.com).

JUNE

DC Jazz Festival. The festival, now in its 10th year, presents more than 125 performances in dozens of venues throughout the city over a 10-day to 2-week period. Some performances are free, some are not. Beginning to mid-June. www.dcjazzfest.org.

Smithsonian Folklife Festival. A major event celebrating both national and international traditions in music, crafts, foods, games, concerts, and exhibits, staged the length of the National Mall. Each Folklife Festival showcases three or four cultures or themes; 2013's festival explored Hungarian Heritage, and the themes of "endangered language and cultural heritage," and "African American diversity, style, and identity." All events are free; most take place outdoors. For details call ☏ **202/633-6440,** visit www.festival.si.edu, or check the listings in the *Washington Post*. Ten days in late June and early July, always including July 4.

JULY

Independence Day. There's no better place to be on the Fourth of July than in Washington, D.C. The all-day festivities include a massive National Independence Day Parade down Constitution Avenue, complete with lavish floats, princesses, marching groups, and military bands. A morning program in front of the National Archives includes military demonstrations, period music, and a reading of the Declaration of Independence. In the evening, the National Symphony Orchestra plays on the west steps of the Capitol with guest artists. And big-name entertainment precedes the fabulous fireworks display behind the Washington Monument. For details or call the National Park

Service at ℂ **202/619-7222** or visit www. nps.gov/mall. July 4.

Capital Fringe Festival. This event debuted in 2005 and celebrates experimental theater in the tradition of the original fringe festival, held annually in Edinburgh, Scotland. More than 130 separate productions take place at some 14 venues daily for 18 days, and it all adds up to about 700-plus individual performances. Local and visiting artists perform in theater, dance, music, and other disciplines. The action centers on the Penn Quarter. All single tickets are $17, plus a one-time fee of $5 for an admission button; purchase them on www.capitalfringe.org, call ℂ **866/811-4111,** or visit the Fort Fringe Box Office, 607 New York Ave. NW. For details call ℂ **202/207-3645.** Eighteen days starting around the second week of July.

AUGUST

Shakespeare Theatre Free for All. This free theater festival presents a different Shakespeare play every year for a 2-week run at the Sidney Harmon Hall, across from the Verizon Center, in the Penn Quarter. Tickets are required, but they're free. Call ℂ **202/547-1122** or visit www. shakespearetheatre.org. Evenings and some matinees late August through early September.

SEPTEMBER

Labor Day Concert. The National Symphony Orchestra closes its summer season with a free performance at 8pm on the West Lawn of the Capitol. For details call the National Park Service at ℂ **202/619-7222.** Sunday before Labor Day. (Rain date: Same day and time at Constitution Hall or the Kennedy Center.)

Library of Congress National Book Festival. The Library of Congress sponsors this festival, welcoming at least 80 established authors and their many fans to the National Mall for readings, author signings, and general hoopla surrounding the love of books.

For details call ℂ **888/714-4696** or visit www.loc.gov/bookfest. A weekend in late September.

OCTOBER

Marine Corps Marathon. Thirty thousand runners compete in this 26.2-mile race (the fifth-largest marathon in the United States). The 2014 running marks its 39th year. It begins at the Marine Corps Memorial (the Iwo Jima statue) and passes many major monuments. For details call ℂ **800/RUN-USMC** (786-8762). Participants must be 14 or older; register online at www.marinemarathon.com. Last Sunday in October.

NOVEMBER

Veterans Day. The nation's fallen heroes are honored with a wreath-laying ceremony at 11am at the Tomb of the Unknowns in Arlington National Cemetery, followed by a memorial service. The president of the United States or his stand-in officiates, as a military band performs. Wreath-laying ceremonies also take place at other war memorials in the city. Call ℂ **703/607-8000** for details about Arlington Cemetery events and **202/619-7222** for details about war memorial events. November 11.

DECEMBER

National Christmas Tree Lighting. At the northern end of the Ellipse, the president lights the national Christmas tree to the accompaniment of orchestral and choral music, and big name performers take the stage. The lighting ceremony inaugurates several weeks of holiday concerts performed mostly by local school and church choruses, afternoons and evenings on the Ellipse. (Brrrr!) For details call ℂ **202/208-1631,** and visit the website, www.thenationaltree.org, to enter the lottery for tickets, which are free but required to attend the tree-lighting ceremony. (No tickets are required to attend the other holiday concerts.) The tree-lighting ceremony takes place at 5pm on a day in early December.

WHERE TO STAY IN WASHINGTON, D.C.

I f your desire for superb accommodations trumps your concern about expense, you should have no trouble discovering just the hotel for you in Washington, D.C.'s stable of upscale properties. In shorter supply are inexpensive and moderately priced hotels. In fact, the cheapest lodging is found more readily outside the District, in suburban Virginia and Maryland motels and hotels. But do I think you should stay there? No. For a full-blooded experience of the capital, you need to stay overnight and wake up within its urban embrace.

4

Washington, D.C., has nearly 130 hotels. In this chapter, I present you with descriptions of about 30 properties, all of which I have visited. The majority of the hotels skew to the more affordable, whose overnight rates can go as low as $99, but seldom higher than $250. I've also included several high-end options, not just for the one percenters, but for those who seek a fabulous deal at a five-star place. (For tips, read "Getting the Best Deal," at the end of this chapter.)

The common denominator is the "distinctly D.C." factor, from the posh **Hay-Adams** (p. 50) showing off its view of the White House to the **Capitol Hill Hotel** (p. 46), the only hotel truly located on "The Hill." For the most part, I've eschewed chains, not because they're not worthy choices, but because the experience is somewhat predictable and usually has more to do with the hotel brand than the city itself.

GETTING THE BEST DEAL

Want the secret for getting the best hotel deal ever in Washington? Easy: Come to Washington when Congress is out, when cherry blossom season is over, or during the blazing hot days of July or August or the icy-cold days of a noninauguration-year January or February. Not possible? Okay, let's put it this way: Don't try to negotiate a good deal for late March or early April (cherry blossom season); hotel reservationists will laugh at you. I've heard them.

PRICE categories

Expensive	$300 and up
Moderate	$200–$300
Inexpensive	Under $200

Consider these tips, too:

o **Visit on a weekend if you can.** Hotels looking to fill rooms vacated by weekday business travelers lower their rates and might be willing to negotiate even further for weekend arrivals.

o **Ask about special rates or other discounts and whether a room less expensive than the first one quoted is available.** You may qualify for substantial corporate, government, student, military, senior, or other discounts. Mention membership in AAA, AARP, frequent-flier programs, or trade unions, which may entitle you to special deals.

o **Book online.** Because booking online is so often the best way to get a discount, we've devoted an entire box to a discussion of how to get the best deals. See p. 42.

o **Look into group or long-stay discounts.** If you come as part of a large group, you should be able to negotiate a bargain rate because the hotel can then guarantee occupancy in a number of rooms. Likewise, if you're planning a long stay (at least 5 days), you might qualify for a discount. As a general rule, expect 1 night free after a 7-night stay.

o **Consider enrolling in hotel "frequent-stay" programs**, which aim to win the loyalty of repeat customers. Frequent guests can accumulate points or credits to earn free hotel nights, airline miles, in-room amenities, merchandise, tickets to concerts and events, and discounts on sporting facilities. Perks are awarded not only by many chain hotels and motels (Hilton Honors and Omni Select Guests, to name two), but also by individual inns and B&Bs.

o **Finally, whether or not you've gotten the best deal possible on your room rate, you can still save money on incidental costs.** D.C. hotels charge unbelievable rates for overnight parking—up to $50 a night at some hotels, plus tax—so if you can avoid driving, you can save yourself quite a bit of money. Avoid dialing direct from hotel phones, which usually have exorbitant rates—as do the room's minibar offerings.

Keep in mind that D.C. hotel sales tax is a whopping 14.5%, merchandise sales tax is 5.75%, and food and beverage tax is 10%, all of which can rapidly increase the cost of a room.

Consider Alternative Accommodations

If your luck and time are running out and you still haven't found a place to stay, and/or if your budget constrains you from choosing one of the selections in this chapter, consider these alternatives:

o **Hostelling International Washington, DC** (1009 11th St. NW, at K St.; *(C)* www. hiwashingtondc.org; 888/464-4872 or 202/737-2333) is well located in the Penn Quarter and nicely equipped, with Wi-Fi, bike racks, and air conditioning. Breakfast is complimentary and the hostel often hosts complimentary dinners. In all, there are

WHAT YOU'LL really PAY

The prices given in this chapter and the price categories given above are rack rates, the maximum that a hotel might charge for a "double" room. At most hotels, you probably won't pay the very highest rate unless you visit in the spring—especially during cherry blossom season in late March and early April—and during inauguration Januarys, every 4 years. These categories are intended as a general guideline only, since rates can rise and fall dramatically, depending on how busy the hotel is. In this chapter, I've tried to show a more realistic picture, providing peak and off-peak rates, sometimes presented as a range, for each hotel.

Discounts are often available online (see p. 42 for tips), or by booking through agencies. When the timing's right, it's not impossible to obtain a room at an expensive property for the same rate as a more moderate one. And if you're persistent, you can try besting the hotel's own discount by searching for a better price on the websites of the major discounters, then calling the hotel and quoting the discovered cheaper rate—it's usually hotel policy to match the lower price.

Two notes: Quoted discount rates almost never include the hefty 14.5 percent hotel sales tax. The word "double" refers to the number of people in the room, not to the size of the bed. Most hotels charge one rate, regardless of whether one or two people occupy the room. In a few cases, a hotel specifies separate rates for "single" and "double" occupancy, and I provide that information.

280 beds, all but a handful without private bath. Dorm rooms and private rooms are available at rates that range from $32 to $152 a night per person, plus $3 Hostelling International daily membership fee.

o **Check out AirBnB,** a website-based rental operation that matches people looking for a place to stay with locals interested in renting out space in their home, or sometimes the entire apartment or house, often for far less than you might pay at a hotel. At the time researched, **AirBnB Washington, D.C.** (www.airbnb.com/locations-dc) had 1,439 listings scattered among 31 neighborhoods. Similarly, **Vacation Rentals by Owner** (www.vrbo.com), **FiipKey.com,** and **HomeAway.com** among others, offers furnished apartments for rent around the city.

o **Consider house swapping.** Try such organizations as **The Home Exchange** (www.homeexchange.com) or **HomeLink International** (www.homelink.org) which offer tens of thousands of would-be swaps worldwide (take into account the membership fees when looking at the overall costs).

o **Call Washington's tourism bureau, Destination D.C.** (② 202/789-7000), and ask the tourist rep for the names and numbers of any **new or about-to-open hotels.** If the rep isn't sure, ask her to check with the marketing director. Up-and-coming hotels may have available rooms, for the simple reason that few people know about them. Hotels scheduled to open in D.C. in 2014 included the **Hilton Garden Inn,** in the West End; **Half Street Hotel,** near Nationals Park, in the Capitol Riverfront neighborhood; and the enormous convention center hotel, the 1,175-room Washington Marriott Marquis, at 901 Massachusetts Avenue, NW.

o **Consider staying outside the city.** In northern Virginia, Rte. 1, also known as Jefferson Davis Highway within Crystal City limits, is lined with hotels for every

TURNING TO THE internet or apps FOR A HOTEL DISCOUNT

Before going online, it's important that you know what "flavor" of discount you're seeking. Currently, there are three types of online reductions and one that's app based.

1. **Extreme discounts on sites where you bid for lodgings without knowing which hotel you'll get.** You'll find these on such sites as Priceline.com and Hotwire.com, and they can be real money-savers, particularly if you're booking within a week of travel (that's when the hotels get nervous and resort to deep discounts to get beds filled). As these companies use only major chains, you can rest assured that you won't be put up in a dump. For more reassurance, visit the website Better Bidding.com. On it, actual travelers spill the beans about what they bid on Priceline.com and which hotels they got. I think you'll be pleasantly surprised by the quality of many of the hotels that are offering these "secret" discounts to the opaque bidding websites.

2. **Discounts on the hotel's website itself.** Sometimes these can be great values, as they'll often include such nice perks as free breakfast or parking privileges. Before biting, though be sure to look at the discounter sites right below.

3. **Discounts on online travel agencies as Hotels.com, Quikbook.com, Expedia.com, and the like.** Some of these sites reserve these rooms in bulk and at a discount, passing along the savings to their customers. But instead of going to them directly, I'd recommend looking at such dedicated travel search engines as **Hipmunk.com, HotelsCombined. com, Momondo.com** and **Trivago. com.** These sites list prices from all the discount sites as well as the hotels directly, meaning you have a better chance of finding a discount. **Note:** Sometimes the discounts these sites find require advance payment for a room (and draconian cancellation policies), so double check your travel dates before booking. **Tingo.com,** a site founded by Trip Advisor.com, is another good source, especially for luxury hotels. Its model is a bit different than the others. Users make a pre-paid reservation through it, but if the price of the room drops between the time you make the booking and the date of arrival, the site refunds the difference in price.

4. **Try the app HotelsTonight.com.** It only works for day of bookings, but WOW, does it get great prices for procrastinators (up to 70% off in many cases). A possible strategy: make a reservation at a hotel, then on the day you're arriving try your luck with HotelsTonight. Most hotels will allow you to cancel without penalty, even on the date of arrival.

It's a lot of surfing, I know, but in the hothouse world of D.C. hotel pricing, this sort of diligence can pay off.

budget. A good listing is available on the Metropolitan Washington Airports Authority website (www.mwaa.com/reagan/reagan.htm). Click on "Travel Tips," and then click on "Local Hotels," in the Local Tourism section on that page to discover the rundown of nearby hotels.

Reservation Services

If you suffer from information overload and would rather someone else do the research and bargaining, you can always turn to one of these two reputable—and free!—local reservations services:

○ **WDCAHotels.com** (www.wdcahotels.com; © **800/503-3330**): This company has been in business for 29 years and, in addition to finding lodgings, can advise you about transportation and general tourist information, and even work out itineraries.

○ **BedandBreakfastDC.com** (www.bedandbreakfastdc.com; © **877/893-3233**): In business since 1978, this organization works with a large selection of private homes, inns, guesthouses, and unhosted furnished apartments to find lodging for visitors.

ON OR NEAR CAPITOL HILL

A handful of hotels form a cluster just north of the Capitol, adjacent to Union Station; just one hotel lies on Capitol Hill itself, a few minutes' walk from the Capitol. These hotels are also within easy reach of the National Mall.

Best for: Travelers who have business at the Capitol and tourists who want to be close to the Capitol and other Hill attractions, as well as to the National Mall.

Drawbacks: These neighborhoods are in the thick of things during the day, but not so much at night.

Expensive

The George, a Kimpton Hotel ★★   The George, which is the best hotel closest to the Capitol, just got a little more whimsically attractive, thanks to a late 2013 renovation. Among the changes in the 260-square-foot guest rooms, look for light cream with parchment and ink-stylized wall graphics of George Washington's inaugural address, and accent pillows based on GW's original uniforms. The George's main clientele are weekday business people and weekend tourists, both of whom have agendas at the Capitol, a very pleasant 8-minute walk away. (Turn left outside the hotel and walk up the block to North Capitol St., turn right on North Capitol St. and then just head toward that big white building up in front of you.) The only other hotel closer to the Capitol is the Capitol Hill Hotel (see below), an entirely different kind of lodging. Celebrities often stay at The George, too, and not just those visiting Congress to plead the case for their pet cause. Big name musicians (ladies and gentlemen, the Rolling Stones!) like The George and this is interesting, because the hotel is not the most obvious choice. Its location is not the hotspot of, say, a Penn Quarter or Georgetown property. Nor is The George associated with the kind of over-the-top luxury of, for instance, a Ritz-Carlton or a Four Seasons. Rather, The George offers playful personality, sumptuously comfortable guest rooms, and total discretion. The hotel's resident restaurant, **Bistro Bis**, is a longtime favorite among locals and visitors, big names or not.

15 E St. NW (at N. Capitol St.). www.hotelgeorge.com. © **800/546-7866** or 202/347-4200. 139 units. Weekdays $289–$489 double; weekends $139–$299 double; $750–$1,050 suite. Children 17 and under stay free in parent's room. Rates include hosted evening wine hour. Extra person $20. Parking $45. Metro: Union Station (Massachusetts Ave. exit). Pets accepted. **Amenities:** Restaurant; bar; children's amenity program; concierge; small exercise room w/steam rooms; room service; Wi-Fi (free).

Washington, D.C., Hotels

Garfield St. NW

Fulton St. NW

Woodley Rd. **2**

1

Woodley Park–Zoo/
Adams Morgan

Calvert St. NW **3**

Harvard St. NW

**NATIONAL
ZOO**

Columbia Rd. NW

Euclid St. NW

**ADAMS
MORGAN**

Woodland Dr. NW

Observatory Circle

**U.S. Naval
Observatory**

E M B A S S Y   R O W

Massachusetts Ave. NW

**ROCK
CREEK
PARK**

Belmont Rd. NW

Kalorama Rd.

Florida Ave.
W St. NW

V St. NW

Florida Ave. NW

4

California St. NW

U STREET

U St. NW

T St. NW

**DUMBARTON
OAKS PARK**

**MONTROSE
PARK**

S St. NW

5
Sheridan
Circle

R St. NW

Corcoran St. NW

**DUPONT
CIRCLE**

13

Q St. NW

Church St. NW

P St. NW

R St. NW
Reservoir Rd.
NW
**GEORGETOWN
UNIVERSITY**

R St. NW

Q St. NW

P St. NW

O St. NW

Dumbarton St. NW

N St. NW

Massachusetts

Dupont
Circle

12

17

16

14 **15**
Scott
Circle

18

GEORGETOWN

Prospect St. NW

M St. NW

6 **7** **8**

9

Washington
Circle

11

L St. NW

K St. NW

Farragut
West

I St. NW

20

Farragut
North

21 **22**

Farragut
Square

23

Thomas
Circle

19

McPherson
Square

Francis Scott
Key Bridge

Whitehurst Fwy. NW

Pennsylvania Ave.

**GEORGE
WASHINGTON
UNIVERSITY**

Virginia Ave.

G St. NW

F St. NW

E St. NW

24

Pennsylvania

**Theodore
Roosevelt
Island**

Georgetown Channel

Rock Creek and Potomac Pkwy. NW

Foggy
Bottom–
GWU

Kennedy
Center

**FOGGY
BOTTOM**

C St. NW

**White
House**

**THE
ELLIPSE**

Little River

George Washington Memorial Pkwy.

Constitution Ave. NW

Theodore Roosevelt
Mem. Bridge

**Lincoln
Memorial**

**Vietnam Veterans
Memorial**

Reflecting Pool

**WWII
Memorial**

**Washington
Monument**

**Iwo Jima
Memorial**

VIRGINIA

**ARLINGTON
NATIONAL
CEMETERY**

**LADY BIRD
JOHNSON
PARK**

Arlington
Cemetery

Arlington Mem. Bridge

WEST POTOMAC PARK

Potomac River

Independence Ave. SW

Ohio Dr. SW

Cherry Trees

Tidal Basin

**FDR
Memorial**

**Jefferson
Memorial**

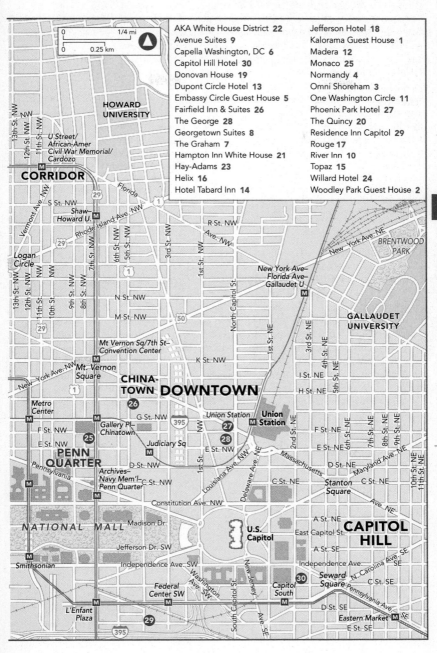

AKA White House District **22**
Avenue Suites **9**
Capella Washington, DC **6**
Capitol Hill Hotel **30**
Donovan House **19**
Dupont Circle Hotel **13**
Embassy Circle Guest House **5**
Fairfield Inn & Suites **26**
The George **28**
Georgetown Suites **8**
The Graham **7**
Hampton Inn White House **21**
Hay-Adams **23**
Helix **16**
Hotel Tabard Inn **14**

Jefferson Hotel **18**
Kalorama Guest House **1**
Madera **12**
Monaco **25**
Normandy **4**
Omni Shoreham **3**
One Washington Circle **11**
Phoenix Park Hotel **27**
The Quincy **20**
Residence Inn Capitol **29**
Rouge **17**
River Inn **10**
Topaz **15**
Willard Hotel **24**
Woodley Park Guest House **2**

Residence Inn Capitol ★ It's no accident that this Residence Inn is located within walking distance of the National Museum of the American Indian. Three Native American tribes are 49 percent owners of the hotel, which made it the first multi-tribal partnership with nontribal partners on land off the reservation, when the hotel opened in 2005. Although certain features, like stonework in the lobby and artwork throughout, hint at its Native American heritage, the hotel is otherwise similar to standard Residence Inns when it comes to amenities. All rooms are spacious suites (studio, one-bedroom, or two-bedroom) equipped with full kitchens. A $4.5-million renovation completed in 2012 added and/or replaced carpeting, granite counters, furniture, and artwork; re-designed the common areas; and expanded the business center. The hotel does lie close to a train track, so be sure to ask for a room on the other side of the hotel if you think you might be disturbed by the sounds of a train whistling by.

333 E St. SW (at 4th St.). www.marriott/wascp. ℂ **800/331-3131** or 202/484-8280. 233 units. Peak $399 studio, $419 1-bedroom suite, $459 2-bedroom suite; off-peak $159 studio, $169 1-bedroom suite, $299 2-bedroom suite. Call about seasonal and long-term rates. Rates include hot breakfast daily, light dinner Mon-Wed, and grocery delivery service. Parking $35 plus tax. Metro: Federal Center SW or L'Enfant Plaza. Pets accepted for a fee. **Amenities:** Concierge, health club with fitness center, indoor pool, whirlpool, and sundeck; Wi-Fi (free).

Moderate

Capitol Hill Hotel ★ This all-suite property occupies two buildings on a residential street lined with old town houses. Neighbors include the Library of Congress, the Capitol, and the Supreme Court; just a block away is Pennsylvania Avenue SE's stretch of fun bars and restaurants. Its location is the hotel's prime attraction, since it is the only hotel truly *on* the Hill (on the House side of the Capitol). The term *suite* denotes the fact that every unit has a kitchenette with coffeemaker, microwave, refrigerator, utensils, and glassware. Most units are efficiencies, with the kitchenette, bed, and sofa all in the same room. Best choices are one-bedroom units, in which the kitchenette and living room are separate from the bedroom. Some rooms have pullout sofas. Whatever the configuration, rooms are generally spacious, ranging in size from 320 to 510 square feet. A renovation begun in late 2013 should be complete by March 2014, replacing furniture, wall coverings, and window treatments throughout the guest rooms. An ample continental breakfast of baked goods, yogurt, boiled eggs, and fruit is laid out each morning in the first floor breakfast room of the hotel's annex; guests staying in the main building must venture outside to enter the neighboring annex. Monday through Thursday evenings, 5 to 6pm, the room serves as the wine social site. Other pluses include a well equipped fitness center, displays of original art by local artists, and restaurant delivery from nearby local favorites, like **Good Stuff Eatery** (p. 68).

200 C St. SE (at 2nd St.). www.capitolhillhotel-dc.com. ℂ **800/814-5983** or 202/543-6000. 152 units. Peak $250–$400 double; off-peak $139–$199 double. Extra person $20. Children 18 and under stay free in parent's room. Rates include continental breakfast daily and wine social Mon-Thurs. Parking $44. Metro: Union Station (Massachusetts Ave. NW exit). Pets accepted. **Amenities:** Fitness center; coin-op washer/dryers; Wi-Fi (free).

Phoenix Park Hotel ★ The flag of Ireland flies outside the entrance to the Phoenix Park, while inside, barkeep Padriac (pronounced "Porick") is pulling drafts of Guinness and Smithwicks (pronounced "Smidicks") in the hotel's lively pub, the **Dubliner** (p. 183). The Irish theme carries over into guest rooms, whose amenities include Irish cotton bathrobes and mahogany furnishings. Guests give top marks to the very high beds and their pillow-topped mattresses. Guest rooms vary in size from 275 to 350 square feet, though rooms in the "new wing," added in 1997, tend to be cozier but not necessarily less expensive. For best views and spaciousness, ask for a room with two queen-size or one king-size bed facing **Union Station** (p. 98) and/or the **National Postal Museum** (p. 96), whose colorful display of "stamped windows" beckons visitors to its new wing, which opened in September 2013. For the quietest rooms, request a room on the top floor, to escape both the sounds drifting up from the Dubliner (live music nightly!) and traffic noise. Families appreciate the bi-level suites, with pullout sofa in the living room and, up the spiral staircase, a loft bedroom. Business and leisure travelers alike choose the Phoenix Park for its convenient proximity to Union Station and to the Capitol.

520 N. Capitol St. NW (at Massachusetts Ave.). www.phoenixparkhotel.com. © **800/824-5419** or 202/638-6900. 149 units. Peak $149–$489 double; off-peak $99–$299 double; from $699 suite. Extra person $30. Children 16 and under stay free in parent's room. Parking $40. Metro: Union Station (Massachusetts Ave. NW exit). **Amenities:** Irish pub; exercise room; room service; Wi-Fi (free).

PENN QUARTER

At the center of the city is this hot locale, jammed with restaurants, bars, museums, theaters, and the Verizon Center sports/concert arena. The plentiful hotels include modern venues catering to convention crowds and historic properties switched up for luxury-loving funseekers.

Best for: Those who love being in the thick of it all. Business travelers are within easy reach of downtown offices, the convention center, and Capitol Hill. Likewise, the Penn Quarter is prime home base for exploring tourists.

Drawbacks: Crowded sidewalks and noisy traffic can be annoying—even overwhelming.

Expensive

Willard InterContinental ★★★ This historic hotel's guest list has always included illustrious figures: President Abraham Lincoln actually lived here in 1861 before moving into the White House, next door. (Lincoln snuck into the hotel dressed as a woman to outwit would-be assassins.) Dr. Martin Luther King, Jr., stayed here in August 1963, in suite 310, where he finished writing his "I Have a Dream" speech. (Dr. King's family stays in this suite whenever they're in town, as they did during the Aug. 28, 2013's 50th anniversary celebration of the delivery of the speech). And from its very start, the Willard has hosted foreign dignitaries, from Japan's 70 Samurai princes in 1860 to . . . well, take a look at the what head of state is on the schedule to visit President Obama, and there's a good chance that dignitary is booked at the Willard.

Guest rooms are handsomely decorated with dark wood furnishings, silk shades on lamps, and inviting flourishes, like the pretty floral throw laid across the end of the plumped-up bed. Ask for courtyard-facing rooms for quiet, and Pennsylvania Avenue-facing rooms for the views. Spring for an oval suite, which look down the avenue to the Capitol.

But you're here as much for the history and ambience as for a place to sleep. You must: enjoy a cocktail at the **Round Robin Bar,** expertly mixed by barman Jim Hewes as he tells tales about Willard guests, from Charles Dickens to Bill Clinton; stroll through the lobby and admire its mosaic floor, marble columns, ornate ceiling; and tour the history gallery filled with memorabilia, like a copy of Lincoln's hotel bill.

1401 Pennsylvania Ave. NW (at 14th St.). www.washington.intercontinental.com. (© **866/487-2537** or 202/628-9100. 335 units. Peak (Mar 1–Jun 30 and Sept 13–Dec 31) weekdays from $459, weekends from $319 double; off-peak (Jan 1–Feb 28 and Jul 1–Sept 12) weekdays from $359, weekends from $259 double. Suites from $434 off-peak to $634 peak. Parking $42. Metro: Metro Center (13th St. exit). Small pets accepted. **Amenities:** Cafe w/seasonal terrace; 2 bars; seasonal afternoon tea in Peacock Alley; babysitting; concierge; thoroughly equipped and luxurious Red Door health club and spa w/steam room, Jacuzzi, and sauna; room service; Wi-Fi ($11/day, $44/week).

Monaco Washington D.C., a Kimpton Hotel ★★

When it was completed in 1866, this historic, four-story, marble building served as the capital's general post office and tariff building for an area that was largely a developing mishmash of big government and smalltown buildings. Hard to imagine now. In 2014, the Monaco is celebrating its 12th year as one of the city's top hotels, in the heart of DC's hottest neighborhood, surrounded by wondrous museums, like the Smithsonian American Art/National Portrait Gallery, and trendy restaurants such as **Azur** and **Hill Country** (p. 71). Ask for an F St. or 7th St.-facing Monte Carlo room (525 square feet) for best views; or a first floor guest room, if quiet is preferred (some guests call this "the basement," since it is nearly subterranean.) Interior rooms overlook the large courtyard, where Poste restaurant and bar patrons sometimes get loud. Always check out special offers posted online, and Loyalty program benefits, which can save you a bunch.

700 F St. NW (at 7th St.). www.monaco-dc.com. (© **800/649-1202** or 202/628-7177. 183 units. Weekdays $299–$499 double, $509–$1,200 suite; weekends $169–$319 double, $269–$800 suite. Extra person $20. Children 17 and under stay free in parent's room. Rates include complimentary organic coffee in morning and a hosted evening wine hour. Parking $42. Metro: Gallery Place (7th and F sts. exit). Pets welcome—they get VIP treatment, with their own registration cards at check-in, maps of neighborhood fire hydrants and parks, and gourmet puppy and kitty treats. **Amenities:** Restaurant; bar; children's amenity program; concierge; spacious fitness center w/flatscreen TVs; room service; Wi-Fi (free, when you sign up for the no-cost Loyalty program).

Moderate

Fairfield Inn & Suites, Washington, D.C./Downtown ★

You're really in the thick of things at this hotel, situated on a busy Chinatown street in the bustling Penn Quarter, a block north of the Verizon Center, and surrounded by hip new eateries, like **Daikiya**, which opened in March 2013 to instant popularity. But this is an old neighborhood, too: The bells of St. Mary Mother of God, the 1890 Catholic Church across 5th Street from the Fairfield, peal from 7am to—don't worry—9pm at night. And if you walk down H Street to #604, you'll notice a historic plaque on the façade of what is now the Wok and Roll restaurant, identifying the structure as Mary Surratt's Boarding House (Surratt conspired here with John Wilkes Booth to assassinate President Lincoln.). The vibrant Fairfield opened in 2011, following a remodeling of the former Red Roof Inn, and the nine-story property plays up the Chinatown connection, with the color red and Chinese symbols predominating in furnishings. Most spacious are ninth floor rooms, which also have high ceilings; and corner suites ending in "25." Fifth Street-facing rooms offer nice city views, including St. Mary's across the street. Deluxe king rooms have pullout sofas. Guests also like the key-only access to elevators, the availability of a coin-operated washer dryer, and, most especially, the complimentary continental breakfast, which in May 2013 expanded to include hot items: eggs, sausage, and waffles.

family-friendly HOTELS

Georgetown Suites

(p. 59)   Georgetown and all its attractions, which include not just restaurants and shops, but the C&O Canal path, tour boats on Washington Harbour, an ice-skating rink in winter at the Harbour Complex, and even a bunch of historical sites (see Georgetown Walking Tour, p. 214), are literally minutes from this hotel. And though Georgetown Suites does not offer a children's program, it does have three things that I, as a parent, have always loved when traveling with kids: spacious suites so you can spread out, full kitchens so you can feed the hungry at any hour, and a nice complimentary breakfast down in the lobby, so you can shoo old-enough children out of the room in the morning, while you get ready for the day.

Monaco Washington, D.C., a Kimpton Hotel (p. 48)   You're in the heart of the city, literally surrounded by attractions (International Spy Museum, two Smithsonian museums, the National Crime and Punishment

Museum, and the Verizon Center), with the National Mall just a few blocks away. The Red Line Metro stop is across the street. Meanwhile the hotel's KimptonKids program offers welcome gifts, a list of kid-friendly activities, and the loan of high chairs, cribs, and other equipment. The hotel's excellent restaurant, **Poste** (p. 48), offers a fun and tasty kid's menu. And as with all Kimptons, you get a goldfish delivered to your room if you so desire.

Omni Shoreham Hotel (p. 60)

With two pools, including a kiddie pool, loads of lawn to wander around and Rock Creek Park beyond that, the National Zoo up the street, as well as the Metro, to take you throughout D.C., the Omni is the best hotel in town for families. The hotel sweetens the deal with its children's amenities: a backpack filled with games and bottled water that the child can wear when you set off sightseeing; and cookies and milk left in the room at turndown the first night. The hotel's restaurant also offers a children's menu.

500 H St. NW (at 5th St.). www.marriott.com/wasfc. ℂ **202/289-5959.** 198 units. Peak (Mar–June and Sept to mid-Nov) weekdays $259–$349 double, weekends $149–$199 double; off-peak (Jan–Feb, July–Aug, and mid-Nov to Dec) weekdays $199–$309 double, weekends $109–$189 double. Add $10 for a deluxe king room and $20 for a suite. Children 17 and under stay free in parent's room. Rates include continental breakfast. Parking $33 (no oversize vehicles). Metro: Gallery Place–Chinatown (7th and H sts. exit). **Amenities:** Restaurant; bar; 24-hr. fitness center; room service; Wi-Fi (free).

MIDTOWN

Think of the White House as center stage, with an array of hotels, law and lobbyist office buildings, and restaurants at its feet. Several historic hotels, as well as less sophisticated, more affordable, contemporary properties, are among the options.

Best for: Travelers interested in a central location that's less raucous than the Penn Quarter at night. Also those on business with the executive branch or at one of the law, lobbying, or association offices that line K Street.

Drawbacks: Urban sounds (traffic, construction, garbage collection) may be part of the experience.

Expensive

Hay-Adams ★★★ Ho hum. In 2013 the Hay-Adams, for the tenth consecutive year, was listed on Travel & Leisure's "World's Best Hotels" list, just one of several recent awards. But excellence is never boring, and, says a staff person on my recent visit to the hotel, "people depend on that consistency and tradition." The 86-year-old hotel's tagline "Where nothing is overlooked but the White House," would be corny if it were not true. The Hay-Adams is known for its sublime service as well as for being the hotel that lies closest to the White House and the only one with such straight-on views, best seen from guest rooms on the top floors six through eight. (One can also see Lafayette Square, the Washington Monument, and the Jefferson Memorial.) Views in other rooms are of historic **St. John's Episcopal Church** (see p. 210) and downtown buildings. So it makes sense that views determine guest room rates. Rooms are similarly sized, about 385 square feet, and furnished with creamy white and tan toile fabrics, European linens, marble bathrooms. The interior designs that were here when Amelia Earhart stayed at the Hay in 1928—intricate plaster moldings, walnut wainscoting, and high ceilings—are still in place. Two things that were not here then are the Top of the Hay, a fabulous rooftop terrace with panoramic views, and the Off the Record bar, a regular hangout for the press and politicos.

1 Lafayette Square (at 16th and H sts.). www.hayadams.com. *C* **800/853-6807** or 202/638-6600. 145 units. Weekdays $425–$1,250 double; weekends $329–$929 double; from $829 junior suite; from $1,299 1-bedroom suite. Two-bedroom suites available. Third person $30. Children 17 and under stay free in parent's room. Valet parking $45. Metro: Farragut West (17th St. exit). Pets under 25 lb. accepted. **Amenities:** Restaurant; bar; concierge; state-of-the-art fitness facility; room service; Wi-Fi (free).

Donovan House, a Kimpton Hotel ★ Like all Kimptons, Donovan House has its own theme going, in this case, espionage, whimsically introduced in the lobby, where classic spy movies play, and where guest service clerks assume secret agent identities, complete with code names. The hotel is known for its hipness, which in guest rooms translates into a provocatively futuristic décor: the opaque-walled, cylindrical shower stall bumps out into the room, a chocolate-brown leather strip canopies the bed, and chairs are podlike. Rooms range in size from 220 to 585 square feet. Best rooms are the largest ones, the king premiers, whose floor-to-ceiling windows overlook Thomas Circle and the John Russell Pope-designed National Christian Church on the other side of the circle. Donovan House is a good pick for couples and solo travelers, but not so much for families, especially in summer when the rooftop pool closes at 5pm and the rooftop bar opens. DNV, as the bar is called (for "Damn Nice View"), attracts local partiers, who crowd the elevators each night on their way to and from the bar. But do try the hotel's first-floor restaurant **Zentan,** which serves pan-Asian tapas with an international flair.

1155 14th St. NW (at Thomas Circle). www.donovanhousehotel.com. *C* **800/383-6900** or 202/737-1200. 193 units. Weekdays $249–$499 double; weekends $179–$459 double; from $449 suite. Third person $30. Children 17 and under stay free in parent's room. Valet parking $42. Metro: McPherson Square (Franklin Square/14th St. exit). Pets welcome. **Amenities:** Restaurant; 2 bars; concierge; state-of-the-art fitness center; rooftop pool; room service; Wi-Fi (free).

Moderate

Hampton Inn Washington, D.C./White House ★ Housed in the former Kiplinger Newspapers Editors building located a block from the White House, the Hampton Inn opened on June 1, 2013 and started selling out immediately. Visitors,

Travelers to Washington, D.C. who plan to visit for a week or longer should know about the centrally located **AKA White House District** ★★★ apartments/hotel, 1710 H St. NW (www.stay-aka.com; ✆ **202/904-2500**). The D.C. location is one of nine AKA properties (others are in NYC, Beverly Hills, Philadelphia, London, and Arlington, VA), all of which offer luxuriously furnished one- and two-bedroom apartments, for short term and extended stays. AKA offers tremendous value, especially when your timing is right: I plugged in some July dates in 2013 and found that a one-bedroom suite was available at the White House District location for $215 a night. Check out the website to see for yourself some of the property's fine appointments and amenities, including fully equipped kitchens, stylish decor, free Wi-Fi, an on-site fitness center, and a washer/dryer in each apartment. K Street law offices, the White House, the Corcoran Gallery, and excellent restaurants, like **BLT Steak**, are just some of the property's notable neighbors. FYI: While it's true that AKA serves mainly as an extended stay property, it also accommodates visitors for nightly or a few nights' stay, as availability allows.

4

whether business or leisure, really like having a budget-friendly option in this part of town, where it's possible to walk most everywhere: to the White House, the National Mall, Georgetown. For spots further away, like the Capitol, the Metro awaits. Look for interior design references (word plays and artful lettering) to the building's journalism roots throughout the expansive lobby/living room, where the popular, complimentary hot breakfast includes eggs, sausages or bacon, and waffles. Families take note: The hotel has 89 standard king rooms, which accommodate a maximum of two people, and 26 double queen rooms, which hold four maximum, and there are no connecting rooms. The hotel has a very urban feel, which means city sounds will be part of your experience, views are of office buildings, and windows don't let in much light. But staff bend over backwards to accommodate you, so if you're not pleased with your room, ask to switch it.

1729 H St. NW (btw. 17th and 18th sts.).www.washingtondcwhitehouse.hamptoninn.com. ✆ **800/ HAMPTON** (426-7866) or 202/296-1006. 116 units. Year-round weekdays $199–$399; weekends $149–$259. Children 17 and under stay free in parent's room. Extra person $10. Rates include "Hot Breakfast Buffet." Parking $35 (height and length limits). Metro: Farragut West (17th and I Sts. exit). No pets. **Amenities:** Concierge; fitness center; small indoor pool; coin-op laundry room; Wi-Fi (free).

Inexpensive

The Quincy ★　The Quincy is nothing fancy, but it's perfectly adequate, especially for its moderate rates, which is saying something in this part of town. The White House is a couple of blocks away, the K Street and Pennsylvania Avenue corridors of lobbying, law, and international organization offices are directly south of The Quincy's L Street location. Weekdays, The Quincy's clientele draws from these segments—the World Bank has an ongoing contract here. Weekends, the hotel belongs to "tourists and partiers," according to one longtime staffer. The Quincy calls all of its rooms "suites," which are of 2 types: open-plan king studios with wet bars (minifridge, microwave, and Keurig coffeemaker) and queen efficiencies, in which the full kitchen is in a separate room. All of the suites are 400 square feet in size. Good to know: Ask for an L

Street-facing room weekdays, or you'll be woken at dawn by garbage trucks in the alley behind The Quincy.

1823 L St. NW (btw. 18th and 19th sts.). www.thequincy.com. ℂ **800/424-2970** or 202/223-4320. 99 units. Year-round weekdays $189–$289; weekends $99–$149. Children 17 and under stay free in parent's room. Parking $30 (in adjoining garage). Metro: Farragut North (L St. exit). Pets under 25 lb. accepted for $150 nonrefundable deposit. **Amenities:** Free passes to nearby full-service Results Gym; room service from Mackey's restaurant (next door); Wi-Fi (free).

ADAMS MORGAN

The hotel listed here is situated just north of Dupont Circle, at the mouth of Adams Morgan rather than within its actual boundaries.

Best for: Travelers who want to stay "in" the city but out of the fray.

Drawbacks: The closest Metro stop (Dupont Circle) is several blocks away.

Moderate

The Normandy Hotel ★★ This boutique hotel is charming, it's Parisian, it's pretty. The six-floor Normandy lies on a tree-shaded street lined with embassies, Macedonia's, Algeria's, and Senegal's among them; not surprisingly, the clientele is an international mix. You're a peaceful detour right off of busy Connecticut Avenue and only minutes away, by foot, from the heart of the Dupont Circle, Adams Morgan, and Woodley Park neighborhoods. The Normandy's 75 rooms are small, measuring between 220 and 270 square feet, but each makes good use of the space with cleverly designed and positioned furnishings: long, skinny desks, clever little reading lamps whose stems you can twist out of the walls just so; and compact Nespresso coffee machines and glass-fronted refrigerators placed out of the way. Front-facing rooms overlook tranquil Wyoming Avenue, while those at the back survey the courtyard. Three first floor rooms open to a private garden terrace. Also on the first level is the parquet-floored lounge, with little sofas, armchairs, round tables, and a fireplace. Guests enjoy the $12 continental breakfast here or in the petite courtyard each morning and the complimentary wine and cheese hour held every evening.

While The Normandy is perfect for couples and solo travelers, Avenue Suites (see listing in Foggy Bottom), in the same hotel family, might be a better choice for groups, large families, and those who crave a lot of space.

2118 Wyoming Ave. NW (at Connecticut Ave.). www.thenormandydc.com. ℂ **202/483-1350.** 75 units. $129–$299 double. Call or go online for best deals, which can fall well below the rack rate. Rates include evening wine and cheese hour and coffee and tea throughout the day. Extra person $20. Children 12 and under stay free in parent's room. Limited parking $25 plus tax. Metro: Dupont Circle (North/Q St. exit). Dogs 20 lb. or under allowed. **Amenities:** Access to the neighboring hotel's pool and exercise room for a $10 fee; Wi-Fi (free).

DUPONT CIRCLE

This neighborhood of quaint town houses and beautiful embassies, bistro restaurants, art galleries, and bars is home to more hotels than any other neighborhood in the city. Boutique hotels reign supreme, though a few chains have outposts here, too.

Best for: Travelers who love a city scene minus the office buildings. Also for gay and lesbian visitors, since Dupont Circle is LGBT Central.

Drawbacks: If you have business on Capitol Hill or in the Penn Quarter, this might not be your first choice, since there are plenty of closer options.

Expensive

The Jefferson ★★★ If you can afford to, stay at The Jefferson, which I consider to be D.C.'s best hotel. And if you can't afford to, at least stop in at **Quill** (p. 185), the hotel's delightful bar, where the bartender will invent a cocktail to please you, right on the spot, or serve you a concoction, like the Sparkling Sakura (sake, cherry puree, cherry blossom syrup, and Prosecco), created to celebrate the 2013 National Cherry Blossom Festival. Located slightly off the beaten track, about ½ mile north of the White House, The Jefferson is an exclusive refuge for privacy seekers, and truly exudes the ambience of a country house hotel. Décor throughout pays homage to Thomas Jefferson in all his passions, from Quill's display of 18th century maps tracing the oenophile's journeys through the wine regions of France, to guest room fabrics imprinted with architectural and agricultural scenes of Monticello. A handful of rooms catch glimpses of the Washington Monument a mile away, another few look to the White House, at the end of 16th Street; none, alas, capture the sight of the Jefferson Memorial a bit beyond. In addition to Quill and the lovely, skylit Greenhouse restaurant, the hotel's dining options include the sublime Plume restaurant, which serves artful French cuisine in its sumptuous, 17-table dining room.

1200 16th St. NW (at M St.). www.jeffersondc.com. © **202/448-2300.** 99 units. $350–$600 double; $650–$11,000 suite. Extra person $30. Children 12 and under stay free in parent's room. Parking $45. Metro: Farragut North (L St. and Connecticut Ave. exit). Dogs welcome. **Amenities:** 2 restaurants; bar/lounge; children's amenities; concierge; 24-hr. on-site fitness center; spa w/hair salon, massages, and facials; room service; Wi-Fi (free).

Moderate

The Dupont Circle Hotel ★★ The Dupont Circle Hotel is now the sole D.C. property of the Dublin-based hotel company, the Doyle Collection, which, in 2013, sold its two other hotels here. Doyle intends to hold on to the Dupont—it spent $52 million on a grand renovation in 2009-2010, after all. You'll hear some Irish accents here, for sure, as well as various languages of the Dupont's international clientele, some of whom have business at nearby embassies. (Most of the capital's embassies are headquartered along Massachusetts Avenue in this Dupont Circle neighborhood.). Guest rooms are quite chic, with frosted glass doors separating bathroom from bedroom, wooden blinds on windows, and leather-wrapped headboards on beds. Level Nine is the hotel's concierge floor, offering the choice of luxury service and suites (glass balconies! hardwood floors!) at an otherwise moderately priced property. No other hotel sits right on Dupont Circle, which is the name not only for the neighborhood but also for the urban park around which the traffic swirls. The park is a performance space in its own right. So don't miss the chance to sit in the lobby lounge or outside on the terrace of the Café Dupont and enjoy a drink or a meal and watch the goings-on.

1500 New Hampshire Ave. NW (across from Dupont Circle). www.thedupontcirclehotel.com. © **866/534-6835** or 202/483-6000. 327 units. From $239 double; from $650 suite. Extra person $20. Children 17 and under stay free in parent's room. Parking $32. Metro: Dupont Circle (either exit). Dogs 20 lb. or under allowed, with flat $150 nonrefundable fee. **Amenities:** Restaurant; bar; concierge; concierge-level rooms; state-of-the-art fitness center; room service; Wi-Fi (free).

Embassy Circle Guest House ★ "The average reservation [in 2013] is for 4 nights," says innkeeper Laura Saba, by way of noting the enduring popularity of both Washington, D.C., and the Embassy Circle Guest House, which Laura and husband Raymond Saba opened in 2007. The Sabas also own the lovely Woodley Park Guest House near the National Zoo. (The www.dcinns.com website links you to both inns.) Of the two, Embassy Circle, housed in a turn-of-the-20th-century mansion, is the more upscale and sophisticated option, reflecting its Embassy Row neighborhood of chancelleries and embassies and the artistic vibe of Dupont Circle, with its galleries and hip cafés. Guests are welcome to enjoy complimentary wine and snacks each evening in the elegant parlor, and an extensive complimentary breakfast, including a hot entrée, every morning in the dining room. Guest rooms take their decorative cues and their names from the antique Persian carpet displayed in each. So room no. 124, the Pearl Gazvin, presents the carpet of that name and a creamy, tranquil décor to complement it. The Red Kashan carpet adds vivid color to its namesake, room no. 111, further enhanced by the room's brilliant paintings and furnishings. As at the Woodley Park Guest House, all of the Embassy Circle's artworks are original pieces created by artists who have stayed there. The inn also has an elevator, a rare feature of older buildings and one that comes in handy for guests with heavy luggage or disabilities.

2224 R St. NW (at Massachusetts Ave.). www.dcinns.com. © **877/232-7744** or 202/232-7744. 11 units, each with private bathroom. $200–$295 double. Rates include extensive continental breakfast and evening wine and snacks. Limited parking; call for specific dates and information. Metro: Dupont Circle (Q St. exit) or Foggy Bottom. (Well-behaved) children 8 and older. **Amenities:** Impromptu dinner parties, at the whim of the owners or even guests; Wi-Fi (free).

Helix, a Kimpton Hotel ★★ The Helix is the perfect place to stay if you're interested in exploring the city's hottest neighborhood, the U Street Corridor. Simply venture a few yards to your right on exiting the hotel, and you reach 14th Street, one of the two heartbeats (U Street being the other) of this district. Turn in either direction at the corner and start your engine: Estadio, Birch and Barley, Churchkey, and many other happenin' eateries and bars await. The Helix is perfect because it is the hotel closest to the action, but also because it speaks the same trendy language. Take your cues from the neon green-colored furniture, striped fabrics, the PEZ and Pop Rocks candies in the minibar, the Andy Warholish artwork, and other attention-grabbing decor, and have fun, fun, fun! Guest rooms, averaging 400 square feet, aim for uncluttered comfort: thick-mattressed platform beds sit inside alcoves (in king deluxe rooms), a petite settee backs up against a triangular desk, leaving much wide open space. There are 18 suites, each with bedroom separate from the living room. The Kimpton Specialty rooms here feature "Eats" rooms, which have fully equipped kitchenettes; and "Bunk" rooms, popular with families. And just so you know: The closest Metro stop is about a half-mile away, so the DC Circulator bus, which stops a couple of blocks away every 10 minutes might be a better bet. But this is compact Washington, so you're never far from many attractions.

1430 Rhode Island Ave. NW (btw. 14th and 15th sts.). www.hotelhelix.com. © **800/706-1202** or 202/462-9001. 178 units. $149–$329 double. Add $30 for specialty rooms, $100 for suites. Best rates usually Fri–Sun. Extra person $20. Children 17 and under stay free in parent's room. Rates include hosted evening "bubbly hour" (champagne). Parking $42. Metro: McPherson Square (Vermont St./White House exit). Pets welcome. **Amenities:** Bar/cafe; bikes; children's amenity program; exercise room; room service; Wi-Fi (free).

Madera, a Kimpton Hotel ★ A 2013 renovation held on to the Madera's overall earthy vibe but switched out animal prints and dark woods, replacing them with colorful Polynesian accents. Red nubby, terrycloth wraps the rippled headboards and vibrant batik fabrics cover pillows and bed throws. Rooms are still large and comfortable, with some offering balconies overlooking New Hampshire Avenue and the Dupont Circle neighborhood, others on floors six and higher, at the rear of the hotel, overlooking some of Rock Creek Park, and northwest to the Washington National Cathedral. Best are the executive king rooms, which have a small sitting area with a pullout sofa. Firefly remains a favorite restaurant, enjoyed as much for its craft cocktails as for its seasonally driven menu.

1310 New Hampshire Ave. NW (btw. N and O sts.). www.hotelmadera.com. ℂ **800/430-1202** or 202/296-7600. 82 units. $149–$439 double. Add $40 for a specialty room. Extra person $20. Children 17 and under stay free in parent's room. Rates include complimentary morning coffee (6–9am) and hosted evening wine hour. Parking $42. Metro: Dupont Circle (South/19th St. exit). Pets welcome. **Amenities:** Restaurant/bar; babysitting; bikes; children's amenity program; concierge; complimentary access to the gym at nearby sister hotel, Hotel Palomar; room service; Wi-Fi (free).

Rouge Hotel ★ An extensive renovation in 2011 traded out the Rouge's retro feel and replaced it with a more chic look, but don't worry—the place is more rouge than ever, from the red terrazzo tile floor in the lobby to the guestrooms' red faux-leather headboards and bed frames covered with red-piping-bordered white duvets. As before, the dressing room holds a brilliant orange dresser, with contents including a built-in minibar and goofy goodies like red wax lips. Spacious rooms easily accommodate Italian-style lounge chairs, pedestal nightstands modeled after Grecian columns, a huge mirror positioned to reflect the living-room-like space, and a 10-foot-long mahogany desk. Specialty rooms are available, including the Bunk Room, which has a space for Mom and Dad and a separate, cozy little nest of a bunk bed for the kids, with drapes to pull closed for privacy and secrets, and a tiny fridge that one can stock with kiddie treats.

1315 16th St. NW (at Massachusetts Ave. and Scott Circle). www.rougehotel.com. ℂ **800/738-1202** or 202/232-8000. 137 units. $149–$359 double. Add $40 for a specialty room. Best rates available on the website or by calling the toll-free reservations number and asking for promotional price. Extra person $20. Rates include complimentary Bloody Marys and cold pizza weekend mornings 10–11am and hosted evening wine hour weeknights 5–6pm. Children 17 and under stay free in parent's room. Parking $42. Metro: Dupont Circle (South/19th St. exit). Pets welcome and pampered. **Amenities:** Restaurant/bar; children's amenity program; bikes; modest-size fitness center; room service; Wi-Fi (free).

Topaz, a Kimpton Hotel ★ Other hotels may be dispensing with in-room minibars, but not Kimptons and not the Topaz, whose honor bars in 2013 held goodies such as Honest Tea, Luna bars, and mineral water. And as with all Kimpton hotels, guests who sign up for the no-cost loyalty program receive a $10 credit toward a minibar purchase, as well as free Wi-Fi access. The minibar's exotic teas and other soothing items are emblematic of the Topaz's "Eastern orientation, creating an atmosphere of balance and calm," as the website helpfully points out. Décor throughout guest rooms leans toward tranquility, too: Comfy platform beds are triple-sheeted and topped with down comforters; furnishings are done in inky black and mesmerizing shades of purple, blue, pale green; a yoga mat comes with the room. Rooms measure a generous 375 square feet; some have alcoves and dressing rooms. Best spots for quiet and views are N Street-facing rooms on the upper floors. Best spots for revelry are the Topaz bar to start with, then out to nearby Dupont Circle clubs for heartier times.

1733 N St. NW (btw. 17th and 18th sts., next to the Hotel Tabard Inn [see below]). www.topazhotel. com. ℂ **800/775-1202** or 202/393-3000. 99 units. $149–$369 double; $40 more for specialty

All That Jazz

For a pleasurable evening's entertainment, you sometimes need look no further than the bar/lounge or in-house restaurant of your hotel—or one nearby. The genre is usually jazz, the performers are top-notch, and the admission is free, for guests and non-guests alike. So if it's a Sunday night, you might want to plant yourself in the paneled parlor of the **Hotel Tabard Inn** (see below) to listen to bassist Victor Dvoskin play world-class jazz, usually accompanied by a guitarist or pianist. And every single night starting at 9pm, the **Phoenix Park Hotel's** (p. 46) Dubliner restaurant is the place to be if you enjoy hoisting a pint to the tune of "Danny Boy" and rowdier Irish ballads, performed live by musicians with names like "Conor Malone" and "Andy O'Driscoll."

rooms. It is very likely you can get a much lower rate by calling direct to the hotel or by booking a reservation online. Extra person $20. Children 17 and under stay free in parent's room. Rates include complimentary morning coffee and tea service, and hosted evening wine reception. Parking $43. Metro: Dupont Circle (North/Q St. NW). Pets welcome. **Amenities:** Bar/restaurant; baby-sitting; bikes; children's amenity program; concierge; complimentary access to nearby health club; room service; Wi-Fi (free).

Inexpensive

Hotel Tabard Inn ★ A generational family feud was raging in the summer of 2013 at the family-owned Tabard. I tell you this just in case the wrangling has affected the operation and services of the Inn, by the time you read this. But aside from the absence of a number of longtime staff, a doting and solicitous bunch who were fired or resigned (and everyone's hoping they'll return), I don't think anything essential will change, actually. Fans of quaintness and quirks will continue to find them throughout the three joined 19th century town houses that make up the inn. Nooks, bay windows, exposed brick walls, vibrant colored walls (shades of purple, or Chartreuse, or periwinkle, for instance), flea market finds, and antiques are some of the characteristics of individual guest rooms. Quaintness also means that there are no televisions in guestrooms and no elevator, which can pose a challenge to those trudging upstairs with or without luggage to lodging on the third or fourth floors. The Tabard is a beloved institution to locals, who flock to the Tabard Inn's charming and highly acclaimed restaurant (p. 79) and to the adjoining, paneled lounge for drinks and, on Sunday nights, jazz.

Note: Its narrow hallways and lack of elevators means the inn is not a good choice for guests with disabilities.

1739 N St. NW (btw. 17th and 18th sts.). www.tabardinn.com. © **202/785-1277.** 38 units, 29 with private bathroom (6 with shower only). $125–$155 single with shared bathroom; $165–$265 single with private bathroom. Add $20 for 2nd person. Rates include continental breakfast. Limited street parking, plus nearby public parking garages. Metro: Dupont Circle (South/19th St. exit). Small and confined pets accepted for a $20 fee. **Amenities:** Restaurant w/lounge (free live jazz Sun evenings); free computer access in lobby (fax and printing available for small fee); free access to nearby YMCA w/extensive facilities that include indoor pool, indoor track, and racquetball/basketball courts; Wi-Fi (free).

FOGGY BOTTOM/WEST END

This section of town is halfway between the White House and Georgetown; Foggy Bottom lies south of Pennsylvania Avenue, and the West End north. Together the neighborhoods are home to town-house-lined streets, the George Washington University, International Monetary Fund offices, World Bank headquarters, and mostly all-suites and upscale lodging choices.

Best for: Parents visiting their kids at GW, international business travelers, and those who desire proximity to the Kennedy Center, also located here.

Drawbacks: There are 11,000 students who attend GW and who sometimes make their presence known throughout the Foggy Bottom neighborhood in ways you'd rather they wouldn't. On the flip side, the West End might seem too quiet if you like being where the action is.

Moderate

Avenue Suites ★★ When Avenue Suites debuted in the spring of 2012, it garnered as much press for its bar, A BAR, as for its transformation of the old Washington Suites hotel. Granted, the terrace lounge with its comfy furniture, fire pit, and green garden wall is a charming place to enjoy the nightly happy hour, as the city's 20-somethings often do. But let's cut to the chase: All of the 124 suites in this all-suite hotel are one-bedroom, measure a remarkably spacious 600 to 650 square feet, and include a sleep sofa in the separate living room, a fully equipped kitchen (Whole Foods and Trader Joe's stores are nearby), and a trendy but comfortable décor, all at quite an affordable rate, though that varies by peak/off-peak times. A helpful feature on the hotel's website is an availability chart that also posts daily rates. Other things to recommend the hotel are its prime location on the cusp of Georgetown and within walking distance of the White House, a Metro stop, and other attractions; and pool privileges at nearby sister hotel, One Washington Circle (see below). By the way, interior rooms at the back of the house overlook A Bar, so during the warm seasons, especially, you might want to try for a top floor room on the 25th Street side.

2500 Pennsylvania Ave. NW (at 25th St.). www.avenuesuites.com. ℂ **888/874-0100** or 202/333-8060. 124 units. Peak: $295–$349, off-peak: $129–$269. Extra person $20. Children 12 and under stay free in parent's room. Parking $34 plus tax. Pets: $25 per day fee. Metro: Foggy Bottom. **Amenities:** Bar; concierge; fitness center; room service; Wi-Fi (free).

The River Inn ★★★ Nestled among quaint town houses on a quiet side street a short walk away from the Kennedy Center, Georgetown, the White House, and the Foggy Bottom Metro station, The River Inn is a comfortable refuge for all sorts except rabble-rousers. Most of the units in the all-suite property are studios, in which the bedroom and living room are combined; 31 units, the Potomac Suites, are one-bedrooms, which are roomier and include a king-size bed and a second TV in the separate bedroom. All guest rooms provide a full kitchen, bed topped with pillowtop mattress, cushy armchair, a sophisticated décor, and a sleep sofa. Upper floor suites offer views of the Potomac River and two, nos. 702 and 802 catch sight of the Washington Monument, currently enshrouded in scaffolding as workers continue to repair damage done during the August 2011 earthquake. Complimentary bikes (based on availability), on-site coin-operated laundry machines, and an especially gracious staff are among the pluses that keep the inn steeped in bookings from happy repeat customers.

924 25th St. NW (btw. K and I sts.). www.theriverinn.com. ℂ **888/874-0100** or 202/337-7600. 125 units. Peak weekdays $299–$354 double, weekends $149–$199 double; off-peak weekdays $159–

$255 double, weekends $99–$149 double. Add $35 for 1-bedroom suite. Extra person $20. Children 17 and under stay free in parent's room. Parking $34 plus 18% tax. Metro: Foggy Bottom. Pets under 40 lb. welcome for nonrefundable $150 fee. **Amenities:** Restaurant; bar; bikes; concierge; small fitness center; room service; Wi-Fi (free).

Inexpensive

One Washington Circle Hotel ★ Even this hotel's smallest room (measuring 390 square feet) is more spacious than the largest room at some other D.C. hotels. The biggest suites here encompass more than 700 feet. All of the rooms are suites, with separate full kitchens in 90 percent of the units and kitchenettes in the remainder. Families especially, but also business travelers, love the chance to spread out, the outdoor pool, the on-site restaurant, and the location near the Foggy Bottom Metro stations, Georgetown, and the White House. All rooms have walkout balconies. One Washington Circle is situated, as it sounds, right on Washington Circle, and across from the George Washington University Hospital. Double-paned windows help screen some of the siren sounds, but for quietest sleep, ask for a room on the 8th or 9th floor facing L Street or New Hampshire Avenue. George Washington University-affiliated guests may be eligible for discounts.

1 Washington Circle NW (btw. 22nd and 23rd sts. NW). www.thecirclehotel.com. ⓒ**800/424-9671** or 202/872-1680. 151 units. Weekdays $159–$299 smallest suites, $199–$339 largest suites; weekends $109–$199 smallest suites, $159–$239 largest suites. Call hotel or look on the website to get best rates, including special offers. Extra person $20. Pets accepted. Children 12 and under stay free in parent's room. Rates include complimentary wine and appetizers 5–6pm nightly in the lobby. Parking $40. Metro: Foggy Bottom. **Amenities:** Restaurant; bar; fitness center; outdoor pool; room service; Wi-Fi (free).

GEORGETOWN

Bustling day and night with shoppers and tourists, Georgetown's handful of hotels range from the city's most sublime accommodations to one that I believe offers the best value in town.

Best for: Shopaholics, tourists, and parents, students, and academics visiting Georgetown University.

Drawbacks: Crowds throng sidewalks; cars snarl traffic daily. College kids and 20-somethings party hearty here nightly, but especially on weekends.

Expensive

Capella Washington, D.C. ★★★ One of the capital's newest hotels (it opened April 2013) is also its most decadently luxurious. Personal assistants are at your service 24/7. The hotel has a resident stylist, who is available to take you on after-hours shopping sprees at Saks Fifth Avenue and other upscale retailers, or will shop for you. A hair stylist is on call just for Capella Hotel guests at the nearby Luigi Parasmo Salon, or the hairmeister will come to you at the hotel. Would you like to surprise your little ballerina with a walk-on role in The Washington Ballet's performance of The Nutcracker? Done. And then there are the practical pluses, like the hotel's flexible check-in/checkout policy. The Capella sits alongside the C&O Canal and some of its 49 rooms overlook the canal, as do the bar and the seasonal outdoor terrace: very nice. Rooms range in size from 359 to 504 square feet; suites go up from there. Guest room furnishings make fashion statements with their mix of black and white accents, dark hardwood floors, and pewter lamps. A rooftop lounge includes a fitness center, indoor/

outdoor relaxation pool, and views of Georgetown, the Kennedy Center, a bit of the Potomac River, and the Washington Monument. The Capella's Rye Bar is already a hot spot, while the Grill Room restaurant is still settling in.

1050 31st St. NW (below M St.). www.capellawashngtondc.com. © **855/922-7355** or 202/617-2400. 49 units. Off peak: from $595 double, from $1,545 suite; Peak: from $745 double, from $2,295 suite. Extra person $50. Children under 12 stay free in parent's room. Parking $48. Metro: Foggy Bottom. Pets accepted with refundable $250 deposit. **Amenities:** restaurant; 2 bars; babysitting; children's programs; concierge; rooftop fitness center and relaxation pool; in-room spa services; room service; Wi-Fi (free).

The Graham ★★ Following the multimillion dollar renovation of the property previously known as The Monticello, The Graham Georgetown opened April 15, 2013 and it's a stunner. Named for the inventor of the telephone, Alexander Graham Bell, who once lived and worked nearby (who knew?), the seven-story hotel holds 57 rooms, nearly half of them standard guest rooms with either a king bed or two queens; the rest suites, either junior or full king. Largest are king suites, which have a king-size pullout sofa in the separate living room. Each unit is similarly and stylishly decorated in shades of grays, whites, and reds, with white, tufted-leather headboards on beds made up in Irish linens. The pretty bathrooms feature white and gray marbled floors and walls, Italian handtiles, and Bulgari amenities. There's a darling restaurant on the lower level, A.G.B. (after you know who), whose exposed brick, paneled walls and dark hardwood floors add pubby charm. Meanwhile, locals are ga-ga about the Observatory rooftop bar, which wraps around the entire building, so you're able to view Georgetown and the city, including the Washington Monument, from various angles. The fact that the bar is open not just to hotel guests but to Washington's rowdy drinking crowd means 1. You must reserve a spot, and 2. You might want to consider requesting a room on a middle floor on the canal side of the hotel to keep bar noise at a remove. (The bar closes at 2am weekends, 1am weeknights.) The hotel website turn up some pretty good deals, especially if you can be flexible and are able to book your stay in advance.

1075 Thomas Jefferson St. NW (just below M St.). www.thegrahamgeorgetown.com. © **855/341-1292** or 202/337-0900. 57 units. Rates: from $300 for a king or double queen room off-peak to $600 for a king suite in peak times; check the website for best rates. Extra person $25. Children under 8 stay free in parents' room. Extra person. Parking $48. Pets not allowed. Metro: Foggy Bottom. **Amenities:** Restaurant, 2 bars, bikes, concierge, exercise room; room service; Wi-Fi (free).

Inexpensive

Georgetown Suites ★★ The pros: The location is unbeatable, just off busy M Street in Georgetown, seconds away from the picturesque C&O Canal and its towpath, but also nearby posh shops and fun restaurants and bars. Staff are cheery. Suites are quite spacious (studios measure 500 square feet, one-bedrooms 800 square feet), are clean, and have full kitchens equipped with everything from dishwasher to oven, and beds with new duvets and skirting. In 2013, the hotel expanded its complimentary breakfast options to include egg sandwiches, and expanded the space and seating where breakfast is enjoyed, in the lobby. The hotel's second location at the Harbour Building on 29th Street lies just across from the Washington Harbour Complex, whose attractions include tour boats that cruise the Potomac River and an ice skating rink that opened in 2013, the largest outdoor rink in the city.

The cons: The hotel's overall décor could use some updating: less college dorm, more urban apartment. The noise of traffic and revelers is an annoying factor for rooms on the lower floors of the 30th Street building, despite the hotel's recessed position off the street. The Harbour Building lies right next to the Whitehurst Freeway, so rooms facing the freeway get those unattractive views and the racket of traffic.

Conclusion: You won't find better value in the city, and certainly not in Georgetown. At the 30th Street location, ask for a room on an upper floor, or, if budget allows, consider one of the two-level, two-bedroom townhouses or one of the penthouse suites, whose terraces overlook Georgetown rooftops. At the 29th Street location, ask for a courtyard-side suite.

Note: Online reviews seem to suggest that Georgetown Suites allows smoking in some rooms. It does not. The property is entirely non-smoking.

1111 30th St. NW (just below M St.) and 1000 29th St. NW (at K St.). www.georgetownsuites.com. ℂ **800/348-7203** or 202/298-7800. 220 units. Weekdays $185 studio, $215 1-bedroom suite; weekends $155 studio, $185 1-bedroom suite; penthouse suites from $350; town houses from $425. Rollaway or sleeper sofa $10 extra. Rates include continental breakfast. Limited parking $20. Metro: Foggy Bottom. **Amenities:** Executive-level rooms; small exercise room; Wi-Fi (free).

4 WOODLEY PARK

This Connecticut Avenue–centered upper northwest enclave is a residential neighborhood of little stores and restaurants, the National Zoo, and Washington's biggest hotel.

Best for: Families who like a tamer experience than found downtown and proximity to Rock Creek Park and the zoo. Business travelers attending a meeting in one of Woodley Park's big hotels.

Drawbacks: This area may be a little too quiet for some, especially at night.

Moderate

Omni Shoreham Hotel ★★★ Step from the jammed up streets of D.C. into the Omni's lovely and enormous lobby and it really does feel like you've arrived at a resort. It's the towering ceiling, the chandeliers, and the sheer expanse of lobby leading back, down through the dining room and out the French doors to the terrace and the acres of landscaped lawns, all backing up to Rock Creek Park. Truly, one of the pleasures of staying here is exploring the premises. Poke your head in the Palladian Ballroom to inspect its muralled scenes of Monticello; the Palladian and the Diplomat (modeled after the East Room of the White House) ballrooms were spruced up in 2013. The Omni was built in 1930 as an apartment building, so its guest rooms are of varying sizes and interesting shapes. For best views and quiet, ask for a parkview room at the back of the house, preferably with a balcony (15 percent of the rooms have them), and within sight of the Washington Monument. You should also sign up (it's free) for the Omni Loyalty program, which allows you a complimentary bundle of worth-it privileges, like Wi-Fi, morning beverage room service, pressing service, and shoe shine. The Omni attracts a lot of groups, thanks to its size (11 acres, 836 rooms, 24 meeting rooms, several ballrooms), but families love it, too, for its large seasonal pool and smaller kiddie pool, children's amenities (backpack of games given at check-in, cookies and milk in the evening), its onsite restaurants, and its proximity to Rock Creek Park and the National Zoo.

2500 Calvert St. NW (near Connecticut Ave.). www.omnishorehamhotel.com. ℂ **800/843-6664** or 202/234-0700. 836 units. $199–$359 double; from $350 suite. Call the hotel directly for best rates. Extra person $30. Children 17 and under stay free in parent's room. Valet parking $30. Metro: Woodley Park–Zoo. Pets under 25 lb. allowed; $50 cleaning fee. **Amenities:** Restaurant; bar/

lounge; children's amenities program; concierge; fitness center w/heated outdoor pool, separate kids' pool, whirlpool, and spa services by appointment; room service; Wi-Fi (free).

Inexpensive

Kalorama Guest House ★ Kalorama's rambling red-brick house blends right in among the large town houses and family dwellings in this residential neighborhood. Built in 1910, the house retains an old-timey feeling about it. That's partly due to its 114-year old design (old wood floors, fireplaces (decorative only) in lots of rooms, paneled wainscoting along the stairwell, a tin ceiling here and there. And it's partly due to the furnishings, which come from flea markets and antiques auctions. Owner Jack Shrestha adds to the homey feel, fussily offering cookies and coffee and pointing out the communal family room, kitchen and laundry room facilities, even as he's pulling out photos to show you of his 2-year-old daughter. (Speaking of children, Shrestha notes that the inn is best for well-behaved children over 6.) Least expensive rooms are two in the basement that share a bathroom; these two rooms, plus a large room on this floor with its own television (the only room to have one besides the communal family room), have their own entrance from the street. Basement rooms, by the way, do have windows, and are as pleasantly furnished as any upstairs. Nicest, in my opinion, is the sole room on the first floor; built-in bookcases and a sleigh bed are part of its charm. You're in a great area, with the zoo, good restaurants, Rock Creek Park, and the Woodly Park Metro stop all within a short walk.

2700 Cathedral Ave. NW (off Connecticut Ave.). www.kaloramaguesthouse .com. ⓒ **202/588-8188**. 10 units, 8 w/private bath. $79–$249 single or double. Rates include expansive breakfast and complimentary wine and cookies. Extra person (including children) $25. Limited parking $15 plus tax. Metro: Woodley Park–Zoo. **Amenities:** Access to gym at nearby Marriott with $10 pass; Wi-Fi (free).

HOTELS BY PRICE

EXPENSIVE
Capella Washington, DC ★★★, p. 60
Donovan House, a Kimpton Hotel ★, p. 51
The George, a Kimpton Hotel ★★, p. 44
The Graham ★★, p. 60
Hay-Adams ★★★, p. 51
The Jefferson ★★★, p. 54
Monaco Washington, DC, A Kimpton Hotel, p. 49
Residence Inn Capitol ★, p. 45
Willard InterContinental ★★★, p. 49

MODERATE
Avenue Suites ★★, p. 59
Capitol Hill Hotel ★, p. 45
Dupont Circle Hotel ★★, p. 55
Embassy Circle Guest House ★, p. 55
Fairfield Inn & Suites ★, p. 49

Hampton Inn Washington, DC ★★, p. 51
Helix, a Kimpton Hotel ★, p. 55
Madera, A Kimpton Hotel ★, p. 56
The Normandy Hotel ★★, p. 53
Omni Shoreham Hotel ★★★ p. 61
Phoenix Park Hotel ★, p.45
Rouge Hotel ★, p. 56
The River Inn ★★★, p. 59
Topaz, a Kimpton Hotel ★, p. 56

INEXPENSIVE
Georgetown Suites ★★, p. 60
Hostelling International Washington, DC, p. 42
Hotel Tabard Inn ★, p. 57
Kalorama Guest House ★ p. 62
One Washington Circle ★, p. 59
The Quincy ★, p. 52

WHERE TO EAT IN WASHINGTON, D.C.

Finding the cuisine of your dreams is easy in Washington, where upward of 1,000 (!) restaurants present a world's choice of options, whether you crave sushi or a luscious boeuf bourguignon. Scoring a table can be the tricky part: Washingtonians dine out a lot. A LOT. Wheeler-dealers and socializing urbanistas fill restaurants throughout the city, from the 14th and U Street corridors, where the newest and hottest eateries proliferate, to the White House neighborhood's upscale fine dining establishments. Be sure to make a reservation, whenever possible. Two services are very helpful in booking a table: www.opentable.com and www.cityeats.com. Most D.C. restaurants belong to one or the other service, and some are registered with both. Use them.

The city is also notable for its casual dining, and often the food is as sensational in these places as at the higher priced D.C. restaurants. (If you're a fan of tacos, pizza, and burgers, you'll love the appealing versions at Tacqueria Nacionale (p. 77), Graffiato (p. 70), and Good Stuff Eatery (p. 68). Asian cuisine is increasingly a favorite with newcomer Daikaya (p. 74) taking the popular lead. Bistros serving "small plates" of delicious tastes are clearly here to stay, Bandolero (p. 81) being among the latest to join standard-bearers Jaleo (p. 71) and Zaytinya (p. 73). Finally, you should know that a boisterous bar scene is now a dining-out fact of life. And it can get loud.

Good restaurants are in every neighborhood and this chapter leads you to a range of options, spanning diverse cuisines and budget considerations.

D.C. RESTAURANTS BY CUISINE

AMERICAN
Ben's Chili Bowl ★, p. 76
Cork ★, p. 75
Five Guys Burger and Fries ★, p. 74

Founding Farmers ★, p. 80
Good Stuff Eatery ★, p. 68
Komi ★★★, p. 78
Le Bon Café ★, p. 68
Market Lunch ★, p. 68

Martin's Tavern ★, p. 82
Matchbox ★, p. 72
Old Ebbit Grill ★, p. 72
1789 ★★, p. 81
Tabard Inn ★★, p. 79
Ted's Bulletin ★, p. 65
The Monocle ★, p. 65
Unum ★, p. 83

ASIAN FUSION
Teaism ★, p. 79

BARBECUE
Hill Country Barbecue Market ★★, p. 71

CHINESE
Ching Ching Cha ★, p. 83

ETHIOPIAN
Ethiopic ★, p. 64

FRENCH
Central Michel Richard ★★, p. 69
Le Chaumiere ★, p. 81
Montmartre ★★, p. 65
Paul ★, p. 80

GREEK
Komi ★★★, p. 78
Zaytinya ★★, p. 73

INDIAN
Bombay Club ★★, p. 74
Indique ★, p. 84
Rasika ★★★, p. 73

ITALIAN
Al Tiramisu ★★, p. 78
Fiola ★★★, p. 70
Graffiato ★, p. 70
Pizza Paradiso ★, p. 79
Posto ★, p. 76

JAPANESE
Daikaya ★, p. 74
Kushi Izakaya and Sushi ★, p. 71
Sticky Rice ★, p. 64

LATIN AMERICAN
Las Canteras ★, p. 77
Oyamel ★★, p. 72
Surfside ★, p. 83

LIGHT FARE
Sweetgreen ★, p. 75

MEXICAN
Bandolero ★, p. 81
Tacqueria Nacionale ★, p. 77

MIDDLE EASTERN
Amsterdam Falafelshop ★, p. 78
Lebanese Taverna ★, p. 85
Zaytinya ★★, p. 73

SEAFOOD
Johnny's Half Shell ★★, p. 64
Market Lunch ★, p. 68
Pearl Dive Oyster Palace ★, p. 76
Surfside ★, p. 83

SPANISH
Jaleo ★★★, p. 71

PRICE categories

Keep in mind that the price categories refer to dinner prices, and that some very expensive restaurants offer affordable lunches, early-bird dinners, tapas, or bar meals. The prices within each review refer to the **average cost of individual entrees,** not the entire meal.

Expensive	$20–plus
Moderate	$10–$19
Inexpensive	$10 and under

ATLAS DISTRICT

Inexpensive

Ethiopic ★ ETHIOPIAN According to the Ethiopian Embassy, approximately 200,000 Ethiopian émigrés live in the D.C. area, making it the largest Ethiopian community in the world, outside of Africa. Ethiopian cuisine, likewise, has found a place for itself in D.C.'s expansive dining scene, as immigrants eager to introduce Washingtonians to the authentic tastes of their country open restaurants here. In other words, if you're already a fan of Ethiopian food or are curious to try it, D.C. is the place. And currently, Ethiopic is the best. Vegetarians, especially, rave about the vegetarian sampler: simmered collard greens; curried potatoes simmered with red onion, garlic, jalapeno pepper, olive oil, and herbs; split lentils in a spicy sauce; and yellow split peas cooked with onions and herbs. Located at the corner of H and 4th streets, it's also a great people watching spot, as the restaurant overlooks both streets through front and side wall windowfronts (in good weather ask for sidewalk seating). In 2013, Ethiopic owners Samuel Ergete and Meseret Bekele decided to try something completely different: a European bakery/café. Open daily 8am to 8pm, **Batter Bowl Bakery** (www. the-bbb.com) is located right next door at 403 H St. NE, and serves the pastries and breads, as well as breakfast items, sandwiches, and salads. Prices range from $3.50 for Belgian waffles to $7.95 for an open-faced smoked salmon sandwich.

401 H St. NE (at 4th St.). www.ethiopicrestaurant.com. ☏ **202/675-2066.** Main courses $15–$24. Tues–Thurs 5–10pm; Fri–Sat noon–10pm. Drive or take a taxi.

Sticky Rice ★ SUSHI Turns out tater tots are a fabulous accompaniment to sushi, sashimi, noodles, and Sapporo beer. That's one of the lessons learned at Sticky Rice, one of the older restaurants in the Atlas District (it's been around for 6 years) but still one of the hottest. All sorts—girlfriend groups, families, couples, and hipsters full of attitude—flock to this sprawling, casual, three-storefront Asian eatery. Lesson #2? Entertainment along with food will keep a place popular. So when you head to Sticky Rice, expect all sorts of interesting things to be going on, like screenings of old Jamie Lee Curtis movies and karaoke nights. All of this doesn't overshadow the food, which includes elaborately presented and fresh-tasting sushi; noodle dishes of all sorts (like one with a topping of spicy shrimp and coconut, or the noodles in a mock chicken Szechuan entrée that vegetarians love); and those terrific tater tots. Order a bucket ($8) for the table or a side ($4) for two people, of either regular or sweet potato tots.

1224 H St. NE (btw. 12th and 13th sts.). www.stickyricedc.com. ☏ **202/397-7655.** Main courses at lunch/dinner/brunch $14 and under. Sun–Thurs 11:30am–2am; Fri–Sat 11:30am–3am. Drive or take a taxi.

CAPITOL HILL & BARRACKS ROW

Also see "Eating with the Insiders," below.

Expensive

Johnny's Half Shell ★★ AMERICAN/SEAFOOD Johnny's offers the movers-and-shakers buzz of Capitol Hill, along with excellent crab cakes, soft shell crabs, and crabmeat imperial, all regional specialties. Expensive, yeah, but few restaurants serve soft shell crabs done just right as they are here, and sided with fresh corn spoonbread;

and fewer still even offer crab imperial. If budget allows and you love seafood, put Johnny's on your list. Of course there are ways to economize here: the appetizer crab-cake, $16.25 at both lunch and dinner, is entrée size, in my opinion. Or you could stop by at happy hour, 4:30 to 7:30pm weeknights, when the bar menu options range from $3 mini burgers to $14 crabcakes, and drinks are a discounted, too. The folks behind Johnny's have also opened a swell tacqueria (p. 77) in the U Street corridor area.

400 N. Capitol St. NW (at E St.). www.johnnyshalfshell.net. ⟨℘⟩ **202/737-0400.** Main courses lunch $8.95–$32.50, dinner $18.25–$32.50. Mon–Fri, 11:30am–2:30pm; Mon–Sat 5–10pm. Happy hour Mon–Fri 4:30–7:30pm. Metro: Union Station (Massachusetts Ave. exit).

The Monocle ★ AMERICAN   Is the Monocle another branch of the U.S. government? It sometimes feels that way. Senators, representatives, Supreme Court justices, and their staffs all dine here at lunch and dinner, as they have since 1960, when The Monocle opened. (The Monocle backs up to Senate Office Building property.) Owner John Valanos, maitre'd Nick, and longtime staff greet frequent customers by name and with warmth, whether the patron is a lobbyist or a Senator. There's no other place like it in the capital. The food's pretty good, too. Usually the best picks are the specials, the salads (especially the Federal Salad and the BLT Salad), and the shrimp and asparagus orzo. Enjoy "Luncheon at the Bar," served 11:30am to 3pm, for the best deal going: a pair of cheddar cheese and bacon-topped angus beef sliders, for $6.50.

107 D St. NE. (at 2nd St.). www.themonocle.com. ⟨℘⟩ **202/546-4488.** Main courses lunch $12–$28; dinner $17–$38. Mon–Fri 11:30am–midnight. Metro: Union Station (Massachusetts Ave. exit).

Moderate

Montmartre ★★ FRENCH   When it opened down the street from Eastern Market in 2002, Montmartre stood out for being so good and so genuinely French. (Capitol Hill's restaurant scene wasn't much to speak of back then). Its wooden tables, yellow-splashed walls, ceiling fans, tiny bar, and sidewalk café looked like a little bistro you'd find in Paris. The French owner welcomed you and the chef served up French country specialties of duck paté, cassoulet, braised rabbit, crème brulée, gratins of this and that. None of that has changed. Should you pop by without reservations and the place is full, you'll be directed next door to Seventh Hill, Montmartre's pizza bistro, which also serves fine salads, sandwiches, and soups.

327 7th St. SE (at Pennsylvania Ave.). www.montmartredc.com. ⟨℘⟩ **202/544-1244.** Main courses brunch $11–$14, lunch $11–$25, dinner $19–$23. Tues–Fri 11:30am–2:30pm; Sat–Sun 10:30am–3pm; Tues–Thurs 5:30–10pm; Fri–Sat 5:30–10:30pm; Sun 5:30–9pm. Metro: Eastern Market.

Ted's Bulletin ★ AMERICAN   Ted's Bulletin calls itself a family restaurant, and it is, it is, but what you should be prepared for is that some of the "children" who come here are in their 20s and 30s and they're drinking milkshakes laced with rum and raspberry schnapps ("Buzzed Berries") or maybe vodka and Kahlúa ("Nutty Professor"). So it can get rowdy. What you'll enjoy, besides the retro décor, is the well-done, comfort food menu: grilled cheese, tomato soup, creamed corn, mac and cheese, barbecued chicken, ribs, chili, sloppy joes and breakfast items (which are served all day). Ted's Bulletin is so popular that it opened a second location in summer of 2013 at 1818 14th St. NW, in the U Street Corridor. *One warning:* Sometimes those waiting in line to get in have attitude problems (think the movie "Mean Girls"), so save yourself from possible aggravation by making a reservation.

505 8th St. SE (at E St.). www.tedsbulletin.com. ⟨℘⟩ **202/544-8337.** Main courses breakfast $9–$13, lunch $10–$15, dinner $14–$25. Daily 7am–10:30pm. Metro: Eastern Market.

Washington, D.C., Restaurants

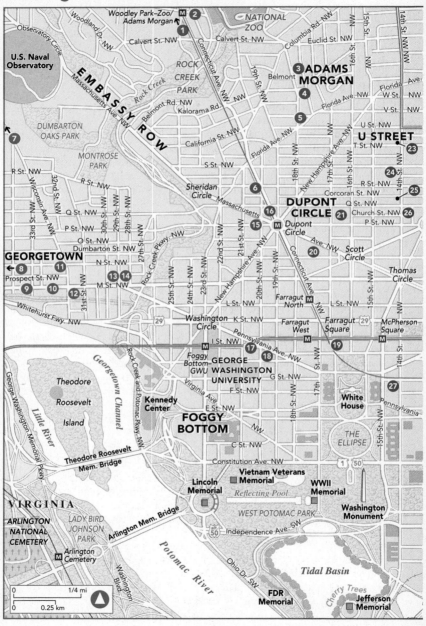

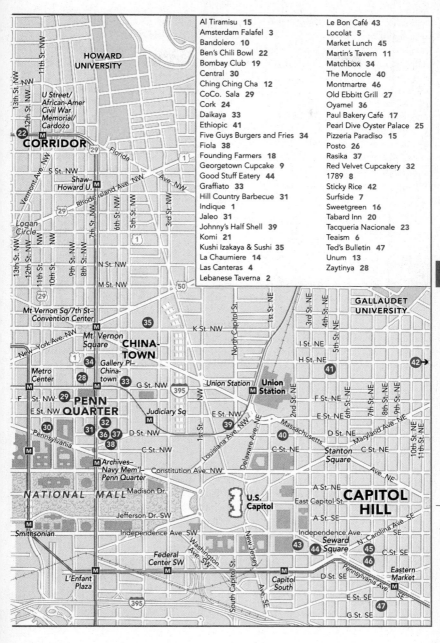

Al Tiramisu **15**
Amsterdam Falafel **3**
Bandolero **10**
Ben's Chili Bowl **22**
Bombay Club **19**
Central **30**
Ching Ching Cha **12**
CoCo. Sala **29**
Cork **24**
Daikaya **33**
Ethiopic **41**
Five Guys Burgers and Fries **34**
Fiola **38**
Founding Farmers **18**
Georgetown Cupcake **9**
Good Stuff Eatery **44**
Graffiato **33**
Hill Country Barbecue **31**
Indique **1**
Jaleo **31**
Johnny's Half Shell **39**
Komi **21**
Kushi Izakaya & Sushi **35**
La Chaumiere **14**
Las Canteras **4**
Lebanese Taverna **2**

Le Bon Café **43**
Locolat **5**
Market Lunch **45**
Martin's Tavern **11**
Matchbox **34**
The Monocle **40**
Montmartre **46**
Old Ebbitt Grill **27**
Oyamel **36**
Paul Bakery Café **17**
Pearl Dive Oyster Palace **25**
Pizzeria Paradiso **15**
Posto **26**
Rasika **37**
Red Velvet Cupcakery **32**
1789 **8**
Sticky Rice **42**
Surfside **7**
Sweetgreen **16**
Tabard Inn **20**
Tacqueria Nacionale **23**
Teaism **6**
Ted's Bulletin **47**
Unum **13**
Zaytinya **28**

Inexpensive

Good Stuff Eatery ★ AMERICAN   This is the "baby" of Spike Mendelsohn, who shot to fame as a *Top Chef* contestant and remains renowned thanks to the scrumptiousness of his burgers, fries, and shakes. (Mendelsohn also appears in the reality show, *Life after Top Chef*.) The Prez Obama Burger (with applewood bacon, onion marmalade, Roquefort cheese, and horseradish mayo sauce) is the most popular item on the menu, according to the staff; but the toasted marshmallow milkshake will always be the #1 milkshake, to my mind. Spike's other restaurants include the pizza place next door, although **We The Pizza** (☏ 202/544-4008), good as its pies are, never gets the crowds that Good Stuff does. Go one more storefront past We The Pizza and you reach **Bearnaise** (315 Pennsylvania Ave. SE; www.bearnaiserestaurant.com; ☏ 202/450-4800), the French bistro that Spike opened with his sister Micheline in late June 2013. A Georgetown Good Stuff opened in July 2013 at 3291 M St. NW. **Warning: Good Stuff Eatery** is always jumping, with people in line on the first floor and filling upstairs and outdoor patio tables. The line moves fast and table turnover is fairly quick, but just the same, you might consider getting the burgers to go, as so many do.

303 Pennsylvania Ave. SE (at 3rd St.). www.goodstuffeatery.com. ☏ **202/543-8222.** Reservations not accepted. Burgers $6–$9; milkshakes and sundaes $4–$6. Mon–Sat 11:30am–11pm. Metro: Capitol South.

Le Bon Café ★ AMERICAN/CAFE   Is Le Bon Café truly French? I wouldn't say so. The menu includes French café staples, like a croque monsieur, quiche, and croissants, but they're Americanized versions, and the rest of the menu includes things like Tandoori chicken wraps and smoked turkey club sandwiches. A little bit of this, little bit of that. That being said, I can vouch for the tastiness of Le Bon Café's offerings, great value for the price. And it's conveniently located, right behind the Madison Building of the Library of Congress, a short walk from the Capitol. Look for the blue-and-white striped awning shading a cluster of round tables outside. Inside are about eight marble-topped bistro tables and, usually, a line of Hill staffers and locals from the neighborhood waiting to place their orders. *FYI:* If you prefer diner fare and livelier local color, head right next door to **Pete's Diner and Carryout**.

210 2nd St. SE (at Pennsylvania Ave. SE). www.leboncafedc.com. ☏ **202/547-7200.** Breakfast items $2–$5; salads/sandwiches/soups $5–$9. Mon–Fri 7am–3pm; Sat 8am–3pm; Sun 8:30am–2pm. Metro: Capitol South.

Market Lunch ★ AMERICAN/SEAFOOD   Market Lunch, like Eastern Market (p. 169), where it resides, is an institution, a little slice of D.C. life. For the best insider experience, come here on weekends and you'll see senators and representatives in line with their Capitol Hill neighbors to eat the famous blueberry buckwheat pancakes ("bluebucks"), softshell crab sandwiches, or crabcakes. The eatery consists of a few small tables and 26 stools pulled up to a wooden counter at the end of Eastern Market's main hall. You choose what you want from the chalkboard menu and then queue to the right of the register to place your order. Once you're seated, you get to watch all that's going on in the market hall, as vendors and residents barter and chat. Market Lunch is open weekdays, too, but is a much quieter experience, so not nearly as much fun.

225 E. 7th St. SE, inside Eastern Market (at Pennsylvania Ave. SE). www.easternmarket-dc.org. ☏ **202/547-8444.** Breakfast items $5–$13; lunch items $5–$20. Cash only. Tues–Fri 7:30am–2:30pm; Sat 8am–3pm; Sun 9am–3pm. Metro: Capitol South.

EATING WITH THE insiders

You just can't beat the atmosphere (political) and value (cheap—your meal isn't taxed!) of the all-American food served in dining spots inside the Capitol, its office buildings, and the Supreme Court. Keep these places in mind while touring the Hill:

○ The **Supreme Court** and its **Cafeteria** (☏ **202/479-3246**), where you may spy a famous lawyer or member of the press but not any of the justices, who have their own dining room. The cafeteria is open weekdays 7:30am to 4pm (though it may be closed briefly between noon and 1pm to accommodate Supreme Court employees).

○ The House of Representatives' immense, full-service **Rayburn Café** (☏ **202/226-9067**), which is Room B357, in the basement of the Rayburn House Office Building, at 1st Street and Independence Avenue SW). Adjoining the cafeteria is a carryout that sells pizza and sandwiches.

○ The **Longworth Café** (in the Longworth Building's Basement, Independence Ave. and S. Capitol St. SE; ☏ **202/225-6372**), where you can grab a bite from a fairly nice food court.

○ **Southside Buffet** (in the Dirksen Office Building, 1st St. and Constitution Ave. NW; ☏ **202/224-4249**) The fried chicken, a

carvery station, and a dessert station, are highlights and popular among the Senate staffers who dine here. All of these eateries are open weekdays only. The carryouts stay open until late afternoon, while the other dining rooms close at 2:30pm. For a complete listing of **House of Representatives** dining services, go to http://go.compass-usa.com/house/content/menus.asp, and for **Senate** dining services, go to http://go.compass-usa.com/senate/content/menus.asp.

A final, less insidery suggestion:

○ The **Capitol Visitor Center's** (☏ **202/593-1785**) mammoth dining hall, which is open 8:30am to 4pm Monday through Saturday, seats 530 people, and serves "meals and snacks that reflect the diverse bounty of America," which translates into the usual hamburgers and hot dogs, croissants and bagels, pizza and pasta, but also specialty sandwiches associated with different pockets of the country, like the New England lobster roll and the Philly cheese steak. You won't see any members of Congress or other political types at the CVC restaurant, but you'll be dining in good company with fellow tourists.

DOWNTOWN & PENN QUARTER

Expensive

Central Michel Richard ★★ FRENCH BISTRO   Ever since flooding caused Michel Richard's renowned, creatively fun restaurant, Citronelle to close in July 2012, Washingtonians have had only one place to go to enjoy the culinary treats invented by our adopted Frenchman. Central is it. And it is always full. The reason may be that Michel, who has lived here for 40 years, has adopted us, Washingtonians, as much as we have adopted him. The menu speaks to both French and American cultures, listing devilled eggs, fried chicken, mashed potatoes, and meatloaf, alongside trout almandine, and mussels in white wine with garlic. Diners complain about the loudness of the dining room, but noise seems to be a fact of life when eating out in D.C. nowadays. At Central, the commotion signifies the happy time that most are enjoying. *A couple of tips:* For best value, order from the $21 three-course Lunch Special menu, or stop by the bar and lounge any night 5 to 6:30pm, and choose items from the bar menu, from $3 for a slider to $8 for house smoked Arctic char with potato salad.

1001 Pennsylvania Ave. NW (at 11th St.). www.centralmichelrichard.com.© **202/626-0015.** Reservations recommended. Main courses lunch $14–$30, dinner $17–$34. Mon–Fri 11:30am–2:30pm; Mon–Thurs 5:30–10:30pm; Fri–Sat 5–11pm. Metro: Metro Center (12th and F sts. exit).

Fiola ★★★ ITALIAN For a splash-out D.C. dining experience, book a table at Fiola, a favorite among the glitterati, but also locals who simply love inventive Italian cuisine and lively atmosphere. With its wide swath of bar at the front, white banquettes, and modern art, the dining room has a glamorous, head-turning, New York feel about it, maybe informed by chef Fabio Trabocchi's stint there not so long ago. But it's got a friendly vibe, too, helped along by Trabocchio's charming wife, Maria, who is usually on the scene. The main event is the seasonal Italian cuisine, which might include lobster ravioli in cream sauce, goat cheese fritters, lasagna with morels and truffles, or arugula salad with figs. The main menu changes frequently—and the variety of menus is always changing, too. There's a real sense that Fabio and Maria are having fun as they create the light "Maria's Lunch" menu, "Presto! Lunch@Fiola Bar for Busy Professionals," "Bar Bites" menu, a special menu for Valentine's Day, and a menu to celebrate spring. Fabio and Maria opened a casual Italian restaurant in summer 2013, Casa Luca, at 1099 New York Ave. NW, in the Penn Quarter, and were expected to open an Italian seafood eatery in Georgetown's waterfront complex, Washington Harbour, by early 2014.

601 Pennsylvania Ave. NW (entrance on Indiana Ave., between 6th and 7th sts.). www.fioladc.com. © **202/628-2888.** Reservations recommended. Lunch main courses $14–28, $28 prix-fixe light lunch menu, and $19 prix-fixe business lunch menu; dinner main courses $24–$44, 4-course tasting menu $110, 5-course tasting menu $120. Mon–Fri 11:30am–2:30pm; Mon–Thurs 5:30–10:30pm; Fri 5:30–11:30pm; Sat 5–11:30pm. Metro: Archives–Navy Memorial or Gallery Place/Verizon Center (7th and F sts. exit).

Moderate

Graffiato ★ ITALIAN The chef/owner of Graffiato is Mike Isabella, of *Top Chef* fame and you'll understand why he was the runner-up on *Top Chef All-Stars* after dining here. He knows how to take classic Italian dishes and up the ante. At Graffiato, his pizzas are topped with gourmet ingredients, like fried calamari and cherry pepper aioli ("The Jersey Shore") and then cooked in a woodburning oven, just as good pizza should be. In addition, Graffiato serves flavorful small plates: charred asparagus with hazelnuts, wild striped bass with bourbon peaches, sweet corn agnolotti—you get the picture. Best seats in the two floor restaurant are upstairs at the "ham counter" in front of the open kitchen, or downstairs at the back bar, where you can watch pizzas come and go from the oven. And the restaurant's location can't be beat: right across from the Verizon Center, steps away from Chinatown.

707 6th St. NW (at G St.) www.graffiatodc.com. © **202/289-3600.** Pizzas $13-$18, small plates $9-$14 each. Daily 11:30am–5pm; Sun–Tues 5–11pm; Wed–Sat 5pm–2am. Metro: Judiciary Square (F St. exit) or Gallery Place–Chinatown (7th and F sts. exit).

Hill Country Barbecue Market ★★ BARBECUE   Enter Hill Country Barbecue and you leave both hip D.C. and official Washington at the door. It's just not possible to cleave to lofty attitudes and politicking when the Red Dirt Rangers or some such band are playing up a storm, as you make your way through a mess of dry-rubbed Texas barbecued ribs ("smoked low and slow over Texas oak"), skillet corn bread and sweet potato bourbon mash. Upstairs is where you place your order in the cafeteria/ kitchen, and then carry it to your seat, either in the large dining room adjoining the cafeteria, or to your table downstairs. I recommend the downstairs. That's where the bands play and where the lively Boots Bar is. The restaurant often hosts summer "backyard barbecues" on the lawn of the nearby **National Building Museum** (p. 136), selling barbecued pulled pork or chicken sandwiches or hot dogs, plus a side, for $10. Cocktails and sodas are also for sale. The barbecues, in 2013, took place Wed through Sat noon to 11pm, Sun noon to 9pm, and bands performed Thurs through Sat, 5:30 to 8:30pm.

410 7th St. NW (at D St.) © **202/556-2050.** www.hillcountrywdc.com. Main courses $8.50–$29. Daily 11:30am–2am (kitchen closes 10pm Sun–Thurs, 11pm Fri–Sat; late-night menu available to 1am). Metro: Archives–Navy Memorial or Gallery Place–Chinatown (7th and F sts. exit).

Jaleo ★★★ SPANISH   Jaleo, at age 21, is ancient in terms of restaurant years, but she sure doesn't act it . . . or look it. A creative re-design in 2012 added artwork by contemporary Spanish artists, foosball tables with chairs made from Vespa scooter seats, "love tables" closed off by metal curtains, and whimsical touches everywhere, even in the restrooms, where photographed faces smile up at you from the floor. Chef extraordinaire José Andrés is 21 years older as well, and in that time has grown into a culinary and personal phenomenon, with restaurants here (Zaytinya, p. 73, and Oyamel, p.72, as well as the chef's unique and avant garde dining experience, **minibar by José Andrés**) and elsewhere, a cooking show, courses at Harvard, and a number of cookbooks. But it all started here at Jaleo, when Andrés introduced his versions of Spanish tapas to the capital. Andrés or his staff may fiddle with the menu of some 60 individual small plates, but you always know you're enjoying the best tapas in the city (some say in the country, and some of the best dining in D.C.). Look for fried dates wrapped in bacon and served with an apple-mustard sauce; mini-burgers made from the "legendary, acorn-fed, black-footed Iberico pigs of Spain"; and roasted sweet onions, pine nuts, and valdeon blue cheese. Be adventurous.

480 7th St. NW (at E St.). www.jaleo.com.© **202/628-7949.** Reservations accepted. Main courses $8.50–$19; tapas $5–$15; pretheater menu (Sun–Thurs 5–6:30pm) $30. Sun–Mon 11:30am–10pm; Tues–Thurs 11:30am–11pm; Fri–Sat 11:30am–midnight. Metro: Archives–Navy Memorial or Gallery Place–Chinatown (7th and F sts. exit).

Kushi Izakaya & Sushi ★ JAPANESE   The effortlessly jaunty Kushi is part grill room, sushi bar, sake pub, and oyster house. Its enormous dining room serves up seared fatty salmon negiri, skewered duck breast, grilled oysters, and the like, as well as performances of sushi chefs and grill masters in their open kitchens. You can sit at counters in front of different work areas and be entertained while you dine on small plates of sushi, as well as grilled meats, vegetables, and seafood. Thoroughly Japanese, from paper lanterns to hachimaki head wraps, Kushi draws Japanese expats and youngish others for this lively taste of cuisine and culture. (FYI: Kushi lies in the

Mount Vernon Triangle, just outside the Penn Quarter, but close enough to be considered in the same geographic discussion.)

465 K St. NW (at 5th St). www.eatkushi.tumblr.com. © **202/682-3123.** Reservations recommended. Sushi and small plates $3–$15. Mon–Fri 11:30am–2:30pm; Sat–Sun noon–2:30pm; Sun–Thurs 5:30–11pm; Fri–Sat 5:30–11:30pm. Metro: Mt. Vernon Square.

Matchbox ★ PIZZA/AMERICAN   Look for the flickering flame above the restaurant entrance and the line queuing up in front of it. That line could be people waiting for a table—Matchbox *is* awfully popular, and there's not a lot of extra space inside for hanging out. Then again, it could be the line for the Chinatown bus, which happens to pick up New York-bound passengers at this exact spot. The sight of those lines may have prompted the owners finally to accept reservations; better yet for last-minute types, you can call ahead and put your name on the list, which reduces your wait time when you arrive. Matchbox won early acclaim for its thin-crust pizzas cooked in 900°F wood-fired brick ovens (try the spicy meatball with crispy bacon and crushed red pepper), its appetizer of mini burgers on toasted brioche topped with onion "straws" (skinny fried onion strands), its chopped salad, and entrées like the honey miso salmon, and diners keep coming back for more. Saturday and Sunday brunch is big, too. This outlet, the original, is now one of six; at the Barracks Row location, accomplished jazz combos often play during the meal.

713 H St. NW (btw. 7th and 8th sts.). www.matchboxchinatown.com. © **202/289-4441.** Reservations accepted. Main courses $14–$28; pizzas and sandwiches $12–$22; brunch $6–$15. Mon–Thurs 11am–10:30pm; Fri 11am–11:30pm; Sat 10am–11:30pm; Sun 11am–10:30pm Metro: Gallery Place–Chinatown (H and 7th sts. exit).

Old Ebbitt Grill ★ AMERICAN   It's midnight and you're starving. Where you gonna go? Or maybe it's 8am and you want to get a good jump on the day ahead. Who serves a full breakfast at this hour not too far from the National Mall? Or you want a taste of both the capital's regional dishes and insider's culture. Who brings that to the table? It's the Ebbitt.

Old Ebbitt is that rare place that attracts tourists and the city's movers and shakers in equal numbers. It could so easily be a tourist trap, with its saloon décor and old fashioned ambience, only it's not fake. Old Ebbitt has been around since 1856, first in another nearby location, and here since 1983, and some of its furnishings date from the early days. Regulars come here precisely because they find the atmosphere genuinely comfortable. Those regulars, by the way, include Secret Service agents, as well as the people they're protecting; hotshot attorneys from nearby law firms; and politicos visiting the White House a block away.

It's comforting to have a conveniently located place that's nearly always open, has four capacious bars, and a menu that's known for its untrendy dishes, like the burgers, the trout parmesan, and the house pasta, which is stuffed with spinach, mortadella ham, and three cheeses and baked in a cream sauce. Oysters are the standout, among the best and freshest in town. (Daily 3-6pm and after 11pm, all raw bar items are half off.)

675 15th St. NW (btw. F and G sts.). www.ebbitt.com. © **202/347-4800.** Reservations recommended. Main courses breakfast $12–$19, brunch $6–$18, lunch and dinner $11–$21; late night: $9–$26. Mon–Fri 7:30am–1am; Sat–Sun 8:30am–1am. Bar until 2am Sun–Thurs, until 3am Fri–Sat. Metro: Metro Center (13th and F sts. exit).

Oyamel ★★ LATIN AMERICAN/MEXICAN   Oyamel is another of José Andrés's "small plates" restaurants (see Jaleo, p. 71, and Zaytinya, p. 73). Another winning one,

I should add. First thing you do is order a margarita and the guacamole, so you can sip and munch on dipped chips while mulling over the list of *antojitos*, or Mexican "little dishes from the streets." Need some suggestions? Try the *ceviche* (marinated seafood salad), *papas al moles* (fried potatoes in an almond and chili sauce with a touch of chocolate), house specialty *chapulines* (sauteed grasshoppers!), and *quesadilla de chicharrones* (fried pork belly in a tortilla with cheese and chile sauce). This may sound like a lot of food, but remember these are small plates meant to share. Oyamel's carnival atmosphere is part of the fun. Window-fronted on two sides, Oyamel over-looks the Penn Quarter's busiest artery, 7th Street; sit at the miniscule ceviche bar in the southwest pocket of the restaurant and you're in the best spot for people-watching, inside and out.

401 7th St. NW (at D St.). www.oyamel.com. ✆ **202/628-1005.** Limited reservations. Main courses lunch and dinner $9–$19, brunch $6–$12; small plates and tacos $3–$12. Sun–Mon 11:30am–10pm; Tues–Thurs 11:30am–11pm; Fri–Sat 11:30am–midnight. Metro: Gallery Place–Chinatown (7th and F sts. exit) or Archives–Navy Memorial.

Rasika ★★★ INDIAN Try to get a reservation here, I dare you. It's not that it's impossible, but you do have to book far in advance. Here's why you'd want to: Rasika serves exquisite modern Indian food in an intimate, soft-lit, shimmering, champagne-hued setting, that's frequented by a who's who of the Capitol, and the world beyond. Simple as that. Its specialties are griddle, open barbecue, Tandoori, and regional dishes; I personally find the *palak chaat* (crisped spinach in a yogurt sauce) irresistible as is the honey ginger duck, and the Tandoori salmon. Intrigued? Better get out your calendar. You can dine in the bar/lounge without advanced reservations but that, too, is usually pretty full and the lounge seating too low for comfortable eating. Rasika has a sister in the West End, at 1190 New Hampshire Ave. NW (✆ 202/466-2500, www.rasikarestaurant.com/westend). It serves a similar menu but the restaurant is larger and doesn't have the same vibe as the Penn Quarter location.

633 D St. NW (btw. 6th and 7th sts.). www.rasikarestaurant.com. ✆ **202/637-1222.** Reservations recommended. Main courses $14–$28; pretheater menu $35. AE, DC, DISC, MC, V. Mon–Fri 11:30am–2:30pm; Mon–Thurs 5:30–10:30pm; Fri 5:30–11pm; Sat 5–11pm. Lounge stays open throughout the day serving light meals. Metro: Archives–Navy Memorial or Gallery Place/Verizon Center (7th and F sts. exit).

Zaytinya ★★ GREEK/TURKISH/MIDDLE EASTERN When it opened in 2002, Zaytinya, with its full-on, authentic, and wide-ranging tastes of the Middle East, Greece, and Turkey, was quite the culinary adventure for Washingtonians. (Crispy brussel sprouts with coriander seed, barberries, and garlic, oh my! Olive oil ice cream. How interesting!). But Washington was a different place then. Twelve years and a world-rush of restaurant openings later, Zaytinya is an old friend. Those Brussels sprouts are a favorite among the dishes that appear on the four-page menu, which, in truth, has barely changed over the years. It consists, primarily, of *mezze*, which are Mediterranean small dishes, although some entrees appear as well. Other signature dishes include scallops in yogurt and dill sauce; roasted cauliflower with sultans, caper berries, and pine nut puree; spanakopita with house made filo, and *kibbeh nayeh* (Lebanese-style beef tartare with bulgur wheat, radishes, mint and pita chips). Zayti-nya is enormous, seating 230 in the attractive dining rooms, another 52 on stools at the bar, and 65 outside on the patio. Is it any surprise that Zaytinya is a José Andrés property?

701 9th St. NW (at G St.). www.zaytinya.com. © **202/638-0800.** Reservations recommended. Mezze items $6–$14; brunch items $6–$7. Sun–Mon 11:30am–10pm; Tues–Thurs 11:30am–11pm; Fri–Sat 11:30am–midnight. Metro: Gallery Place–Chinatown (9th St. exit).

Inexpensive

Daikaya ★ JAPANESE   Asian cuisine, especially Japanese, is all the rage in Washington, with Daikaya being the trend's current go-to hotspot. Located right next door to another local favorite, Graffiato (see above), you'll know you've found Daikaya when you spot the enormous steel screen with wavelike cutouts covering the façade. The restaurant is an upstairs/downstairs affair, two different places with two separate entrances, but both offering authentic Japanese specialties. Downstairs is the ramen noodle house, a 40-seat, sparsely decorated joint that lets you concentrate on slurping up one of four broths, meat-based or vegetable, filled with aged wheat noodles and topped with a bouquet of briefly stir-fried garnishes. On the second floor, which you reach via an outside staircase to the left of the ramen house, is the larger izakaya, or Japanese tavern. This dimly lit bar and grill's decorative woodwork and Japanese fabrics lend an exotic feel, which tastes from the menu only amplify. You might try grilled avocado with fresh wasabi, crab croquettes, miso cod with pickled carrot, monk fish liver, and finally everyone's favorite, the seaweed-covered rice balls, whose center holds a kind of sticky rice stew. Both upstairs and downstairs are always crowded, always noisy, always a thrill.

705 6thSt. NW (at G St.). www.daikaya.com. © **202/589-1600.** Ramen noodle soups $11–$13; Japanese small plates $2–$9. Ramen noodle house Sun–Mon 11:30am–11pm, Tues–Thurs 11:30am–11pm, Fri–Sat 11:30am–midnight. Upstairs izakaya Sun 11:30am–3pm, Mon 5–10pm, Tues–Thurs 5–11pm, Fri–Sat 5pm–midnight. Metro: Gallery Place (H St./Chinatown exit).

Five Guys Burgers and Fries ★ AMERICAN   Five Guys is taking over the world! Yeah, I know it's a chain, but it's our chain, a family operation that got started in Arlington 28 years ago. At last count, Five Guys had more than 1,000 of its joints in 47 states and six Canadian provinces. You've got your hamburgers, cheeseburgers, bacon burgers, and bacon cheeseburgers, all of which come in two sizes; assorted hot dogs; a veggie sandwich and a grilled cheese for vegetarians; and your choice of regular or Cajun-style fries. One immediate difference between Five Guys and most other popular burgeries, like D.C.'s Good Stuff Eatery (p. 68), is the absence of a "magic sauce." You do get to add as many as 15 toppings, grilled onions to tomatoes, for free. D.C. currently has ten Five Guys, including this Penn Quarter/Chinatown location.

808 H St. NW (at 9th St.).© **202/393-2900.** www.fiveguys.com.© **202/393-2900.** Burgers $4–$7; fries $2–$5. Daily 11:30am–10pm. Metro: Gallery Place (H St./Chinatown exit).

MIDTOWN

Moderate

Bombay Club ★★ INDIAN   Located directly across Lafayette Square from the White House, Bombay Club has been a favorite of one administration after the other, since it opened in 1988. This was Ashok Bajaj's first restaurant in D.C., and though he has added other well-reviewed dining rooms since, most notably **Rasika** (p. 73), Bombay Club is special, a gracious veteran that seems to appeal to everyone. A pianist plays nightly in the dining room, which is decorated in hues of pale pink and yellow. You don't have to be Indian to appreciate the cuisine (although the Indians I know say it is the real thing). Among the popular dishes are the crispy spinach and arugula *chaat*, a savory snack served with date-tamarind chutney; the chicken *tikka*, prepared with coriander, cumin, garlic, black pepper, and yogurt; and tandoor-oven roasted eggplant served with sauteed onions, ginger, and yogurt. If you like spicy, try the chilis and ginger infused duck kebab appetizer. To sample an assortment of tastes, order a house *thali*.

815 Connecticut Ave. NW (H St.). www.bombayclubdc.com. ⓒ **202/659-3727.** Reservations recommended. Main courses $16–$32; Sun brunch $21. Mon–Fri and Sun brunch 11:30am–2:30pm; Mon–Thurs 5:30–10:30pm; Fri–Sat 5:30–11pm; Sun 5:30–9pm. Metro: Farragut West (17th St. exit).

Inexpensive

Sweetgreen ★ LIGHT FARE Sweetgreen was the brainchild of three eco-conscious Georgetown University students who wanted to provide homegrown, healthy options for their neighbors. Today, these eateries are popping up all over town, and in other cities, too. The eatery "sources local and organic ingredients from farmers we know" to create seasonal salads and wraps. Choose one of the eight or so signature salads (my fave: the kale caesar with roasted chicken) or create your own using organic greens and all sorts of interesting fresh ingredients, like spicy pickles and roasted sweet potatoes. All Sweetgreens favor the same modern and streamlined look, but size and seating capacity vary greatly. This location has seating for about 14 inside and 40 more on the sidewalk in pleasant weather. *Note:* **Teaism** (p. 79) has a location at 800 Connecticut Ave. NW, that presents another excellent option for healthy dining in, or for a carryout picnic lunch (weekdays only, and it closes at 5:30pm).

1901 L St. NW (at 19th St.). www.sweetgreen.com. ⓒ **202/331-3355.** Salads $7–$12; yogurt $4–$6. Mon–Fri 10:30am–8pm. Metro: Farragut North (L St. exit).

U STREET CORRIDOR

Beyond the suggestions below, you may want to try two new restaurants in one locale from local celeb chef Mike Isabella (see p. 70): **Kapnos** (2201 14th St. NW at the corner of W Street; ⓒ 202/234-5000; dinner only) serving Greek food, and **Sandwich Shop/Tasting Menu** (see above for address; ⓒ 202/234-5015; lunch and dinner), which will feature sandwiches by day and a $40 tasting menu at night.

Moderate

Cork ★ AMERICAN If I lived in this neighborhood, I would probably hang out here all the time. It's a cozy little wine bar with 160 bottles on offer (most from unusual, small producers), and a whopping 50 wines by the glass. And since wine always tastes better with food, the menu features about 20 dishes nightly, half cold, half hot, meant to be shared. Cheese and charcuterie; carrot and marcona almond salad with golden raisins and toasted cumin; a pan-crisped brioche sandwich of prosciutto, fontina, and Path Valley egg; and french fries tossed with parsley, garlic, lemon always seem to be available, and you should order them, as they're delish. Consider the nightly specials, too, which on my last visit included a memorably rich moussaka. Cork was a pioneer when it opened in 2008, but just these few years later, the neighborhood has more eateries and bars than one can keep up with. Nothing like Cork, though. By the way, if you like a particular wine, you can buy it across the street at **Cork Market and Tasting Room,** 1805 14th St. NW (ⓒ **202/265-2674**).

1720 14th St. NW (at S St.). ✆ **202/265-2675.** www.corkdc.com. ✆ **202/265-2675.** Reservations accepted. Brunch items and dinner small plates $5–$15. Sun 11am–3pm and 5pm–10pm; Tues–Wed 5pm–midnight; Thurs–Sat 5pm–1am. Metro: U St./Cardozo (13th St. exit).

Pearl Dive Oyster Palace ★ AMERICAN/SEAFOOD   The Kitchen at Pearl's turns out some of the city's best oyster dishes, appropriately enough, including the oyster po' boy (cornmeal-fried oysters, house pickles, and aioli), oyster gumbo, and something called *mariscos de Campechana*, which is a stack of oyster, blue crab and shrimp, salsa, and avocado. But you don't have to be a bivalve lover to come here: excellent non-oyster dishes include wood-grilled redfish and grass fed hanger steak. The only downside (which will be an upside for some): the crowd of rambunctious 20-something patrons who fill Pearl Dive's gated front patio, like children in a play-pen. Know that the dining room, with its nautical theme and friendly waitstaff, is a perfectly civilized place to eat, once you walk through the rowdy bar crowd.

1612 14th St. NW. ✆ **202/319-1612.** www.pearldivedc.com. ✆ **202/319-1612.** Reservations not accepted. Brunch main courses $9–$19, dinner main courses $13–$27. Fri–Sun 11am–3pm, daily 5–10pm. Metro: U St./Cardozo (13th St. exit).

Posto ★ ITALIAN   Posto is the little sister of upscale, top-table restaurant Tosca, and the same level of excellence is on offer here, only served up in pizzas, pastas, and grilled main courses. The setting is much different, too: Located on happenin' 14th Street, the casual trattorio is one large modern and high-ceilinged room, combining seats by the windowfront, a communal table, and an open kitchen. The wood-burning oven emits tantalizing aromas of pizzas cooking, like my personal favorite, the Parma (mozzarella, fresh sliced tomatoes, arugula, and prosciutto). It's difficult to choose between pasta dishes, like the three meat ravioli with red wine and sage butter sauce—melts in your mouth—or specials, which always include a "chef's interpretation of the best fish available." If you're wandering the 14th Street strip in search of a place to eat, and striking out everywhere, Posto may be your ace in the hole—not because it's not popular, but because of the quick turnover of tables as some diners hurry to make showtime at **Studio Theatre** next door.

1515 14th St. NW (at P St.). www.postodc.com. ✆ **202/332-8613.** Reservations recommended. Pizzas $15–$17; main courses $18–$26. Mon–Thurs 5:30–10:30pm; Fri–Sat 5–11:30pm; Sun 5–10pm. Metro: U St./Cardozo (13th St. exit).

Inexpensive

Ben's Chili Bowl ★ AMERICAN   Ben's opened in 1958 and it looks like it, too, with its old-fashioned storefront, Formica counters, and red bar stools. Its staying power is impressive enough, but Ben's history is also compelling: When riots broke out throughout the city following the assassination of Dr. Martin Luther King, Jr. in April 1968, Ben's stayed open to serve police officers, firefighters, and anyone who needed sustenance, even as surrounding establishments closed or were destroyed.

On that basis alone, a visit to Ben's is warranted, and some locals do continue to stop by out of an ongoing respect for the place, and for the Ali family who own it. Walls are hung with photographs that cover the history of the city and of Ben's, and include snapshots of the many celebrities who've dined here, from President Obama to Mary K. Blige.

Of course, most folks go to Ben's for the food, which is ultra cheap and usually tasty. Most famous is the half-smoke sandwich, which is a ¼ pound, half-beef, half-pork smoked sausage, served inside a warm bun, and, if you so desire, smothered with mustard, chopped onions, and a spicy chili sauce. I went to Ben's recently with a friend and tried the half-smoke for the first time. And though it is near sacrilege in this city to admit it, I didn't care for it. My friend, who ordered the half-smoke plus cheese fries, says it's because I chose not to top off my half-smoke with the chili sauce and onions. Maybe. What I enjoy most at Ben's are other items on the menu, like the flavorful turkey burger sub and the vegetarian chili (vegetarians take note: Ben's has a few veggie-friendly options).

1213 U St. NW (btw. 12th and 13th sts.). www.benschilibowl.com. © **202/667-0909.** Reservations not accepted. Main courses $3–$10. No credit cards (there's an ATM here). Mon–Thurs 6am–2am; Fri 6am–4am; Sat 7am–4am; Sun 11am–11pm. Metro: U St./Cardozo (13th St. exit).

Tacqueria Nacionale ★ MEXICAN   Johnny's Half Shell (p. 64), on Capitol Hill, long had a little tacos joint operating on the side, or more literally, behind Johnny's, tucked inside an office building. In 2013, Johnny's owners, Ann Cashion and John Fulchino, bestowed real restaurant status upon their popular tacqueria, took over a former post office on this side street in the U Street Corridor, and decorated the interior with beautiful Mexican tiles and grillwork, an old chandelier, and a vision of the Blessed Mother painted upon a worn plaster wall. It seats 45 max at a jumble of brightly colored tables, so from the moment it opens, the tacqueria stays busy. The menu is short but affordable, featuring fresh, authentic tacos, and custom-made quesadillas and tostadas. Yucca fries, salads, guacamole, and other sides are available. (Personally, I think the guacamole could be a little spicier, and I'm a wuss when it comes to hot stuff, so that's saying something.) Saturday/Sunday brunch (breakfast quesadilla, huevos rancheros, and Mexican fritters) is also a big hit. The beverage list is mostly nonalcoholic but does include draft beer and a $5.75 Margarita.

1409 T St. NW (at 14th St.) © **202/299-1122.** www.tacquerianacionale.com. Reservations not accepted. All items: $3–$8. Sun 10am–10pm; Mon–Wed 11am–10pm; Thurs 11am–11pm; Fri 11am–midnight; Sat 10am–midnight. Metro: : U St./Cardozo (13th St. exit) or take the D.C. Circulator.

ADAMS MORGAN

Moderate

Las Canteras ★ LATIN AMERICAN/PERUVIAN   This little sleeper of a restaurant is not about trendiness, thankfully. Instead, Las Canteras introduces diners to the delights of Peruvian culture in the form of food, drinks, and atmosphere. Chef/co-owner Eddy Ancasi is from southern Peru and has decorated his intimate dining room and downstairs bar with photographs of scenes from modern Peru and with colorful handcrafts of local Peruvian artisans. His menu spans both traditional and contemporary Peruvian cuisine, but I'd recommend you go the traditional route: a pisco sour cocktail to start, followed by *cebiche* (fresh white fish marinated in citrus, and garnished with sweet potatoes, roasted corn, and red onions), and *lomo saltado* (morsels of beef wok-fried in soy sauce and served with garlic rice and French fries). Try happy hour Tues through Fri 5 to 7:30pm or the three-course $24 early bird special Tues through Thurs 5 to 7pm for best value.

2307 18th St. NW (at Kalorama Rd.). © **202/265-1780.** www.lascanterasdc.com. Main courses lunch $12–$19, dinner $16–$23. Tues–Fri 11am–3pm; Tues–Thurs and Sun 5–10pm; Fri–Sat 5–11pm; Sat–Sun brunch noon–5pm. Metro: Woodley Park–Zoo, with a walk.

Inexpensive

Amsterdam Falafelshop ★ MIDDLE EASTERN/DUTCH Inspired by the falafel shops of Holland, the owners opened their own D.C. version in 2004, and franchises recently in Annapolis, MD, and in Boston. If you're out clubbing in the neighborhood, do what D.C.'s barhoppers do, and stop here for a snack at, 2, 3, even 4am. The shop does a steady business all day among people who just love these toasted pita sandwiches stuffed with fried balls of mashed chickpeas, topped with as many of the 21 self-serve garnishes, from crunchy onion to hummus. You'll want to add an order of double-fried potatoes, which go best with a dab of Dutch mayo and a shake of Old Bay Seasoning. You can dine in or on the patio, but most customers carry out.

2425 18th St. NW (at Belmont Rd.) www.falafelshop.com. © **202/234-1969.** Reservations not accepted. Falafel $5–$7; Dutch fries $3–$4. Sun–Mon 11am–midnight; Tues–Wed 11am–2:30am; Thurs 11am–3am; Fri–Sat 11am–4am. Metro: Woodley Park–Zoo, with a walk.

DUPONT CIRCLE

Expensive

Al Tiramisu ★★ ITALIAN Al Tiramisu is a find, and those who have found it include George Clooney and dad Nick Clooney, Hillary Clinton, Magic Johnson, Ethel Kennedy, and Catherine Zeta-Jones. I imagine celebrities like it for the same reason everyone else does: the infectious ebullience of chef/owner Luigi Diotaiuti, who bounces out from behind a curtain to greet you as you enter; the unpretentious feeling of this snug little restaurant, which is essentially one long room in the bottom of a Dupont Circle townhouse (people do complain that it feels cramped, but I like it); and a menu that includes excellently prepared fresh grilled fish, house-made spinach-ricotta ravioli with butter and sage sauce, and veal Milanese. This is a place to come for romance, for cheering up, for having a good time with friends, and Tiramisu has been so obliging since it opened in 1996. Check out the restaurant's website for a hint of its personality. A little hokey, maybe, but fun. By the way, reservations are accepted by phone only.

2014 P St. NW (btw. 19th and 20th sts.). www.altiramisu.com. © **202/467-4466.** Reservations recommended. Main courses $19–$30 at lunch and dinner. Mon–Fri noon–2pm, nightly 5–10pm. Metro: Dupont Circle (19th St./South exit).

Komi ★★★ NEW AMERICAN/GREEK Dining at Komi is a simply delicious experience in an intimate, somewhat casual dining room, where the best servers in the city make you feel fully at home and encourage you to focus on the food, your companions, and the exquisite pleasure of tasting the best cuisine in the capital. Because Komi's is the best; critics tend to agree about that. Chef/owner Johnny Monis may be young, but he knows exactly what he's doing, filling dates with mascarpone, or a brioche with monkfish liver, or charring octopus with tomato and fig. There is no printed menu. Monis just sends out 15 or more tastes of his divine inspirations, and if you know what's good for you, you savor it. (Komi will accommodate those with allergies or dietary restrictions; just be sure to call ahead.) This is not a place for loud conversation, nor is it hoity-toity. I wouldn't even describe it as the domain of foodies, although foodies certainly flock here. A dinner at Komi is really about slowing down for a short while, focusing, and being renewed. *FYI:* If you can't book a table at Komi, try Monis's **Little Serow,** a stools-only, walk-ins only, family-style restaurant in the basement of the building next door to Komi. The Northern Thai menu is prix fixe, $45 for seven courses and authentic. You'll know you've found Little Serow when you see the line.

1509 17th St. NW (near P St.). www.komirestaurant.com.© **202/332-9200.** Reservations a must (call a month in advance). Prix fixe $135 per person. Tues–Sat 5:30–9:30pm. Metro: Dupont Circle (Q St. exit).

Tabard Inn ★★ AMERICAN   When a brunch reservation is as difficult to get as it is here, one has to wonder what all the commotions about. My guess? The freshly-made doughnuts served with whipped cream. The Tabard Inn bakes all its breads, pastries, and desserts in-house, and they're scrumptious. Other items also prove a potent lure, like the buttermilk fried chicken sandwich, crab cakes with fried green tomatoes, and the eggs Benedict served with house-smoked salmon. The fact that all of this is served in an absolutely charming, sky-lit room (just past the comfy, old, wood-paneled lounge, where live jazz performances are offered on Sunday evenings) doesn't hurt. If you can't get in for a meal (and they serve more than brunch), do stop in for a cocktail, just so you can experience the inn's lovely ambiance (it's also a hotel; see p. 56).

1739 N St. NW (at 17th St., in the Hotel Tabard Inn). www.tabardinn.com.© **202/331-8528.** Reservations recommended. Main courses breakfast $5–$10, lunch and brunch $11–$18, dinner $24–$36. Mon–Fri 7–10am and 11:30am–2:30pm; Sat 8–9:45am; Sun 8–9:15am; Sat brunch 11am–2:30pm; Sun brunch 10:30am–2:30pm; Sun–Thurs 6–9:30pm; Fri–Sat 6–10pm. Metro: Dupont Circle (19th St./South exit).

Inexpensive

Pizzeria Paradiso ★ PIZZA/ITALIAN   Pizzeria Paradiso has been around since before you were born. Okay, well, certainly before the gourmet pizza trend was born. It's 23 years old and remains a favorite among a wide field of contenders. Paradiso cooks its pizzas in a wood-burning, domed, stone oven that can withstand 650 degree heat, which gives the light but doughier crust than its rivals. The pies come in 8" and 12" sizes, and the 47-item toppings list includes anything you might imagine, from mussels to vegan mozzarella. Paninis and salads, too, get high marks. Pizzeria Paradiso also has a Birreria, where patrons interested in microbrews and handcrafted beers can select from 12 drafts and 200 bottles. Paradiso's other locations are in Georgetown, at 3282 M St. NW (© **202/337-1245**), and in Old Town Alexandria, at 124 King St. (© **703/837-1245**).

2003 P St. NW (btw. 20th and 21st sts.). www.eatyourpizza.com.© **202/223-1245.** Reservations not accepted. Pizzas $10–$19; sandwiches and salads $6–$12. DC, DISC, MC, V. Mon–Thurs 11:30am–11pm; Fri–Sat 11:30am–midnight; Sun noon–10pm. Metro: Dupont Circle (19th St./South exit).

Teaism Dupont Circle ★ ASIAN FUSION   I have long been a fan of this home-grown teahouse enterprise, which in 2012 added a fourth location, in Old Town Alexandria. The District's Teaisms are mostly alike in their menus of bento boxes, aromatic teas, savory sandwiches, and sweets, though they differ in appearance. (Old Town's is an exception, a bit more sophisticated in its menu.) This one, in Dupont Circle, is the original, a homey, two-level restaurant and shop tucked inside a century-old building with French windows that overlook the tree-lined street. The Penn Quarter's Teaism is busier, as you might expect from the neighborhood, and its shop is situated separately, one storefront away from the restaurant. No matter the Teaism, you'll find these are casual eateries, where you order from a menu that might include curried chicken salad,

Vietnamese wrapped sandwiches (of chicken with spicy lime mayo), udon noodle soup, daily specials (such as Korean beef tacos), and a constantly updated inventory of about 36 teas.

Visit **Teaism Lafayette Square,** 800 Connecticut Ave. NW (📞 **202/835-2233**), near the White House; and **Teaism Penn Quarter** ★, 400 8th St. NW (📞 **202/638-6010**), which is the only branch that serves beer, wine, and cocktails; and **Teaism Old Town** at 682 N. Asaph St. (📞 **703/684-7777**).

2009 R St. NW (btw. Connecticut and 21st sts.). www.teaism.com. 📞 **202/667-3827.** All items $3–$12. Mon–Thurs 8am–10pm; Fri 8am–11pm; Sat 9am–11pm; Sun 9am–10pm. Metro: Dupont Circle (Q St. exit).

FOGGY BOTTOM/WEST END
Moderate

Founding Farmers ★ AMERICAN   An international clientele gathers at Founding Farmers, thanks to the fact that the restaurant is located on the ground floor of the International Monetary Fund, one block from World Bank Headquarters, and within a short walk of the Pan American Health Organization and the State Department. But the real reason for its popularity may be that it's one of only a few good dining room restaurants (as opposed to fast food joints and delis) in this neck of the woods. So expect a full house, a frenetic ambience, and noise. That's especially true downstairs which holds a big bar and communal farm tables, as well as booths, and tables. Upstairs tends to be quieter, with silo-shaped booths and small clusters of more intimate seating. So what to order? Founding Farmers fans enthuse about the fancy cocktails, the New Orleans-style French toast available at brunch, and, at lunch and dinner, the crispy shrimp and the griddled farm bread topped with Brie, onion jam, and sliced apples. But the options are endless and include meatless entrées that the menu describes as "Prepared on dedicated meatless equipment." The restaurant is also committed to eco-friendly practices, and uses them even in the restaurant's design.

1924 Pennsylvania Ave. NW (at 20th St.). www.wearefoundingfarmers.com. 📞 **202/822-8783.** Reservations recommended. Main courses breakfast and brunch $5–$15, lunch and dinner $8–$35 (most under $20). Mon 7am–10pm; Tues–Thurs 7am–11pm; Fri 7am–midnight; Sat 9am–midnight; Sun 9am–10pm. Metro: Foggy Bottom.

Inexpensive

Paul ★ FRENCH BAKERY/CAFE   Talk about an appreciative audience! French expats, embassy staff, francophiles like moi—and everybody else who loves croissants, gateau, baguettes, brioche, crepes, eclairs, and macarons—plan their runs to Paul with quiet regularity. I am not embarrassed to say that I have visited all four District shops of this French chain. I'm partial to this one because it is so large and has so many places to perch. There are hundreds of Pauls around the world, all descendants of the one that opened in 1889 in Croix, near the city of Lille in northern France. Besides bread and pastries, Paul sells soups, salads, and sandwiches. In the D.C. area you'll find Paul's in Penn Quarter (801 Pennsylvania Ave. NW; 📞 **202/524-4500**), Georgetown (1078 Wisconsin Ave. NW; 📞 **202/524-4630**), and in Midtown (1000 Connecticut Ave. NW; 📞 **202/524-4860**).

2000 Pennsylvania Ave. NW (entrance on 20th St.). www.paul-usa.com. 📞 **202/524-4655.** Reservations not accepted. Breads and pastries $1–$8; sandwiches and salads $7–$14. Mon–Fri 7am–8pm; Sat–Sun 8am–6pm. Metro: Foggy Bottom.

GEORGETOWN

The closest Metro stop to Georgetown is the Blue Line's Foggy Bottom station; from there you can walk or catch the D.C. Circulator bus on Pennsylvania Avenue.

Expensive

1789 ★★ AMERICAN   One of the city's top tables, the 1789 is the standard bearer for Old World charm. The restaurant's six dining rooms occupy a renovated Federal period house on a back street in Georgetown. Equestrian and historical prints, tables laid with Limoges china and silver, and antique furnishings throughout add touches of elegance. Women usually dress up and men are advised to wear jackets (the staff have lender attire for those who forget). Romancing couples, like Nicole Kidman and Keith Urban, world leaders, like Pres. Obama and German Chancellor Angela Merkel, and locals celebrating birthdays and anniversaries, are among those who dine here for the intimate atmosphere and sense of momentousness the 1789 confers upon any occasion.

The kitchen has seen chefs come and go in the past few years, but the 1789, at 54 years old, is an old hand at handling change. Its cuisine has always been and always will be American, the emphasis more and more on produce purchased from local farms, and meats, seafood, and poultry bought "direct from their native regions." The menu tells you where everything comes from, listed in categories such as "Sustainable Seafood," where you learn that the potato-crusted rockfish is from Rock Hall, MD; in the "Humanely Farmed Animals" section you find country ham from Waynesboro, VA, served with creamy collard greens.

1226 36th St. NW (at Prospect St.). www.1789restaurant.com. © **202/965-1789.** Reservations recommended. Jacket suggested for men. Main courses $35–$48. Mon–Thurs 6–10pm; Fri 6–11pm; Sat 5:30–11pm; Sun 5:30–10pm.

La Chaumiere ★ FRENCH   Sometimes you just are not in the mood for trendy. Sometimes you simply want: delicious food, service that is solicitous but not in the way, a pretty but not splashy dining room, and tables set enough apart to allow for private conversation. La Chaumiere is the answer. A "grown-up" restaurant in Georgetown that's been around for 37 years, it pleases with its French country décor, its white tablecloth-covered tables and rushbottomed chairs arranged around the large center hearth, where a fire crackles in winter. Le Chumiere's menu is a joy for lovers of French classics, like French onion soup, lobster bisque, steak au poivre, and St. Jacques provencale (sea scallops with garlic and tomatoes). The clientele usually skews older, but young couples, families, and business people are among the grateful patrons, too.

2813 M St. NW (at 28th St.) www.lachaumieredc.com. © **202/338-1784.** Reservations accepted. Main courses lunch $17–$21, dinner $17–$37 (most under $30). Mon–Fri 11:30am–2:30pm; Mon–Sat 5:30–10:30pm.

Moderate

Bandolero ★ MEXICAN   Bandolero is one of those places where it always seems like a party's in progress. This small plates eatery has figured out how to make people happy: Combine conversation-making décor (look for depictions of mustachioed Mexican bad guys, skulls, and graveyard posts and tombstones); strong drinks (Tequila gets its own menu, with 26 kinds listed, and there are seven versions of Margaritas); and most importantly, shareable, familiar cuisine that's done differently enough to

HUNGRY? MAKE LIKE A LOCAL & FOLLOW THE food trucks

"Meet you at McPherson Square—lobster rolls!" "Time for a cupcake break—corner of 3rd and D." All day long weekdays and somewhat on weekends, D.C. workers of all trades and echelons text, tweet, e-mail, or phone friends to arrange a food-on-the-move rendezvous. They track the routes of favorite "food trucks," that most unappetizing name for the legion of mobile cook-and-serve vendors, each hocking its own irresistible specialty: gourmet macaroni and cheese, empanadas, Philly cheesesteaks, Maine lobster rolls, all sorts of desserts—you get the idea.

Traditional sidewalk and roadway merchants selling hot dogs and T-shirts still abound in all the usual sightseeing places, including in clusters around the National Mall. These are not them. This next generation of food trucks switches up street fare, tweets its location so hungry patrons know where to go, and still

manages to keep prices reasonable (generally ranging from $3 for a Curbside Cupcake to $15 for a Red Hook Lobster Pound lobster roll). These days, close to 200 different trucks roll around town, setting up shop at designated spots before driving on to their next location.

For a complete list of D.C.'s food trucks, go to **www.foodtruckfiesta.com**, which also displays a map in real time of food-truck stops and messages. The website includes links to each truck's website, where menus, travel routes, and prices are posted.

Laws prohibit gourmet food trucks from parking and serving on federal property, so you won't find these trucks parked along the National Mall (though the aforementioned stationary vendors selling hot dogs and T-shirt vendors are allowed, for some reason). They're never far away, though.

inspire oohs and aahs. Some of the highlights here are suckling pig with apple and habanero sauce, queso fundido (cheese dip) served with a sunny-side-up egg on top, and crispy Brussels sprouts in lemon vinaigrette with coconut-habanero sauce. Diners have complained about the noise level and the dim lighting, though the last time I visited, the dining room did seem better lit. Noise level? Remains loud.

3241 M St. NW (btw. Potomac St. and Wisconsin Ave.). www.bandolerodc.com. © **202/625-4488.** Reservations accepted. Small plates $8–$15 each. Mon–Thurs 5–10pm Fri noon–11pm; Sat 10am–11pm; Sun 10am–10pm. Bar stays open later.

Martin's Tavern ★ AMERICAN   Martin's turns 81 in 2014, and in its lifetime has served every president from Harry Truman to George W. Bush. The tavern is best known as the place where JFK, then a U.S. Senator, proposed to Jacqueline Bouvier on June 24, 1953. Hardbacked wooden booths line the walls of the restaurant and many bear a plaque identifying the former President or famous person who dined within; #3 is the "Proposal Booth." Fourth generation Billy Martin is usually behind the bar, attending to the regulars who frequent the place. That's largely what Martin's is these days: a restaurant for folks from the neighborhood, many of them generational iterations of earlier customers. People who aren't regulars sometimes feel left out, but that's part of the experience, too. "Tavern" is exactly the word to describe Martin's food, which is OK American and, in some cases, Colonial American: Shepherd's Pie and Brunswick Stew are listed and so is Martin's Delight, which is roasted turkey on toast, smothered in rarebit sauce. Martin's offers a bit of old-guard Washington and George-town you're not going to get anywhere else, and that's mostly why I recommend it.

1264 Wisconsin Ave. NW (at N St.). www.martins-tavern.com. © **202/333-7370.** Reservations accepted. Main courses breakfast $8–$18, lunch/brunch $8–$27; dinner $12–$35. Sun 8am–1:30am; Mon–Thurs 11am–1:30am; Fri 11am–2:30am, Sat 9am–2:30am.

Unum ★ AMERICAN Unum as in "E pluribus unum," meaning "Out of many, one," the Latin phrase that appears on the seal of the United States. Only in the nation's capital. But the name hints at the fact that one of the owners has government creden-tials—and, in fact, Laura Schiller hasn't quit her day job working for California Sena-tor Barbar Boxer (husband and co-owner Phillip Blane is the chef). Open since February 2012, Unum is ensconced in the space of the former Mendocino Grille and has retained its lovely features: rough-textured walls, painted wooden floors, and the layout with a bar at the front and banquettes lining the walls in back, with a little nook to the side. It's cozy, a good place for couples. Among the standouts on the menu are a rockfish bouillabaisse which tastes fresh from the sea, smoked duck breast with whipped potatoes, and rosemary gnocchi.

2917 M St. NW (btw. 29th and 30th sts.). www.unumdc.com.© **202/621-6959.** Reservations rec-ommended. Main courses $10–$25. Sun–Thurs 5:30–10pm; Fri–Sat 5:30–11pm.

Inexpensive

Ching Ching Cha ★ CHINESE You'd never guess this kind of place might exist in wild and woolly Georgetown, and it's right in the thick of things, too, on Wisconsin Ave., just past Blues Alley. Although it's been here since 1998, many locals don't even know about Ching, and maybe that's why there's never a line. You're here for an authentic tearoom experience, where the emphasis is on enjoying tea in a tranquil environment. The skylit space is furnished with cushioned platform seating and chairs set at rosewood tables. Try one of the flowering teas, listed among Artisan Teas, in which the brewed tea opens up a jasmine or orange blossom. Seventy teas in all are listed: scented, black, green, oolong, decaffeinated, tisanes, you name it. A short list of menu options ranges from the $5 Mongolian dumpling to the $14 tea meal (soup, rice, marinated cold vegetables, and a main dish, such as mustard miso salmon.) A fine selection of teaware products gifts is for sale.

1063 Wisconsin Ave. NW (near M St.). www.chingchingcha.com.© **202/333-8288.** Reservations not accepted. All food items $4–$12; pot of tea $6–$20. Daily 11am–9pm.

Surfside ★ AMERICAN/LATIN/SEAFOOD Here it is that 20- and 30-some-things gather on the rooftop deck to sip margaritas and dive into guacamole, while down in the colorful and casual eatery, their married-with-children peers, families in tow, nosh on tacos, quesadillas, burritos, and salads. Surfside is especially known for its fresh grilled fish tacos, but its menu covers assorted options, including a pork car-nitas taco served with pineapple jalapeño salsa on corn tortillas, that I like. But if the menu combinations don't appeal, you fill out a form indicating your desired ingredi-ents so the cook can custom-prepare your order. Good to know: Surfside does a brisk takeout business, too, and it now operates a food truck—look for its signature ocean-blue van prowling downtown streets. Technically, Surfside is in a neighborhood called Glover Park, which is just north of Georgetown, so not far.

2444 Wisconsin Ave. NW (near Calvert St.). www.surfsidedc.com.© **202/337-0004.** Reservations accepted. Main courses dinner $7–$14, brunch $7–$10. Sun–Thurs 11am–9pm; Fri–Sat 11am–9:30pm. Bar daily until midnight.

chocolate LOUNGES & CUPCAKE SHOPS

Busted! Washingtonians are finally exposed for what we are: all chocoholics and sweet-cake addicts. An explosion of chocolate lounges and cupcake shops has forced us to come clean. Outposts of Sprinkles and Crumbs keep popping up around town, as do those of Paul Bakery (see p. 80). But let's talk about excellent homegrown sweet shops, shall we? If you answer to the same passion for something desserty, join the queue at one of these four personally vouched-for places:

Co Co. Sala, 929 F St. NW (www.cocosala.com; *𝄢* **202/347-4265**): This chocolate lounge and boutique is a sweet refuge in the heart of the Penn Quarter, dispensing coffees, cocoas, pastries, and small plates of light fare throughout the day. Dessert cocktails and chocolate-spiked liqueurs are on tap into the wee hours.

Georgetown Cupcake, 3301 M St. NW (www.georgetowncupcake.com; *𝄢* **202/333-8448**): Two sisters, 12 daily flavors, darling designs and packaging, and superb baked goods. Locals vote the chocolate ganache the best cupcake in the city; I love the lemon cupcake with lemon cream cheese frosting. Georgetown Cupcake is so popular that the TLC network developed a reality TV show featuring the lovely cupcake makers, Sophie LaMontagne and Katherine Kallinis. Georgetown Cupcake now has locations in New York, Los Angeles, Atlanta, and Boston.

Locolat Café, 1781 Florida Ave. NW (www.belgiumlocolat.com; *𝄢* **202/518-2570**): The Adams Morgan–based Locolat was already a Belgian chocolate *confiserie* when it launched its cafe with sidewalk seating. Chocoholics can sip chocolate-enhanced coffee and hot cocoas, and savor an assortment of cakes, Belgian waffles, pastries, and created-on-the-premises chocolate bonbons.

Red Velvet Cupcakery, 501 7th St. NW (www.redvelvetcupcakery.com; *𝄢* **202/347-7895**): Located in the heart of the Penn Quarter, Red Velvet stays open until 11pm nightly, happy to accommodate the bar and club crowd when a yen for a sweet something hits. It also serves hot chocolate to go.

WOODLEY PARK & CLEVELAND PARK

Moderate

Indique ★ INDIAN   Staff from the Indian Embassy and others who know authentic Indian cuisine consider Indique's regional dishes the real deal. Favorite dishes are too many to mention, but definitely order the vegetable samosa chaat, the chicken curry, and the tandoori shrimp. The two-level townhouse offers two different dining spaces: Upstairs is a beautiful room of red and gold walls and blue painted ceilings, with best tables overlooking the atrium; downstairs includes the lively windowfronted bar area, a good spot for watching commuters emerging from the Cleveland Park subway station and all else that's happening on busy Connecticut Avenue.

3512–14 Connecticut Ave. NW (btw. Porter and Ordway sts.). www.indique.com. *𝄢* **202/244-6600.** Reservations accepted. Main courses $12–$23. Fri–Sun noon–3pm; Sun–Thurs 5:30–10:30pm; Fri–Sat 5:30–11pm. Metro: Cleveland Park (Connecticut Ave. west exit).

Lebanese Taverna ★ MIDDLE EASTERN   Open since 1990, the family-owned Lebanese Taverna received a much-needed renovation in 2012. The re-design added the inevitable bar (13 seats) and lounge, and created a contemporary look in the dining room that now intersperses natural walnut wood panels with hand-laid fieldstone walls, and crowns the room overall with a high sweep of white double-vaulted ceiling. The place feels streamlined and airy. The menu continues to emphasize traditional Middle Eastern dishes, but presents them in more up-to-date ways. For instance, the hummus bar offers three flavors (traditional, spicy, garlic), 11 toppings, and four dippers (crackers, vegetables, fries, and pita toasts). Entrees, like the lamb sharhat (sliced lamb loin with three green-herb sauce), and mezza items, from tabbouleh to spinach pastries, continue to draw the neighborhood here. All meals begin with fresh-from-the-oven puffs of pita bread, with olive oil. The proper ending is an order of Turkish doughnuts, honey-drizzled creamy pudding on the side for dipping.

2641 Connecticut Ave. NW (near Woodley Rd.). www.lebanesetaverna.com. ⓒ **202/265-8681.** Reservations recommended. Main courses $8–$24 (most $15–$17); *mezze* items $6–$11. Sun–Thurs 11:30am–10pm; Fri–Sat 11:30am–11pm. Metro: Woodley Park–Zoo (Connecticut Ave. south exit).

FAMILY-FRIENDLY RESTAURANTS

Nearly every restaurant welcomes families these days, starting, most likely, with the one in your hotel. What you need to know, Mom and Dad, is that many D.C. restaurants are playgrounds for the city's vast population of young professionals, so you want to avoid having to wait for a table, especially when the waiting area is often in the bar! So make reservations, that's my strongest advice. Or consider dining early and getting a table away from the bar scene. Chinese restaurants and museum cafes are always a safe bet, and so are these:

Lebanese Taverna (see above)   Its location down the hill from the National Zoo and its Kids Menu of $6.50 items, each served with hummus, rice, carrots, and celery, make the Taverna attractive to Mom, Dad, and the whole caboodle. Around for 24 years, the Taverna is a favorite among locals, as are its sister locations—there are six now, but this is the only one in D.C.

Five Guys Burgers and Fries (p. 74)   Duh. Burgers. Fries. Hot dogs. Sodas. Grilled cheese. Indestructible environment. And the Guys are everywhere you turn. Last but not least, the price is right: burgers are $4–$7; fries $2–$5.

Ted's Bulletin (p. 65)   This boisterous, laid-back place in the Barracks Row section of Capitol Hill welcomes children of all ages with a retro menu of comfort food, like grilled cheese, Pop-Tarts®, mac and cheese, and tomato soup. Breakfast is served all day, so that might decide things right there. Or how about this: thick and creamy milkshakes in awesome flavors like Oreo and Heath bar almond. (Just don't share your alcohol-infused adult milkshake with your little partner.) There's always a lot going on here, so you never have to worry about your children making too much noise. Prices: $9–$13, lunch $10–$15, dinner $14–$25. Milkshakes are $6.49 each.

EXPLORING WASHINGTON, D.C.

I f you've never been to Washington, D.C., your mission is clear: Get thee to the National Mall and Capitol Hill. Within this roughly 2.5-by-.3-mile rectangular plot lie the lion's share of the capital's iconic attractions (see "Iconic Washington, D.C.," in chapter 3), including presidential memorials, the U.S. Capitol, the U.S. Supreme Court, the Library of Congress, most of the Smithsonian museums, the National Gallery of Art, and the National Archives.

In fact, even if you have traveled here before, you're likely to find yourself returning to this part of town, to pick up where you left off on that long list of sites worth seeing and to visit new ones. The Smithsonian's Arts and Industries Building on the National Mall re-opens in summer 2014 following a years-long renovation that has added a new Innovation Pavilion within the structure. By mid-June, the Washington Monument should be fully repaired and open for public tours again, after suffering damage during the August 2011 earthquake.

And that's just a taste of all there is to absorb in this living, breathing exploratorium of a city: neighborhoods, standalone museums, historic houses, and beautiful gardens. Tour national landmarks and you'll gain a great sense of what this country is about, politically and culturally. Tour off-the-Mall attractions and neighborhoods and you'll get a taste of the vibrant, multicultural local scene that is the real D.C. This chapter will help you do both.

WASHINGTON'S ICONIC SIGHTS

- Arlington National Cemetery ★★ (p. 150)
- The Capitol ★★★ (p. 88)
- Ford's Theater ★★ (p. 133)
- Jefferson Memorial ★★ (p. 105)
- Library of Congress ★★ (p. 93)
- Lincoln Memorial ★★★ (p. 106)
- National Archives ★★ (p. 109)
- National Air and Space Museum ★★ (p. 107)
- National Museum of Natural History ★★ (p. 115)
- National Zoological Park ★★★ (p. 145)
- The Pentagon ★ (p. 152)
- The U.S. Supreme Court ★★★ (p. 97)
- Vietnam Veterans Memorial ★★ (p. 119)

- The Washington Monument ★★★ (p. 120)
- Washington National Cathedral ★★ (p. 146)

- The White House ★★★ (p. 128)

MONUMENTS

- D.C. War Memorial ★ (p. 100)
- FDR Memorial ★★ (p. 102)
- George Mason Memorial ★ (p. 103)
- Korean War Memorial ★ (p. 105)

- Martin Luther King, Jr. Memorial ★★ (p. 107)
- National World War II Memorial ★★ (p. 116)

MUSEUMS

- African American Civil War Memorial and Museum ★ (p. 144)
- Art Museum of the Americas ★ (p. 125)
- Corcoran Gallery of Art ★★ (p. 125)
- Daughters of the American Revolution Museum ★ (p. 126)
- Dumbarton Oaks ★ (p. 148)
- Freer Gallery of Art ★★ (p. 103)
- Heurich House Museum ★ (p. 141)
- Hillwood Museum and Gardens ★ (p. 145)
- Hirshhorn Museum ★★ (p. 104)
- International Spy Museum ★★ (p. 135)
- Kreeger Museum ★ (p. 149)
- Madame Tussauds Washington, DC ★ (p. 135)
- Marian Koshland Science Museum ★ (p. 136)
- Mary McLeod Bethune Council House National Historic Site ★ (p. 144)
- National Building Museum ★ (p. 136)
- National Gallery of Art ★★★ (p. 110)
- National Geographic Museum ★ (p. 142)

- National Museum of American History ★★★ (p. 113)
- National Museum of African Art ★ (p. 112)
- National Museum of Crime and Punishment ★ (p. 137)
- National Museum of the American Indian ★ (p. 114)
- National Museum of Women in the Arts ★ (p. 138)
- National Portrait Gallery ★★★ (p. 140)
- National Postal Museum (p. 96)
- The Newseum ★★ (p. 138)
- Phillips Collection ★★ (p. 142)
- Renwick Gallery ★ (p. 126)
- Sackler Gallery ★ (p. 117)
- Smithsonian American Art Museum ★★★ (p. 140)
- Smithsonian Information Center (the Castle) ★ (p. 118)
- Textile Museum ★ (p. 143)
- U.S. Holocaust Memorial Museum ★★ (p. 123)
- Woodrow Wilson House Museum ★ (p. 143)

OTHER ATTRACTIONS

- Anderson House ★ (p. 141)
- Arts and Industries Building ★ (p. 100)
- Bureau of Engraving & Printing ★ (p. 121)
- Dumbarton House ★ (p. 148)
- Enid A. Haupt Gardens ★ (p. 101)

- Eastern Market ★ (p. 92)
- Folger Shakespeare Library (p. 93)
- Octagon House ★ (p. 126)
- Old Post Office Clock Tower ★ (p. 140)
- Old Stone House ★ (p. 149)
- Ripley Center ★ (p. 117)

CAPITOL HILL

The **U.S. Capitol** with its surrounding Senate and House office buildings dominate this residential neighborhood of tree-lined streets, 19th-century town houses, and pubs and casual eateries. Across the street from the Capitol lie the **U.S. Supreme Court** and the **Library of Congress**; close by are the smaller but fascinating **Folger Shakespeare Library,** the **Sewall-Belmont House,** and **Eastern Market**. A bit farther away is **Union Station,** doing triple duty as historical attraction, shopping mall, and transportation hub. But the neighborhood itself is a pleasure. Explore.

The Capitol ★★★ GOVERNMENT BUILDING   In Washington, D.C. the Capitol Dome can be seen from just about everywhere. That's no accident: by law, no building in the District can be taller than the dome. Its importance, and the importance of Congress, is meant to be unmistakable. Incontrovertible, too, is the fact that a tour of this iconic American symbol is a necessary stop on any first time tour of D.C. When you visit here, you understand, in a very visceral way, just what it means to govern a country democratically. The fights and compromises, the din of differing opinions, the necessity of creating "one from the many" (*e pluribus unum*), without trampling on the rights of that one. It's a powerful experience. And the ideals of the Congress are not just expressed in the debates on the floor of the House and Senate (though you should try to hear those if you can; see below), but in the collection of art and artifacts that litter this massive building (the largest in the world when it was first erected).

Before you get too close to the Capitol, stand back to take a look at the "Statue of Freedom," the 19-foot, 6-inch bronze female figure crowning the Capitol's dome. (You'll get to see the plaster model for the statue on display in the Capitol Visitor Center's Emancipation Hall.) December 2, 2013, marked the 150th anniversary of the placement of the statue upon the top of the dome.

The Capitol is as majestic up close as it is from afar. For 135 years it sheltered not only both houses of Congress, but also the Supreme Court and, for 97 years, the Library of Congress. The hourlong guided tour (for procedures, see below) starts in the Capitol Visitor Center, where you'll watch a 13-minute orientation film, then takes you to the Rotunda, National Statuary Hall, down to the Crypt, and back to the Visitor Center. Here's some of what you'll see:

The **Rotunda**—a huge 96-foot-wide circular hall capped by a 180-foot-high dome—is the hub of the Capitol. The dome was completed, at Lincoln's direction, while the Civil War was being fought: "If people see the Capitol going on, it is a sign we intend the Union shall go on," said Lincoln. Eleven presidents have lain in state here, with former President Gerald Ford, in 2006, being the most recent; when Kennedy's casket was displayed, the line of mourners stretched 40 blocks. On rare occasions, someone other than a president, military hero, or member of Congress receives this posthumous recognition. In October 2005, Congress paid tribute to Rosa Parks by allowing her body to lie in state here, the first woman to be so honored. (Parks was the black woman who in 1955 refused to relinquish her seat to a white man on a bus in Montgomery, Alabama, thereby helping to spark the civil rights movement. On February 27, 2013, Congress further honored Parks by adding a full-sized statue of the civil rights hero to **National Statuary Hall.** The statue is located in Statuary Hall, but is not part of the state collection—see below.)

Embracing the Rotunda walls are eight immense oil paintings commemorating great moments in American history, such as the presentation of the Declaration of Independence and the surrender of Cornwallis at Yorktown. Inside the eye, or inner dome, of the Rotunda is an allegorical fresco masterpiece by Constantino Brumidi, *The Apotheosis of Washington,* a symbolic portrayal of George Washington surrounded by Roman gods and goddesses watching over the progress of the nation. Brumidi was known as the "Michelangelo of the Capitol" for the many works he created throughout the building. (Take another look at the fresco and find the woman directly below Washington; the triumphant *Armed Freedom* figure is said to be modeled after Lola Germon, a beautiful young actress with whom the 60-year-old Brumidi conceived a child.) Beneath those painted figures is a *trompe l'oeil* frieze depicting major developments in the life of America, from Columbus's landing in 1492 to the birth of the aviation age in 1903. Don't miss the sculptures in the Rotunda, including: a pensive Abraham Lincoln; a dignified Rev. Dr. Martin Luther King, Jr.; a ponderous trinity of suffragists Elizabeth Cady Stanton, Susan B. Anthony, and Lucretia Mott; a bronze statue of President Ronald Reagan, looking characteristically genial; and the newest arrival, a likeness in granite of President Gerald Ford.

The **National Statuary Hall** was originally the chamber of the House of Representatives; in 1864 it became Statuary Hall, and the states were invited to send two statues each of native sons and daughters to the hall. There are 100 state-represented statues in all, New Mexico completing the original collection with its contribution in 2005 of Po'Pay, a Pueblo Indian, who in 1680 led a revolt against the Spanish that helped to save Pueblo culture. States do have the prerogative to replace statues with new choices, which is what Michigan did in 2011, swapping out the 1913 choice of Detroit mayor and U.S. Senator Zachariah Chandler for President Ford. Because of space constraints, only 38 statues or so reside in the Hall, with the figures of presidents displayed in the Rotunda, 24 statues placed in the Visitor Center, and the remaining scattered throughout the corridors of the Capitol. Statues include Ethan Allen, the Revolutionary War hero who founded the state of Vermont, and Missouri's Thomas Hart Benton—not the 20th-century artist famous for his rambunctious murals, but his namesake and uncle, who was one of the first two senators from Missouri and whose antislavery stance in 1850 cost him his Senate seat. Nine women are represented, including Alabama-born Helen Keller and Montana's Jeannette Rankin, the first woman to serve in Congress.

As of June 19, 2013, the District of Columbia now has a statue representing it: a full-sized bronze depiction of abolitionist Frederick Douglass stands in Emancipation Hall of the Capitol Visitor Center. Congress has yet to recognize the District as its own state, but at least granted its constituents this representation!

The **Crypt** of the Capitol lies directly below the Rotunda and is used mainly as an exhibit space.

In slow seasons, usually fall and winter, your public tour may include a visit to the **Old Supreme Court Chamber,** which has been restored to its mid-19th-century appearance. The Supreme Court met here from 1810 to 1860. Busts of the first four chief justices are on display—John Marshall, John Rutledge, John Jay, and Oliver Ellsworth—and so are some of their desks, believed to have been purchased in the 1830s. The justices handed down a number of noteworthy decisions here, including *Dred Scott v. Sandford,* which denied the citizenship of blacks, whether slaves or free, and in so doing precipitated the Civil War.

THE CAPITOL visitor center

The enormous, 4,000-person-capacity **Capitol Visitor Center** is underground, which means that as you approach the East Front of the Capitol, you won't actually see it. But look for signs and the sloping sets of steps on either side of the Capitol's central section, leading down to the center's entrances. Once inside you'll pass through security screening and then enter the two-level chamber.

If you have time before or after your tour, you'll find plenty to do here. (Most visitors find it works best to explore the center after touring the Capitol.) You can admire the 24 Statuary Hall statues scattered throughout and tour **Exhibition Hall**, which is a minimuseum of historic document displays; check out interactive kiosks that take you on virtual tours of the Capitol, filling you in on history, art, and architecture; and marvel at exhibits that explain the legislative process. **Emancipation Hall** is the large central chamber where you line up for tours; this is also where you'll find the 26 restrooms and 530-seat restaurant.

The visitor center is open Monday through Saturday year-round from 8:30am to 4:30pm, but closed on Thanksgiving, Christmas, New Year's Day, and Inauguration Day.

You will not see them on your tour, but the **south and north wings** of the Capitol hold the House and Senate chambers, respectively. The House of Representatives chamber is the setting for the president's annual State of the Union addresses. (See below for info on watching Senate and House sessions.)

A note on the area right outside the building: Immediately surrounding the Capitol itself are 59 acres of beautifully kept grounds, originally landscaped in 1892 by Frederick Law Olmsted, who also planned New York City's Central Park. Stroll these winding paths and admire the flower plantings and memorial trees.

Procedures for Touring the Capitol: Tours of the Capitol are free and take place year-round, Monday through Saturday between 8:50am and 3:20pm. Capitol Guide Service guides lead the hourlong, general public tours, which can include as few as one or two people or as many as 40 or 50, depending on the season. Here I must sing the praises of these guides, who are often historians in their own right, repositories of American lore, traditions, anecdotes, and, of course, actual fact. Got a question? Ask away. These guides know their stuff.

You and everyone in your party must have a **timed pass,** which you can order online at www.visitthecapitol.gov. During peak spring and summer sessions, you should order tickets at least 2 weeks in advance. But same-day passes are also available daily from the "public walk-up" near the information desks on the lower level of the visitor center—in limited supply during peak times, but plentiful at off-peak times, particularly in January and February. You can also contact your representative or senator in Congress and request passes for constituent tours, which are usually limited to groups of 15 and conducted by congressional staff, who may take you to notable places in the Capitol beyond those seen on the general public tour. No matter what, call © **202/225-6827** in advance of your visit; that way you'll know for sure whether the Capitol is open.

The Capitol has quite a list of items it prohibits; you can read the list online at www.visitthecapitol.gov or listen to a recitation by calling the phone number above. Items

Security precautions and procedures are a post-9/11 fact of life everywhere in America, but especially in the nation's capital, thanks to the preponderance of federal structures and attractions that are open to the public. What that means for you as a visitor is that you may have to stand in line to enter a national museum (like one of the Smithsonians) or a government building (like the Library of Congress). At many tourist sites, you can expect staff to search handbags, briefcases, and backpacks, either by hand or by X-ray machine. Some sites, including the National Air and Space Museum, require you to walk past metal detectors. During the busy spring and summer seasons, you may be queuing outside as you wait your turn to pass through security. So pack your patience, but otherwise carry as little as possible, and certainly no sharp objects. Museums and public buildings rarely offer lockers for use by visitors.

ranging from large bags of any kind to food and drink are prohibited; leave everything you can back at the hotel.

The Capitol Guide Service also offers other special tours and talks on an ongoing basis, though the specific topics might change. Recent offerings included tours of the Brumidi Corridors and tours that focused on the Capitol and Congress during the Civil War. Look online or ask at the visitor center information desk for details about these presentations.

Procedures for Visiting the House Gallery or Senate Gallery: Both the Senate and House galleries are open to visitors whenever either body is **in session** ★–★★★, so do try to sit in. (The experience receives a range of star ratings because a visit can prove fascinating or deathly boring, depending on whether a debate is underway and how lively it is.) Otherwise the Senate Gallery is open to visitors during scheduled recesses of one week or more, Monday to Friday 9am to 4:15pm, and the House Gallery is open to visitors year-round Monday to Friday 9am to 4:15pm. Children 5 and under are not allowed in the Senate gallery. You can obtain visitor passes at the offices of your representative and senator, or in the case of District of Columbia and Puerto Rico residents, from the office of your delegate to Congress. To find out your member's office location, go online at www.house.gov or www.senate.gov and follow the links to your state representative's or your senators' information, or call © 202/225-3121 to speak to a Capitol operator. You must have a separate pass for each gallery. Once obtained the passes are good through the remainder of the Congress. *Note:* International visitors can obtain both House and Senate gallery passes by presenting a passport or a valid driver's license with photo ID to staff at the House and Senate Appointments desks on the upper level of the visitor center, near the main entrance.

The main, staffed offices of congressional representatives and delegates are in House buildings on the south (Independence Avenue) side of the Capitol; senators' main, staffed offices are located in Senate buildings on the north (Constitution Avenue) side. You should be able to pick up passes to both the Senate and House galleries in one place, at either your representative's office or one of your senators' offices. Visit the Architect of the Capitol's website, **www.aoc.gov**, the Visitor Center website, **www. visitthecapitol.gov**, or call your senator or congressperson's office for more exact information about obtaining passes to the House and Senate galleries.

Here's a crucial piece of advice: **Call ahead or check the websites of the places you plan to tour each day before you set out.** Many of Washington's government buildings, museums, memorials, and monuments are open to the general public daily, year-round—except when they're not.

Because buildings like the Capitol, the Supreme Court, and the White House are offices as well as tourist destinations, the business of the day always poses the potential for closing one of those sites, or at least sections, to sightseers. There's also the matter of maintenance. The steady stream of visitors to Washington's attractions necessitates ongoing caretaking, which may require closing an entire landmark, or part of it, to the public, or changing the hours of operation or procedures for visiting. Washington's famous museums, grand halls, and public gardens sometimes double as settings for press conferences, galas, special exhibits, festivals, and even movie sets. You might arrive at, say, the National Air and Space Museum on a Sunday afternoon, only to find some or all of its galleries off-limits because a movie shoot is underway. (Have you seen *Night at the Museum: Battle of the Smithsonian,* by the way?) And then there is the sequester, the term for the budget cuts enacted by Congress that affect various federally funded government programs, including most notably here in D.C., the cancellation of White House tours open to the public. (I've noted the few other sequester-related changes within the individual write-ups for affected attractions.) The sequester went into effect in March 2013 and is designed to continue for a decade, but you just never know; perhaps the cuts will be cancelled, or the White House will resume its public tour schedule. To avoid frustration and disappointment, call ahead or check online for up-to-the-minute information.

You'll know that the House and/or the Senate is in session if you see flags flying over their respective wings of the Capitol (*Remember:* House, south side; Senate, north side), or you can visit their websites, **www.house.gov** and **www.senate.gov,** for an in-depth education on the legislative process; schedules of bill debates in the House and Senate, committee markups, and meetings; and links to your Senate or House representative's page.

Capitol and Capitol Visitor Center: E. Capitol St. (at 1st St. NW). www.visitthecapitol.gov, www.aoc.gov, www.house.gov, www.senate.gov. ℂ **202/225-6827** (recording), 202/593-1768 (Capitol Guide Service Office), or 202/225-3121 (Capitol operator). Free admission. Year-round Mon–Sat 8:30am–4:30pm (first tour at 8:50am, last tour at 3:20pm). Closed for tours Sun and Jan 1, Thanksgiving, Dec 25, and Inauguration Day. Parking at Union Station or on neighborhood streets. Metro: Union Station (Massachusetts Ave. exit) or Capitol South, then walk to the Capitol Visitor Center, located on the East Front of the Capitol.

Eastern Market ★ MARKET   A mainstay of the historic Capitol Hill neighborhood and of the city itself, Eastern Market has been operating continuously since 1873, not even pausing after a fire in 2007 (indoor vendors moved to a parking lot across the street until the building re-opened in 2009.) Inside, 13 vendors in their separate stalls sell fresh produce, pasta, seafood, meats, cheeses, sweets, flowers, and pottery Tues–Sun. Weekends is when things get really lively, when about 140 arts and crafts merchants, plus an additional 20 or so farmers and open air food-vendors sell their wares on the market's outdoor plaza. The street is closed to traffic in front of the market and the block teems with families doing their weekly grocery shopping, hipsters attracted to this cool attraction, and even the occasional congressperson (many live in the neighborhood). For a real hometown experience, come for blueberry buckwheat pancakes ("bluebucks") served at Market Lunch inside the Market on Saturdays (see p. 68), or for lunch Tues–Sun.

225 7th St. SE (at North Carolina Ave.). www.easternmarket-dc.org. © **202/698-5253.** Free admission. Indoor market: Tues-Fri 7am–7pm, Sat 7am–6pm, Sun 9am–5pm. Closed Thanksgiving, Dec 25, and New Year's Day. Metro: Union Station or Capitol South.

Folger Shakespeare Library ★ LIBRARY   "Shakespeare taught us that the little world of the heart is vaster, deeper, and richer than the spaces of astronomy," wrote Ralph Waldo Emerson in 1864. A decade later, Amherst student Henry Clay Folger was profoundly affected by a lecture Emerson gave similarly extolling the Bard. Folger purchased an inexpensive set of Shakespeare's plays and went on to amass the world's largest (by far) collection of the Bard's works, today housed in the Folger Shakespeare Library. By 1930, when Folger and his wife, Emily, laid the cornerstone of a building to house the collection, it comprised 93,000 books, 50,000 prints and engravings, and thousands of manuscripts. The Folgers gave it all as a gift to the American people. The library opened in 1932.

The building itself has a marble facade decorated with nine bas-relief scenes from Shakespeare's plays; it is a striking example of Art Deco classicism. An **Elizabethan garden** on the east side of the building is planted with flowers and herbs of the period. Most remarkable here are eight sculptures, each depicting figures from a particular scene in a Shakespeare play. Each work is welded onto the top of a pedestal, on which are inscribed the play's lines that inspired the sculptor, Greg Wyatt. Inquire about **guided tours** scheduled at 10 and 11am on every first and third Saturday from April to October. The garden is also a nice, quiet place to have a picnic.

The facility, which houses some 256,000 books, 116,000 of which are rare (pre-1801), is an important research center not only for Shakespearean scholars, but also for those studying any aspect of the English and continental Renaissance. Other features entertain the general public: A multimedia computer exhibition called "The Shakespeare Gallery" offers users a close-up look at some of the Folgers' treasures, as well as Shakespeare's life and works. The white-oak-paneled, Tudor-ish **Great Hall** rotates exhibits of items from the permanent collection—Renaissance musical instruments to centuries-old playbills—to highlight a particular theme. Plan on spending at least 30 minutes here.

At the end of the Great Hall is a theater designed to suggest the yard of an Elizabethan inn, where plays, concerts, readings, and Shakespeare-related events take place (see chapter 8 for details).

201 E. Capitol St. SE. www.folger.edu. © **202/544-4600.** Free admission. Mon–Sat 10am–5pm; Sun noon–5pm. Free walk-in tours Mon–Fri 11am and 3pm; Sat 11am and 1pm; Sun 1pm. Closed federal holidays. Metro: Capitol South or Union Station.

Library of Congress ★★ LIBRARY   You're inside the main public building of the Library of Congress—the magnificent, ornate, Italian Renaissance–style **Thomas Jefferson Building.** Maybe you've arrived via the tunnel that connects the Capitol and the Library of Congress, or maybe you've entered through the 1st Street doors. In any case, you'll likely be startled—very startled—to find yourself suddenly inside a government structure that looks more like a palace. Before you stop in the **Orientation**

Galleries to line up for the tour, take time to stroll around the building and just gape. Admire the stained-glass skylights overhead; glance down to the Italian marble floors inlaid with brass and concentric medallions; gaze right, left, and all around to try to take in the gorgeous murals, allegorical paintings, stenciling, sculptures, and intricately carved architectural elements. This building, more than any other in the city, is a visual treasure.

Now for the history lesson: Established in 1800 by an act of Congress, "for the purchase of such books as may be necessary for the use of Congress," the library today also serves the nation, with holdings for the visually impaired (for whom books are recorded on cassette and/or translated into Braille), scholars in every field, college students, journalists, teachers, and researchers of all kinds. Its first collection of books was destroyed in 1814 when the British burned the Capitol (where the library was then housed) during the War of 1812. Thomas Jefferson then sold the institution his personal library of 6,487 books as a replacement, and this became the foundation of what would grow to become the world's largest library.

The Jefferson Building was erected between 1888 and 1897 to hold the burgeoning collection and to establish America as a cultured nation with magnificent institutions equal to anything in Europe. Originally intended to hold the fruits of at least 150 years of collecting, the Jefferson Building was, in fact, filled up in a mere 13 years. It is now supplemented by the **James Madison Memorial Building** and the **John Adams Building.**

Today the collection contains a mind-boggling 151.8 million items. Its buildings house more than 34.5 million cataloged books; 63 million manuscripts; millions and millions of prints and photographs, audio holdings (discs, tapes, talking books, and so on), movies, and videotapes; musical instruments from the 1700s; and the letters and papers of everyone from George Washington to Groucho Marx. Its archives also include the letters, oral histories, photographs, and other documents of war veterans from World War I to the present, all part of its **Veterans History Project;** go to www. loc.gov/vets to listen to or read some of these stories, especially if you plan on visiting the National World War II Memorial (p. 116).

In addition to its art and architecture, the Library displays ongoing exhibits of objects taken from its permanent collections; Exploring the Early Americas and Thomas Jefferson's Library were two shows going on at press time. The concerts that take place in the Jefferson Building's elegant **Coolidge Auditorium** are free but require tickets, which you can obtain through Ticketmaster (www.ticketmaster.com). Across Independence Avenue from the Jefferson Building is the **Madison Building,** which houses the Copyright Office and the **Mary Pickford Theater,** a venue for classic film screenings.

Using the library: Anyone 16 and over may use the library's collections, but first you must obtain a user card with your photo on it. You can get the process started by pre-registering online at https://wwws.loc.gov/readerreg/remote. Whether pre-registered or not, you must go to Reader Registration in Room LM 140 (street level of the Madison Building) and present your driver's license or passport. Staff will verify your identity, take a photo, and present you with your user card. Then head to the Information Desk in either the Jefferson or the Madison building to find out about the research resources available to you and how to use them. Most likely, you will be directed to the Main Reading Room. All books must be used on-site.

Jefferson Building: 1st St. SE, between Independence Ave. and E. Capitol St. Madison Building: 101 Independence Ave. SE (at 1st St. SE). www.loc.gov. © **202/707-8000.** Free admission.

Capitol Hill

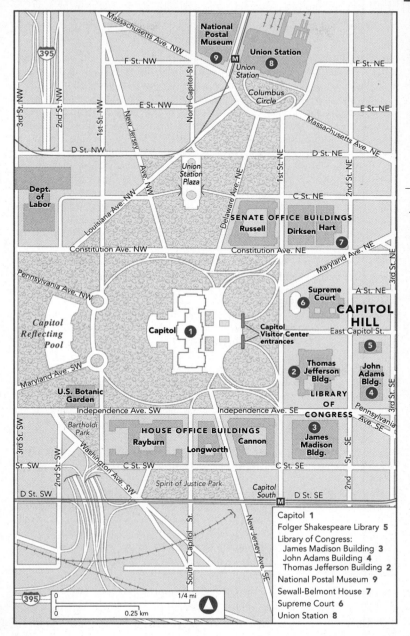

Capitol **1**
Folger Shakespeare Library **5**
Library of Congress:
  James Madison Building **3**
  John Adams Building **4**
  Thomas Jefferson Building **2**
National Postal Museum **9**
Sewall-Belmont House **7**
Supreme Court **6**
Union Station **8**

Madison Building Mon–Fri 8:30am–9:30pm; Sat 8:30am–5pm. Jefferson Building Mon–Sat 8:30am–4:30pm. Closed federal holidays. Stop at an information desk on the 1st floor of the Jefferson Building. Docent-led tours of the Jefferson Building are free, require no reservations or tickets, and take place Mon–Fri 10:30 and 11:30am, and 12:30, 1:30, 2:30, and 3:30pm; Sat 10:30 and 11:30am, and 1:30 and 2:30pm. Contact your congressional representatives to obtain tickets for congressional, or "VIP," tours (slightly more personalized tours). Metro: Capitol South.

National Postal Museum ★ MUSEUM This Smithsonian museum is somewhat off the standard sightseeing route (most other Smithsonians are located on or near the National Mall), so it doesn't capture as many visitors as the other attractions. That's set to change, however, thanks to the September 22, 2013 opening of the **William H. Gross Stamp Gallery.** The new Gallery's design adds much needed visibility and appeal to the original Postal Museum, with a wall of windows featuring replicas of 54 historic U.S. stamps. The display transforms the building's façade and catches the attention of passersby, especially at night when the artwork is illuminated.

The curious who venture in off the street find themselves immediately in the elegant lobby of the historic structure (home of the Old City Post Office), where a welcome center and the new gallery are located. The gallery's 12,000 square feet of exhibits is a 50 percent increase in total exhibit space for the museum, and covers themes that will make philatelists' hearts go pitter pat. The **World of Stamps,** for example, features a hit list of famous stamps, starting with the very first postage stamp, the 1840 Penny Black, bearing a young Queen Victoria's profile; **Stamps Around the Globe,** displays international stamps, which make up half the Postal Museum's overall collection. Lots of pullout cases containing more than 20,000 items, interactive kiosks, and videos should keep even the non-stamp-collector visitor interested, even amused. For example, you can build a virtual stamp collection and email it to yourself.

But don't neglect the original museum, where America's postal history is on display, from 1673 to the present. Stop at the entrance, which is one floor down, and grab the self-guide tour flyer, one side mapping out a tour for kids, the other for everyone else. (Personally, I liked using both versions.) Children usually make a beeline to the enormous, blue freightline truck front over in the corner, and climb up into the driver's seat. This is part of the central exhibit area called **Moving the Mail,** and you'll see planes, trains, and other postal vehicles, even a handcrafted hickory Alaskan dogsled, that have been used at one time or another to transport the mail. In **Binding the Nation,** visitors can follow a path through a forest to trace the steps of mail carriers who traveled from New York to Boston in 1673, and climb into a stagecoach headed West. The exhibit introduces famous figures, like Buffalo Bill, of Pony Express renown, and Henry "Box" Brown, who "mailed" himself, a slave, to an abolitionist in 1856.

Other exhibits cover stamp collecting (**Alphabetilately**), mail's impact on city streets and rural routes (**Customers & Communities**), the journey a single letter takes through the postal system and how that process has changed over time (**Systems at Work**), and the history and current practice of getting mail delivered to and from military personnel (**Mail Call**). Don't miss the colorful display of mailboxes from around the world: Sweden, the Vatican, Taiwan, Denmark, and Ireland among them.

2 Massachusetts Ave. NE (at 1st St.). www.postalmuseum.si.edu. © **202/633-5555.** Free admission. Daily 10am–5:30pm. Closed Dec 25. Metro: Union Station.

Sewall-Belmont House ★ MUSEUM This unassuming old brick house betwixt the Capitol and the Supreme Court has been the home of the National Woman's Party since 1929. Suffragist and organizer extraordinaire Alice Paul founded the NWP in 1917 to fight for women's rights, including the right to vote. (In 1997, the NWP switched from being a political party to an organization focusing on education and advocacy.) The house is a repository of suffragist memorabilia, banners, political buttons, photos of events and main characters in the life of the women's equal rights movement, and other artifacts, 2,600 in all, of which 250 are on view. Visits here are by guided tour only, but that's a good thing, since the power and point of the site is best conveyed through hearing the stories of individual heroines. Susan B. Anthony you will have heard of. But Alva Belmont, Inez Mulholland Boissevain, and Febb Burn?

144 Constitution Ave. NE (at 2nd St.). www.sewallbelmont.org. ℂ **202/546-1210.** Admission $8. Open for tours Thurs–Sat at 11am, 1pm, and 3pm. Sign up online or just show up on a scheduled day and time. Entrance is on 2nd St.—look for the signs. Closed Thanksgiving, Dec 25, and New Year's Day. Metro: Union Station or Capitol South.

The Supreme Court of the United States ★★★ GOVERNMENT BUILD- ING   On many days, the Supreme Court is the most exciting place to be in town. Beginning each annual session on the first Monday in October, the nine justices hear cases and render opinions that can dramatically affect every American. Visitors are invited to sit in on arguments between lawyers for opposing sides, who are typically questioned sharply and repeatedly by the justices. It's a grand show, fast-paced, sometimes heated, and always full of weighty import (the justices hear only about 100 of the most vital of the 10,000 or so petitions filed with the Court every year). The Court's rulings are final, reversible only by an Act of Congress. And you, the visitor, get a close-up seat . . .if you're lucky (see below for more on how to get in).

But even when the court isn't in session, touring the building is still a worthwhile experience. During these periods, docents offer 30-minute lectures inside the Supreme Court chamber, to introduce visitors of all ages to the Court's judicial functions, the building's history, and the architecture of the courtroom. Lectures take place every hour on the half-hour, beginning at 9:30am on days when the Court is not sitting and at a later time on Court days. You can also tour the building on your own; architect Cass Gilbert, best known for his skyscrapers (like New York's 761-foot-high Woolworth building), designed the stately Corinthian marble palace that houses the Court today. First stop by the ground-floor Information Desk to pick up a helpful flyer, view exhibits, and watch a film on the workings of the Court. In fact, that short film is a good preliminary to the docent lecture, so you may want to time your visit accordingly.

Getting in to see a case being argued: Starting the first Monday in October and continuing through late April, the Court "sits" for 2 weeks out of every month to hear two 1-hour arguments each day Monday through Wednesday, from 10am to noon, with occasional afternoon sessions scheduled as necessary from 1 to 2 or 3pm. You can find out the specific dates and names of arguments in advance by calling the Supreme Court (℃ **202/479-3211**) or by going to the website, **www.supremecourt.gov,** where the argument calendar and the "Merits Briefs" (case descriptions) are posted.

Plan on arriving at the Supreme Court at least 90 minutes in advance of a scheduled argument during the fall and winter, and as early as 3 hours ahead in March and April, when schools are often on spring break and students lengthen the line. (Dress warmly; the stone plaza is exposed and can be witheringly cold.) Controversial cases also attract crowds; if you're not sure whether a particular case has created a stir, call the Court information line to reach someone who can tell you. The Court allots only about **150 first-come, first-served seats** to the general public, but that number fluctuates from case to case, depending on the number of seats that have been reserved by the lawyers arguing the case and by the press. The Court police officers direct you into one line initially; when the doors finally open, you form a second line if you want to attend only

3 to 5 minutes of the argument. Seating begins at 9:30am for those attending the full argument and at 10am for those who want to catch just a few minutes.

The justices are always at work on their opinions following Court arguments, and release these completed opinions in the courtroom throughout the argument term, October through April, and into May and June. If you attend an oral argument, you may find yourself present as well for the release of a Supreme Court opinion, since the justices precede the hearing of new oral arguments with the announcement of their opinions on previously heard arguments, if any opinions are ready. What this means is, if you're visiting the Court on a Monday in May or June, you won't be able to attend an argument, but you might still see the justices in action, delivering an opinion, during a 10am, 15-minute session in the courtroom. To attend one of these sessions, you must wait in line on the plaza, following the same procedure outlined above.

Leave your cameras, recording devices, and notebooks at your hotel—they're not allowed in the courtroom. *Note: Do* bring quarters. Security procedures require you to leave all your belongings, including outerwear, purses, books, sunglasses, and so on, in a cloak room where there are coin-operated lockers that accept only quarters.

1 1st St. NE (btw. E. Capitol St. and Maryland Ave. NE). www.supremecourt.gov. ℭ **202/479-3000** or 202/479-3030 (recording)**.** Free admission. Mon–Fri 9am–4:30pm. Closed all federal holidays. Metro: Capitol South or Union Station.

Union Station ★ ARCHITECTURAL ICON/MARKET   When it opened in 1907, this was the largest train station in the world. It was designed by noted architect Daniel H. Burnham, who modeled it after the Baths of Diocletian and the Arch of Constantine in Rome. Its facade includes Ionic colonnades fashioned from white granite, and 100 sculptured eagles. Graceful 50-foot Constantine arches mark the entryways, above which are poised six carved fixtures representing Fire, Electricity, Freedom, Imagination, Agriculture, and Mechanics. Inside is the **Main Hall,** a massive rectangular room with a 96-foot barrel-vaulted ceiling, an expanse of white-marble flooring, and a balcony adorned with 36 Augustus Saint-Gaudens sculptures of Roman legionnaires. Off the Main Hall is the **East Hall,** shimmering with scagliola marble walls and columns, a gorgeous hand-stenciled skylight ceiling, and stunning murals of classical scenes inspired by ancient Pompeian art. (Today this is the station's most pleasant shopping venue: less crowded and noisy, with small vendors selling pretty jewelry and other accessories.)

In its time, this "temple of transport" has witnessed many important events. President Wilson welcomed General Pershing here in 1918 on his return from France. South Pole explorer Rear Admiral Richard Byrd was also feted at Union Station on his homecoming. And Franklin D. Roosevelt's funeral train, bearing his casket, was met here in 1945 by thousands of mourners.

But after the 1960s, with the decline of rail travel, the station fell on hard times. Rain caused parts of the roof to cave in, and the entire building—with floors buckling, rats running about, and mushrooms sprouting in damp rooms—was sealed in 1981. That same year, Congress enacted legislation to preserve and restore this national treasure, to the tune of $160 million. A remarkable 2-year restoration involved hundreds of European and American artisans who were meticulous in returning the station to its original design. A new and improved Union Station re-opened in 1988 (2013 marked the 25th anniversary of that event.)

By 2014 Union Station's grand front circle, Columbus Plaza, will have been enhanced, allowing for easier traffic flow and safer pedestrian access. (Funds ran out before the fountain was fixed, unfortunately.) Many more improvements are in the works, as part of a decades-long plan. If you see scaffolding and construction areas,

express bus service AROUND THE NATIONAL MALL & MEMORIAL PARKS

It's easy to access the National Mall and Memorial Parks on foot or by bike, but be aware that bus transportation is also available. In addition to various sightseeing services (see p. 243 for narrated options), you might consider **Mall Express** trams (www.anctours.com/mallexpress.php; © **202/488-1012**) which provide a fast, unnarrated shuttle service. These open-air trams travel between Union Station and Arlington Cemetery, stopping at the National World War II and the Lincoln memorials in one direction and at the Martin Luther King memorials and Smithsonian Metro station on the return trip. The trams are blue and white and display the name "Mall Express." These trams do not provide a hop-on hop-off service; you'll pay $5 each time you board or $9 for a round-trip journey. Buy your ticket in person when you board or online. The trams operate daily, 9am to 6:30pm March through September, 9am to 4:30pm October to February. They depart Union Station every 30 to 45 minutes.

however, they are likely related to the repair work that is still going on to fix damage done by the Aug. 23, 2011 earthquake.

Union Station just keeps on going. At least 32 million people come through Union Station's doors yearly. About 120 retail and food shops on three levels offer a wide array of merchandise and dining options. The sky-lit **Main Concourse,** which extends the entire length of the station, is the primary shopping area, as well as a ticketing and baggage facility. You could spend half a day here shopping or about 20 minutes touring. Several tour companies use the station as a point of arrival and departure; at least three, **Double Decker Tours, Old Town Trolley,** and **Open Top Sightseeing** operate ticket booths inside the front hall of the main concourse. (See p. 243 for more information about tours.)

50 Massachusetts Ave. NE. www.unionstationdc.com. © **202/289-1908.** Free admission. Station daily 24 hr. Shops Mon–Sat 10am–9pm; Sun noon–6pm. Machines located inside the station near the exit/entrance to the parking garage will validate your ticket for $1 for 2 hr. of parking; after that fees are as follows: $7 for 1 hr. or less, up to $22 for 24 hr. Metro: Union Station.

THE NATIONAL MALL & MEMORIAL PARKS

This one's the biggie, folks. More than one-third of the capital's major attractions lie within this complex of parkland that the National Park Service calls **National Mall and Memorial Parks.** The National Mall (see below) is the centerpiece of this larger plot that extends from the Capitol to the Potomac River, and from Constitution Avenue to down and around the cherry-tree-ringed Tidal Basin. Presidential and war memorials, the Washington Monument, the Dr. Martin Luther King, Jr. Memorial, 10 Smithsonian museums, the National Gallery of Art, the National Archives, and the U.S. Botanic Garden are here waiting for you. So let's get started. FYI: The National Mall and Memorial Parks has its own telephone number, © **202/485-9880,** and website, www.nps.gov/nama.

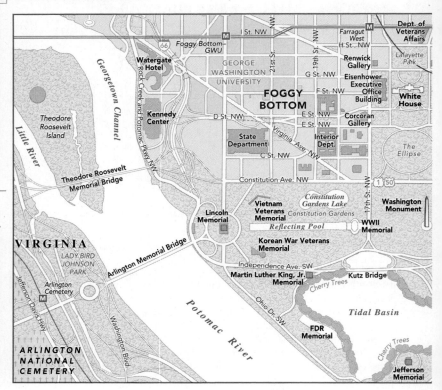

Arts and Industries Building ★ ARCHITECTURE   The building is closed for an extensive renovation, as you'll no doubt guess if the dramatic scaffolding is still in place by the time you visit. When it re-opens in summer 2014, the museum will offer a new Innovation Pavilion. The Smithsonian has partnered with the U.S. Patent and Trademark Office to develop exhibits and programs related to innovation. Completed in 1881 just in time to host President James Garfield's inaugural ball, this red-brick and sandstone structure was the first Smithsonian museum on the Mall, and the first U.S. National Museum. More recently, from 1976 to the mid-1990s, it housed exhibits from the 1876 U.S. International Exposition in Philadelphia—a celebration of America's centennial that featured the latest advances in technology.

Weather permitting, and regardless of the construction underway, a 19th-century **carousel** operates across the street on the Mall.

900 Jefferson Dr. SW (on the south side of the Mall). www.si.edu.

D.C. War Memorial ★ MONUMENT/MEMORIAL   This long-neglected and often overlooked memorial commemorates the lives of the 499 citizens of Washington, D.C. who died in the First World War. Newly restored in 2011, the memorial is surely

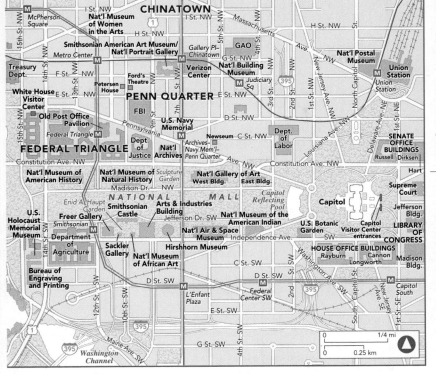

worth a stop on your way to grander, more famous edifices. President Herbert Hoover dedicated the memorial in 1931; John Phillip Sousa conducted the Marine band at the event. The structure is a graceful design of 12 Doric columns supporting a classical circular dome. The names of the 499 dead are inscribed in the stone base.

On the north side of Independence Ave. SW, between the National World War II and Lincoln memorials. www.wwimemorial.org.

Enid A. Haupt Garden ★ GARDEN Named for its donor, a noted supporter of horticultural projects, this pretty 4-acre garden presents elaborate flower beds and borders, plant-filled turn-of-the-20th-century urns, 1870s cast-iron furnishings, and lush baskets hung from reproduction 19th-century lampposts. The garden is planted on the rooftops of the subterranean Ripley Center and Sackler and African Art museums. The tranquil **Moongate Garden** near the Sackler Gallery employs water and granite in a landscape design inspired by a 15th-century Chinese temple. Two 9-foot-tall pink-granite moon gates frame a pool paved with half-rounds of granite. Benches backed by English boxwoods sit under the canopy of weeping cherry trees.

A **"Fountain Garden"** outside the African Art Museum provides granite seating with walls overhung by hawthorn trees. Three small terraces, shaded by black sour-gum trees, are located near the Arts and Industries Building. And five majestic linden trees shade a seating area around the **Downing Urn,** a memorial to American landscapist Andrew Jackson Downing, who designed the National Mall. Elaborate cast-iron carriage gates made according to a 19th-century design by James Renwick, flanked by four red sandstone pillars, salute the Independence Avenue entrance to the garden.

10th St. and Independence Ave. SW. ℂ **202/633-1000.** Free admission. Daily dawn–dusk. Free tours May–Sept Wed 1pm. Closed Dec 25. Metro: Smithsonian (12th St. and Independence Ave. exit).

Franklin Delano Roosevelt Memorial ★★ MONUMENT/MEMORIAL   The

FDR Memorial has proven to be one of the most popular of the presidential memorials since it opened in 1997. Its popularity has to do as much with its design as the man it honors. This 7½-acre outdoor memorial stretches out, mazelike, rather than rising up, across the stone-paved floor. Granite walls define the four "galleries," each representing a different term in FDR's presidency, from 1933 to 1945. Architect Lawrence Halprin's design includes waterfalls, sculptures (by Leonard Baskin, John Benson, Neil Estern, Robert Graham, Thomas Hardy, and George Segal), and Roosevelt's own words carved into the stone.

The many displays of cascading water can sound thunderous, as the fountains recycle an astonishing 100,000 gallons of water every minute. The presence of gushing fountains and waterfalls aren't a random choice. Instead, they reflect FDR's appreciation for the importance of H_2O. As someone afflicted by polio, he understood the rehabilitative powers of water exercises and established the Warm Springs Institute in Georgia to help others with polio. As president, FDR supported several water projects, including the creation of the Tennessee Valley Authority.

When the memorial first opened, adults and children alike arrived in bathing suits and splashed around on warm days. Park rangers don't allow that anymore, but they do allow you to dip your feet in the various pools. A favorite time to visit is at night, when dramatic lighting reveals the waterfalls and statues against the dark parkland.

Conceived in 1946, the FDR Memorial had been in the works for 50 years. Part of the delay in its construction can be attributed to the president himself: FDR had told his friend Supreme Court Justice Felix Frankfurter, "If they are to put up any memorial to me, I should like it to be placed in the center of that green plot in front of the Archives Building. I should like it to consist of a block about the size [of this desk]." In fact, such a plaque sits in front of the National Archives. Friends and relatives struggled to honor Roosevelt's request to leave it at that, but Congress and national sentiment overrode them.

As with other presidential memorials, this one opened to some controversy. Advocates for people with disabilities were incensed that the memorial sculptures did not show the president in a wheelchair, which he used after he contracted polio. President Clinton asked Congress to allocate funding for an additional statue portraying a wheelchair-bound FDR. You will now see a small statue of FDR in a wheelchair, placed at the very front of the memorial, to the right as you approach the first gallery. Step inside the gift shop to view a replica of Roosevelt's wheelchair, as well as one of the rare photographs of the president sitting in a wheelchair. The memorial is probably the most accessible tourist attraction in the city; as at most of the National Park Service locations, wheelchairs are available for free use on-site. Rangers conduct interpretive tours every hour on the hour. Thirty minutes is sufficient time for a visit.

On West Basin Dr., alongside the Tidal Basin in West Potomac Park (across Independence Ave. SW from the Mall). www.nps.gov/frde. ✆ **202/426-6841**. Free admission. Ranger on duty daily 9:30am–11:30pm, except for Dec 25. Limited parking. Metro: Smithsonian (12th St./Independence Ave. exit), with a 20-min. walk.

Freer Gallery of Art ★★ MUSEUM   Thanks to a wealthy donor of varied passions, a single museum houses one of the world's finest permanent collections of Asian art as well as the most comprehensive assemblage of the works of American artist James McNeill Whistler. This somewhat schizophrenic entity, which opened in 1923, was the first Smithsonian museum devoted to the fine arts.

The museum's namesake, Charles Lang Freer, was a self-taught connoisseur, who started out in the 1880s collecting American art, specifically living American artists, including his friend, the British-based Whistler. It was Whistler and his affinity for Japanese and Chinese art, that got Freer interested in collecting Asian art. (Galleries near the Peacock Room display other works by Whistler that clearly show the influence of Asian art and techniques upon his own style.) Soon Freer's Asian art collection outgrew his American art collection; today, of the 25,000 objects spanning 6,000 at the Freer (from China, Japan, Korea, Syria, Iraq, Iran, India, Pakistan, Turkey, Central Asia, and Egypt) only a small number, 1,708, to be exact, consists of American works.

The Freer, unlike many of its Smithsonian sisters, is usually blessedly uncrowded, making it a wonderful place to escape D.C.'s throngs. The Italian-Renaissance-style building's main galleries lie on one level and encircle a lovely, landscaped central courtyard. It's possible to stroll unhurried through the skylit rooms, which hold astonishingly a wide array of wonders. Such as: fine jewelry from the Chinese Liangzhu culture (which flourished during the late Neolithic and Bronze ages—we're talking 6,000 years ago); a 1760 Japanese handscroll depicting "One Hundred Old Men Gathering for a Drink Party"; 12th century illuminated manuscripts of sacred texts created by Jain artists of western India; a monumental hammered brass Iranian candlestick from the late 12th century; exquisite Japanese screens; a beautiful, turquoise-glazed jar, from late 12th century Syria; giant and forbidding-looking Japanese wooden figures that face each other at either end of a corridor, but which stood guard in the early 14th century outside the entrance to a temple near Osaka; and the Freer's single permanent installation, Whistler's famous (and drop-dead gorgeous) **Harmony in Blue and Gold, the Peacock Room**, conceived of as a dining room for the London mansion of wealthy client F. R. Leyland.

When you enter from the National Mall into the museum, you'll see stairs to your left that take you to the neighboring Sackler Gallery and the two museums' shared performance space, the **Meyer Auditorium**, where Asian-themed films, concerts, and other programs are frequently staged. But when you get to the bottom of the stairs, before you continue on to those destinations, turn right to see what's on view in the small exhibit area dedicated to Whistler drawings and watercolors. Precious. "Whistler's Neighborhood: Impressions of a Changing London" is the one I toured in the summer of 2013, but I'm looking forward to the Sept 2013–Sept 2014 exhibit, "Off the Beaten Path: Whistler's Early Works on Paper." Stop at the information desk or check online for info about highlights tours, children's activities, and so on.

Jefferson Dr. SW at 12th St. SW (on the south side of the Mall). www.asia.si.edu. ✆ **202/633-1000**. Free admission. Daily 10am–5:30pm. Closed Dec 25. Metro: Smithsonian (Mall/Jefferson Dr. exit).

George Mason Memorial ★ MONUMENT/MEMORIAL   Though his name is not famous today, George Mason is considered, along with James Madison, one of the two "Fathers of the Bill of Rights". It was his efforts that got those first 10 lines of the U.S. Constitution added; indeed they were based upon the Virginia Declaration of Rights, which Mason authored. Dedicated on April 9, 2002, the memorial consists of a bronze statue of Mason, dressed in 18th century garb, from buckled shoes to tricorner hat, set back in a landscaped grove of trees and flower beds (lots and lots of pansies). Two stone slabs are inscribed with some of Mason's words, like these, referring to Mason's rejection of slavery: THAT SLOW POISON, WHICH IS DAILY CONTAMINATING THE MINDS & MORALS OF OUR PEOPLE. An interesting stand for a slave-owner to take, wouldn't you say? Wooden benches at the site present a pleasant opportunity to learn about Mason and take a break before moving on. *Note:* The memorial is easy to miss, since it does not lie on the Tidal Basin path. As you approach the Jefferson Memorial from the direction of the FDR Memorial, or as you approach the FDR Memorial from the direction of the Jefferson, you'll come to the bridge that arches over the inlet leading from the Tidal Basin to the Potomac River; look straight across from the bridge, and there you'll see it.

E. Basin and Ohio drives SW (btw. the Jefferson and FDR memorials). www.nps.gov/gemm. ☏ **202/426-6841.** Free admission. Open daily, though rangers generally are not posted here. To find out more about George Mason, visit the Jefferson Memorial, a 5-min. walk away, on the Tidal Basin, where a park ranger is on duty 9:30am–11:30pm. Limited parking. Metro: Smithsonian (12th St./Independence Ave. exit), with a 25-min. walk.

Hirshhorn Museum and Sculpture Garden ★★ ART MUSEUM This cylindrically shaped, concrete-and-granite building holds provocative art at its best, from de Kooning to Jeff Koons. Look for Thomas Hart Benton's dizzying sprawl of figures in the 1920 painting "People of Chilmark," Ellsworth Kelly's vivid minimalist paintings, Dan Steinhilber's sculpture made out of paper-clad wire hangers, Henri Matisse's bronze casts, and Damian Hirst's "The Asthmatic Escaped II, 1992," in which one of two conjoined glass cases holds a camera on a tripod, and the other holds the clothing, inhaler, and other personal effects of "the escaped." The museum rotates works from its near 12,000-piece collection, 600 at any one time, so if these exact artworks are not on view, others in their avant-garde family will be.

Some of the Hirshhorn's most famous art is on display outside, on the grounds surrounding the museum plaza and across Jefferson Drive in the sunken Sculpture Garden. Sadly, a lot of people miss the garden, maybe because it's below ground, but also because, in my opinion, the Hirshhorn doesn't point it out well enough. Also, sadly, the place seemed ill kept when I visited recently, and some of the sculptures are missing identifying placards. Let's blame it on Congress's 2013 sequester, shall we? With any luck, by the time you read this, the sequester will have ended and funding been found to better maintain the garden. The sculptures themselves stand up well: Rodin's *Monument to the Burghers of Calais*, Giacometti's *Monumental Head*, and Henry Moore's *Reclining Figure No. 4*, among them. *Note:* The Hirshhorn's Sculpture Garden and the **National Gallery of Art's Sculpture Garden** (see p. 111), located directly across the Mall from each other, **are not the same!** It astonishes me how often people confuse the two. They offer two very different experiences, and you should visit both.

The Hirshhorn exists thanks to a man named Joseph H. Hirshhorn, who was born in Latvia in 1899, but immigrated to the United States as a boy. In 1966, Hirshhorn donated his collection of more than 6,000 works of modern and contemporary art to the United States in gratitude for the country's welcome to him and other immigrants, and bequeathed an additional 5,500 upon his death in 1981. The museum opened in 1974.

In addition to films, concerts, and lectures, the Hirshhorn holds **Hirshhorn After Hours** events three or four times a year, ultra-popular parties for 20-somethings, with cocktails, live music, art, and dance (tickets available in advance online at www. hirshhorn.tumblr.com).

Stop by the museum noon to 4pm daily for docent-led, free, 30-minute tours.

Independence Ave. at 7th St. SW (on the south side of the Mall). www.hirshhorn.si.edu. ℭ **202/633-4674.** Free admission. Museum daily 10am–5:30pm. Sculpture Garden daily 7:30am–dusk. Closed Dec 25. Metro: L'Enfant Plaza (Smithsonian Museums/Maryland Ave. or Smithsonian exit).

Jefferson Memorial ★★ MONUMENT/MEMORIAL   President John F. Kennedy, at a 1962 dinner honoring 29 Nobel Prize winners, told his guests that they were "the most extraordinary collection of talent, of human knowledge, that has ever been gathered together at the White House, with the possible exception of when Thomas Jefferson dined alone." Jefferson penned the Declaration of Independence and served as George Washington's secretary of state, John Adams's vice president, and America's third president. He spoke out against slavery—although, like many of his countrymen, he kept slaves himself. He also established the University of Virginia and pursued wide-ranging interests, including architecture, astronomy, anthropology, music, and farming.

Franklin Delano Roosevelt, a great admirer of Jefferson, spearheaded the effort to build him a memorial, although the site choice was problematic. The Capitol, the White House, and the Mall were already located in accordance with architect Pierre L'Enfant's master plan for the city, and there was no spot for such a project that would maintain L'Enfant's symmetry. So the memorial was built on land reclaimed from the Potomac River, perched upon the lip of the manmade reservoir now known as the Tidal Basin. Roosevelt laid the memorial cornerstone in 1939 and had all the trees between the Jefferson Memorial and the White House cut down so that he could see the memorial every morning.

The memorial is a columned rotunda in the style of the Pantheon in Rome, whose classical architecture Jefferson himself introduced to this country (he designed his home, Monticello, and the earliest University of Virginia buildings in Charlottesville). On the Tidal Basin side, the sculptural group above the entrance depicts Jefferson with Benjamin Franklin, John Adams, Roger Sherman, and Robert Livingston, all of whom worked on drafting the Declaration of Independence. The domed interior of the memorial contains the 19-foot bronze statue of Jefferson standing on a 6-foot pedestal of black Minnesota granite. The sculpture is the work of Rudolph Evans, chosen from among more than 100 artists in a nationwide competition. Jefferson is depicted wearing a fur-collared coat given to him by his close friend, the Polish General Tadeusz Kosciuszko. If you follow Jefferson's gaze, you see that, sure enough, the Jefferson Memorial and the White House have an unimpeded view of each other.

Rangers present 20- to 30-minute programs throughout the day as time permits.

Ohio Dr. SW, at the south shore of the Tidal Basin (in West Potomac Park). www.nps.gov/thje. ℭ **202/426-6841.** Free admission. Ranger on duty daily 9:30am–11:30pm, except Dec 25. Limited parking. Metro: Smithsonian (12th St./Independence Ave. exit), with a 20- to 30-min. walk.

Korean War Veterans Memorial ★ MONUMENT/MEMORIAL   This privately funded memorial, founded in 1995, honors those who served in the Korean War, a 3-year conflict (1950–53) that produced almost as many casualties as Vietnam. It consists of a circular "Pool of Remembrance" in a grove of trees and a triangular "Field of Service," highlighted by lifelike statues of 19 infantrymen who appear to be trudging across fields. A 164-foot-long black granite wall depicts the array of combat and support troops that served in Korea (nurses, chaplains, airmen, gunners, mechanics, cooks, and others); a raised granite curb lists the 22 nations that contributed to the UN's effort there; and a commemorative area honors KIAs, MIAs, and POWs. Plan to spend 15 minutes here.

Southeast of the Lincoln Memorial, on the Independence Ave. SW side of the Mall. www.nps.gov/kowa. ✆ **202/426-6841.** Free admission. Ranger on duty daily 9:30am–11:30pm, except Dec 25. Limited parking. Metro: Foggy Bottom, with 30-min. walk.

Lincoln Memorial ★★★ MONUMENT/MEMORIAL   When famed architect Charles Follen McKim (of McKim, Meade, and White) was asked to work on the 1902 McMillan commission to reshape the overall design for the Mall, he made his views clear on what he felt would be an important addition. "As the Arc de Triomphe crowns Place de l'Etoile in Paris, so should stand a memorial erected of the memory of that one man in our history as a nation who is worthy to be joined with George Washington—Abraham Lincoln." Twenty years later, in 1922, the Lincoln Memorial was dedicated. As the McMillan commission envisioned, it was set on a direct axis to the Washington Monument, symbolically anchoring the Mall with a monument to the nation's founding President at one end and the memorial honoring the President who saved the Union at the other.

The neoclassical templelike structure, similar in architectural design to the Parthenon in Greece, has 36 fluted Doric columns representing the states of the Union at the time of Lincoln's death, plus two at the entrance. On the attic parapet are 48 festoons symbolizing the number of states in 1922, when the monument was erected. (Hawaii and Alaska are noted in an inscription on the terrace.) Due east is the Reflecting Pool, lined with American elms and stretching 2,000 feet toward the Washington Monument and the Capitol beyond.

The memorial chamber has limestone walls inscribed with the Gettysburg Address and Lincoln's second inaugural address. Two 60-foot-high murals by Jules Guerin on the north and south walls depict, allegorically, Lincoln's principles and achievements. On the south wall, an Angel of Truth freeing a slave is flanked by groups of figures representing Justice and Immortality. The north-wall mural portrays the unity of North and South, and is flanked by groups of figures symbolizing Fraternity and Charity. Most powerful, however, is Daniel Chester French's 19-foot-high seated statue of Lincoln. Lincoln sits, gazing down on the visitors at his feet, the burdens of guiding the Union through the Civil War etched deeply in his face. Though 19 feet tall, the figure is eerily lifelike and exudes a fatherly compassion. Some say that his hands create the sign-language shapes for A (Abraham) and L (Lincoln), as a tribute to the fact that Lincoln signed legislation giving Gallaudet University, a school for the deaf, the right to confer college degrees. The Parks Department denies the symbolism, but it should be noted that French's son was deaf, so the sculptor *did* know sign language.

Lincoln's legacy has made his memorial the site of numerous demonstrations by those seeking justice. Most notable was a peaceful demonstration of 200,000 people on August 28, 1963, at which Martin Luther King, Jr. proclaimed, "I have a dream." Look for the words I HAVE A DREAM. MARTIN LUTHER KING, JR., THE MARCH ON

WASHINGTON FOR JOBS AND FREEDOM, AUGUST 28, 1963, inscribed and centered on the 18th step down from the chamber. The inscription, which the National Park Service added in July 2003, marks the precise spot where King stood to deliver his famous speech. Be sure to visit the National Museum of American History to tour the exhibit, "Changing America: The Emancipation Proclamation, 1863, and the March on Washington, 1963."

Rangers present 20- to 30-minute programs as time permits throughout the day. Thirty minutes is sufficient time for viewing this memorial.

On the western end of the Mall, at 23rd St. NW (btw. Constitution and Independence aves.). www. nps.gov/linc. © **202/426-6841.** Free admission. Ranger on duty daily 9:30am–11:30pm, except Dec 25. Limited parking. Metro: Foggy Bottom, then a 30-min. walk.

Martin Luther King, Jr. National Memorial ★★ MONUMENT/MEMORIAL   I must confess my disappointment in the Martin Luther King, Jr. Memorial, which provides little context for King's life and work as, arguably, the United State's most important Civil Rights activist. I would have preferred a memorial more like the one for FDR, whose panels illustrate scenes from FDR's presidency; or like Lincoln's or Jefferson's, whose remarkable words are rendered more fully in the stone walls. Still, the very fact of its existence is sign of changed times.

Authorized by Congress in 1996, this memorial pays tribute to the Baptist minister who was committed to nonviolence and direct action to force social change, and whose efforts and compelling speeches profoundly moved the country toward that achievement. The memorial debuted on Oct. 16, 2011. Hurricane Irene prevented it from opening on its originally planned date, August 28, exactly 48 years after the Rev. Dr. Martin Luther King, Jr. delivered his momentous "I Have a Dream" speech on the steps of the nearby Lincoln Memorial. On that original date, some 200,000 people gathered on the Mall during the "March on Washington" to pressure Congress to pass the Civil Rights Act. King was assassinated on April 4, 1968, at the age of 39.

The memorial's site along the northwest lip of the Tidal Basin is significant for the "visual line of leadership" it creates between the Lincoln Memorial, representing the principles of equality and civil rights as embodied in the personage of Abraham Lincoln and carried forward in King, and the Jefferson Memorial, which symbolizes the democratic ideals of the founding fathers. Set on a crescent-shaped, 4-acre parcel of land surrounded by the capital's famous cherry trees, the mammoth sculpture (created in China, a controversial decision) rests on 300 concrete piles driven into the muddy basin terrain. A 28-foot, 6-inch statue of Dr. King in a business suit, arms folded, stands front and center, representing the "Stone of Hope"; he is flanked by two enormous background pieces, representing the "Mountain of Despair." A curving boundary wall enclosing the grounds perhaps commemorates the slain civil rights leader best, with inscriptions of excerpts from his remarkable sermons and speeches.

Ranger talks are held frequently throughout the day, and those are probably the best way to get the most out of a visit here. The memorial includes a bookstore, a ranger station, and restrooms.

Adjacent to the FDR Memorial, along the northwest side of the Tidal Basin, at Independence Ave. SW, in West Potomac Park. www.nps.gov/mlkm. © **202/426-6841.** Free admission. Ranger on duty daily 9:30am–11:30pm, except Dec 25. Limited parking. Metro: Smithsonian (12th St./Independence Ave. exit), with a 25-min. walk.

National Air and Space Museum ★★ MUSEUM   The second most popular museum in all of Washington—and that's saying a lot!—The National Air and Space

Museum manages to taps into that most primordial of human impulses: the urge to fly. And it does so in a multi-layered fashion, mixing extraordinary artifacts with IMAX movies, videos, computer terminals with quizzes, even flight simulators.

The seeds of this museum were planted when the Smithsonian Institution acquired its first aeronautical objects in 1876, with the purchase of 20 kites from the Chinese Imperial Commission. By the time the National Air and Space Museum opened on the National Mall one hundred years later, the collection had grown to tens of thousands of objects. Today, the inventory of historic aircraft and spacecraft artifacts numbers 60,000, the world's largest such collection.

I have never visited the National Air and Space Museum when it was not a frenzied scene, so bring your patience. This is the second most visited museum of the Smithsonians (Natural History, see below, is first), attracting nearly 7 million people, many of them children and teenagers. The place is huge, as is much of its collection. Enormous aircraft and spacecraft dangle from the ceiling or are placed in floor exhibits throughout both levels. Visitors of all ages, but as I say, mostly families, are chattering away, taking pictures of each other against the backdrops of the towering Pershing (34.8') and SS20 (54.10') missiles, or the Apollo II Command Module *Columbia,* or just about anything in the museum, since most of the artifacts dwarf humans. Tours and demonstrations are going on simultaneously in different areas of the museum.

And there are lines—many, many lines. The first is just to enter the building. (*Tip:* Fewer people tend to enter through the Independence Avenue doors; if you are in line reading this on the National Mall side, why not break away and go around the west side of the building to the Independence Avenue entrance?) Then there are lines to get tickets for **IMAX films ★**, or a show at the **Einstein Planetarium ★**, to take a ride on a flight simulator, and to enter the cockpit of the Northwest Airlines Boeing 747 on display in the **America by Air** exhibit (FYI: You enter the nose of the plane from the second floor). So take a moment when you enter to grab a flyer and strategize which exhibits will be most interesting for you.

I recommend starting your visit by looking for the 12 items listed as highlights in the flyer. The very first mentioned object is the touchable moon rock, which is located in the **Milestones of Flight** gallery, just inside the museum when you enter from the National Mall. There's so much going on in this section, that people often walk right past the unobtrusive upright display case, despite its being clearly marked "Moon Rock." Stick your hand in the little slot and run your finger over the small triangle of black volcanic rock. You've touched a four billion year-old piece of basalt! The Apollo 17 mission astronauts collected the rock in December 1972.

Other points of interest include the second floor exhibit, **Pioneers of Flight,** where Amelia Earhart's brilliant red Lockheed Vega plane is on view. Earhart piloted her "little red bus," as she called it, alone and nonstop in 1932 from Canada to Northern Ireland. Next door to Pioneers of Flight is the **Wright Brothers** exhibit, where the highlight, naturally, is the Wright brothers' 1903 Flyer, the world's first successful airplane.

Additional exhibits cover **Flight and the Arts**, **Apollo to the Moon**, **Exploring the Planets**, **World War II Aviation,** and much, much more, everything in sync with the museum's mission, "…to commemorate the national development of aviation and spaceflight, and [to] educate and inspire the nation." Get off your feet for a while and take in an IMAX film, like the ever popular *To Fly*, or *Hubble 3-D*, or watch a show at the **Albert Einstein Planetarium** ★, where you have the sensation that you're traveling through space. IMAX and planetarium films require tickets, which range from $7.50 per child to $9 per adult per film.

This location is also home to the Smithsonian's largest gift shop (three levels, 12,000 square feet), and fast food favorites McDonald's, Boston Market, and Donato's Pizzeria.

Haven't had enough? Drive the 25 miles or so to the National Air and Space Museum's companion location, the **Steven F. Udvar-Hazy Center**, which celebrated its 10th anniversary in 2013. Here you can explore one huge hangar filled with aviation objects, another with space objects, each arranged by subject (Commercial Aviation, Korea and Vietnam Aviation, Sport Aviation, and so on), and you can tour an observation tower that gives you a bird's eye view of planes landing and departing at Washington Dulles International Airport. IMAX movies and simulator rides are options here, as well.

Mall museum: Independence Ave. SW, btw. 4th and 7th sts. (on the south side of the Mall, with 2 entrances, one on Jefferson Dr. and the other on Independence Ave.). Udvar-Hazy Center: 14390 Air and Space Museum Pkwy., Chantilly, VA. www.nasm.si.edu. ℂ **202/633-1000** (for both locations), or 877/932-4629 for IMAX ticket information. Free admission. Both locations daily 10am–5:30pm (Mall museum often until 7:30pm in summer, but call to confirm). Free 1½-hr. highlight tours daily 10:30am and 1pm. Closed Dec 25. Metro: L'Enfant Plaza (Smithsonian Museums/Maryland Ave. exit) or Smithsonian (Mall/Jefferson Dr. exit).

National Archives ★★ GOVERNMENT BUILDING The Rotunda of the National Archives displays the country's most important original documents: the Declaration of Independence, the Constitution of the United States, and the Bill of Rights (collectively known as the Charters of Freedom), as part of its exhibit **The National Archives Experience.** Fourteen document cases trace the story of the creation of the Charters and the ongoing influence of these fundamental documents on the nation and the world. Be sure not to miss viewing the original 1297 Magna Carta, on display as you enter the Rotunda; the document is one of only a few known to exist, and the only original version residing permanently in the United States.

But those documents, though the most famous in the Archives, are just the beginning of the fun here. Don't skip the **Public Vaults,** an area introduces visitors to the heart of the archives: its 9 billion records, covering 2 centuries worth of documents, from patent searches to genealogical records to census records, passport applications, governmental records and more.

I know, I know: it sounds dry, but the way the curators have laid it all out is anything but. Using the very latest in interactive museum design—listening booths, computer terminals, videos, you name it—the curators have mined the material for drama (and often presented it in a very kid-friendly fashion). In an area on patents, for example, the process is turned into a game: you read the patent application and then try and guess what well-known gadget it was for. A section on immigration presents the search for genealogical data as a cliffhanger mystery, detailing the steps and missteps of several Archives' users. President Nixon makes several eerie appearances: you read his resignation letter and listen to disturbing excerpts from the Watergate tapes. During the day, the **William C. McGowan Theater** continually runs dramatic films illustrating the relationship between records and democracy in the lives of real people, and at night it serves as a premier documentary film venue for the city. The **Lawrence F. O'Brien Gallery** rotates exhibitions of Archives documents.

Beyond its exhibits, the Archives are a vital resource for those doing research. Anyone 16 and over is welcome to use the National Archives center for genealogical research. Call for details.

The National Archives' building itself is worth an admiring glance. The neoclassical structure, designed by John Russell Pope (also the architect of the National Gallery of Art and the Jefferson Memorial) in the 1930s, is an impressive example of the Beaux Arts style. Seventy-two columns create a Corinthian colonnade on each of the four facades. Great bronze doors mark the Constitution Avenue entrance, and four large sculptures representing the Future, the Past, Heritage, and Guardianship sit on pedestals near the entrances. Huge pediments crown both the Pennsylvania Avenue and Constitution Avenue entrances to the building.

In peak season, you may want to reserve a spot on a guided tour (Mon–Fri 9:45am) or simply a timed visit entry, to help avoid a long wait in line. Admission is always free, but you'll pay a $1.50 convenience fee when you place your order online.

700 Constitution Ave. NW (btw. 7th and 9th sts. NW; tourists enter on Constitution Ave., researchers on Pennsylvania Ave.). www.archives.gov/nae. (𝐶 **202/357-5000.** Free admission. Daily 10am–5:30pm. Call for research hours. Closed Dec 25. Metro: Archives–Navy Memorial.

National Gallery of Art ★★★ ART MUSEUM   Best. Art Museum. Ever. That's my opinion, but let me quickly say that world-renowned critics also consider the National Gallery of Art to be among the best museums in the world. Its collection of more than 130,000 paintings, drawings, prints, photographs, sculpture, decorative arts, and furniture trace the development of Western art from the Middle Ages to the present in a manner that's both informative and rapturously beautiful.

The original West Building is devoted to works by European (13th to early 20th century) and American (18th to early 20th century) artists; across the street from the West Building is a Sculpture Garden that features 18 sculptures created by an international roster of artists in the last few decades. The I.M. Pei-designed East Building normally showcases modern and contemporary art, but is closed until 2017 for a grand renovation that will add 12,260 square feet of new exhibit space and two skylit Tower galleries, connected by an outdoor sculpture terrace. Some of the East Building's modern art may find temporary homes in the West Building and in other D.C. museums, like the Corcoran Galley of Art (p. 125), so check the website for latest news.

Now let me tell you why this is my favorite art museum, even one of my favorite places in Washington. I love the many ways the Gallery's design and programs make the artworks and the museum itself accessible to the ordinary visitor. Architect John Russell Pope (of Jefferson Memorial fame, see p. 105) modeled his design after the Pantheon in Rome, anchoring the main floor's interior with a domed rotunda, and then centered a colonnaded fountain beneath the dome. The overall feeling is of spaciousness and grace, especially when the huge fountain is encircled with flowers, as it often is. Visitors gravitate here, resting on stone benches set against the curving walls. Extending east and west of this nexus are long and wide, light-filled, high-ceilinged halls, off which the individual **paintings galleries** lie, nearly 100 in all, leading eventually to lovely garden courts and more places to sit.

One hundred galleries? Yes, but the 1,000-some paintings are arranged in easy to understand order, in separate rooms by age and nationality: 13th century Italian to 18th century Italian, Spanish, and French artists on the west side; 18th and 19th century Spanish, French, British, and American masters on the east side. You may recognize some names: Leonardo da Vinci (whose painting, *Ginevra de' Benci,* that hangs here,

The beauteous National Mall is showing its age. But help is on the way! You may notice construction areas and fencing in different locations around the Mall, in some cases obstructing the way to a landmark you'd hoped to visit. Just know it's all for a good cause. Improvements that will be underway or completed by the time you visit in 2014 include updated signage and maps on the National Mall; a new, amphitheater, wooded canopy for performances, and café pavilion on the grounds of the Washington Monument; scaffolding (that lights up at night) shrouding the Washington Monument as repairs continue on masonry that was damaged by the August 2011 earthquake; a complete overhaul of the area known as Constitution Gardens, which sits between Constitution Avenue and the Lincoln Memorial Reflecting Pool; and construction of the newest Smithsonian, the National Museum of African American History and Culture, on Constitution Avenue NW, between 14th and 15th streets.

is the only da Vinci on public view in the Americas), Rubens, Raphael, Cassatt, El Greco, Bruegel, Poussin, Vermeer, Van Dyck, Gilbert Stuart, Winslow Homer, Turner, and so on.

Down the sweep of marble stairway lies the ground floor's fewer chambers. The light-filled, vaulted ceilinged sculpture galleries include standouts by Bernini, Rodin, Degas, and Honoré Daumier, whose 36 small, bronze busts of French government administrators are highly amusing caricatures. Other galleries display decorative arts, prints and drawings, photographs, even Chinese porcelain. *Here's a tip:* Don't skip the tiny **Armand Hammer Drawings** antechamber, located on the ground floor in Galleries 22 and 22A, not far from the 7th Street entrance. The National Gallery rotates precious drawings from the Hammer collection and you never know what you'll find. I viewed a rare 1507 Raphael drawing here, *The Madonna and Child with John the Baptist*, in March 2013, and little sketches by Watteau later that summer. I always have the chapel-like room to myself.

If you exit the West Building onto 7th Street, you are directly across from the **Sculpture Garden.** Go! Positioned throughout its lushly landscaped 6 acres you'll find a stalking *Spider* by Louise Bourgeois, a shiny stainless steel and concrete tree called *Graft*, by Roxy Paine, and 16 other modern sculptures. At the center of the garden is an expansive pool, which turns into an ice rink in winter. The garden is famous for its summer Friday Jazz in the Garden series of concerts, which are free and draw a crowd, no matter how hot it is. Everyone just drinks more of the sangria sold by the Pavilion Café, whose food is rather good, by the way.

The National Gallery also mounts killer special exhibits, like the Andrew Wyeth (May 4–Nov. 30) and Degas/Cassatt (May 11–Oct. 5) shows coming our way in 2014. And then there's the robust schedule of films, tours, talks, and Sunday evening concert series (now in its 72nd year), plus four recommendable dining options, the best of which are the Garden Café, whose menu is often tied to the theme of a current exhibit, and the Sculpture Garden's Pavilion Café. So add it all up: world-class art, gorgeous setting, jazz concerts, films, classical music performances, tours in several languages, good eats, and ice skating—every bit of this free, except for the food and ice skating, and just see whether the National Gallery of Art isn't one of your favorite places, too.

One other thing you should know is that we have a man named Andrew W. Mellon to thank for the museum. The financier/philanthropist, who served as ambassador to England (1932-33), was inspired so much by London's National Gallery that he decided to give such a gift to his own country. The National Gallery of Art's West Building opened in Washington, D.C., in 1941, the East Building in 1978, and the Sculpture Garden in 1999.

Constitution Ave. NW, btw. 3rd and 7th sts. NW (on the north side of the Mall). www.nga.gov. ✆ **202/737-4215.** Free admission. Gallery: Mon–Sat 10am–5pm; Sun 11am–6pm. Sculpture Garden: Memorial Day to Labor Day Mon–Thurs and Sat 10am–7pm, Fri 10am–9:30pm, Sun 11am–7pm; Labor Day to Memorial Day Mon–Sat 10am–5pm, Sun 11am–6pm. Ice Rink: Mid-Nov to mid-Mar Mon–Thurs 10am–9pm, Fri–Sat 10am–11pm, Sun 11am–9pm. Rink fees: $8 adults, $7 children, plus $3 skate rental. Closed Dec 25 and Jan 1. Metro: Archives–Navy Memorial, Judiciary Square (either exit), or Gallery Place/Verizon Center (Arena/7th and F sts. exit).

National Mall ★★★ ICON   As part of his vision for Washington, Pierre L'Enfant conceived of the National Mall as a bustling ceremonial avenue of embassies and other distinguished buildings. Today's 2-mile, 700-acre stretch of land extending westward from the base of the Capitol to the Potomac River, just behind the Lincoln Memorial, fulfills that dream to some extent. Ten Smithsonian buildings, plus the National Gallery of Art and its Sculpture Garden, and a stray government building (Department of Agriculture), stake out the Mall's northern border along Constitution Avenue and southern border along Independence Avenue. More than 2,000 American elm trees shade the pebbled walkways paralleling Jefferson and Madison drives. In a single year, more than 25 million tourists and locals crisscross the Mall as they visit the Smithsonian museums; hustle to work; pursue exercise; participate in whatever festival, event, or demonstration is taking place on the Mall that day; or simply go for a stroll—just as L'Enfant envisioned, perhaps.

What L'Enfant did not foresee was the toll that all of this activity might take on this piece of parkland. In recent years, visitors to the Mall often have been dismayed to see an expanse of browned rather than green grass, crumbling walkways, and an overall worn appearance. The National Park Service maintains the land but struggles to keep up with needed repairs and preservation work, mostly due to lack of sufficient funds, despite monies from Congress and from the Trust for the National Mall (**www .nationalmall.org**), the Park Service's official fundraising partner. A third organization called the National Coalition to Save Our Mall (**www.savethemall.org**), made up of professional and civic groups as well as assorted concerned artists, historians, and residents, advocates for a public voice in Mall enhancement decisions, and for more support from Congress. These organizations don't necessarily agree on their visions for the Mall.

From the foot of the Capitol to the Lincoln Memorial. www.nps.gov/mall. ✆ **202/426-6841.** Public space, open 365/24/7. Metro: Smithsonian.

National Museum of African Art ★ MUSEUM   This inviting little museum does not get the foot traffic of its larger, better-known sister Smithsonians, but that only makes for a better experience for those who do visit. Find it by strolling through the Enid Haupt Garden, under which the subterranean museum lies, and enter via the doors of the domed pavilions to descend to the galleries, picking up a self-guided tour flyer at the Information Desk, as you go.

Traditional and contemporary African music plays lightly in the background as you tour the dimly lit suite of rooms on three sublevels. The galleries rotate works from the museum's 9,100-piece permanent inventory of ancient and modern art, spanning art forms and geographic areas. (The museum owns the largest public holdings of contemporary African art in the United States.) Sometimes the museum emphasizes a particular theme in its choice of exhibited art, as in 2013 when a selection of South African artworks was on view to honor Nelson Mandela. A 1943 oil painting by Gerard Sekoto, *Boy and the Candle*, a late 19th century wooden male figure by a Tsongan artist, and a special exhibit of drawings by South African photographer Roger Ballen, were among the highlights. Themed or not, a tour of the museum turns up diverse discoveries: a 13th–15th century ceramic equestrian figure from Mali, face masks from Congo and Gabon, a 15th century Ethiopian manuscript page, and a commanding, mixed media sculpture of Haiti's liberator, Toussaint Louverture, *Toussaint Louverture et La Vieille Slave*, by Senegalese artist Ousmane Sow.

A special exhibit on view until March 2, 2014 celebrates the 40th anniversary of the museum's **Eliot Elisofon Photographic Archives.** "Africa Re-Viewed: The Photographic Legacy of Eliot Elisofon" pairs photographs selected from the archives' 80,000 prints and transparencies with objects from the museum's collection.

The African Art Museum was founded in 1964, joined the Smithsonian in 1979, and moved to the Mall in 1987. If you descend to sublevel 3, you will reach the subterranean passage that takes you to the **Ripley Center** (p. 117) and to the **Sackler Gallery.**

950 Independence Ave. SW. www.nmafa.si.edu. ✆ **202/633-4600.** Free admission. Daily 10am–5:30pm. Closed Dec 25. Metro: Smithsonian.

National Museum of American History ★★★ MUSEUM How does one museum possibly sum up the history of a nation that is 238-years-old, 3.8 million square miles in size, and has a population of 316 million people? And how does the museum sort through its collection of 3.3 million artifacts, which include every imaginable American object, from George Washington's uniform to an 1833 steam locomotive, from the Star Spangled Banner to a 1960s lunchbox, and choose which to display? And finally, how does the museum serve it up in such a way as to capture both the essence of American history and culture, and the attention of a diverse and international public?

As the National Museum of American History celebrates its 50th birthday in 2014, it is in the midst of re-inventing itself so as to live up to these daunting but joyful challenges. And though the strategic plan involves another 6 years or so to complete, I can tell you that a visit to the National Museum of American History today is already much more fun and interesting than it ever was before.

Presentation is everything, isn't it? I recommend you enter from the National Mall into the museum's first floor, a light-filled space thanks to the skylit central atrium and free-flowing design. (If you enter from Constitution Avenue, you'll be on the lower level; you can just start touring the exhibits there or take the escalator or grand staircase up.) Stop at the welcome center to your right to pick up museum maps and find out what's going on that day . . . and there's always tons going on, from live music to theatrical performances. My favorite performance is the one staged at the Greensboro lunch counter taken from the Woolworth's in Greensboro, N.C., where, on Feb. 1, 1960, students held a sit-in to protest segregated eating places. (The counter is on the second floor, east wing.)

But head to the **Flag Hall** first, for this is the location of the museum's star (or should I say, "starred"?) attraction: the original Star-Spangled Banner. This 30×34-foot wool and cotton flag is the very one that Francis Scott Key spied at dawn on September 14,

The **National Museum of African American History and Culture** won't open until 2015 (across 14th St. from the American History Museum, at Constitution Ave., northeast of the Washington Monument). In the meantime, tour the American History Museum's gallery dedicated to exhibits that eventually will be on display in the completed museum. On view in 2014, for example, is a fabulous exhibit, *Changing America: The Emancipation Proclamation, 1863, and The March on Washington, 1963.*

1814, flying above Fort McHenry in Baltimore's harbor, signifying an American victory over the British during the War of 1812. Key memorialized that moment in a poem, which became the country's official National Anthem in 1931. The thread-bare 200-year-old treasure is on view behind a window in an environmentally controlled chamber, just beyond the atrium wall; terrific, interactive displays bring to life the significance and grandeur of this important artifact.

The west wing is entirely closed for renovations until 2016, which makes your visit from this point a simple matter of touring the east wing's three floors, each of which follows its own theme: exhibits on transportation, technology, and innovation are on the first floor, exhibits to do with American ideals and individual stories are on the second floor, and exhibits related to American wars and politics are on the third floor.

From Flag Hall, stay on the second floor to see Dorothy's ruby slippers, a fragment of Plymouth rock and 100 other objects in **American Stories.** The other highlight of the second floor is a partially reconstructed, 200+ year-old house transplanted from Ipswich, Mass., the centerpiece of **Within These Walls . . . ,** which tells the stories of the families who lived here. Also here: a small stand-in exhibit for the National Museum of African American History and Culture, which is under construction (see "Preview the Next Smithsonian," below).

Assorted transportation vehicles command a lot of space and attention in the first floor's exhibit **America on the Move,** but to my mind they're not nearly as interesting as the exhibit titled "FOOD: Transforming America's Table, 1950–2000." Its *piece de resistance* is **Julia Child's home kitchen,** kitchen sink to favorite skillet, which Child donated to the museum in late 2001.

On the third floor is the museum's most visited exhibit, **The First Ladies,** featuring 26 first ladies' gowns and other objects, which round out our perceptions about the roles and personalities of these singular women. Also on this floor is **The American Presidency: A Glorious Burden,** which displays of 900 objects, including Thomas Jefferson's lap desk, shining a more personal light on those who have held the office. Continue on to **The Price of Freedom: Americans at War,** which explores military history and the idea of wars as defining episodes in American history.

Constitution Ave. NW, btw. 12th and 14th sts. NW (on the north side of the Mall, with entrances on Constitution Ave. and Madison Dr.). www.americanhistory.si.edu. *©* **202/633-1000.** Free admission. Daily 10am–5:30pm. Closed Dec 25. Metro: Smithsonian or Federal Triangle.

National Museum of the American Indian ★ MUSEUM   This striking building, located at the Capitol end of the National Mall, stands out for the architectural contrast it makes with neighboring Smithsonian and government structures. It is the first national museum in the country dedicated exclusively to Native Americans and Native Americans consulted on its design, both inside and out; the main architect was a Blackfoot Indian. The museum's rippled exterior is clad in golden, sand-colored, Kasota limestone, the building standing five stories high within a landscape of wetland grasses, water features, and 40 large uncarved rocks and boulders known as "grandfather rocks."

While the interior design is as breathtaking (you enter into a 120-foot high domed "Potomac," or rotunda, a place for performances and ceremonies) the experience of visiting here can be bewildering, thanks to the vast number of artifacts and the variety of tribes and tribal traditions portrayed. Perhaps this dizzying effect is intentional, but I've found that going through on one of the highlights tours is far superior to navigating the museum on one's own.

But if a tour isn't starting when you arrive, or you prefer exploring on your own, begin with the 13-minute Who We Are orientation film that plays throughout the day in the Lelawi Theater on the fourth level. It offers a good introduction to the variety of lifestyles the museum covers. Then descend to tour the main galleries on the third and second floors. Approximately 8,000 objects are on display in five exhibits. **"Our Universes"** focuses on Native cosmologies and the spiritual connection between man and nature. **"Our Peoples"** relates historical events from a Native point of view. **"Our Lives,"** to my mind the most revealing exhibit, explores the identities and choices of Native peoples in the 21st century. **"Window on the Collections"** is for art lovers, showcasing 3,500 objects arranged in seven categories, including animal-themed figurines and objects, beadwork, dolls, and peace medals. **"Return to a Native Place"** tells the story of the Algonquian peoples of the Chesapeake Bay region, which is now Washington, D.C., Maryland, Virginia, and Delaware. Also look for displays of totem poles and other landmark objects and art throughout the museum.

When you return to the first floor, make sure to stop by the museum's restaurant, Mitsitam (one of the best places to eat on the mall), which is a popular lunch spot for nearby office workers. Newly opened is the Mitsitam Espresso Coffee Bar, which serves fair trade coffee breed from beans that have been imported and roasted by the Eastern Band of Cherokee of North Carolina.

The National Museum of the American Indian celebrates its 10th anniversary in 2014, so be sure to check its calendar for celebratory events, which are bound to take place.

4th St. and Independence Ave. SW. www.nmai.si.edu. © **202/633-1000.** Free admission. Daily 10am–5:30pm. Closed Dec 25. Metro: Federal Center Southwest or L'Enfant Plaza (Smithsonian Museums/Maryland Ave. exit).

National Museum of Natural History ★★ MUSEUM   I'll be blunt: This museum is just too much. And I mean that in, unfortunately, a negative way. Not only is it the most popular museum in town (get ready to fight the crowds!) there are so many exhibits, and so many items within the exhibits, that the average visitor experiences an uncomfortable sensory overload while visiting.

Let me give you some numbers: The museum's collection has 12.3 million artifacts and specimens (only a small percentage on display); the building measures 1.32 million square feet, of which 325,000 square feet is public space; and about 7.38 million people visit annually, making this the most visited natural history museum *in the world.*

If you find yourself overwhelmed, do as I did on a recent visit to the crowded museum: Go up to one of the green vested "Visitor Concierges" you'll see roaming the exhibit areas and ask them to name the two must-see things they would recommend in the particular exhibit (naturally, you should tailor this to your liking: five must-sees, or the concierge's particular favorites, or the ones best for children, and so on). A concierge I approached in the Sant Ocean Hall, responded immediately with the "live coral reef" and the "shark mouth," pointing me to them in the vast hall. Perfect suggestions. The variously colored coral reef tank holds fish of brilliant blue, purple, yellow, and pink hues. The enormous jaw of a *Carcharodon megalodon*, a shark that lived 5 million years ago, is enclosed in a glass case; the idea is for you to pose behind the glass case so that it appears as if you're "inside the mouth" of the sharp-toothed shark and your partner/mom/friend/passing guidebook writer snaps a photo of you.

Preparing of the abundance of the museum will also be a help; you may want to make your choices about what to see before you arrive. So here's the scoop: the museum has 17 different galleries, whose exhibits cover the story of natural history from the earliest beginnings of life to the present, from dinosaurs to whales, to earliest mammals, to the origins of man. All manner of enormous creatures are on display, whether in live, skeleton, fossil, or taxidermied form: giant squids swim in **Ocean Hall**; a large skeleton of a woolly mammoth with enormous curled tusks and five fingerlike toes faces off with you in the Ice Age exhibit; the sight of the three-horned triceratops and other dinosaurs (the word dinosaur is the Latin name for "terrible lizard") stops traffic in **Dinosaur Hall**; and a rearing African bush elephant greets you in the museum's central Rotunda. And there's more: a gems and geology exhibit that displays the **Hope Diamond** and other fine bling; a walk-through live butterfly pavilion, where exotically colored butterflies alight upon you; a discovery room of hands-on exhibits for young children; and simulator rides and 2-D and 3-D IMAX movies (*Dinosaurs 3-D: Giants of Patagonia* was one shown in 2013) for thrill seekers.

And that doesn't even cover the special exhibits on tap in 2014, "Fragile Beauty: The Art and Science of Sea Butterflies" and "Beyond Bollywood: Indian Americans Shape the Nation," to name just two.

What to pick? That's up to you. Enjoy.

Constitution Ave. NW, btw. 9th and 12th sts. (on the north side of the Mall, with entrances on Madison Dr. and Constitution Ave.). www.mnh.si.edu. © **202/633-1000,** or 633-4629 for information about IMAX films. Free admission. Daily 10am–5:30pm (in summer often until 7:30pm, but call to confirm). Closed Dec 25. Metro: Smithsonian (Mall/Jefferson Dr. exit) or Federal Triangle.

National World War II Memorial ★★ MONUMENT/MEMORIAL   When this memorial was dedicated on May 29, 2004, 150,000 people attended: President Bush; members of Congress; Marine Corps General (retired) P. X. Kelley, who chaired the group that spearheaded construction of the memorial; actor Tom Hanks and now-retired news anchor Tom Brokaw, both of whom had been active in soliciting support for the memorial; and last, but most important, thousands of World War II veterans and their families. These legions of veterans—some dressed in uniform, many wearing a cap identifying the name of their division—turned out with pride, happy to receive the nation's gratitude, 60 years in the making, expressed profoundly in this memorial.

Designed by Friedrich St. Florian and funded mostly by private donations, the memorial fits nicely into the landscape between the Washington Monument grounds to the east and the Lincoln Memorial and its Reflecting Pool to the west. St. Florian purposely situated the 7½-acre memorial so as not to obstruct this long view down the Mall. Fifty-six 17-foot-high granite pillars representing each state and territory stand to either side of a central plaza and the Rainbow Pool. Likewise 24 bas-relief panels divide down the middle so that 12 line each side of the walkway leading from the entrance at 17th Street. The panels to the left, as you walk toward the center of the memorial, illustrate seminal scenes from the war years as they relate to the Pacific front: Pearl Harbor, amphibious landing, jungle warfare, a field burial, and so on. The panels to the right are sculptured scenes of war moments related to the Atlantic front: Rosie the Riveter, Normandy Beach landing, the Battle of the Bulge, the Russians meeting the Americans at the Elbe River. Architect and sculptor Raymond Kaskey sculpted these panels based on archival photographs.

Large open pavilions stake out the north and south axes of the memorial, and semi-circular fountains create waterfalls on either side. Inscriptions at the base of each pavilion fountain mark key battles. Beyond the center Rainbow Pool is a wall of 4,048 gold stars, one star for every 100 American soldiers who died in World War II. People often leave photos and mementos around the memorial, which the National Park Service gathers up daily for an archive. For compelling, firsthand accounts of World War II experiences, combine your tour here with an online visit to the **Library of Congress's Veterans History Project,** at www.loc.gov/vets; see the Library of Congress entry (p. 93) for more information.

From the 17th Street entrance, walk south around the perimeter of the memorial to reach a ranger station, where there are brochures as well as registry kiosks for looking up names of veterans. Better information and faster service is available online at **www.wwiimemorial.com.**

17th St., near Constitution Ave. NW. www.nps.gov/nwwm. ✆ **800/639-4992** or 202/426-6841. Free admission. Ranger on duty daily 9:30am–11:30pm, except Dec 25. Limited parking. Metro: Farragut West, Federal Triangle, or Smithsonian, with a 20- to 25-min. walk.

Ripley Center ★ CULTURAL INSTITUTION   Part of the Smithsonian complex but not officially counted as a museum, the S. Dillon Ripley Center is notable for housing **Discovery Theater**, which stages children's plays and entertainment, and the International Gallery, which hosts rotating exhibits of works from various Smithsonian museums. Look for the copper-domed hutlike structure next to the Smithsonian Castle. Galleries and the Discovery Theater are actually subterranean and connect underground to the Freer, Sackler, and African Art museums.

1100 Jefferson Dr. SW. www.si.edu/museums/ripley-center. ✆ **202/633-1000.** Free admission. Daily 10am–5:30pm. Closed Dec 25. Metro: Smithsonian (Mall exit).

Sackler Gallery ★ MUSEUM   The Sackler is one-half of what is formally known as the National Museum of Asian Art in the United States (the Freer Gallery, p. 103 is the other half). And though the two museums are connected by purpose, research, staff—and subterranean passageway—they occupy separate buildings.

The Sackler Gallery exists because primary benefactor Arthur M. Sackler gave the Smithsonian Institution 1,000 works of Asian art and $4 million to put toward museum construction. When it opened in 1987, the gallery held mostly ancient works, including early Chinese bronzes and jades, centuries-old Near East ceramics, and sculpture from South and Southeast Asia. Pieces from that stellar permanent collection continue to be on rotating view in several underground galleries, along with other precious works acquired over the years, like an assemblage of Persian book artistry and 20th century Japanese ceramics and works on paper. The collection now numbers nearly 9,000 objects. Special exhibits, like "Yoga: The Art of Transformation" (Oct. 19, 2013-Jan. 26, 2014), which displays 120 temple sculptures, icons, court paintings, and other works, also explore Asian art of old.

But a big focus today is on the works of contemporary Asian artists, as you'll notice upon entering the museum's street-level pavilion. This floor is home to a gallery reserved for rotating installations of contemporary works by contemporary Asian and Asian Diaspora artists. **Perspectives**, as the series is known, hosts an exhibit in 2014 of art by India-born, New York-based artist Rina Bannerjee, who works with textiles, tourist souvenirs, and other objects to touch on themes of migration and transformation.

Once you've viewed Perspectives, descend the stairs to tour exhibits on sublevels 1, 2 and 3 that include the arts of China and sculptures of South Asia and the Himalayas. Notice as you go the monumental sculpture suspended from the sky-lit atrium, through the stairwell, and down to the reflecting pool at bottom. Entitled *Monkeys Grasping for the Moon*, the sculpture was designed specifically for the gallery by Chinese artist Xu Bing. The work links 21 laminated wood pieces, each of which spells the word "monkey" in one of a dozen languages.

The Sackler and the Freer Gallery frequently host public programs, partnering on some of them, like the hugely popular Asia After Dark parties aimed at those under 40. An August 2013 party screened Chinese martial arts movies and staged live hip-hop performances, and kung fu martial arts and tai chi demonstrations. With cocktails, naturally. Tickets cost $25 to $30 and sell out. For information visit www.asia.si.edu/asiaafterdark.

1050 Independence Ave. SW. www.asia.si.edu. (C) **202/633-4880.** Free admission. Daily 10am–5:30pm. Closed Dec 25. Metro: Smithsonian (Mall/Jefferson Dr. exit).

Smithsonian Information Center ("The Castle") ★ MUSEUM Beautiful on the outside, the 1855 Medieval-style building with its eight crenellated towers and rich red sandstone facade, lives up to its nickname. Its Great Hall interior is pretty unattractive, but that doesn't matter, since you're here for information, possibly restrooms, and perhaps a bite to eat. Watch the 10-minute orientation video, take a look at the National Mall models in the middle of the room, and, most important, stop by the information desk to ask the multilingual staff of volunteers to help you plan your Smithsonian itinerary.

There's not much else in this big building that's open to the public. The remains of Smithsonian benefactor James Smithson are buried in that big crypt in the Mall-side entrance area, which includes a small exhibit about the man. The pretty south-side entrance has been repainted to appear as it did in the early 1900s, when children's exhibits were displayed here. **The Commons** area and **Schermer Hall,** on the west side of the building, sometimes are used as small exhibit areas highlighting works from surrounding Smithsonian museums. On the east side of the building is the **Castle Café,** which opens at 8:30am, earlier than any other building on the Mall. Coffee, pastries, sandwiches, and even beer and wine are sold. Situate yourself at a table inside, where there's free Wi-Fi, or outdoors in the lovely Enid A. Haupt Garden, and plot your day.

1000 Jefferson Dr. SW. www.si.edu. (C) **202/633-1000.** Daily 8:30am–5:30pm (info desk 9am–4pm). Closed Dec 25. Metro: Smithsonian (Mall exit).

United States Botanic Garden ★ GARDEN For the feel of summer in the middle of winter, the sight of lush, breathtakingly beautiful greenery and flowers year-round, stop in at the Botanic Garden, located at the foot of the Capitol and next door to the National Museum of the American Indian. The grand conservatory devotes half of its space to exhibits that focus on the importance of plants to people, and half to exhibits that focus on ecology and the evolutionary biology of plants. But those finer points may escape you as you wander through the various chambers, outdoors and indoors, upstairs and down, gazing in stupefaction at so much flora. The conservatory holds about 1,300 living species (about 3,000 plants); a high-walled enclosure, called "the Jungle," of palms, ferns, and vines; an Orchid Room; a meditation garden; a primeval garden; and gardens created especially with children in mind. Stairs and an elevator in the Jungle take you to the top of this windowed tower, where you can admire the sea of greenery 24 feet below and, if condensation on the glass windows doesn't prevent it, a view of the Capitol Building rising up on Capitol Hill. Just outside the conservatory is the National Garden, which includes the First Ladies Water Garden, a formal rose garden, a butterfly garden, and a lawn terrace. Tables and benches make this a lovely spot for a picnic anytime but in winter, though you should keep in mind that the entire garden is unshaded.

Ask at the front desk about tours. The USBG sometimes offers entertainment and special programs.

Also visit the garden annex across the street, **Bartholdi Park.** The park is about the size of a city block, with a cast-iron classical fountain created by Frédéric Auguste Bartholdi, designer of the Statue of Liberty. Flower gardens bloom amid tall ornamental grasses, benches are sheltered by vine-covered bowers, and a touch and fragrance garden contains such herbs as pineapple-scented sage.

100 Maryland Ave. SW (btw. 1st and 3rd sts. SW, at the foot of the Capitol, bordering the National Mall). www.usbg.gov. ⓒ **202/225-8333.** Free admission. Conservatory and National Garden daily 10am–5pm. Bartholdi Park dawn–dusk. Metro: Federal Center SW (Smithsonian Museums/Maryland Ave. exit).

Vietnam Veterans Memorial ★★ MONUMENT/MEMORIAL   The Vietnam Veterans Memorial is possibly the most poignant sight in Washington: two long, black-granite walls in the shape of a V, each inscribed with the names of the men and women who gave their lives, or remain missing, in the longest war in American history. Even if no one close to you died in Vietnam, it's moving to watch visitors grimly studying the directories to find out where their loved ones are listed, or rubbing pencil on paper held against a name etched into the wall. The walls list close to 60,000 people, most of whom died very young.

Because of the raging conflict over U.S. involvement in the war, Vietnam veterans had received almost no recognition of their service before the memorial was conceived by Vietnam veteran Jan Scruggs. The nonprofit Vietnam Veterans Memorial Fund raised $7 million and secured a 2-acre site in tranquil Constitution Gardens to erect a memorial that would make no political statement about the war and would harmonize with neighboring memorials. By separating the issue of the wartime service of individuals from the issue of U.S. policy in Vietnam, the VVMF hoped to begin a process of national reconciliation.

Yale senior Maya Lin's design was chosen in a national competition open to all citizens ages 18 and over. Erected in 1982, the memorial's two walls are angled at 125 degrees to point to the Washington Monument and the Lincoln Memorial. The walls' mirrorlike surfaces reflect surrounding trees, lawns, and monuments. The names are inscribed in chronological order, documenting an epoch in American history as a series of individual sacrifices from the date of the first casualty in 1959. The National Park Service continues to add names as Vietnam veterans die eventually of injuries sustained during the war. A movement is underway to create a visitor center for the Vietnam Veterans Memorial on the plot of land across Henry Bacon Drive from the memorial.

Northeast of the Lincoln Memorial, east of Henry Bacon Dr. (btw. 21st and 22nd sts. NW, on the Constitution Ave. NW side of the Mall). www.nps.gov/vive. ⓒ **202/426-6841.** Free admission.

Where were you on August 23, 2011? That's when a 5.8-magnitude earthquake struck the East Coast. Here in Washington, D.C., the earthquake's rumbling damaged several buildings, most notably the Washington Monument and the Washington National Cathedral, which were forced to close to the public. The cathedral was deemed structurally sound and reopened November 12, 2011, although repairs of pinnacles, flying buttresses, and gargoyles will continue for years. The Washington Monument's interior and exterior masonry has taken a bit longer to pass the safety test; repairs are still ongoing. The monument is expected to reopen to the public in spring 2014, although the exact date was not known at the time of this writing. Furthermore, even if the monument reopens, procedures for visiting may have changed. Call the National Park Service at (*C*) **202/426-6841** for the latest information. The information below was accurate at press time.

Ranger on duty daily 9:30am–11:30pm, except Dec 25. Limited parking. Metro: Foggy Bottom, with 25-min. walk.

Washington Monument ★★★ MONUMENT/MEMORIAL   The idea of a tribute to George Washington first arose 16 years before his death, at the Continental Congress of 1783. But the new nation had more pressing problems and funds were not readily available. It wasn't until the early 1830s, with the 100th anniversary of Washington's birth approaching, that any action was taken.

First there were several fiascoes. A mausoleum under the Capitol Rotunda was provided for Washington's remains, but a grandnephew, citing Washington's will, refused to allow the body to be moved from Mount Vernon. In 1830, Horatio Greenough was commissioned to create a memorial statue for the Rotunda. He came up with a bare-chested Washington, draped in classical Greek garb. A shocked public claimed he looked as if he were "entering or leaving a bath," and so the statue was relegated to the Smithsonian. Finally, in 1833, prominent citizens organized the Washington National Monument Society. Treasury Building architect Robert Mills's design was accepted.

The cornerstone was laid on July 4, 1848, and construction continued for 6 years, until declining contributions and the Civil War brought work to a halt at an awkward 153 feet (you can still see a change in the color of the stone about one-third of the way up). It took until 1876 for sufficient funds to become available, thanks to President Grant's authorization for use of federal moneys to complete the project, and another 4 years after that for work to resume on the unsightly stump. The Washington Monument's dedication ceremony took place in 1885, and the monument finally opened to the public in 1888.

Assuming the Washington Monument has reopened since the earthquake (see "Washington Monument–goers: Read This First," above), here's what you need to know:

Visiting the Washington Monument: A series of security walls encircles the Washington Monument grounds, a barrier to vehicles but not to people; the National Park Service has gone to a good bit of trouble to incorporate these 33-inch-high walls into a pleasing landscape design. Please be aware that large backpacks and open containers of food or drink are not allowed inside the monument. You'll need a ticket (see

> ### Impressions
>
> *May the spirit which animated the great founder of this city descend to future generations.*
>
> —John Adams

below), and then you'll pass through a small screening facility before entering the monument's large elevator, which whisks you upward for 70 seconds.

When you reach the top of this 555.5-foot-tall obelisk, you'll be standing in the tip of the world's tallest freestanding work of masonry. The Washington Monument lies at the very heart of Washington, D.C. landmarks, and its 360-degree views are spectacular. Due east are the Capitol and Smithsonian buildings; due north is the White House; due west are the World War II and Lincoln memorials (with Arlington National Cemetery beyond); due south is the Martin Luther King, Jr. and Jefferson memorials, overlooking the Tidal Basin and the Potomac River. On a clear day, you can see west probably 60 miles, as far as the Shenandoah Mountains, according to a National Park Service ranger I spoke to.

The glass-walled elevator slows down in its descent, to allow passengers a view of some of the 192 carved stones inserted into the interior walls that are gifts from foreign countries, all 50 states, organizations, and individuals. One stone you usually get to see is the one given by the state of Alaska in 1982—it's pure jade and worth millions. There are stones from Siam (now Thailand), the Cherokee Nation, the Vatican, and the Sons of Temperance, to name just a few.

Ticket Information: Admission to the Washington Monument is free, but you still have to get a ticket. The ticket booth is located in the Monument Lodge, at the bottom of the hill from the monument, on 15th Street NW between Madison and Jefferson drives; it opens daily at 8:30am. Tickets are often gone by 9am, so plan to get there by 7:30 or 8am, especially in peak season. The tickets grant admission at half-hour intervals between the stated hours on the day you visit. If you want to get tickets in advance, call the **National Park Reservation Service** (✆ 877/444-6777) or go to www.recreation.gov and type "Washington Monument" into the "Search for Places" field on the left-hand side of the page. You'll pay $1.50 per ticket in a service fee if you order in advance, plus $2.85 for shipping and handling if you order 10 or more days in advance and want the tickets mailed to you; otherwise you can pick up the tickets at the "will call" window at the ticket kiosk. To make sure that you get tickets for your desired date, reserve these tickets at least 2 weeks in advance. You can order up to six tickets.

15th St. NW, directly south of the White House (btw. Madison Dr. and Constitution Ave. NW). www.nps.gov/wamo. ✆ **202/426-6841.** Free admission. Labor Day to Memorial Day 9am–4:45pm; Memorial Day to Labor Day 9am–10pm (until noon July 4). Last elevators depart 15 min. before closing (arrive earlier). Closed Dec 25. Limited parking. Metro: Smithsonian (Mall/Jefferson Dr. exit), with a 10-min. walk.

SOUTHWEST OF THE MALL

Two top attractions are located on 15th Street SW, across Independence Avenue from the National Mall. These sites are not National Park Service properties, so I separate them from other attractions located nearby in the southwest section of the National Mall and Memorial Parks category.

Bureau of Engraving & Printing ★ GOVERNMENT BUILDING   This is where they will literally show you the money: A staff of about 2,000 works round-the-clock Monday through Friday churning it out at the rate of nearly $500 million a day.

You must be wondering by now: How did the Smithsonian Institution come to be? It's rather an unlikely story, concerning the largesse of a wealthy English scientist named James Smithson (1765–1829), the illegitimate son of the duke of Northumberland. Smithson willed his vast fortune to the United States, to found "at Washington, under the name of the Smithsonian Institution, an establishment for the increase and diffusion of knowledge." Smithson never explained why he left this handsome bequest to the United States, a country he had never visited. Speculation is that he felt the new nation, lacking established cultural institutions, most needed his funds.

Smithson died in Genoa, Italy, in 1829. Congress accepted his gift in 1836; 2 years later, half a million dollars' worth of gold sovereigns (a considerable sum in the 19th c.) arrived at the U.S. Mint in Philadelphia. For the next 8 years, Congress debated the best possible use for these funds. Finally, in 1846, James Polk signed an act into law establishing the Smithsonian Institution and authorizing a board to receive "all objects of art and of foreign and curious research, and all objects of natural history, plants, and geological and mineralogical specimens . . . for research and museum purposes." In 1855 the first Smithsonian building opened on the Mall, not as a museum, but as the home of the Smithsonian Institution. The red sandstone structure suffered a fire and several reconstructions over the years, to serve today as the Smithsonian Information Center, known by all as "the Castle." Smithson's remains are interred in the Crypt located inside the north vestibule (National Mall side) of the Castle,

Today the Smithsonian Institution's 19 museums (D.C. has 17, soon to be 18, when the National Museum of African American History and Culture opens in 2015), nine research centers, and the National Zoological Park comprise the world's largest museum complex. Millions of people visit the Smithsonians annually—more than 30 million toured the museums in 2012. The Smithsonian's collection of nearly 137 million objects spans the entire world and all of its history, its peoples and animals (past and present), and our attempts to probe into the future.

So vast is the collection that Smithsonian museums display only about 1% or 2% of the collection's holdings at any given time. Artifacts range from a 3.5-billion-year-old fossil to inaugural gowns worn by the first ladies. Thousands of scientific expeditions sponsored by the Smithsonian have pushed into remote frontiers in the deserts, mountains, polar regions, and jungles.

Individually, each museum is a powerhouse in its own field. The National Museum of Natural History and the National Air and Space Museum are the most visited of the Smithsonians, each welcoming more than seven million people in 2012. The National Air and Space Museum maintains the world's largest collection of historic aircraft and spacecraft. The Smithsonian American Art Museum is the nation's first collection of American art and one of the largest in the world. And so on.

To find out information about any of the Smithsonian museums, call ℭ **202/633-1000** or 633-5285. The Smithsonian museums also share a website, **www.si.edu**, which helps you get to their individual home pages.

Everyone's eyes pop as they walk past rooms overflowing with new greenbacks. But the money's not the whole story. The bureau prints security documents for other federal government agencies, including military IDs and passport pages. FYI: The Bureau, which is an agency of the Treasury Department, celebrated its 150th anniversary in August 2012.

The 40-minute guided tour begins with a short introductory film. Large windows allow you to see what goes into making paper money: inking, stacking of bills, cutting, and examining for defects. Most printing here is done from engraved steel plates in a process known as intaglio; it's the hardest to counterfeit, because the slightest alteration will cause a noticeable change in the portrait in use. Additional exhibits display bills no longer in circulation and a $100,000 bill designed for official transactions. (Since 1969 the largest-denomination bill issued for the general public is $100.)

After you finish the tour, allow time to explore the **visitor center,** open from 8:30am to 3:30pm (until 7:30pm in summer), with additional exhibits and a gift shop, where you can buy bags of shredded money, uncut sheets of currency in different denominations, and copies of historic documents, like a hand-engraved replica ($200) of the Declaration of Independence.

Many people line up each day to get a peek at all the moolah, so arrive early, especially during the peak tourist season. To save time and avoid a line, consider securing VIP, also called "congressional," tour tickets from one of your senators or your congressperson; write or call at least 3 months in advance for tickets. These tours take place at 8:15am and 8:45am May through Aug., with additional tours added in the summer.

Tickets for general public tours are generally not required from September to February; simply find the visitors entrance at 14th and C streets. March through August, however, every person taking the tour must have a ticket. To obtain a ticket, go to the ticket booth on the Raoul Wallenberg (formerly 15th St.) side of the building and show a valid photo ID. You will receive a ticket specifying a tour time for that same day and be directed to the 14th Street entrance of the bureau. You are allowed as many as four tickets per person. The ticket booth opens at 8am and closes when all tickets are dispersed for the day.

14th and C sts. SW. www.moneyfactory.gov. (C) **866/874-2330.** Free admission. Sept–Feb Mon–Fri 9–10:45am and 12:30–2pm (last tour at 1:40pm); Mar–Aug every 15 minutes 9am–2pm Mar 2–22; and 9am–7pm Mar 23–Aug 30. Closed federal holidays and Dec 25–Jan 1. Metro: Smithsonian (Independence Ave. exit).

United States Holocaust Memorial Museum ★★ MUSEUM

The experience you have at the U.S. Holocaust Memorial Museum will be unlike your experiences at other museums in the capital. A visit here will not gladden your heart about men's and women's great accomplishments nor impress you with the awesomeness of our universe and the natural world. Rather, the Holocaust Museum's exhibits document Nazi Germany's systematic persecution and annihilation of six million Jews and others between 1933 and 1945, and present you with individual stories of both horror and courage in the persecuted's struggle to survive. The museum calls itself a "living memorial to the Holocaust," the idea being for people to visit, confront the evil of which mankind is capable, and leave inspired to face down hatred and inhumanity when they come upon it in the world. A message repeated over and over is this one of Holocaust survivor and author Primo Levi, "It happened. Therefore it can happen again. And it can happen everywhere." Since the museum opened

Holocaust Museum Touring Tips

Because so many people want to visit the museum (it has hosted as many as 10,000 visitors in a single day), passes specifying a visit time (in 15-min. intervals) are required during the busiest months, March through August. You can obtain same-day passes, as many as 20 per person, by arriving early and standing in line on the 14th Street side of the museum's alley, where museum staff distribute passes. (If there's no line, head inside to the information desk.) Or you can reserve as many as 40 tickets in advance at https://tix.cnptix.com/Online/ushmm, for $1 per pass (you print your own tickets). Passes are valid for entry within a 1-hour time frame from the time stamped on your pass.

in 1993, more than 35 million visitors have taken home that message, and another: "What you do matters."

You begin your tour of the permanent exhibit on the first floor, where you pick the identity card of an actual Holocaust victim, whose fate you can learn about in stages at different points in the exhibit. Then you ride the elevator to the fourth floor, where Part I: Nazi Assault, 1933-1939 covers events in Germany, from Hitler's appointment as chancellor in 1933 to Germany's invasion of Poland and the official start of World War II in 1939. You learn that anti-Semitism was nothing new, and observe for yourself in newsreels how Germans were bowled over by Hitler's powers of persuasion and propaganda. Exhibits tell stories of desperation, like the voyage of the St. Louis passenger liner in May 1939, which sailed from Germany to Havana with 900 Jews, but was turned away and returned to Europe.

The years 1940 to 1944 reveal the horrors of the Nazi machine's Final Solution, including deportations, the ghetto experience, and life and death within concentration camps. You listen to survivors tell their stories in taped recordings, and view artifacts such as transport rail cars, reconstructed concentration camp barracks, and photographs of "killing squad" executions.

"The Last Chapter," on the second floor, documents the stories of heroes, like the king of Denmark, who was able to save the lives of 90 percent of Denmark's Jewish population. Exhibits also recount the Allies' liberation of the concentration camps and aftermath events, from Jewish emigration to America and Israel, to the Nuremberg trials. At exhibit's end is the hour-long film, *Testimonies,* in which Holocaust survivors tell their stories. The tour finishes in the **Hall of Remembrance,** a place for meditation and reflection.

The museum also houses a Resource Center for educators, a registry of Holocaust survivors, a library, and archives, available to researchers.

The museum's permanent exhibit is not recommended for children 11 and under; for older children, it's advisable to prepare them for what they'll see.

If you visit in the off-peak months, usually September through February, you should be able to enter the museum without a wait and start your tour. During the busy months, you'll need a free, timed pass (See "Touring Tips" box above for more information.) to tour the museum's permanent collection, which occupies the top three floors of the museum. At any time of year, you are welcome to tour the first floor and lower level exhibits, which I recommend. Always on view are **Daniel's Story: Remember the Children**, for children eight and older, and the **Wall of Remembrance** (Children's Tile Wall), which commemorates the 1.5 million children killed in the Holocaust. A special exhibit on view through 2018, is "Some Were Neighbors: Collaboration and Complicity in the Holocaust," which as it sounds, explores the role of ordinary citizens in carrying out Nazi policies.

There's a cafeteria and museum shop on the premises.

100 Raoul Wallenberg Place SW (formerly 15th St. SW; near Independence Ave., just off the Mall). www.ushmm.org. ℂ **202/488-0400.** Free admission. Daily 10am–5:20pm, open later in peak seasons. Closed Yom Kippur and Dec 25. Metro: Smithsonian (12th St. and Independence Ave. SW exit).

MIDTOWN

The **White House** is Midtown's main attraction and offers reason enough to visit this part of town, even if you're only able to admire it from the outside. (As stated throughout this book, the March 2103 sequester closed the White House for public tours, though the sequester may have ended by the time you read this.) But there are many other great reasons. Midtown is where you'll find Washington's oldest art museum, the **Corcoran Gallery of Art;** an off-the-Mall Smithsonian museum, the **Renwick Gallery;** smaller and more specialized art collections; and several historic houses. Pick and choose from the offerings below, or follow the walking tour of the neighborhood outlined in chapter 10.

Art Museum of the Americas ★ ART MUSEUM   Contemporary Latin and American artworks are on display inside this picturesque, red-tiled-roofed, Spanish-colonial style structure. The museum rotates works from its permanent collection of 2,000, but also mounts special exhibits, like the photography exhibit seen in 2013, "Un Lugar sin Reposo" (A Place with No Rest"), in which Guatemalan artist Gonzalez Palma used photographs to explore "the power of communication through the gaze and body language." The Organization of American States opened the museum in 1976 as a gift to the United States in honor of the U.S.'s bicentennial.

201 18th St. NW (at Virginia Ave.). http://museum.oas.org. ℂ **202/458-6016.** Free admission. Tues–Sun 10am–5pm. Closed federal holidays and Good Friday. Metro: Farragut West (18th St. exit) or Farragut North (K St. exit).

The Corcoran Gallery of Art ★★ ART MUSEUM   Established in 1869, and opened to the public in 1874, the Corcoran Gallery of Art is the capital's oldest art museum, and one of the oldest in America. American art created between 1718 and 1945 forms the nucleus of the world-renowned collection, which now numbers more than 17,000 works. Selections from the collection are always on view, but an installation that debuted in September 2013, and continues indefinitely, gathers 110 paintings and a number of sculptures, more than have ever been displayed together. The subject is a fascinating one: the theme of "place" in the history of American art. Entitled "American Journeys—Visions of Place," the installation portrays the new nation's history and landscape with such masterworks as Rembrandt Peale's *Washington Before Yorktown* (1824; reworked 1825) and Frederic Edwin Church's *Niagara* (1857). Other big name artists on display include John Singer Sargent, William James Glackens, George Bellows and Childe Hassam.

The Corcoran's other focuses are on post-1945 American artists, such as Louise Nevelson and Andy Warhol; artists associated with the "Washington Color School," including Sam Gilliam and Kenneth Noland; and the assorted European treasures of Delft porcelain, Impressionist paintings, and a Louis XVI ornately gilded and paneled salon, transported untouched from Paris, and more.

The elegant Beaux-Arts building, located across the street from the White House, and the city's largest non-federal art museum, is worth seeing just for its architecture. Its elegant interior, with double marble staircases and skylit galleries, have long made it a favorite venue for weddings and parties.

The Corcoran has a better-than-average café (operated by Equinox chef Todd Gray, who also creates the menu) and a small but fine gift shop.

500 17th St. NW (btw. E St. and New York Ave.). www.corcoran.org. © **202/639-1700.** Admission $10 adults; $8 seniors, military, and students; always free for children 12 and under. May be higher for special exhibits. Thurs and Fri–Sun 10am–5pm; Wed 10am–9pm. Free highlights tours daily noon, additional tours Wed 7pm, Sat 11am, 1:30pm, 2pm, and 3pm; and Sun noon and 3pm. Closed Mon, Tues, Dec 25, and Jan 1. Metro: Farragut West (17th St. exit) or Farragut North (K St. exit).

Daughters of the American Revolution (DAR) Museum ★ MUSEUM

Americana fans, quilting enthusiasts, and amateur historians like to dawdle here. The DAR Museum gives visitors a glimpse of pre-1840 American life, through its displays of folk art, rocking chairs and other furnishings, silverware, samplers, and everyday objects. Its Americana Collection showcases the paperwork of each period, from Colonial days, through the Revolutionary War, up to the country's beginnings: diaries, letters, and household inventories. Be sure not to miss the Period Rooms. See p. 212 for further information. From time to time, the museum hosts a special exhibit, like its 2012-2013 show, "Fashioning the New Woman," about styles worn by women from 1890 to 1925.

1776 D St. NW (at 17th St.) www.dar.org/museum. **202/628-1776.** Free admission. Museum Mon–Fri 9:30am–4pm; Sat 9am–5pm. Period Rooms Mon–Fri 10am–2:30pm; Sat 9am–4:30pm. Americana Collection Mon–Fri 8:30am–4pm. Closed on federal holidays. Metro: Farragut West (17th St. exit) or Farragut North (K St. exit).

Octagon House ★ HISTORIC HOME This is the country's oldest museum dedi-

cated to architecture and design. Dr. William Thornton, first architect of the Capitol, designed the house in 1801. As its name suggests, the structure is an architectural marvel. Eight sides, though? Nope, try six. Thornton designed the house for Colonel John Tayloe III, a Virginia planter, a breeder of racehorses, and a friend of George Washington, who would come by to inspect the construction site from time to time. Upon its completion (which Washington did not live to see), the Octagon became a favorite social scene, the Tayloes welcoming John Adams, Thomas Jefferson, James Madison, James Monroe, Daniel Webster, Henry Clay, and their ilk.

1799 New York Ave. NW (at 18th St.). © **202/626-7439.** Free admission for self-guided tours or $5 for guided tours. Thurs–Fri 1–4pm. Metro: Farragut West (17th St. exit).

Renwick Gallery of the Smithsonian American Art Museum ★ ART

MUSEUM The Renwick Gallery is closed for renovations until at least 2016. Normally, you'd be trotting inside to gaze at American decorative arts and crafts. Instead, you'll have to be satisfied with admiring the building's French Second Empire style architecture, designed by and named for James W. Renwick, Jr., architect of the Smithsonian Castle (p. 118). The historic mid-1800s mansion, across from the White House, originally was built to house the Corcoran Gallery (p. 125), which quickly outgrew the space.

1661 Pennsylvania Ave. NW (at 17th St.). www.americanart.si.edu/renwick. © **202/633-7970.** Free admission. Daily 10am–5:30pm. Closed Dec 25. Metro: Farragut West or Farragut North.

The White House Area

NOTE: As I write this, the White House is closed for public tours due to Congress-enacted budget cuts, known as "the sequester," that affected funding for the Secret Service detail on staff during White House tours. I'm hopeful that by the time you read this, public tours will have been revived. So read on.

The White House ★★★ GOVERNMENT BUILDING   It's amazing when you think about it: This house has served as residence, office, reception site, and world embassy for every U.S. president since John Adams. The White House is the only private residence of a head of state that has opened its doors to the public for tours, free of charge, a practice that Thomas Jefferson inaugurated. On a typical day, you'll be one of some 1,600 people touring the White House, knowing that meanwhile, somewhere in this very building, the president and his staff are meeting with foreign dignitaries, congressional members, and business leaders, and hashing out the most urgent of national and global decisions. For tour information, see "How to Arrange a White House Tour," below.

An Act of Congress in 1790 established the city now known as Washington, District of Columbia as the seat of the federal government. George Washington and city planner Pierre L'Enfant chose the site for the president's house and staged a contest to find a builder. Although Washington picked the winner—Irishman James Hoban—he was the only president never to live in the White House. The structure took 8 years to build, starting in 1792, when its cornerstone was laid. Its facade is made of the same stone used to construct the Capitol. The mansion quickly became known as the "White House," thanks to the limestone whitewashing applied to the walls to protect them, later replaced by white lead paint in 1818. In 1814, during the War of 1812, the British set fire to the White House and gutted the interior; the exterior managed to endure only because a rainstorm extinguished the fire. What you see today is Hoban's basic creation: a building modeled after an Irish country house (in fact, Hoban had in mind the house of the Duke of Leinster in Dublin).

Note: Tours of the White House exit from the North Portico. Before you descend the front steps, look to your left to find the window whose sandstone still remains unpainted as a reminder both of the 1814 fire and of the White House's survival.

Additions over the years have included the South Portico in 1824, the North Portico in 1829, and electricity in 1891, during Benjamin Harrison's presidency. In 1902 repairs and refurnishing of the White House cost nearly $500,000. No other great change took place until Harry Truman's presidency, when the interior was completely renovated after the leg of Margaret Truman's piano cut through the dining room ceiling. The Trumans lived at Blair House across the street for nearly 4 years while the White House interior was shored up with steel girders and concrete.

In 1961, First Lady Jacqueline Kennedy spearheaded the founding of the White House Historical Association and formed a Fine Arts Committee to help restore the famous rooms to their original grandeur, ensuring treatment of the White House as a museum of American history and decorative arts. "It just seemed to me such a shame when we came here to find hardly anything of the past in the house, hardly anything before 1902," Mrs. Kennedy observed.

Every president and first family put their own stamp on the White House. The Obamas installed in their private residence artworks on loan from the Hirshhorn Museum and from the National Gallery of Art, and chose works to hang in the public rooms of the White House. (Changing the art in the public rooms requires approval from the White House curator and the Committee for the Preservation of the White House.) Michelle Obama planted a vegetable garden on the White House grounds, and

If public tours are once again up and running, it's likely that procedures for signing up for a tour are the same as they were before the sequestration temporarily stopped them. BUT! Check the White House website or call ahead to find out for sure, since at this writing, White House public tours had not yet resumed. Here are the pre-sequestration procedures that were in place:

White House tours are available to the general public year-round from 7:30 to 11am Tuesday through Thursday, 7:30am to noon Friday, and 7:30am to 1pm Saturday, and at other times as well, depending on the president's schedule. If the president is out of town, it's possible that more tours will be allowed past the usual cutoff time. Tours are self-guided, and most people take no more than an hour to go through. You must have a reservation to tour the White House. At least 21 days and as far as 6 months in advance of your trip, call one of your senators' or your representative's office with the names of the people in your group and ask for a specific tour date. The tour coordinator consults with the White House on availability and, if your date is available, contacts you to obtain the names, birth dates, Social Security numbers (for those 14 and over), and other information for each of the people in your party. The Secret Service reviews the information and clears you for the tour, putting the names of the people in your group on a confirmed reservation list; you'll receive a confirmation number and the date and time of your tour well in advance of your trip. (**Note:** International visitors should contact their embassy for help in submitting a tour request.)

On the day of your tour, call *C* **202/456-7041** to make sure the White House is still open to the public that day. Then off you go, to the south side of East Executive Avenue, near the Southeast Gate of the White House, with valid, government-issued photo IDs whose information exactly matches that which you provided to your congressional member's office. Everyone in your party who is 18 or older must have an ID. Be sure to arrive about 15 minutes before your scheduled tour time.

Do not bring the following prohibited items: backpacks, book bags, handbags, or purses; food and beverages; strollers; cameras; video recorders or any type of recording device; tobacco products; personal grooming items, from cosmetics to hairbrushes; any pointed objects, whether a pen or a knitting needle; aerosol containers; guns; ammunition; fireworks; electric stun guns; maces; martial arts weapons/devices; or knives of any kind. Cellphones are okay, but not to be used as cameras. The White House does not have a coat-check facility, so there is no place for you to leave your belongings while you go on the tour. There are no public restrooms or telephones in the White House, and photos and videotaping are prohibited. *Best advice:* Leave everything but your wallet back at the hotel.

President Obama altered the outdoor tennis court so that it can be used for both basketball and tennis games.

Highlights of the public tour include the gold and white **East Room,** the scene of presidential receptions, weddings, major presidential addresses, and other dazzling events. This is where the president entertains visiting heads of state and the place where seven of the eight presidents who died in office (all but Garfield) laid in state. It's also where Nixon resigned. The room's early-18th-century style was adopted

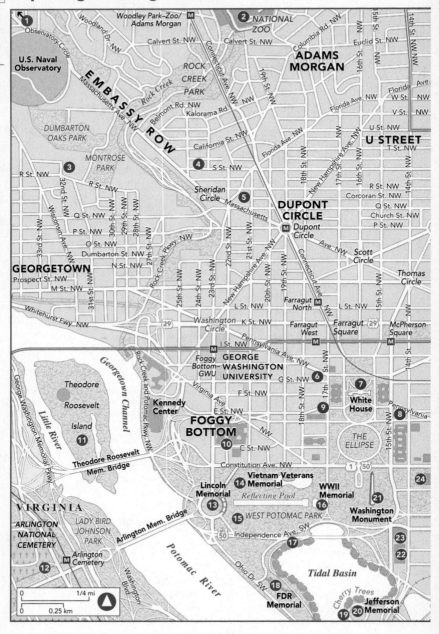

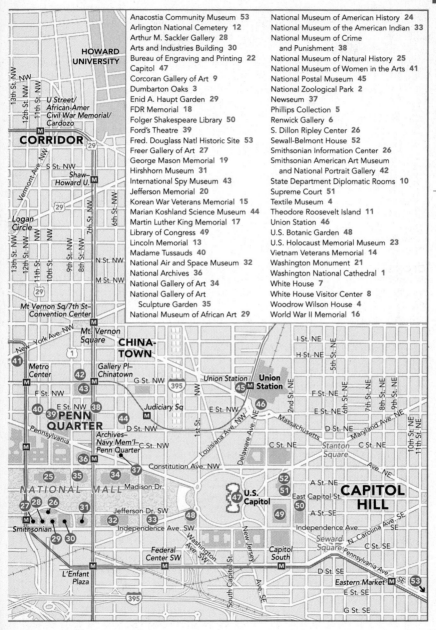

Anacostia Community Museum **53**
Arlington National Cemetery **12**
Arthur M. Sackler Gallery **28**
Arts and Industries Building **30**
Bureau of Engraving and Printing **22**
Capitol **47**
Corcoran Gallery of Art **9**
Dumbarton Oaks **3**
Enid A. Haupt Garden **29**
FDR Memorial **18**
Folger Shakespeare Library **50**
Ford's Theatre **39**
Fred. Douglass Natl Historic Site **53**
Freer Gallery of Art **27**
George Mason Memorial **19**
Hirshhorn Museum **31**
International Spy Museum **43**
Jefferson Memorial **20**
Korean War Veterans Memorial **15**
Marian Koshland Science Museum **44**
Martin Luther King Memorial **17**
Library of Congress **49**
Lincoln Memorial **13**
Madame Tussauds **40**
National Air and Space Museum **32**
National Archives **36**
National Gallery of Art **34**
National Gallery of Art
  Sculpture Garden **35**
National Museum of African Art **29**

National Museum of American History **24**
National Museum of the American Indian **33**
National Museum of Crime
  and Punishment **38**
National Museum of Natural History **25**
National Museum of Women in the Arts **41**
National Postal Museum **45**
National Zoological Park **2**
Newseum **37**
Phillips Collection **5**
Renwick Gallery **6**
S. Dillon Ripley Center **26**
Sewall-Belmont House **52**
Smithsonian Information Center **26**
Smithsonian American Art Museum
  and National Portrait Gallery **42**
State Department Diplomatic Rooms **10**
Supreme Court **51**
Textile Museum **4**
Theodore Roosevelt Island **11**
Union Station **46**
U.S. Botanic Garden **48**
U.S. Holocaust Memorial Museum **23**
Vietnam Veterans Memorial **14**
Washington Monument **21**
Washington National Cathedral **1**
White House **7**
White House Visitor Center **8**
Woodrow Wilson House **4**
World War II Memorial **16**

during the Theodore Roosevelt renovation of 1902; it has parquet Fontainebleau oak floors and white-painted wood walls with fluted pilasters and classical relief inserts. Note the famous Gilbert Stuart portrait of George Washington that Dolley Madison saved from the British torch during the War of 1812; the portrait is the only object to have remained continuously in the White House since 1800 (except during times of reconstruction).

You'll visit the **Green Room,** which was Thomas Jefferson's dining room but today is used as a sitting room. Mrs. Kennedy chose the green watered-silk-fabric wall covering. In the **Oval Blue Room,** decorated in the French Empire style chosen by James Monroe in 1817, presidents and first ladies have officially received guests since the Jefferson administration. It was, however, Martin Van Buren's decor that began the "blue room" tradition. The walls, on which hang portraits of five presidents (including Rembrandt Peale's portrait of Thomas Jefferson and G. P. A. Healy's of John Tyler), are covered in reproductions of early-19th-century French and American wallpaper. Grover Cleveland, the only president to wed in the White House, was married in the Blue Room. This room was also where the Reagans greeted the 52 Americans liberated after being held hostage in Iran for 444 days, and every year it's the setting for the White House Christmas tree.

The **Red Room,** with its red-satin-covered walls and Empire furnishings, is used as a reception room, primarily for afternoon teas. Several portraits of past presidents and a Gilbert Stuart portrait of Dolley Madison hang here. Dolley Madison used the Red Room for her famous Wednesday-night receptions.

From the Red Room, you'll enter the **State Dining Room.** Modeled after late-18th-century neoclassical English houses, this room is a superb setting for state dinners and luncheons. Below G. P. A. Healy's portrait of Lincoln is a quote taken from a letter written by John Adams on his second night in the White House (FDR had it carved into the mantel): I PRAY HEAVEN TO BESTOW THE BEST OF BLESSINGS ON THIS HOUSE AND ON ALL THAT SHALL HERE-AFTER INHABIT IT. MAY NONE BUT HONEST AND WISE MEN EVER RULE UNDER THIS ROOF.

Note: Even if you have successfully reserved a White House tour for your group, you should still call ✆ **202/456-7041** before setting out in the morning, in case the White House is closed on short notice because of unforeseen events. If this should happen to you, consider following the "Stroll Around the White House" walking tour outlined in chapter 10.

1600 Pennsylvania Ave. NW (visitor entrance gate at E St. and E. Executive Ave.). www.whitehouse. gov. ✆ **202/456-7041** or 202/208-1631. Free admission. Tours for groups of 10 or more who have arranged the tour through their congressional offices. Closed federal holidays. Metro: Federal Triangle.

The White House Visitor Center   The Visitor Center underwent a renovation throughout 2013 that shuttered its headquarters here at 1450 Pennsylvania Avenue. The center has been operating temporarily out of the Ellipse Visitor Pavilion, south of the White House, at 15th and E streets. The renovated Visitor Center will include interactive exhibits and a refreshed appearance, among other things. But if it hasn't opened by the time you read this, head across 15th Street to the Visitor Pavilion.

1450 Pennsylvania Ave. NW (in the Department of Commerce Building, btw. 14th and 15th sts.). ✆ **202/208-1631.** Free admission. Daily 7:30am–4pm. Closed Jan 1, Thanksgiving, and Dec 25. Metro: Federal Triangle.

PENN QUARTER

Most of this bustling downtown neighborhood's attractions congregate near the Verizon Center, on or just off 7th Street, the main artery. The ones that aren't there, like Ford's Theatre and the National Museum of Women in the Arts, are just a short walk away. If you enjoy layering your touring experience with stops for delicious meals or snacks, this is your neighborhood. The Penn Quarter is loaded with great restaurants, bars, and bakeries.

Ford's Theatre National Historic Site ★★ HISTORIC SITE On April 14, 1865, President Abraham Lincoln was in the audience at Ford's Theatre, one of the most popular playhouses in Washington. Everyone was laughing at a funny line from Tom Taylor's celebrated comedy, *Our American Cousin,* when John Wilkes Booth crept into the president's box, shot the president, and leapt to the stage, shouting, *"Sic semper tyrannis!"* ("Thus ever to tyrants!"). With his left leg broken from the vault, Booth mounted his horse in the alley and galloped off. Doctors carried Lincoln across the street to the house of William Petersen, where the president died the next morning.

The theater was closed after Lincoln's assassination and used as an office by the War Department. In 1893, 22 clerks were killed when three floors of the building collapsed. It remained in disuse until the 1960s, when the NPS remodeled and restored Ford's to its appearance on the night of the tragedy. Grand renovations and developments completed in phases between 2009 and 2012 have since brought about a wholly new experience for visitors.

Ford's Theatre today stands as the centerpiece of the **Ford's Theatre National Historic Site,** a campus of three buildings straddling a short section of 10th St. and including the **Ford's Theatre** and its **Ford's Theatre Museum; Petersen House,** where Lincoln died; and the **Center for Education and Leadership,** which debuted in 2012 and is dedicated to exploring Lincoln's legacy and promoting leadership.

I recommend visiting all four attractions if you have the time. Briefly, here's what you'll see at the Ford's Theatre National Historic Site:

The Ford's Theatre: The National Park Service presentations vividly recreate the events of that night, so try for a tour that includes one of these. The President's Box is still on view, but no, you are not allowed to enter it and sit where Lincoln sat. A portrait of George Washington hangs beneath the President's Box, as it did the night Lincoln was shot. Ford's remains a working theater, so consider returning in the evening to attend a play. Ford's productions lean toward historical dramas and classic American musicals; the 2013–2014 season includes Charles Dickens's *A Christmas Carol,* and the musical comedy *The 25th Annual Putnam County Spelling Bee.* The production schedule means that the theater, and sometimes the museum, may be closed to sightseers on some days; check the online schedule before you visit.

The **Ford's Theatre Museum,** on the lower level of the theater, displays artifacts that tell the story of Lincoln's presidency, his assassination, and what life was like in Washington and in the United States during that time. Unfortunately, when the museum is crowded, as it often is, it can be hard to get close enough and have enough time at each of the exhibits to properly absorb the information. An exhibit about life in the White House shines a little light on Mary Todd Lincoln; a display of artifacts that includes the Dellinger gun used by John Wilkes Booth connects the dots between the assassin and those who aided him.

Across 10th Street from the theater and museum is **Petersen House**. The doctor attending to Lincoln and other theatergoers carried Lincoln into the street, where boarder Henry Safford, standing in the open doorway of his rooming house, gestured for them to bring the president inside. So Lincoln died in the home of William Petersen, a German-born tailor. Now furnished with period pieces, the dark, narrow town house looks much as it did on that fateful April night. You'll see the front parlor where an anguished Mary Todd Lincoln spent the night with her son, Robert. In the back parlor, Secretary of War Edwin M. Stanton held a cabinet meeting and questioned witnesses. From this room, Stanton announced at 7:22am on April 15, 1865, "Now he belongs to the ages." Lincoln died, lying diagonally because he was so tall, on a bed the size of the one in the room. (The Chicago Historical Society owns the actual bed and other items from the room.) The exit from Petersen House leads to an elevator that transports you to the fourth floor of the:

Center for Education and Leadership, where your tour begins with the sights and sounds in the capital in the days following the assassination of Lincoln. You hear church bells tolling and horseshoes clopping and view exhibits of mourning ribbons, coffin handles, and newspaper broadsheets announcing the tragic news. Details convey the sense of piercing sorrow that prevailed: 25,000 people attended Lincoln's funeral on April 21, 1865, though not Mary Todd Lincoln, who was too overcome with grief. A staircase that winds around a sculptured tower of some 6,800 books all to do with Lincoln leads down to the center's third floor. Here, a short film, videos, and exhibits explore Lincoln's influence and legacy: Lincoln's name and image pop up on all sorts of commercial products, from the children's building game of Lincoln Logs to jewelry. Lincoln's words and life have inspired leaders around the world including, we learn, the founder of modern Chinese government, Sun-Yat Sen, who hung a portrait of Lincoln in his home. Following the staircase another level down takes you to a gallery whose displays use real-life examples of brave individuals, like Rosa Parks, to pose the question "What Would You Do?" in their circumstances.

The how to: You'll need a timed ticket to tour any part of the campus. Tickets are free and tours take place daily. Visit the website, www.fords.org, for a list of "brief visit" and "full experience" offerings, which range from a simple museum and theater walk-through (25 minutes) to a full tour encompassing the museum; the theater, including either a National Park Service ranger's interpretive program or a miniplay (highly recommended); Petersen House; and the Center for Education and Leadership (for a total of about 2 hours and 15 minutes).

A single ticket admits you to all parts of the campus, so don't lose it! Ford's really wants you to order tickets in advance online—only 20% of the daily allotment of tickets are available for same-day pickup. And even though Ford's says tours are free, the fact is that tickets are free only to those 20% lucky enough to get same-day passes. Online tickets cost $3.75 each to cover processing fees; if you want an audio tour, you'll pay $9.75 per ticket. You order the tickets online and can print them yourself or pick them up at the theater's will-call booth. **Good to know:** When the Ford's Theatre website shows same-day tickets as unavailable, that just means they are unavailable to order online; go in person to the box office and you may score one of those same-day passes.

Spring through early fall, Ford's also sells tickets ($15 each, plus $3 processing fee, available online) to its popular "History on Foot" 2-hour walking tours. A costumed actor brings to life the events of April 14 and 15, 1865, leading tourists on a 1½-mile traipse to about eight historically significant locations.

511 10th St. NW (btw. E and F sts.). www.fords.org. ℂ **202/426-6925**. Daily 9am–5pm. Closed Thanksgiving, Christmas and other days subject to the theater's schedule. Timed tickets required for the free tours offered throughout the day. See above for details. Metro: Metro Center (11th and G sts. exit).

International Spy Museum ★★ MUSEUM   A visit to this museum takes on a whole new meaning, following the 2013 disclosures of the National Security Agency's far-flung phone and internet surveillance practices. One can more easily believe the claim made in the museum's five-minute introductory briefing film, that Washington, D.C., has more spies than any other city in the world. Yikes.

Well, if you can't flee them, join them. The International Spy Museum gives you the chance to do just that, learning about the best in the trade and tricks of the trade in interactive exhibits that allow you to test your powers of observation and pretend to be a spy. (Is that a gun in your pocketbook or a lipstick tube?) The history section reveals that the most unlikely of people have acted as spies in their time. Would you believe Moses? George Washington? Julia Child?

The International Spy Museum's inventory of international espionage artifacts numbers about 2,400, one-third of which are on display at any one time, in exhibits that cover history, as noted, as well as training, equipment, the "spies among us," legendary spymasters, spying during the Civil War, and 21st century cyber-spying. The most popular exhibit is the one that was added in late 2012, "Exquisitely Evil: 50 Years of Bond Villains." Originally conceived as a temporary show, Bond will definitely be on exhibit through the end of 2014 and possibly longer. The attraction here is, basically, you get to be Agent 007. Interactive props allow you to use surveillance cameras, design a villain's hideout, and match your skills against the real James Bond. On display throughout the show are 110 artifacts from James Bond movies. For example, in the section on "Weapons of Mass Disruption," look for cyber-villain Raoul Silva's laptop, from the 2012 movie Skyfall.

The Spy Museum is a three-floor affair, its main exhibit occupying the top level, and the James Bond exhibit consuming most of the first floor. Your general admission ticket grants you access to both of these areas. The second floor is devoted to providing the **Operation Spy** experience, which requires a separate ticket and admission fee. Here, participants immerse themselves in spy activities, like decrypting audio conversations and searching for evidence, as they work as part of a team to accomplish a mission.

Note: Operation Spy participants must be 12 or older. In fact, although the museum doesn't specify an age requirement for touring its main exhibits, I think children 10 and older have the most fun here.

You exit the museum directly to its gift shop, which leads to the Spy City Café.

For an extra $2 convenience fee, you can order advance tickets online and print your tickets at home or pick them up at the box office. You can also purchase advance tickets, including for same-day tours, at the box office.

800 F St. NW (at 8th St. NW). www.spymuseum.org. ℂ **866/779-6873** or 202/393-7798. Admission $20 plus tax ages 12–64, $16 plus tax seniors (65 and over), $15 plus tax ages 7–11. Operation Spy $15 plus tax ages 12 and over (combined admission fee $28 plus tax). Open daily 9 or 10am to 6pm, sometimes later, rarely earlier; check website for details. Closed Jan 1, Thanksgiving, and Dec 25. Metro: Gallery Place–Chinatown (9th and G sts. exit) or Archives–Navy Memorial.

Madame Tussauds Washington D.C. ★ MUSEUM   Calling all tweens! Justin Bieber's in the house! And OMG, is that Rihanna? And wait, who's this, Angelina Jolie? Yes and yes. On display throughout this museum are upwards of 100 lifelike wax figures, dressed and poised true to form, and grouped by theme: The Presidents' Gallery, Sports, Glamor, Civil Rights, Media Room, and Behind the Scenes. You can pretend to play golf with Tiger Woods, mingle with Johnny Depp, dance with Beyonce, and shake hands with President Barack Obama. Said to be the most interactive of the 15 Madame Tussauds around the world, the D.C. Madame's best feature is its **3-D Presidential Gallery**, which arranges each of the 43 presidents with important historical figures of that day, at important moments in their presidencies. With the use of interactive devices and fun props, the gallery creates an entertaining learning experience targeted to children, who are allowed up-close and personal access to the wax replicas. (This is a popular school field trip destination.) Kids can try on period costumes and join George Washington in his boat crossing the Delaware River, or stand next to Woodrow Wilson and listen to the crowds cheer his arrival at the end of World War I.

1001 F St. NW (btw. 10th and 11th sts.). www.madametussaudsdc.com. ℭ **866/823-9565** or 202/942-7300. Walk-up admission $21.50 plus tax ages 13 and over, $17 plus tax ages 4–12, children 3 and under free. Purchase advance tickets online and receive a 20% discount. Open daily, but hours fluctuate; call or check the website for exact hours on the day you wish to visit. Metro: Metro Center (11th and G sts. exit).

Marian Koshland Science Museum ★ MUSEUM As small as the **National Museum of Natural History** (p. 115) is large, the Koshland Science Museum serves as a perfect and quieter, more focused counterpoint to the Smithsonian museum's experience. This museum is about helping people use science to solve problems in their community. High-tech, interactive exhibits aim to provoke critical thinking about science and how it can be applied to looming issues from climate change, to healthy aging, to understanding how the brain works. A popular feature is a driving simulator, on the dangers of distracted driving. In the Earth Lab Exhibit: Degrees of Change, museum-goers use interactive tools to devise possible energy policy solutions in order to reduce CO_2 emissions. Families who have scientifically inclined children 14 and over should bop by this museum on weekend afternoons for hands-on science activities, like Energy Efficiency, in which you learn to use your own muscles to power a light bulb. Check out the museum's calendar online to learn about other fun events, like science trivia night. The Koshland Science Museum turns a decade old in 2014.

525 E St. NW. www.koshland-dc.org. ℭ **202/334-1201.** Admission $7, $4 students and military (with ID). Wed–Mon 10am–6pm. Closed Jan 1, Thanksgiving, and Dec 25. Metro: Gallery Place–Chinatown or Judiciary Square.

National Building Museum ★ MUSEUM The first thing you notice about the National Building Museum is the actual building, its pressed red-brick exterior and decorative terra cotta frieze, and its **size**, 400 feet by 200 feet, big enough to hold a football field. It costs nothing to tour the **Great Hall**, which impresses even more with its Italian Renaissance courtyard, colossal Corinthian columns, 15-story-high ceiling, and central fountain. This structure, modeled after an Italian palazzo, was designed to house the Pension Bureau (Its offices were located in those upper arcaded areas, overlooking the atrium.) and to serve as a venue for grand galas. The building hosted its first event, Pres. Grover Cleveland's inaugural ball, in 1885, even before construction was completed in 1887, and it's been the site of such balls and other events ever since. In the 1980s, the site took on new purpose as a museum dedicated to architecture, landscape architecture, engineering, urban planning, and historic preservation and opened to the public in 1985 as the National Building Museum. The museum charges

Washington's museum shops hold a treasure-trove of unusual gifts. Right now I'm loving the set of coffee mugs I bought my husband for Christmas at the **Folger Shakespeare Library** (p. 93) gift shop. They're covered in Shakespeare quotes: both for when you're in a foul mood ("Bolting-hutch of beastliness," "Thou art a boil, a plague sore") and for when you're feelin' the love ("Love is a smoke raised with the fume of sighs"). I've always had a weakness for the shop at the **National Building Museum** (p. 136), which is jammed with surprising, useful, and cleverly designed housewares and interesting games, including bookends embossed with Celtic designs, Bauhaus mobiles, and collapsible strainers. And I can never

visit the **National Gallery of Art** (p. 110) without lingering a little while in the store to admire captivating catalogue books, note cards, posters, children's games, and a slew of other things. The Smithsonian's **National Museum of African Art** (p. 112) has unusual items from all over Africa, but I especially liked the bright colors and interesting designs of the dishtowels, handbags, and headbands from Ghana. And then there's the woman-centric **National Museum of Women in the Arts** (p. 138) gift shop, whose Frida Kahlo notecards and leaning lady bookends I keep looking at online. No matter the museum, stop by the store and see whether a particular item or two calls out to you.

a fee to tour its exhibits, which are mounted in the galleries off the Great Hall on the first and second floors. A typical topic is the one covered in the 2014 show, *Designing for Disaster*, which examines how to assess environment risks so as to develop policies and plans for building disaster-resilient communities. It's not all so serious, though: Memorial Weekend through Labor Day Weekend every year, the museum hosts its mini-golf exhibit inside the Great Hall, setting up two, nine-hole mini golf courses designed and built by area experts in the building arts. In 2013, the museum partnered with nearby restaurant **Hill Country Barbecue** (p. 71) to host summer block party picnic barbecues on its west lawn, and the picnics are likely to return in 2014. PS: The museum gift shop is an especially good one (see box on Museum Shopping, p. 137).

401 F St. NW (btw. 4th and 5th sts.). www.nbm.org. ✆ **202/272-2448.** Free admission to view the inside of the building; exhibit tour $8 adults, $5 students (with ID), children 3–17, and seniors 60 and over. Mon–Sat 10am–5pm; Sun 11am–5pm. Closed Thanksgiving and Dec 25. Metro: Gallery Place (7th and F sts. exit) or Judiciary Square (F St. exit).

National Museum of Crime and Punishment ★ MUSEUM The history of American crime, punishment, crime fighting, crime scene investigation, and crime solving is the subject of this museum (as you might have guessed from the name). By 2014, the museum will have opened two new galleries dealing with anti-counterfeiting and pop culture, and possibly a third permanent exhibit aimed at children ages four and older (details were in the works but not confirmed at press time.). The museum displays more than 100 artifacts, like prison clothing actually worn by prisoners (in the Consequences of Crime area), and items actually confiscated by U.S. Customs (in the Homeland Security exhibit), and employs lots of interactive props to engage the visitor.

The museum's most popular features are the law enforcement driving simulator, in which you experience what it's like to drive a police car in pursuit of a speeding car, the FBI shooting range simulator in which you can test your skills in weapon accuracy and judgment, the section on serial killers, and the forensic science gallery, whose interactive devices puts you to work as a crime scene investigator à la the television show, *CSI*. In fact, so popular is the forensic science exhibit, that the museum offers almost daily forensic science workshops conducted by experts in different areas; tickets cost about $26 per adult, $22 per child, and include admission to the museum.

The museum operates a gift shop, the Cop Shop.

575 7th St. NW (at E St.). www.crimemuseum.org. © **202/621-5550.** Admission online tickets $18 adults (ages 12–59), $14 children 5–11, $16 all others; expect to pay about $4 more per ticket if you purchase in person. Sept to mid-Mar Sun–Thurs 10am–7pm, Fri–Sat 10am–8pm; mid-Mar to Sept 4 Mon–Thurs 9am–7pm, Fri–Sat 9am–8pm, Sun 10am–7pm. Metro: Gallery Place/Verizon Center (7th and F sts./Arena exit) or Archives–Navy Memorial.

National Museum of Women in the Arts ★ ART MUSEUM If you've never heard of Clara Peters, a 16th century Flemish painter of superbly rendered still-lifes, or Renaissance painter Lavinia Fontana, or Russian artist Sonia Delaunay, whose mastery of murals, theater sets, and ceramics, led the Louvre in 1964 to choose her as its first living female artist to hold a retrospective there . . . well, as I say, if you've never heard of these wondrous artists, it's a shame, but not surprising, given the historical short shrift accorded women's contributions to art. Here in Washington, D.C., we have an answer for that: Visit the National Museum of Women in the Arts, where more than 1,000 works by women, 16th century to the present, are on display at any one time. Open since 1987, the museum remains the world's only major museum solely dedicated to recognizing women's creative accomplishments.

Start with the attention-getting series of four outdoor sculptures positioned on a grassy island across New York Avenue from the museum. Artist Chakai Booker's large-scale works weave twisted and sliced pieces of discarded rubber tires into these dynamic and provocative assemblages. (The works are on display through March 9, 2014, and possibly longer, as part of the museum's New York Avenue Outdoor Sculpture Project.)

Inside the white marble Renaissance Revival 1908 museum building, originally a Masonic temple, is a space so elegant it's frequently in demand as a wedding reception venue. Some of the artwork is on display in the Grand Hall, but most exhibits are in upstairs galleries, accessed via the sweeping marble double stairways. Among the works from the permanent collection that you might see are those by Rosa Bonheur, Mary Cassatt, Helen Frankenthaler, Frida Kahlo, Barbara Hepworth, Georgia O'Keeffe, Lila Cabot Perry, and Elaine de Kooning. Most popular is Frida Kahlo's self portrait; it is the only Frida Kahlo on view in Washington. The museum mounts 10 special exhibits annually, which through Apr. 27, 2014 includes "Workt by Hand": Hidden Labor and Historical Quilts; the exhibit explores issues of anonymity versus authorship, and fine art versus craft, in showcasing 35 18th–20th century quilts on loan from the Brooklyn Museum.

Also recommended is the museum's gift shop, which sells clever little items, like leaning ladies bookends and a Dorothy Parker martini glass.

1250 New York Ave. NW (at 13th St.). www.nmwa.org. © **800/222-7270** or 202/783-5000. Admission $10 adults, $8 students 18 and over (with ID) and seniors 65 and over, free for youths 18 and under (general admission rates; special exhibition prices may be higher). Mon–Sat 10am–5pm; Sun noon–5pm. Closed Jan 1, Thanksgiving, and Dec 25. Metro: Metro Center (13th St. exit).

Newseum ★★ MUSEUM With newspapers closing every other week, it seems, a visit to the Newseum takes on not just added poignancy, but may raise feelings of alarm. That's because at the core of this entertaining yet erudite enterprise there's an important message: that journalism is an integral part not just of democracy, but of civilization itself. And the museum makes its case in a much less heavy-handed way than I just have, while at the same time acknowledging the myriad of ways that journalists can screw up! In a town of absorbing museums, this one more than holds its own.

The seven-level museum has 15 galleries highlighting subjects from ethics in journalism to Pulitzer Prize Photographs, 15 theaters, 130 interactive game stations, and two broadcast studios, including one that has the real-life Capitol as its backdrop. When you enter, staff usually direct you to the lower level, to watch orientation films. I'd say that you can skip the 4-minute introductory film and head instead to the theater showing the 8-minute *What's News?*, a topical film that explores the boundaries of journalism. Also on this level is the **Berlin Wall** exhibit, which includes eight 12-foot-high concrete sections of the original wall, and an East German guard tower. Future crime reporters might want to tour the **FBI exhibit's** display of artifacts related to big-name cases from the past 100 years.

From here, take the glass elevator to the sixth floor and stroll the outdoor terrace to admire the view of Pennsylvania Avenue and the Capitol (great photo op). If you have time, peruse the timeline that's posted along the length of this promenade, tracing the history of events that took place up and down the avenue.

Now walk down the stairs to level five to explore the **Putnam Great Books Gallery**, whose interactive touch screens allow you to view pages of the Magna Carta, the Federalist Papers, and other cornerstone works on freedom. The **History Gallery** serves up 5 centuries of journalism and more than 300 historic front pages. The 100-foot-wide video wall plays original programming and breaking news throughout the day.

Down another flight to the fourth floor finds you in the Newseum's newest and most popular exhibit at the moment, the **HP New Media Gallery**, whose interactive exhibits allow you to create your own news homepage and play Dunk the Anchorman. (Your correct answers to a set of increasingly difficult questions about journalism and social media result in the dunking of the virtual anchorman.) For more laughs, tour the aforementioned *Anchorman: The Exhibit*, in this same gallery. Elsewhere on this floor, the **First Amendment Gallery** tells the stories of real people whose experiences illustrate the value of our five First Amendment freedoms. The **9/11 Gallery** highlights the challenges faced by journalists reporting on 9/11 in a seriously moving fashion.

The third floor's **Journalists Memorial** honors the more than 2,246 journalists who have died in the course of reporting their stories, since 1837. Also on this floor are two state-of-the-art broadcast studios frequently in use by media organizations.

Pull up to one of 48 interactive kiosks in the second floor's **NBC News Interactive Newsroom** and test your prowess as a photojournalist, reporter, or editor. Sit in as a news anchor and read from a teleprompter, then play back the tape to see how well you did.

The gallery of **Pulitzer Prize-winning photographs** on the first floor includes a documentary film and interactive kiosks featuring interviews with some of the photographers.

Finish up on the concourse level with a viewing of *I-Witness*, whose 4-D film features put you in the picture with legendary journalists Isaiah Thomas (radical printer, not basketball legend), Nellie Bly, and Edward R. Murrow.

If it's before 3pm, you might want to visit the food court, which has a very kid-friendly (and adult-friendly: wine and beer are on offer) menu designed by Wolfgang Puck. The museum also has several gift shops.

555 Pennsylvania Ave. NW (at 6th St.). www.newseum.org. © **202/292-6100.** Admission $23 plus tax ages 19–64, $19 plus tax seniors (65 and over), $14 plus tax ages 7–18, free for children 6 and under. Daily 9am–5pm. Closed Jan 1, Thanksgiving, and Dec 25. Metro: Judiciary Square (4th St. exit), Gallery Place/Verizon Center (7th and F sts./Arena exit), or Archives–Navy Memorial.

Old Post Office Clock Tower ★ HISTORIC SITE   You may have heard that Donald Trump has bought the historic Old Post Office Pavilion and plans to turn the building into a hotel. This is true. However, the National Park Service, which operates and maintains the pavilion's 1899 Clock Tower, continues to state that the tower is off-limits and will remain open to the public. Hope so. Here's why: The tower offers a fabulous view of Pennsylvania Avenue, from the Capitol to the White House, and all around the town. Though the tower, at 315 feet tall, stands only about half the height of the Washington Monument, the outlook is still panoramic. Plus, inside the tower, you're able to see the clockwork, visible through glass panels. The directions for getting to the top of the tower may change once hotel construction gets underway; for now you should look for signs to the elevator to take you to the ninth floor, where you switch to a second elevator that takes you to the 12th.

1100 Pennsylvania Ave. NW (at 12th St.). www.oldpostofficedc.com or www.nps.gov/opot. © **202/606-8691.** Free admission. Mon-Sat 9am–4:45pm (until 6:30pm Thurs, and 7:45pm Mon-Sat Memorial Day to Labor Day); Sun noon–5:45pm. Metro: Federal Triangle.

Smithsonian American Art Museum and National Portrait Gallery ★★★ ART MUSEUM   Walt Whitman called this historic Greek Revival structure "the noblest of Washington buildings," and if he were around today, he'd likely stick with that opinion. If you've been flitting around the Penn Quarter, you had to have noticed it, with its porticoes modeled after the Parthenon in Athens, and its monumental footprint (405 by 274 feet.)

But it's the inside we're interested in. The magnificent landmark, which served as the nation's Patent Office in the mid-19th century, now houses two distinct Smithsonian museums: the American Art Museum and the National Portrait Gallery, each occupying three levels of galleries that enclose a stunning, light-filled inner courtyard, museum wings meeting seamlessly.

Walt Whitman's name crops up again. He is here, yes he is, in portrait form, painted by John White Alexander, in 1889, appearing rather old and tired, with blindingly white hair, full beard, and fluffy eyebrows, sitting at an angle and staring into the distance. Whitman's portrait hangs in the National Portrait Gallery's first floor section, **American Origins**, whose chronological arrangement of paintings of American notables tells the country's story, from Pocahontas, to Harriet Beecher Stowe, to Thomas Edison in compelling fashion. Other permanent exhibits feature **20th Century Americans** and **America's Presidents**. A temporary exhibit on view through May 31, 2015 is *Matthew Brady's Photographs of Union Generals*.

The American Art Museum resides within these skylit, vaulted halls too. Its collection of American art is one of the largest in the world, and most diverse, with folk art, modern, African American, and Latino art well represented. Standouts include Georgia O'Keeffe's take on *Manhattan*, Albert Bierstadt's idealized vision of the American West, *Among the Sierra Nevada*, a Nam June Paik video installation, *Electronic Superhighway: Continental U.S., Alaska, Hawaii*; and intriguing folk art, like James

Hampton's creation of artwork out of garbage, *The Throne of the Third Heaven of the Nations' Millennium General Assembly*. You'll either love it or you'll hate it, but you won't be able to look away from it.

In all, about 2,000 works are on display throughout both the American Art and Portrait galleries. You'll want to tour the top floor's two-level **Luce Foundation Center for American Art,** too, where thousands more works are stored but still on view, from walking canes to sculptures to dollhouses. In the adjacent **Lunder Conservation Center,** conservators work to preserve art pieces. Finally, make time to visit the museum's courtyard cafe, the setting for concerts, like the monthly free jazz series of performances, *Take Five!.*

One note: These two museums are open later than most in D.C., so you can schedule a visit for the end of the day.

8th and F sts. NW. www.americanart.si.edu or www.npg.si.edu. ✆ **202/633-1000.** Free admission. Daily 11:30am–7pm. Highlights tours are offered; check online or call for exact schedule. Closed Dec 25. Metro: Gallery Place–Chinatown (7th and F sts. Exit, or 9th and G sts. exit).

DUPONT CIRCLE

In a city of national this-and-that attractions, Dupont Circle provides a charmingly personal counterpoint. Within this lively residential neighborhood of old town houses, trendy boutiques, and bistros, are mostly historic houses (like the Christian Heurich House), embassy buildings, and beloved art galleries (like the Phillips Collection).

Anderson House ★ HISTORIC HOME   A visit to Anderson House is about marveling over the palatial architecture and interior design (love the ballroom), the display of artwork—from Flemish tapestries to Asian and European paintings and antiquities—and Revolutionary War artifacts. A bit of background: This limestone-veneered Italianate mansion, fronted by twin arches and a Corinthian-columned portico, was built between 1902 and 1905. Its original owners were career diplomat Larz Anderson III, who served as ambassador to Japan in 1912 and 1913, and his heiress wife, Isabel. The couple traveled a lot and filled their home with beautiful purchases from those journeys. Larz and Isabel were popular hosts in the capital and counted presidents and foreign dignitaries among their guests. Since Larz's death in 1937, the house has served as headquarters for the Society of the Cincinnati, an organization founded in 1783 for descendants of army officers who fought in the Revolutionary War. Anderson's great-grandfather was a founder and George Washington the society's first president-general. Anderson House hosts exhibits, concerts, and lectures throughout the year; all are free and open to the public.

2118 Massachusetts Ave. NW (at Q St.). www.societyofthecincinnati.org. ✆ **202/785-2040.** Free admission. Tues–Sat 1–4pm; highlights tours Tues–Sat 1:15pm, 2:15pm, and 3:15pm. Closed Thanksgiving, Dec 25, and Jan 1. Metro: Dupont Circle (Q St. exit).

Heurich House Museum ★ HISTORIC HOME   Wealthy German businessman and brewer Christian Heurich built this turreted, four-story brownstone and brick Victorian castle in 1894, and lived here with his family until he died in 1945. Old Heurich was a character, as a tour of the 31-room mansion-museum reveals. Allegorical paintings cover the ceilings, silvered plaster medallions festoon the stucco walls, and there's a bierstube (tavern room) in the basement sporting the brewer's favorite drinking mottos—written in German, but here's one translation: "There is room in the smallest chamber for the biggest hangover." The Victorian Garden is a good place to pause for a picnic or to page through your guidebook.

1307 New Hampshire Ave. NW (at 20th St.) www.heurichhouse.org. (📞 **202/429-1894**. Garden free admission; house tours $5, reservations required. Tours Thurs–Sat 11:30am and 1pm, with an additional Sat tour at 2:30pm. Garden weekdays spring–fall 10am–3pm. Metro: Dupont Circle (19th St. exit).

National Geographic Museum ★ MUSEUM   You don't have to be an adventurer to appreciate the exhibits mounted at the National Geographic Society's headquarters. It helps, though, if you're a curious soul and admire the natural world. Consider recent exhibits: "Real Pirates: The Untold Story of the *Wydah* from Slave Ship to Pirate Ship," "Gardens by Night," "Lions & Tigers & Bears: Through the Lens with National Geographic," and "Women of Vision: National Geographic on Assignment." National Geo also offers lectures, films, and performances throughout the year. Certain photography exhibits and events (the once-a-month Tuesdays at noon film series) are free, but most charge what I consider is a pretty hefty admission, $11 per adult and up. 1145 17th St. NW (at M St.). www.nationalgeographic.com/museum. (📞 **202/857-7588**. Free admission to some exhibits; admission to special exhibits usually $11 per adult and up. Daily 10am–6pm. Closed Dec 25. Metro: Farragut North (Connecticut Ave. and L St. exit).

Phillips Collection ★★ ART MUSEUM   The Phillips is beloved in Washington, mostly because of its French Impressionist and Post-Impressionist paintings by van Gogh, Bonnard, Cezanne, Picasso, Klee, and Renoir, whose *Luncheon of the Boating Party* is the most popular work on display. But as familiar and traditional as these paintings may seem now, the works and their artists were considered daring and avant garde, when Duncan Phillips opened his gallery in 1921. The Phillips Collection, indeed, was America's first official museum of modern art.

Founder Phillips's vision for "an intimate museum combined with an experiment station" is one that the museum continually renews, through programs like its Intersections series of contemporary art projects that explore links between old and new artistic traditions; and in exhibits of provocative art. Let me give you a good example:

On March 2, 2013, the Phillips Collection debuted the **Wolfgang Laib Wax Room,** its first permanent artwork installation since its opening of the Rothko Room in 1960. The Laib Room is also the first beeswax chamber that artist Laib has created for a specific museum. That's right: beeswax. You actually smell it before you see it, kind of a musty, faintly honeyish, cloying scent. The artwork is the size of a powder room, with a single light bulb dangling to illuminate walls and ceiling slathered thickly with wax the yellow hue of the fruit of a peach, flecked with bits of orangey brown. I sooo wanted to touch it, but that's not allowed. And a staff sentry stands just outside the entrance to make sure you don't.

What is the Wax Room but an experiment station?

Today, the museum's 3,000-work collection includes European masterpieces, treasures by American masters Dove, Homer, Hopper, Lawrence, and O'Keeffe; and works by living artists, such as Susan Rothenberg and Sean Scully. The Phillips resides in a complex that joins the original 1897 Georgian Revival mansion that served initially as both Phillips family home and public art gallery, with a modern gallery annex that doubles the space. The elegant mansion's graceful appointments—leaded- and stained-glass windows, elliptical stairway, oak-paneled Music Room, and tiled fireplaces—provide a lovely backdrop to the art and add to the reasons that locals love the Phillips.

Other reasons include blockbuster temporary shows, like the Van Gogh exhibit (Oct. 25, 2013-Jan. 26, 2014), that you may arrive in time for; gallery talks; Sunday concerts in the Music Room (October through May; admission $20); and the Phillips After Five events that take place on the first Thursday of each month, combining live music, cash bar, and food ($12 admission and you must make a reservation—very popular). The museum also has a charming café and a small gift shop.

1600 21st St. NW (at Q St.). www.phillipscollection.org. ℂ **202/387-2151.** Admission: Permanent collection free (donation welcome) on weekdays; weekends $12 adults; $10 seniors 62 and older and students 18 and older; free ages 18 and under. Ticketed special exhibits: $12 adults; $10 seniors 62 and older and students 18 and older; free ages 18 and under. Admission price allows entry to both permanent and special exhibits. Tues–Sat 10am–5pm (Thurs until 8:30pm); Sun 11am–6pm. Closed Mon and federal holidays. Metro: Dupont Circle (Q St. exit).

Woodrow Wilson House Museum ★ HISTORIC HOME   America's 28th President, was too ill to attend the inauguration of his successor. Instead he was driven to his new home in the prestigious Kalorama neighborhood. His final residence is preserved as he left it. Guided tours lasting about 60 minutes are scheduled on the hour; you can reserve on the website (above) or join as a walk-in visitor. The tour focuses on Wilson's Washington years (1912–1924), examining his public persona while allowing a peek behind the draperies into his personal life. Furnishings, White House objects, personal memorabilia, and elaborate gifts of state help tell the story. A mosaic of St. Peter hangs in the Drawing Room, a gift from Pope Benedict XV when the Wilsons toured Europe at the conclusion of World War I. Edith's portrait hangs above the mantle. The only presidential home open to the public in Washington, it's a natural stop for students of diplomacy.

2340 S St. NW (at Massachusetts Ave.). www.woodrowwilsonhouse.org. ℂ **202/387-4062.** Admission $10 adults, $8 seniors, $5 students, free for ages 11 and under. Tues–Sun 10am–4pm. Closed federal holidays. Metro: Dupont Circle (Q St. exit).

FOGGY BOTTOM

Known primarily as the locale for the George Washington University campus, the State Department, the International Monetary Fund, and the World Bank, Foggy Bottom in 2014 welcomes the Textile Museum to its neighborhood, whose other two main attractions are the John F. Kennedy Center for the Performing Arts (see chapter 8) and the State Department's Diplomatic Reception Rooms.

State Department Diplomatic Reception Rooms ★ GOVERNMENT BUILDING   This is a fine-arts tour of rooms that serve as our country's stage for international diplomacy and official entertaining. The rooms house a collection of Early American paintings, furniture, and decorative arts dating from 1740 to 1850. The tour is not recommended for children 11 and under. You must bring a valid picture ID, such as a driver's license, to enter the building.

2201 C St. NW (entrance on 23rd St. NW). https://diplomaticrooms.state.gov. ℂ **202/647-3241.** Free admission. Guided tours only: Mon–Fri 9:30am, 10:30am, and 2:45pm. Advance reservations required. Metro: Foggy Bottom.

Textile Museum ★ MUSEUM   The Textile Museum, long located in the Dupont Circle neighborhood, has up and moved to this new and larger location at the intersection of G and 21st streets, on the George Washington University campus. The museum is slated to open in the fall of 2014 and will bear the name The George Washington University Museum and The Textile Museum. In its new, custom-built, 46,000 square-foot space, the museum displays handcrafted historic and contemporary textile arts

In a grove of holly and elm trees at the southwest corner of the National Academy of Science grounds, you'll find this dear memorial displaying the slouching figure of brilliant scientist, great thinker, and peace activist Albert Einstein. He sits slightly bent and sideways, upon a granite bench, leaning on one hand and holding in the other a bronze sheet of paper on which are written mathematical equations for which he is famous. At his feet is a celestial map. His gaze looks worn and warm. The statue measures 12 feet in height and weighs 4 tons, yet children cannot resist crawling upon it and leaning up against this man.

spanning civilizations and centuries. A library and gift shop are also here. Check the website for more information.

G and 21st St. NW. www.textilemuseum.org. Metro: Foggy Bottom.

U STREET CORRIDOR

In these old stomping grounds of Duke Ellington and his fellow Black Broadway jazz greats, the main attractions are of the nightlife and dining variety—jazz clubs, like Twins Jazz, that carry Duke's legacy forward, and many restaurants and bars that cater to a range of appetites and interests. The two museums located here reflect the neighborhood's identity as a stronghold of African-American history and heroes. *Note:* These two museums are located about half a mile from each other.

African American Civil War Memorial and Museum ★ MUSEUM   This modest-sized museum displays old photographs, maps, letters, and inventories, along with ankle shackles worn by slaves, and other artifacts, accompanied by text to tell the stories of the United States Colored Troops and the African American involvement in the American Civil War. Not everyone knows that thousands of African Americans, mostly slaves, fought during the Civil War. Walk across the street to view the African American Civil War Memorial. A semicircular Wall of Honor curves behind the sculpture; etched into the stone are the names of the 209,145 United States Colored Troops who served in the Civil War.

1925 Vermont Ave. NW (at 10th St.; in the Grimke Building). www.afroamcivilwar.org. © **202/667-2667.** Free admission. Tues–Fri 10am–6:30pm; Sat 10am–4pm; Sun noon–4pm. Metro: U St./Cardozo (10th St. exit).

Mary McLeod Bethune Council House National Historic Site ★ HISTORIC HOME   This town house is the last D.C. residence of African-American activist/educator Bethune, who was a leading champion of black's and women's rights during FDR's administration. Born in South Carolina in 1875, the 15th of 17 children of former slaves, Mary McLeod grew up in poverty but learned the value of education through her schooling by missionaries. It was a lesson she passed forward. By the time she died in 1955 at the age of 79, McLeod—now Bethune, from her marriage in 1898 to Albert Bethune—had founded a school for "Negro girls" in Daytona Beach, Florida that would later become the Bethune-Cookman College, today Bethune-Cookman University; received 11 honorary degrees; served on numerous government advisory commissions, including the National Child

Welfare Commission; and acted as Special Advisor on Minority Affairs to President Franklin Delano Roosevelt from 1935 to 1944. Bethune also established this headquarters of the National Council of Negro Women to advance the interests of African-American women and the black community. Maintained by the National Park Service, the Bethune House exhibits focus on the professional achievements of this remarkable woman.

1318 Vermont Ave. NW (at O St.). www.nps.gov/mamc. *②* **202/673-2402.** Free admission. Open daily, Apr 1–Oct 31 9am–5pm, Nov 1–Mar 31 9am–4:30pm. Metro: U St./Cardozo (13th St. exit).

UPPER NORTHWEST D.C.: GLOVER PARK, WOODLEY PARK & CLEVELAND PARK

A handful of attractions lie in these just-beyond-downtown enclaves.

Hillwood Museum and Gardens ★ HISTORIC HOME This magnificent estate of Post cereal heiress, businesswoman, and socialite Marjorie Merriweather Post includes the beautiful mansion, where she lived from 1955 until her death in 1973, and 13 acres of gardens. The Georgian-style manse is filled with Post's collections of art and artifacts from 18th-century France and 18th- and 19th-century Russia, from Fabergé eggs to tapestries. The spectacular gardens include a Japanese-style plot, a Russian dacha, a French parterre, and a pet cemetery.

4155 Linnean Ave. NW (at Connecticut Ave.). www.hillwoodmuseum.org. *②* **202/686-5807.** Admission $15 adults, $12 seniors, $10 college students, $5 students 18 and under. Tues-Sat 10am–5pm; select Sun 1–5pm. Metro: Van Ness/UDC (east side of Connecticut Ave. exit), with a 20-minute walk.

National Zoological Park ★★ ZOO The National Zoo was created by an act of Congress in 1889 and became part of the Smithsonian Institution in 1890. A leader in the care, breeding, and exhibition of animals, the zoo occupies 163 lushly landscaped and wooded acres and is one of the country's most delightful zoos. In all, the park is home to about 400 species—some 2,000 animals, many of them rare and/or endangered. You'll see cheetahs, zebras, camels, elephants, tapirs, antelopes, brown pelicans, kangaroos, hippos, rhinos, giraffes, apes, and, of course, lions, tigers, and bears. But the zoo's biggest draws continue to be two **giant pandas,** Mei Xiang and Tian Tian.

One of its newest exhibits is called the **American Trail.** Located dead center in the zoo, American Trail is home to animals native to the United States and Canada that were once in danger of becoming extinct. Bald eagles, ravens, seals, sea lions, gray wolves, beavers, and river otters are among the creatures living here. An artificial tidal pool is now part of the display, and visitors are welcome to dip their toes in and touch model sea creatures.

At the bottom of the hill is the **Kids' Farm** with ducks, chickens, goats, cows, and miniature donkeys for kids to observe up close. A vegetable garden and pizza sculpture are also popular among the 3-to-8 crowd.

Enter the zoo at the Connecticut Avenue entrance; you'll be right by the Education Building, where you can pick up a map and find out about feeding times and any special activities. *Note:* From this main entrance, you're headed downhill; the return uphill walk can prove trying if you have young children and/or it's a hot day.

Zoo grounds open daily at 6am, which might be too early for a lot of tourists, but not for families whose young children like to rise at the crack of dawn. If you find yourselves trapped and restless in the hotel room, hop on the Red Line Metro, which opens at 5am weekdays, 7am Saturday and Sunday (or drive—the zoo parking lot opens at 6am, too), get off at the Woodley Park–Zoo station, and walk up the hill to the zoo. A Starbucks, which opens at 6am daily, is directly across from the zoo's entrance on Connecticut Avenue. Good morning.

But the zoo rents strollers, and snack bars and ice-cream kiosks are scattered throughout the park.

The zoo animals live in large, open enclosures—simulations of their natural habitats—along easy-to-follow paths. The **Olmsted Walk** winds from the zoo's Connecticut Avenue entrance all the way to the zoo's end, at Rock Creek Park. Stemming off the central Olmsted Walk is the **Asia Trail,** which takes you past sloth bears, frolicking giant pandas, fishing cats, clouded leopards, and Japanese salamanders. You can't get lost, and it's hard to miss a thing. Be sure to catch **Amazonia,** where you can hang out and observe enormous 7-foot-long arapaima fish and itty-bitty red-tailed catfish; and look for monkeys hiding in the 50-foot-tall trees.

Not far from the Amazonia exhibit, stationed in front of the **Great Cats** habitat, is the zoo's new carousel, whose canopy is carved with 58 species of animals. Rides are $3.

The zoo offers several dining options, including the Mane Grill, the Panda Café, and a number of snack stands. Other facilities include stroller rental stations, a handful of gift shops, a bookstore, and several paid-parking lots. The lots fill up quickly, especially on weekends, so arrive early or take the Metro.

3001 Connecticut Ave. NW (adjacent to Rock Creek Park). www.nationalzoo.si.edu. © **202/633-4888.** Free admission. Apr–Oct (weather permitting) grounds daily 6am–8pm, animal buildings daily 10am–6pm; Nov–Mar grounds daily 6am–6pm, animal buildings daily 10am–4:30pm. Closed Dec 25. Metro: Woodley Park–Zoo or Cleveland Park.

Washington National Cathedral ★★ CATHEDRAL   Pierre L'Enfant's 1791 plan for the capital city included "a great church for national purposes." Possibly because of early America's fear of mingling church and state, more than a century elapsed before the foundation for Washington National Cathedral was laid. Its actual name is the Cathedral Church of St. Peter and St. Paul. The church is Episcopal, but it has no local congregation and seeks to serve the entire nation as a house of prayer for all people. It has been the setting for every kind of religious observance, from Jewish to Serbian Orthodox.

A church of this magnitude—it's the sixth-largest cathedral in the world, and the second largest in the U.S.—took a long time to build. Its principal (but not original) architect, Philip Hubert Frohman, worked on the project from 1921 until his death in 1972. The foundation stone was laid in 1907 using the mallet with which George Washington set the Capitol cornerstone. Construction was interrupted by both world wars and by periods of financial difficulty. The cathedral was completed with the placement of the final stone on the west front towers on September 29, 1990, 83 years (to the day) after it was begun.

When you visit in 2014, there's a good chance you'll see exterior scaffolding, and perhaps debris netting inside to catch any stones that might fall due to the construction work. The earthquake of Aug. 23, 2011 damaged some of the pinnacles, flying buttresses, and gargoyles at the very top of the cathedral's exterior, as well as some minor areas of the interior ceiling. Restoration work will probably continue until 2016, but the cathedral is completely safe to visit, and its programs continue as usual.

English Gothic in style (with several distinctly 20th-c. innovations, such as a stained-glass window commemorating the flight of *Apollo 11* and containing a piece of moon rock), the cathedral is built in the shape of a cross, complete with flying buttresses and 110 gargoyles. Along with the Capitol and the Washington Monument, it is one of the dominant structures on the Washington skyline. Its 59-acre landscaped grounds have two lovely gardens (the lawn is ideal for picnicking), three schools, and two gift shops.

Among the many historic services and events that have taken place at the cathedral are: celebrations at the end of World Wars I and II; the burial of President Wilson; funerals for Presidents Eisenhower, Reagan, and Ford; the burials of Helen Keller and her companion, Anne Sullivan, inside the cathedral; the Rev. Dr. Martin Luther King, Jr.'s final sermon; a round-the-clock prayer vigil in the Holy Spirit Chapel when the Iranians held American hostages captive, and a service attended by the hostages upon their release; and President Bush's National Prayer and Remembrance service on September 14, 2001, following the cataclysm of September 11.

The best way to explore the cathedral is to take a 30-minute **guided highlights tour;** the tours leave continually from the west end of the nave. You can also walk through on your own, using a self-guiding brochure available in several languages. Visit the website to find out about group and special interest tours, which require reservations and fees. Allow additional time to tour the grounds and to visit the **Pilgrim Observation Gallery ★**, where 70 windows provide panoramic views of Washington and its surroundings. Among the most popular special interest tours are the Tuesday and Wednesday afternoon **Tour and Tea** events, which start at 1:30pm with an in-depth look at the cathedral and conclude in the Observation Gallery with a lovely "high tea," in both the British and literal sense—you're sitting in the cradle of one of the highest points in Washington, gazing out at the cathedral and the city below, while noshing on scones and Devon cream. The cost is $30 per person, and reservations are required. Call ✆ **202/537-8993** or book online at https://commerce. cathedral.org/exec/cathedral/tourtea.

The cathedral hosts numerous events: organ recitals; choir performances; an annual flower mart; calligraphy workshops; jazz, folk, and classical concerts; and the playing of the 53-bell carillon. Check the cathedral's website for schedules.

Massachusetts and Wisconsin aves. NW (entrance on Wisconsin Ave.). www.nationalcathedral.org. ✆ **202/537-6200.** Requested donation $10 per adult, $5 per child and senior. Cathedral Mon–Fri 10am–5:30pm (nave level until 8pm May to Labor Day); Sat 10am–4:30pm; Sun 1–3pm. Gardens daily until dusk. Regular tours Mon–Fri 10–11:30am and 1–3:30pm; Sat 10–11:30am and 1–3pm; Sun 1–2:30pm. No tours on Palm Sunday, Easter, Thanksgiving, Dec 25, or during services. Services vary throughout the year, but Mon–Thurs Evensong service at 5:30pm is usually on throughout the academic year. Check the website for all other service times. Metro: Tenleytown, with a 20-min. walk. Bus: Any N bus up Massachusetts Ave. from Dupont Circle, or any 30-series bus along Wisconsin Ave. This is also a stop on the Old Town Trolley Tour. Parking garage $6 per hr./$22 maximum weekdays until 11pm and a flat rate of $7 if you arrive after 4pm; flat rate of $9 on Sat; free on Sun.

GEORGETOWN

One of the oldest parts of the city has long been best known for its major shopping opportunities, and you should make the most of it, if that interests you. Nearly all of the stores are located along Georgetown's main streets, M Street and Wisconsin Avenue.

Historic Georgetown still exists, however, and a walking tour in chapter 10 will lead you to centuries-old estates and dwellings, including **Tudor Place,** the **Old Stone House,** and **Dumbarton House.** Whether or not you take this tour, you might want to seek out the other two places included in this chapter: Dumbarton Oaks, a historic mansion, museum, and formal gardens; and the Kreeger Museum, located slightly northwest of Georgetown proper and most easily accessible by car or taxi. But very cool.

Dumbarton House ★ HISTORIC HOME   Built between 1799 and 1805, Dumbarton House is the headquarters for the National Society of Colonial Dames of America. Stop here to admire gorgeous architecture and antique decorative arts, and to glean a bit of early American history. Self-guide your way or call to arrange in advance for a docent-guided tour.

2715 Q St. NW (at 27th St.). www.dumbartonhouse.org. © **202/337-2288.** Admission $5; free for students. Tues–Sun 11am–3pm. Closed federal holidays. Metro: Dupont Circle (Q St. exit, with a 20-min. walk) or take the DC Circulator, two of whose routes run close by the house.

Dumbarton Oaks ★ MUSEUM   One block off the main drag of Wisconsin Avenue in upper Georgetown delivers you far from the madding crowds, to the peaceful refuge of Dumbarton Oaks. The estate includes a museum devoted to Byzantine and Pre-Columbian art, a research center and library, and 10 acres of formal and informal gardens. Frankly, many people skip the museum altogether to wander along the garden's hedge-lined walkways, into the orangery, past the weeping cherry trees, and all around the garden plots, admiring what's in bloom as they go. If it's February, you may see English daisies. April? Bluebells. August? Dahlias. (Just to name a few.) The gardens are romantic, have several pretty places to perch, and also are adorned here and there with garden ornaments and artwork. The gardens can get crowded in spring and early summer, when they are at their loveliest.

Do try to make time for the museum, whose galleries display 1,200 Byzantine artifacts, including jewelry, lamps, icons, and illuminated manuscripts from the 4th to the 15th centuries; and Pre-Columbian objects such as Aztec stone carvings, Inca gold ornaments, and Olmec heads. A special exhibit, "Inspiring Art: The Dumbarton Oaks Birthing Figure," continuing until March 2, 2014, explores the changing perceptions of an Aztec birthing statue. (Some think it a fake, others believe it to be a masterpiece.) Other highlights include the Flemish tapestries and an El Greco painting, *The Visitation*, on display in the Renaissance-style Music Room, which you'll have to admire from the roped-off entryway. Like the Phillips Collection (p. 142), the museum's mansion setting adds to its charm.

The country house and gardens, which are situated at the highest point of Georgetown, belonged to a couple named Mildred and Robert Woods Bliss, who initiated these collections and gardens in the first half of the 20th century. The couple gave Dumbarton Oaks to Harvard University in 1940. Harvard University students, staff, and faculty can visit the gardens for free.

1703 32nd St. NW (garden entrance at 31st and R sts.). www.doaks.org. © **202/339-6401.** Gardens admission Mar 15–Oct 31 $8 adults, $5 children 12 and under and seniors; free Nov–Mar 14. Museum free admission. Gardens Tues–Sun year-round (weather permitting): Mar 15 to Oct 31

2–6pm; Nov 1 to Mar 14 2–5pm. Museum Tues–Sun 2–5pm. Closed national holidays and Dec 24. Metrobus nos. 31, 32, 36, D1, D2, D3, D6, and G2, plus the D.C. Circulator bus all have stops close to the site.

Kreeger Museum ★ ART MUSEUM You have to make an effort to visit the Kreeger, since it's located in a residential neighborhood away from the downtown and public transportation. But if you don't mind driving, taking a taxi, or riding the D6 bus from Dupont Circle, then walking a half-mile up the hill to the museum, you'll be well rewarded. On view throughout this unique Philip Johnson-designed building, besides the stunning architecture itself, are paintings, sculptures, prints, and drawings by 19th and 20th century European artists, Picasso (early and late works), Kandinsky, Monet, Renoir, Munch, Pissarro, Rodin among them. American works are on view, too, including some by Washington, D.C., artists, like Sam Gilliam and Gene Davis. Downstairs lies a small collection of traditional African masks and figures and Asian pieces. Outdoors are a sculpture terrace and sculpture garden, where large works by Maillol and Henry Moore, and the sight of the distant Washington Monument, are some of the pleasures at hand. This summit-situated, 5½ acre estate, once the residence of collectors Carmen and David Kreeger, opened to the public in 1994. In celebration of its 20th anniversary in 2014, the Kreeger is installing three large-scale sculptures by John L. Dreyfuss, completing his *Inventions* series on view around the museum's new reflecting pool.

2401 Foxhall Rd. NW (off Reservoir Rd.). www.kreegermuseum.org. © **202/337-3050.** Admission $10 adults, $7 seniors and students, free for children 12 and under. Fri–Sat 10am–4pm; Tues–Thurs by reservation only, for guided tours at 10:30am and 1:30pm. Closed federal holidays and Aug. About 2 miles from Reservoir Rd. and Wisconsin Ave. in Georgetown (a pleasant walk on a nice day); otherwise drive, take a taxi, or ride the D6 bus from Dupont Circle.

Old Stone House ★ HISTORIC HOME This 1765 structure is said to be the oldest in Washington. The National Park Service owns and operates the house, and National Park Service rangers provide information and sometimes demonstrations related to the site's pre-Revolutionary history. See p. 220.

3051 M St. NW (at 30th St.). www.nps.gov/olst. © **202/895-6070.** Free admission. Daily noon–5pm. Garden open during daylight hours. Closed Dec 25. Metro: Foggy Bottom with a 15-min. walk, or take the D.C. Circulator.

Tudor Place ★ HISTORIC HOME Designed by Dr. William Thornton, architect of the Capitol, Tudor Place was constructed between 1796 and 1816 for Martha Parke Custis, who was George Washington's step-granddaughter. Family descendants lived here until 1983. Tour the garden on your own; house tours are docent-led only. See p. 218.

1644 31st St. NW (at R St.). www.tudorplace.org. © **202/965-0400.** House admission $10 adults, $8 seniors, $3 students. Garden admission $3. House Tues–Sat 10am–4pm; Sun noon–4pm. Garden Mon–Sat 10am–4pm; Sun noon–4pm. Closed Dec 25. Metro: Dupont Circle (Q St. exit, with a 20-min. walk).

NORTHERN VIRGINIA
Arlington

The land that today comprises Arlington County, Virginia, was included in the original parcel of land demarcated as the nation's capital. In 1847 the state of Virginia took its territory back, referring to it as "Alexandria County" until 1920, when Arlington at last

MUSEUMS IN anacostia

This historic, largely black residential neighborhood located east of the Capitol and away from the center of the city is not a tourist destination, but two attractions do draw visitors. The **Frederick Douglass National Historic Site** (1411 W St. SE, at 14th St. SE; www.nps.gov/frdo; ☎ 202/426-5961) is by far the more compelling. Crowning one of the highest hills in Washington is Cedar Hill, abolitionist Frederick Douglass's home for the last 18 years of his life. A National Park Service ranger takes you upstairs and down, and fills you in on the life of the brilliant, brave, and charismatic abolitionist here at this house, but with detours to Douglass's life story: his love of reading, his escape from slavery, his married life, and his embrace of emancipation for all oppressed people. See website for hours and admission.

The **Anacostia Community Museum** (1901 Fort Place SE, off Martin Luther King Jr. Ave.; www.anacostia. si.edu; ☎ 202/633-4820) primarily serves the neighborhood and the local black community with exhibits that focus on social, cultural, and historical themes that resonate with area residents.

became "Arlington," a name change made to avoid confusion with the city of Alexandria.

And where did the county pick up the name "Arlington"? From its famous estate, Arlington House, built by a descendant of Martha Washington, George Washington Parke Custis, whose daughter married Robert E. Lee. The Lees lived in Arlington House on and off until the onset of the Civil War in 1861. After the First Battle of Bull Run, at Manassas, several Union soldiers were buried here; the beginnings of Arlington National Cemetery date from that time.

The Arlington Memorial Bridge leads directly from the Lincoln Memorial to the Robert E. Lee Memorial at Arlington House, symbolically joining these two figures into one Union after the Civil War.

Beyond Arlington the cemetery, is Arlington, a residential community from which most residents commute into Washington to work and play. In recent years, however, the suburb has come into its own, booming with businesses, restaurants, and nightlife, giving residents reasons to stay put and tourists more incentive to visit. Here are some sites worth seeing:

Arlington National Cemetery ★★ CEMETERY   Like the Mall, Arlington National Cemetery is an essential part of the itinerary for first time visitors to D.C. It is, without hyperbole, the United State's most important burial ground. This shrine occupies approximately 624 acres on the high hills overlooking the capital from the west side of Memorial Bridge. More than 400,000 people are buried here, including veterans of all national wars, from the American Revolution to the Iraq and Afghanistan conflicts; Supreme Court justices; literary figures; slaves; presidents; astronauts; and assorted other national heroes. Many graves of the famous at Arlington bear nothing more than simple markers.

Upon arrival head over to the visitor center, where you can view exhibits, pick up a detailed map, use the restrooms (there are no others until you get to Arlington House), and purchase an **ANC Tours by Martz Gray Line ticket** ($10 adults, $7.75 seniors, $4.50 children 3–11), which stops at the Kennedy gravesites, the Tomb of the

Unknowns, and Arlington House. You can also purchase tickets online at www. anctours.com. Service is continuous, and the narrated commentary is informative; this is the only guided tour of the cemetery. If you've got plenty of stamina, consider doing part or all of the tour on foot. Remember as you go that this is a memorial frequented not just by tourists but also by those attending burial services or visiting the graves of beloved relatives and friends who are buried here.

Cemetery highlights include the **Tomb of the Unknowns,** which contains the unidentified remains of a service member from World War I in a massive, white marble sarcophagus; just west of the sarcophagus are three white marble slabs flush with the plaza, marking the graves of unknown service members from World War II, the Korean War, and the Vietnam War. But the crypt for the Vietnam War service member contains no remains. In 1998 the entombed remains of the unknown soldier from Vietnam were disinterred and identified as those of Air Force 1st Lt. Michael Blassie, whose A-37 was shot down in South Vietnam in 1962. The Blassie family buried Michael in his hometown of St. Louis. The crypt honoring the dead but unidentified Vietnam War soldiers remains empty. A 24-hour honor guard watches over the marble Tomb of the Unknowns and its companion gravesites with the changing of the guard taking place every half-hour April to September, every hour on the hour October to March, and every hour at night year-round.

Within a 20-minute walk, all uphill, from the visitor center is **Arlington House** (www.nps.gov/arho; © **703/235-1530**), whose structure was begun in 1802, by Martha and George Washington's adopted grandson, George Washington Parke Custis. Custis's daughter, Mary Anna Randolph, inherited the estate, and she and her husband, Robert E. Lee, lived here between 1831 and 1861. When Lee headed up Virginia's army, Mary fled, and federal troops confiscated the property. An ongoing restoration was at last completed in 2013 and the house, fully furnished with Lee and Custis family artifacts, is open to the public for self-guided tours. Slave quarters and a small museum adjoin. Park rangers are on-site to answer your questions. Admission is free. It's open daily from 9:30am to 4:30pm (closed Dec 25 and Jan 1).

Pierre Charles L'Enfant's grave was placed near Arlington House at a spot that is believed to offer the best view of Washington, the city he designed.

Below Arlington House is the **gravesite of Pres. John Fitzgerald Kennedy,** which is a three-acre lawn terrace paved with irregular-sized stones of Cape Cod granite, bits of grass growing between the stones. At the head of the gravesite is a 5-foot, circular fieldstone, with the Eternal Flame burning in the center. Embracing the terrace is a low crescent wall inscribed with quotations from President Kennedy's presidency. Slate headstones mark the actual graves for President Kennedy, Jacqueline Kennedy Onassis, and two infant children. President Kennedy's two brothers, Senators Robert Kennedy and Edward Kennedy, are buried close by. The Kennedy graves attract streams of visitors. Arrive close to 8am to contemplate the site quietly; otherwise it's often crowded. Looking north, there's a spectacular view of Washington.

In 1997 the **Women in Military Service for America Memorial** (www.womens memorial.org; © **800/222-2294** or 703/533-1155) was added to Arlington Cemetery to honor the more than 2.5 million women who have served in the armed forces from the American Revolution to the present. The impressive memorial lies just beyond the gated entrance to the cemetery, a 3-minute walk from the visitor center. As you approach, you see a large, circular reflecting pool, perfectly placed within the curve of the granite wall rising behind it. Arched passageways within the 226-foot-long wall lead to an upper terrace and dramatic views of Arlington National Cemetery and the monuments of

Washington; an arc of large glass panels (which form the roof of the memorial hall) contains etched quotations from famous people about contributions made by service-women. Behind the wall and completely underground is the **Education Center,** housing a **Hall of Honor,** a gallery of exhibits tracing the history of women in the military, a theater, and a computer register of servicewomen, which visitors may access for the stories and information about 250,000 individual military women, past and present. Hours are 8am to 5pm. Stop at the reception desk for a brochure that details a self-guided tour through the memorial. The memorial is open every day but Christmas.

Just across the Memorial Bridge from the base of the Lincoln Memorial. www.arlingtoncemetery. mil. © **877/907-8585.** Free admission. Apr–Sept daily 8am–7pm; Oct–Mar daily 8am–5pm. Metro: Arlington National Cemetery. If you come by car, parking is $1.75/hr. for the 1st 3 hr., $2.50/ hr. thereafter. The cemetery is also accessible via the ANC Tours by Martz Gray Line Express bus.

The Pentagon ★ GOVERNMENT BUILDING   Completed in January 1943, after a mere 16 months of construction, the structure is the world's largest low-rise office building in the world. The Capitol could fit inside any one of its five wedge-shaped sections. 23,000 people work at the Pentagon, which holds 17½ miles of corridors, 19 escalators, 284 restrooms, and 691 water fountains. Tours of this headquarters for the American military establishment were suspended for a while following the September 11 2001, attack in which terrorists hijacked American Airlines Flight 77 and crashed it into the northwest side of the Pentagon, killing 125 people working at the Pentagon and 59 people aboard the plane. In the years since, the Pentagon has been completely restored and its tour program reinstated, in accordance with certain procedures (see below). More than 100,000 visitors tour the Pentagon annually.

An active duty staff person from the National Capital Region's ceremonial unit conducts the free, 60-minute tour that covers 1½ miles and is required to memorize 20 pages of informational material, outlining the mission of each military branch. It's a fascinating introduction, as is seeing the building itself, its corridors commemorating the history, people, and culture of the Air Force, Navy, Army, Marine Corps, and Coast Guard. You'll see historical photos, the Hall of Heroes for Medal of Honor recipients, an exhibit recognizing U.S. prisoners of war and the missing in action, paintings depicting the country's founding fathers and the signing of the Declaration of Independence.

The tour does not include a visit to the **Pentagon Memorial,** better known as the **9/11 Memorial,** which is located outside, on the northwest side of the building, near where the plane crashed. The memorial opened to the public on the seventh anniversary of the 9/11 attacks, September 11, 2008. On view are 184 granite-covered benches, each engraved with a victim's name, and arranged in order of birth date. The names are written in such a way on each bench that you must face the Pentagon to be able to read the names of those killed there and face away from the Pentagon, toward the western sky, to read the names of those who perished on the plane. *Please note:* You do not need to sign up for a Pentagon tour to visit the 9/11 Memorial, which is outside and open to the public 24 hours a day, every day. The best way to reach the memorial is to take the Metro to the Pentagon station and follow the signs that lead from the station to the northwest side of the Pentagon. Memorial staff are on hand to answer questions daily between 10am and 8pm.

Pentagon tours are available Monday to Friday 9am to 3pm, and you must book your tour no sooner than 14 days and no later than 90 days in advance. You request the tour online at **pentagontours.osd.mil,** providing your Social Security number, birth date and other information for each of the people in your party. You can also fax a request to © 703/614-1642 or email a request to tourschd.pa@osd.mil. There is no public parking at the Pentagon, so it's best to arrive by Metro, since the Pentagon has its own Metro stop. Once you exit the Pentagon Metro station, look for the Pentagon Visitors Center near the station entrance, and go to the Pentagon Tour Window.

Department of Defense, 1155 Defense Pentagon. pentagontours.osd.mil, www.whs.mil/memorial. © **703/697-1776.** Free admission, but reservations required; guided tours only. Pentagon Mon–Fri 9am–3pm. Pentagon Memorial Daily 24 hr. Metro: Pentagon.

Parks

More than 27 percent of Washington's land space is national parkland. When you add in the parks and gardens maintained by the D.C. Department of Parks and Recreation, as well as private estates that are open to the public, you're talking thousands and thousands of green acres!

POTOMAC PARK

The National Mall and Memorial Parks' individual spaces known as West and East Potomac parks are 720 riverside acres divided by the Tidal Basin. The parkland is most famous for its display of **cherry trees,** which bloom for a mere 2 weeks, tops, every spring, as they have since the city of Tokyo first gave the U.S. capital the gift of the original 3,000 trees in 1912. Today there are more than 3,750 cherry trees planted along the Tidal Basin in West Potomac Park, East Potomac Park, the Washington Monument grounds, and other pockets of the city.

The sight of the delicate cherry blossoms is so special that the whole city joins in cherry-blossom-related hoopla, throwing the **National Cherry Blossom Festival** (the 2014 festival is scheduled for March 20 through April 13). The National Park Service devotes a home page to the subject, **www.nps.gov/cherry**, and the National Cherry Blossom Festival officials another: **www.nationalcherryblossomfestival.org.** The trees usually begin blooming sometime between March 20 and April 17; April 4 is the average date.

To get to the Tidal Basin by car (*not* recommended in cherry-blossom season—actually, let me be clear: *impossible* in cherry-blossom season), you want to get on Independence Avenue and follow the signs posted near the Lincoln Memorial that show you where to turn to find parking. If you're walking, you'll want to cross Independence Avenue where it intersects with West Basin Drive and follow the path to the Tidal Basin. There is no convenient Metro stop near here. If you don't want to walk or ride a bike, your best bet is the National Park Service's newly authorized express trams.

West Potomac Park encompasses Constitution Gardens; the Vietnam, Korean, Lincoln, Jefferson, World War II, and FDR memorials; the D.C. World War I Memorial; the Reflecting Pool; the Tidal Basin and its paddle boats; and countless flower beds, ball fields, and trees. It has 1,678 cherry trees bordering the Tidal Basin, some of them Akebonos with delicate pink blossoms, but most are Yoshinos with white, cloudlike flower clusters.

East Potomac Park has 1,681 cherry trees in 10 varieties. The park also has picnic grounds, tennis courts, three golf courses, a large swimming pool, and biking and hiking paths by the water. East Potomac Park's **Hains Point** is located on a peninsula extending into the Potomac River; locals love to ride their bikes out to the point; golfers love to tee up in view of the Washington Monument. See "Outdoor Activities," below, for further information.

Part of National Mall and Memorial Parks, bordering the Potomac River along the west and south-west ends. www.nps.gov/nama. ℭ **202/426-6841.** Free admission. Daily 24 hr. Metro: Smithsonian (12th St./Independence Ave. exit).

Lower Rock Creek Park

Created in 1890, **Rock Creek Park** was purchased by Congress for its "pleasant valleys and ravines, primeval forests and open fields, its running waters, its rocks clothed with rich ferns and mosses, its repose and tranquility, its light and shade, its ever-varying shrubbery, its beautiful and extensive views," according to a Corps of Engineers officer quoted in the National Park Service's administrative history. A 1,750-acre valley within the District of Columbia, extending 12 miles from the Potomac River to the Maryland border, it's one of the biggest and finest city parks in the nation. Parts of it are still wild; coyotes have been sighted here, joining the red and gray foxes, raccoons, and beavers already resident. Most tourists encounter its southern tip, the section from the Kennedy Center to the National Zoo, but the park widens and travels much farther from there.

The park's offerings include D.C.'s oldest standing structure, the 1765 **Old Stone House** (see p. 149) in Georgetown (located on a busy street in Georgetown, outside the park but considered a park property, nonetheless); playgrounds; an extensive system of hiking and biking trails; sports facilities; remains of Civil War fortifications; and acres and acres of wooded parklands. In upper Georgetown, Rock Creek Park includes the family-friendly Montrose Park, a favorite place for picnicking and playing tennis, and Dumbarton Oaks Park, a 27-acre rustic preserve. Both Montrose and Dumbarton Oaks parks adjoin each other and the Dumbarton Oaks estate and formal gardens (p. 148).

For full information on the wide range of park programs and activities, visit the **Rock Creek Nature Center and Planetarium,** 5200 Glover Rd. NW (ℭ **202/895-6070**), Wednesday through Sunday from 9am to 5pm. To get to the center by public transportation, take the Metro to Friendship Heights and transfer to bus no. E2 to Military Road and Oregon Avenue/Glover Road, then walk up the hill about 100 yards.

The Nature Center and Planetarium is the scene of numerous activities, including weekend planetarium shows, nature films, crafts demonstrations, live animal demonstrations, guided nature walks, plus a daily mix of lectures, films, and other events. Self-guided nature trails begin here. All activities are free, but for planetarium shows you need to pick up tickets a half-hour in advance. The Nature Center is closed on federal holidays.

At Tilden Street and Beach Drive, you can see the recently refurbished, water-powered 19th-century gristmill, used until not so long ago to grind corn and wheat into flour. It's called **Peirce Mill** (a man named Isaac Peirce built it). The mill is open for tours Nov 1–Dec 21 and Jan 1–Mar 31 Sat–Sun 10am to 4pm; and Apr 1–Oct 31 Wed–Sun 10am–4pm. Check the website, www.nps.gov/pimi, or call ℭ 202/895-6070.

You'll find convenient free **parking** throughout the park.

From the Potomac River near the Kennedy Center northwest through the city into Maryland. www.nps.gov/rocr. ℭ **202/895-6070.** Free admission. Daily during daylight hours. Metro: Access points near the stations at Dupont Circle, Foggy Bottom, Woodley Park–Zoo, and Cleveland Park.

THEODORE ROOSEVELT ISLAND PARK ★

A serene, 91-acre wilderness preserve, Theodore Roosevelt Island is a memorial to the nation's 26th president in recognition of his contributions to conservation. During his administration, Roosevelt, an outdoor enthusiast and expert field naturalist, set aside a total of 234 million acres of public lands for forests, national parks, wildlife and bird refuges, and monuments.

Native American tribes were here first, inhabiting the island for centuries until the arrival of English explorers in the 1600s. Over the years, the island passed through many owners before becoming what it is today—an island preserve of swamp, marsh, and upland forest that's a haven for rabbits, chipmunks, great owls, foxes, muskrats, turtles, and groundhogs. It's a complex ecosystem in which cattails, arrow arum, and pickerel-weed grow in the marshes, and willow, ash, and maple trees root on the mud flats. You can observe these flora and fauna in their natural environs on 2.5 miles of foot trails.

In the northern center of the island, overlooking a terrace encircled by a water-filled moat, stands a 17-foot bronze statue of Roosevelt. Four 21-foot granite tablets are inscribed with tenets of his conservation philosophy.

To drive to the island, take the George Washington Memorial Parkway exit north from the Theodore Roosevelt Bridge. The parking area is accessible only from the northbound lane; park there and cross the pedestrian bridge that connects the lot to the island. You can also rent a canoe at Thompson Boat Center (p. 158) and paddle over, or take the pedestrian bridge at Rosslyn Circle, 2 blocks from the Rosslyn Metro station. Expect bugs in summer and muddy trails after a rain.

In the Potomac River, btw. Washington and Rosslyn, VA (see above for access information). www.nps.gov/this. (C) **703/289-2500.** Free admission. Daily 6am–10pm. Metro: Rosslyn, then walk 2 blocks to Rosslyn Circle and cross the pedestrian bridge to the island.

CHESAPEAKE & OHIO CANAL NATIONAL HISTORICAL PARK ★

One of the great joys of living in Washington is the **C&O Canal** and its unspoiled 185-mile towpath. You leave urban cares and stresses behind while hiking, strolling, jogging, cycling, or boating in this lush, natural setting of ancient oaks and red maples, giant sycamores, willows, and wildflowers. But the canal wasn't always just a leisure spot for city people. It was built in the 1800s, when water routes were considered vital to transportation. Even before it was completed, though, the canal was being rendered obsolete by the B&O Railroad, which was constructed at about the same time and along the same route. Today its role as an oasis from unrelenting urbanity is even more important.

A good source of information about the canal is the National Park Service office at **Great Falls Tavern Visitor Center,** 11710 MacArthur Blvd., Potomac, Maryland ((C) **301/767-3714**). The center is open Wednesday through Sunday year round, 9am–4:30pm. At this 1831 tavern, you can see museum exhibits and a film about the canal; there's also a bookstore on the premises. The park charges an entrance fee: $5 per car, $3 per walker or cyclist.

In Georgetown the **Georgetown Information Center,** 1057 Thomas Jefferson St. NW ((C) **202/653-5190**), can also provide maps and information. The center is open weekends, June through August 9:30am–4:30pm.

The park offers many opportunities for outdoor activities (see below), but if you or your family would prefer a less strenuous form of relaxation, consider the park's **mule-drawn 19th-century canalboat trip,** led by Park Service rangers in period dress. They regale passengers with canal legend and lore, and sing period songs. Georgetown barge rides have been suspended for the foreseeable future, but boats operate at Great Falls April 15 to October 31. Barge rides last about 1 hour and 10 minutes, and cost $8 per adult, $6 for seniors, $5 per child, and free for children 3 and under.

Check for special children's events at museum information desks when you enter. As noted within the listings for individual museums, some children's programs are also great fun for adults. I recommend the programs at the **Folger Shakespeare Library** (p. 93), the **Phillips Collection** (p. 142), and the **Sackler Gallery** (p. 117) in particular. (The gift shops in most of these museums have wonderful toys and children's books.) Call ahead to find out what programs are running. Here's a rundown of great kid-pleasers in town:

o **Madame Tussauds Washington D.C.** (p. 135): There are two kinds of people in this world: those who think wax museums are hokey, and children. Yeah, watch your offspring pretend to sing with Beyoncé, box with Evander Holyfield, stand tall next to George Washington, and whoop it up with Whoopi. Maybe you'll find your inner child and start loving these wax figures, too.

o **Discovery Theater, inside the S. Dillon Ripley Center** (p. 117):

Right next to the Smithsonian Castle is this underground children's theater that puts on live performing arts entertainment for the kiddies, about 30 productions each season, including puppet shows, storytelling, dances, and plays.

o **National Museum of Crime and Punishment** (p. 137): Your little darlings can pretend to be little Dillingers and test their safecracking skills, or little Elliot Nesses as they learn how to take fingerprints and gather clues. By 2014, the museum should have added a special exhibit geared specifically to children 4 and older. Can't tell you more than that, since I promised to keep a secret.

o **Newseum** (p. 138): Proceed directly to one of two areas: the interactive newsroom on the second floor, where your children will happily, endlessly play computer games while testing their news knowledge and journalism skills, and where they'll have the

Enter the towpath in Georgetown below M Street via Thomas Jefferson Street. If you hike 14 miles, you'll reach **Great Falls,** a point where the Potomac becomes a stunning waterfall plunging 76 feet.

Enter the towpath in Georgetown below M St. via Thomas Jefferson St. www.nps.gov/choh. © **301/767-3714.** Free admission. Daily during daylight hours. Metro: Foggy Bottom, with a 20-min. walk to the towpath in Georgetown.

Especially for Kids

As far as I know, Pierre L'Enfant and his successors were not thinking of children when they incorporated the long, open stretch of the Mall into their design for the city. But they may as well have been. This 2-mile expanse of lawn running from the Lincoln Memorial to the Capitol is a playground, really, and a backyard to the Smithsonian museums and National Gallery of Art, which border it. You can visit any of these sites assured that if one of your little darlings starts to misbehave, you'll be able to head right out the door to the National Mall, where numerous distractions await. Vendors sell ice cream, soft pretzels, and sodas. Festivals of all sorts take place on a regular basis, whether it's the busy **Smithsonian Folklife Festival** for 10 days at the end of chance to play an on-camera reporter; or to the New Media Gallery for similar activities.

o **Lincoln Memorial** (p. 106): Kids know a lot about Lincoln and enjoy visiting his memorial. A special treat is visiting after dark.

o **National Air and Space Museum** (p. 107): Spectacular IMAX films (don't miss), thrilling flight simulators, planetarium shows, missiles, rockets, and a walk-through orbital workshop.

o **National Museum of American History** (p. 113): Living-history performances and lively musical numbers staged in public areas throughout the museum switch a typical museum visit into something more fun and memorable. And the museum has gotten into simulators, offering rides on machines that make you believe you're driving a race car or riding on a roller coaster.

o **National Museum of the American Indian** (p. 114): Children, and their parents, too, enjoy themselves in the museum's imagiNATIONS Activity Center, where visitors learn basket weaving, kayak balancing, and other Native American skills, and play games to discover more about Indian culture.

o **National Museum of Natural History** (p. 115): A Discovery Room just for youngsters, the Butterfly Pavilion and exhibit, an insect zoo, shrunken heads, dinosaurs, and the IMAX theater showing 2-D and 3-D films.

o **National Zoological Park** (p. 145): Pandas! Cheetahs! Kids always love a zoo, and this is an especially good one.

o **Washington Monument** (p. 120): Spectacular 360-degree views from the center of Washington, D.C.—when the monument opens to the public again, which may not be until mid-2014.

June into July (see "Washington, D.C. Calendar of Events," in chapter 2), or the **Kite Festival** in spring. Weather permitting, a 19th-century carousel operates in front of the Arts and Industries Building, on the south side of the Mall. Right across the Mall from the carousel is the children-friendly National Gallery Sculpture Garden, whose shallow pool is good for splashing one's feet in summer and for ice-skating in winter.

The truth is that many of Washington's attractions hold various enchantments for children of all ages. It might be easier to point out which ones are not recommended for your youngest: the Supreme Court, the chambers of Congress, the U.S. Holocaust Memorial Museum, and the Marian Koshland Science Museum; the International Spy Museum is now recommending that its museum is most suitable for children 10 and over. Generally speaking, the bigger and busier the museum, the better it is for kids (see box below).

For more ideas, consult the online or print version of the Friday "Weekend" section of the *Washington Post,* which lists numerous activities (mostly free) for kids: special museum events, children's theater, storytelling programs, puppet shows, video-game competitions, and so forth. Call the Kennedy Center and the National Theatre to find out about children's shows; see chapter 8 for details.

Outdoor Activities

For information about spectator-sports venues, see chapter 8. But if you prefer to work up your own honest sweat, Washington offers plenty of pleasant opportunities in many lush surroundings. See "Parks," earlier in this chapter, for complete coverage of the city's loveliest green spaces.

BIKING

Biking is big in D.C., not just as a leisure activity but as an environmentally friendly form of transportation. So much of the city is flat, and paths are everywhere, notably around the National Mall and Memorial Parks. Rock Creek Park has an **11-mile paved bike route** ★ from the Lincoln Memorial through the park into Maryland. Or you can follow the bike path from the Lincoln Memorial and go over Memorial Bridge to pedal to Old Town Alexandria and on to Mount Vernon (see chapter 9). On weekends and holidays, a large part of Rock Creek Parkway is closed to vehicular traffic. The C&O Canal park's towpath, described in "Parks," earlier in this chapter, is a popular bike path. The **Capital Crescent Trail** takes you from Georgetown to the suburb of Bethesda, Maryland, following a former railroad track that parallels the Potomac River for part of the way and passes by old trestle bridges and pleasant residential neighborhoods. You can pick up the trail at the **Thompson Boat Center**, in Georgetown, and at **Fletcher's Cove**, along the C&O Canal; visit **www.cctrail.org** for maps and more information.

Bike rental locations include:

○ The **Boat House at Fletcher's Cove,** 4940 Canal Rd. NW (www.fletcherscove. com; ✆ **202/244-0461**).

○ **Bike and Roll/Bike the Sites** (www.bikethesites.com; ✆ **202/842-2453**), with three locations: 1100 Pennsylvania Ave. NW, at the rear plaza of the Old Post Office Pavilion (Metro: Federal Triangle, on the Blue and Orange lines); Union Station (✆ **202/962-0206**); or Old Town Alexandria, 1 Wales Alley, off of King Street at the waterfront (✆ **703/548-7655**). Bike and Roll is best known for its Bike the Sites guided tours (see p. 244), but also rents bikes. Rates vary depending on the bike you choose but always include helmet, bike, lock, and pump; there's a 2-hour minimum. Note: The Union Station location is the only year-round operation; The Old Post Office Pavilion and Old Town Alexandria locations close in late November until early March.

○ **Thompson Boat Center,** 2900 Virginia Ave. NW, at Rock Creek Parkway (www. thompsonboatcenter.com; ✆ **202/333-9543**; Metro: Foggy Bottom, with a 10-min. walk). Both Fletcher's and Thompson rent bikes, weather permitting, from about mid-March to mid-October.

○ **Big Wheel Bikes,** 1034 33rd St. NW, right near the C&O Canal just below M Street (www.bigwheelbikes.com; ✆ **202/337-0254**). You can rent a bike here year-round Tuesday through Sunday.

BOATING & FISHING

Look to the same places that rent bikes for rental boats: **Thompson Boat Center** and the **Boat House at Fletcher's Cove** (see above for both); they follow the same schedule as their bike rental season, basically March to November. Thompson has canoes, kayaks, and rowing shells (recreational and racing), and is open for boat and bike rentals daily in season from (generally) 7am to 7pm. Fletcher's is right on the C&O Canal, about 3¼ miles from Georgetown. In addition to renting bikes, canoes, rowboats, and kayaks, Fletcher's also sells fishing licenses, bait, and tackle. Open daily 7am to 7pm in season, Fletcher's is accessible by car (west on M St. NW to Canal Rd. NW) and has plenty of free parking.

Key Bridge Boathouse, 3500 K St. NW (www.keybridgeboathouse.com; ☏ 202/337-9642), located along the Georgetown waterfront beneath Key Bridge, is open daily mid-April to October (check website for hours) for canoe and kayak rentals. Foggy Bottom is the closest Metro station.

From mid-March to mid-October, weather permitting, you can rent **paddle boats** ★ on the north end of the Tidal Basin off Independence Avenue (www.tidalbasinpaddle boats.com; ☏ **202/479-2426**). Four-seaters are $19 an hour, two-seaters $12 an hour, from 10am to 6pm daily mid-March to Labor Day, Wednesday to Sunday Labor Day to mid-October.

GOLF

The District's best and most convenient public golf course is the historic **East Potomac Golf Course** on Hains Point, 972 Ohio Dr. SW, in East Potomac Park (www. golfdc.com; ☏ **202/554-7660**). Golfers use the Washington Monument to help them line up their shots. The club rents everything but shoes. In addition to its year-round 36-hole green, the park offers a miniature golf course; open since 1930, this is the oldest continually operating miniature golf course in the country.

HIKING & JOGGING

Joggers can enjoy a run on the Mall or along the path in Rock Creek Park.

Washington has numerous **hiking paths.** The C&O Canal offers 185 miles stretching from D.C. to Cumberland, Maryland; hiking any section of the flat dirt towpath or its more rugged side paths is a pleasure (and it's free). There are picnic tables, some with barbecue grills, about every 5 miles on the way to Cumberland. Theodore Roosevelt Island has more than 88 wilderness acres to explore, and Rock Creek Park boasts 20 miles of hiking trails (visit www.nps.gov/rocr/planyourvisit/brochures.htm for maps).

ICE-SKATING

Georgetown's waterfront complex, **The Washington Harbour,** at 3050 K St. NW (☏ 202/706-7666; www.thewashingtonharbour.com/skating), opened an ice rink in 2012 that, at 11,800 square feet, is the largest outdoor skating venue in the city. (The view of the Potomac River ain't bad either.) The season runs November to March, and the rink is open Monday through Thursday noon to 9pm, Friday noon to 10pm, Saturday 10am to 10pm, and Sunday 10am to 7pm.

For a truly memorable experience, head to the **National Gallery Sculpture Garden Ice Rink** ★, on the Mall at 7th Street and Constitution Avenue NW (☏ **202/289-3360**), where you can rent skates, twirl in view of the sculptures, and enjoy hot chocolate in the Pavilion Café next to the rink.

SWIMMING

If it's summer and your hotel doesn't have a **pool,** you might consider one of the neighborhood pools, including a large outdoor pool at 25th and N streets NW (☏ **202/727-3285**) and the Georgetown outdoor pool at 34th Street and Volta Place NW (☏ **202/645-5669**). Keep in mind that these are likely to be crowded.

One of the best places open to the public for swimming in summer and for other outdoor sports year-round is East Potomac Park's **Hains Point,** which lies within walking distance of Independence Avenue and has a large outdoor swimming pool (✆ **202/727-6523**; http://app.dpr.dc.gov/dprmap/details.asp?cid=14).

TENNIS

Hains Point also has 24 tennis courts (10 clay, 9 outdoor hard courts, and 5 indoor hard courts), including three illuminated at night; the park rents rackets as well; contact East Potomac Park Tennis (www.eastpotomactennis.com; ✆ **202/554-5962**). Fees vary with court surface and time of play.

Finally, one other tennis option: **Montrose Park,** right next to Dumbarton Oaks (p. 148), in Georgetown, has several courts available free on a first-come, first-served basis, but they're often in use.

SHOPPING

Washington, D.C.'s shopping scene is thriving, thanks to the city's strong economy. With its low unemployment rate, high-income population, and vigorous spending statistics for both visitors and residents, Washington continues to attract major retailers to open stores here, with the Apple Store in Georgetown (p. 168) and a new Anthropologie store in the Penn Quarter (p. 171) among the latest enticing additions. Local entrepreneurs, meanwhile, are doing quite nicely, at long-established stores, like The Phoenix (p. 168) in Georgetown, and in newer boutiques, like Hill's Kitchen (p. 174) on Capitol Hill. Wherever you are in the city, shops present a variety of wares, prices, and styles. This chapter leads you to some of the best.

THE SHOPPING SCENE

Most Washington-area stores are open from 10am to 5 or 6pm Monday through Saturday. Sunday hours tend to vary, with some stores opting not to open at all and others with shorter hours of noon to 5 or 6pm. Two neighborhoods prove the exception to these rules: Many stores in the Penn Quarter and in Georgetown keep later hours and are also open on Sunday. Other exceptions include suburban shopping malls, which are open late nightly, and antiques stores and art galleries, which tend to keep their own hours.

Sales tax on merchandise is 6% in the District, 6% in Maryland, and 5% in Virginia. Most gift, arts, and crafts stores, including those at the Smithsonian museums, will handle shipping for you; clothing stores generally do not.

GREAT SHOPPING AREAS

UNION STATION   It's a railroad station, a historic landmark, an architectural marvel, a Metro stop, and a shopping mall. Yes, the beauteous Union Station offers some fine shopping opportunities; it's certainly the best on Capitol Hill, with more than 100 clothes, specialty, and souvenir shops, and more than 40 eateries. **Metro:** Union Station.

PENN QUARTER   The area bounded east and west by 7th and 14th streets NW, and north and south by New York and Pennsylvania avenues NW, continues to develop as a central shopping area, despite the economic crisis. Look for a long list of "name" stores, including Urban Outfitters, Bed, Bath & Beyond, Banana Republic, H&M, Forever 21, Zara, and, by the time you read this, my personal favorite, Anthropologie (950 F St. NW; see Fashion section, p. 170). One-of-a-kind places include museum shops at the National Building Museum, the Smithsonian American Art Museum and Portrait Gallery, and the International Spy Museum; and the delightful jewelry store,

Mia Gemma (p. 175). Macy's (formerly "Hecht's"), at 12th and G streets, continues as the sole department store downtown. **Metro:** Metro Center, Gallery Place–Chinatown, or Archives–Navy Memorial.

ADAMS MORGAN Centered on 18th Street and Columbia Road NW, Adams Morgan is a neighborhood of ethnic eateries and nightclubs interspersed with the odd secondhand bookshop and eclectic collectibles stores. It's a fun area for walking and shopping. Parking is possible during the day but impossible at night. For the closest **Metro,** you have a few choices: Woodley Park–Zoo/Adams Morgan, then walk south on Connecticut Avenue NW until you reach Calvert Street, cross Connecticut Avenue, and follow Calvert Street across the Duke Ellington Memorial Bridge until you reach the junction of Columbia Road NW and 18th Street NW. Second choice: Dupont Circle; exit at Q Street NW and walk up Connecticut Avenue NW to Columbia Road NW. Best bet: the D.C. Circulator bus, which runs between the McPherson Square and the Woodley Park–Zoo/Adams Morgan Metro stations.

CONNECTICUT AVENUE/DUPONT CIRCLE Running from K Street north to S Street, Connecticut Avenue NW is a main thoroughfare, where you'll find traditional clothing at Brooks Brothers, Ann Taylor, and Burberry's; casual duds at Gap; and haute couture at Rizik's. Closer to Dupont Circle are coffee bars and neighborhood restaurants, as well as art galleries; funky boutiques; gift, stationery, and book shops; and stores with a gay and lesbian slant. **Metro:** Farragut North at one end, Dupont Circle at the other.

U STREET CORRIDOR/14TH STREET Urbanistas have been promoting this neighborhood for years, but now the number of cool shops, restaurants, and bars has hit the critical mass mark, winning the area widespread notice. If you shun brand names and box stores, you'll love the vintage boutiques and affordable fashion shops along U and 14th streets. Look for provocative handles, like Pulp, then step inside to inspect their equally intriguing merchandise. **Metro:** U Street/African American Civil War Memorial/Cardozo.

GEORGETOWN Georgetown is the city's main shopping area. Most of the stores sit on the two main, intersecting streets, Wisconsin Avenue and M Street NW. (For a tour of Georgetown that combines historic houses, shopping, and dining, see "The Roads Less Traveled" box on p. 164.) You'll find both chain and one-of-a-kind shops, chic as well as thrift. Sidewalks and streets are almost always crowded, and parking can be tough. Weekends, especially, bring out all kinds of yahoos, who are mainly here to drink. Visit Georgetown on a weekday morning, if you can. Weeknights are another good time to visit, for dinner and strolling afterward. **Metro:** Foggy Bottom, then catch the D.C. Circulator bus from the stop at 22nd Street and Pennsylvania Avenue (see p. 240 for more information). Metro buses (the no. 30 series) travel through Georgetown from different parts of the city. Otherwise, consider taking a taxi. If you drive, you'll find parking lots expensive and tickets even more so, so be careful where you plant your car.

UPPER WISCONSIN AVENUE NORTHWEST In a residential section of town known as Friendship Heights on the D.C. side and Chevy Chase on the Maryland side (7 miles north of Georgetown, straight up Wisconsin Ave.) is a quarter-mile shopping district that extends from Saks Fifth Avenue at one end to Sur La Table at the other. In between are Lord & Taylor, Neiman Marcus, Bloomingdale's, and Versace (to name just a few stores), and three malls (the Mazza Gallerie, Chevy Chase Pavilion, and the Shops at Wisconsin Place). The street is too wide and traffic always too snarled to make this a pleasant place to stroll, although teenagers do love to loiter here. Drive if you want and park in the garages beneath the Mazza Gallerie, Chevy Chase Pavilion, or Bloomingdale's. Or take the **Metro;** the strip is right on the Red Line, with the "Friendship Heights" exits leading directly into each of the malls.

OLD TOWN ALEXANDRIA   Old Town, a Virginia neighborhood beyond National Airport, resembles Georgetown in its picturesque location on the Potomac, historic-home-lined streets, and plentiful shops and restaurants, as well as in its less desirable aspects: heavy traffic, crowded sidewalks, difficult parking. Old Town extends from the Potomac River in the east to the King Street Metro station in the west, and from about 1st Street in the north to Green Street in the south, but the best shopping is in the center, where King and Washington streets intersect. Weekdays are a lot tamer than weekends. It's always a nice place to visit, though; the drive alone is worth the trip. See chapter 9 for full coverage of Alexandria. **Metro:** King Street, then take a free King Street Trolley to reach the heart of Old Town.

SHOPPING A TO Z
Antiques

Georgetown has a concentration of great antiques stores, with other neighborhoods claiming the outliers.

Brass Knob Architectural Antiques ★   When old homes and office buildings are demolished in the name of progress, these savvy salvage merchants spirit away salable treasures, from lots and lots of light fixtures and chandelier glass to wrought-iron fencing. 2311 18th St. NW. ℭ **202/332-3370.** www.thebrassknob.com. Metro: Woodley Park or Dupont Circle.

Cote Jardin Antiques ★★   This very pretty shop just off busy Wisconsin Avenue specializes in 18th- and 19th-century French formal and country antique home furnishings and late 19th/early 20th antique French garden ornaments and furniture. 3218 O St. NW. ℭ **800/505-3067.** www.cotejardinantiques.com. Metro: Foggy Bottom, then take the D.C. Circulator.

The French Apartment ★   The inventory housed in this mid-19th-century town house changes weekly but always offers a mix of antique early-20th-century vintage and modern French and French-influenced home furnishings. 1671 Wisconsin Ave. NW. ℭ **202/625-9199.** www.thefrenchapartment.com. Metro: Foggy Bottom, then take the D.C. Circulator.

Marston-Luce ★   Stop in here at least to admire, if not buy, a beautiful 18th- or 19th-century French furnishing or two. 1651 Wisconsin Ave. NW. ℭ **202/333-6800.** www.marstonluce.com. Metro: Foggy Bottom, then take the D.C. Circulator.

Millennium Decorative Arts ★★   This is antiques shopping for the TV genera-tion, where anything made between the 1930s and the 1970s is considered collectible. The shop works with nearly a score or so of dealers; stock changes weekly. Funky wares run from Bakelite to Heywood-Wakefield blond-wood beauties to toasters to used drinking glasses. 1528 U St. NW. ℭ **202/483-1218.** www.millenniumdecorativearts.com. Metro: U St./Cardozo (13th St. exit).

Old Print Gallery ★★★   Open since 1971, this gallery carries original American and European prints from the 17th to the 19th century, including political cartoons, maps, and historical documents. It's one of the largest antique print and map shops in

THE ROADS LESS TRAVELED: A BACK-STREET TOUR OF historic georgetown, WITH STOPS AT SHOPS

Most people who visit Georgetown never get off the beaten track of the M Street/lower Wisconsin Avenue axis. Too bad for them, but good for you: While they bump into each other in the crowded bottom of Georgetown, you can tour the lovely, quiet streets in upper Georgetown, where a number of historic houses and beautiful gardens lie close to fun boutiques and delectable cafes.

Tudor Place, Dumbarton House, and the garden at Dumbarton Oaks are open for tours, but not all day, every day, so call for hours if you want to incorporate house and garden tours into your back-street stroll; please note that all other houses on the tour are privately owned and not open to the public.

From the corner of Q Street and Wisconsin Avenue (a stop on the D.C. Circulator's Wisconsin Ave. line), walk east along Q Street to 31st Street and take a left on 31st Street to **Tudor Place** (© 202/965-0400), an 1816 mansion and gardens where Martha Washington's descendants lived until 1984. From Tudor Place, return to Q Street and walk

farther east to **Dumbarton House** (© 202/337-2288), a Federal-style mansion built in 1805 and filled with 18th- and 19th-century furnishings and decorative arts.

Retrace your steps as far as 28th Street and proceed north on 28th Street, stopping to admire the 18th-century estate **Evermay,** built by a Scottish merchant, as you continue on your way to **Dumbarton Oaks Museum and Gardens** (© 202/339-6401; p. 148) at 31st and R streets. From the gardens, walk westward on R Street to Wisconsin Avenue, passing en route **3238 R St. NW,** an early-19th-century Federal brick building once used as a summer White House by President Ulysses S. Grant—its high elevation made it cooler than 1600 Pennsylvania Ave.

You have now reached Wisconsin Avenue, just a little farther north of the hustle-bustle, but a sweet spot for shopping at one-of-a-kind shops and for enjoying a scrumptious repast. Turn south on Wisconsin Avenue to find Italian and French home and garden acces-

the United States. Prices range from $45 to $10,000. 1220 31st St. NW. © **202/965-1818.** www.oldprintgallery.com. Metro: Foggy Bottom, then take the D.C. Circulator.

Susquehanna Antiques ★★ This is Georgetown's largest collection of fine American, English, and European furniture, paintings, and garden items of the late 18th and early 19th centuries. The shop turns 100 in 2013. 3216 O St. NW. © **202/333-1511.** www.susquehannaantiques.com. Metro: Foggy Bottom, then take the D.C. Circulator.

Art Galleries

Art galleries used to center on the Dupont Circle neighborhood but now are scattered throughout the city. The following are among the best and most interesting.

Addison/Ripley Fine Art ★ This gallery represents internationally, nationally, and regionally recognized artists, from the 19th century to the present; works include paintings, sculpture, photography, and fine arts. 1670 Wisconsin Ave. NW (Reservoir Rd.). © **202/338-5180.** www.addisonripleyfineart.com. Metro: Foggy Bottom, then take the D.C. Circulator.

sories at **A Mano**
((☏ **202/298-7200**), and a variety of
women's trendy clothing boutiques at
Sassanova ((☏ **202/471-4400**), **Sherman
Pickey** ((☏ **202/333-4212**), and, across
the street, **Urban Chic** ((☏ **202/338-
5398**). For refreshment, cross back to the
other side to find (no. 1645): **Patisserie
Poupon** ((☏ **202/342-3248**)—I highly
recommend that you pause for a ham-
and-cheese sandwich and, *absolument,*
for a pastry dessert: Choose from tarts,
éclairs, individual little cakes, and chocolate in all its forms.

Cross Wisconsin Avenue to continue
your tour on the other side. Walk south
on Wisconsin Avenue to N Street and
turn right, following the street to **no.
3307,** the brick town house where John
and Jacqueline Kennedy lived when
Kennedy was a U.S. senator. In the same
block, a few houses up at **nos. 3327–
3339,** are five charming houses known
collectively as **"Cox's Row,"** for owner
John Cox, who built the dwellings in
1817. Cox, who was the first elected
mayor of Georgetown, lived at no. 3339;

Revolutionary War hero the Marquis de
Lafayette stayed at no. 3337 on a visit in
1824. Follow N Street to 36th Street, and
turn left and again left on Prospect
Street to reach **Prospect House,** at no.
3508. This restored Georgian-style house
was built in 1788 by Revolutionary War
hero and wealthy tobacco merchant
James McCubbin Lingan; the house, like
the street, was named for the views one
once had here of the Potomac River.
From here, it's a short stroll to **Halcyon
House,** at 3400 Prospect St., whose original owner, Benjamin Stoddert, was a
Revolutionary War cavalry officer and first
secretary of the Navy. Two hundred years
ago, the Potomac River lapped right up
to Stoddert's terraced garden, designed
by Pierre L'Enfant.

If you still have some energy left, finish the tour by visiting a perennial Washington hot spot, the **Cafe Milano,** 3251
Prospect St. NW ((☏ **202/333-6183**).
Then go home knowing that you've seen
more of the "real" Georgetown than
most Washingtonians.

Burton Marinkovich Fine Art ★★   One of the city's leading art galleries,
this one showcases fine prints, drawings, and paintings by modern and contemporary international artists, including Jim Dine, Alexander Calder, and Helen Frankenthaler. 1506 21st St. NW (P St.). ☏ **202/296-6563.** www.burtonmarinkovich.com. Metro:
Dupont Circle (19th St. exit).

Flashpoint ★   Flashpoint is a dance studio, theater lab, office space, and art gallery
all in one. Its art gallery is dedicated to nurturing emerging local artists, who tend to
use a variety of mediums, including video, sculpture, photography, and drawings to tell
their personal stories. 916 G St. NW (9th St.). ☏ **202/315-1305.** www.flashpointdc.org. Metro:
Gallery Place (9th and G sts. exit).

Foundry Gallery ★   In business since 1971, this gallery is artist-owned and -oper-
ated and features the works of local artists, who work in various media and styles, from
abstract painting on silk, to mixed-media collages. 1314 18th St. NW (Massachusetts Ave.).
☏ **202/463-0203.** www.foundrygallery.org. Metro: Dupont Circle (19th St. exit).

Govinda Gallery ★   This place, a block from the campus of Georgetown University, generates a lot of media coverage because it often shows artwork created by famous names and features photographs of celebrities, also pop and contemporary art. 1227 34th St. NW (Prospect St.). © **202/333-1180.** www.govindagallery.com. Metro: Foggy Bottom, then take the D.C. Circulator.

Hillyer Art Space ★   This hip little two-room gallery lies in an alley behind the Phillips Collection. Its shows of contemporary art fulfill its mission to "increase cross-cultural understanding and exposure to the arts internationally." Hillyer hosts monthly events that draw social 20-somethings. 9 Hillyer Court NW (21st St.). © **202/338-0680.** www.artsandartists.org/hillyer.html. Metro: Dupont Circle (Q St. exit).

Studio Gallery ★   This artist-owned gallery—the longest-running of its kind in the area—shows the works of some 30 local and professional artists, fine arts in all mediums. Don't miss the sculpture garden. Open Wednesday through Saturday. 2108 R St. NW (20th St.). © **202/232-8734.** www.studiogallerydc.com. Metro: Dupont Circle (Q St. exit).

Susan Calloway Fine Arts ★   On display are antique European and American oil paintings; contemporary art by local, regional, and international artists; and a carefully chosen selection of 17th- to 19th-century prints. 1643 Wisconsin Ave. NW (Q St.). © **202/965-4601.** www.callowayart.com. Metro: Foggy Bottom, then take the D.C. Circulator.

Beauty

The city's best hair salons and cosmetic stores are in Georgetown, while spas are more evenly scattered throughout the city. Here's a sampling of recommended places to go for beauty treatments and products.

Aveda Georgetown Salon and Spa ★   If your hotel doesn't have a hair salon or spa, visit this ultracool, one-stop spot for top to bottom renewal. Hair care, Swedish massage, and beauty treatments are available for men and women. Waxing, facials, pedicures, the works. 1325 Wisconsin Ave. NW. © **202/965-1325.** www.avedageorgetown.com. Metro: Foggy Bottom, then take the D.C. Circulator.

Beauty 360   CVS pharmacies are known as drugstores, mainly, where you can buy all your essentials, from candy to cold medicine. With the launching of Beauty 360 (D.C.'s was the first to open), CVS ventures into the high-end cosmetics and skin treatment market. Trained and licensed professionals provide signature services including minimanicures and express facials, while trying to interest you in buying, say, Juicy Couture fragrance, Paula Dorf makeup, or Payot skincare items. A regular old CVS lies just around the corner, if you need something not quite so chi-chi. 1350 Connecticut Ave. NW (Dupont Circle). © **202/331-1725.** www.beauty360.com. Metro: Dupont Circle (19th St. exit).

Blue Mercury   Half "apothecary," half spa, this chain's two D.C. locations offer a full selection of facial, massage, waxing, and makeup treatments, as well as a smorgasbord of high-end beauty products, from Acqua di Parma fragrances to Kiehl's skincare line. Very popular, so you might want to call before your trip. Georgetown: 3059 M St. NW. © **202/965-1300.** Metro: Foggy Bottom, then take the D.C. Circulator. Dupont Circle: 1619 Connecticut Ave. NW (© **202/462-1300)** and 1145 Connecticut Ave. NW (© **202/628-5567).** Metro: Dupont Circle (Q St. exit). www.bluemercury.com.

The Grooming Lounge   Not your father's barbershop. Famous for its 30-minute "hot lather shave," the Grooming Lounge also dispenses treatments with names like "the Commander in Chief" and sells beauty accessories, um, I mean, grooming tools, from nail clippers to special shaving brushes. Or you can just get a haircut. 1745 L St. NW. © **202/466-8900.** www.groominglounge.com. Metro: Farragut North (L St. exit).

Violet Hair and Skin Care A favorite of both men and women, especially those in media and politics, who like the owners' expertise in coloring and cuts. White wine and tea on hand help put you at ease. 1513 Wisconsin Ave. NW. © **202/337-3477.** www. violetsalondc.com. Metro: Foggy Bottom, then take the D.C. Circulator.

Books

Real-live bookstores still have their fans. Here are some favorite shops in general, used, and special-interest categories.

GENERAL

Barnes & Noble ★★★ This three-story shop in Georgetown is remarkably well stocked in all genres, including sizable software, travel-book, children's-title, and music sections. The store has a cafe on the second level. 3040 M St. NW. www.bn.com. © **202/965-9880.** Metro: Foggy Bottom, then take the D.C. Circulator. Other area locations include 555 12th St. NW (© **202/347-0176**), Union Station (© **202/289-1724),** and 4801 Bethesda Ave. in Bethesda, MD (© **301/986-1761**).

Books A Million ★★ A friendly staff, excellent and unusual gift items and, of course, tons of books makes this store a go-to choice in the Dupont Circle area. 11 Dupont Circle NW; © **202/319-1374.** Metro: Dupont Circle.

Bridge Street Books ★ A small, serious shop specializing in politics, poetry, literature, history, philosophy, and publications you won't find elsewhere. Bestsellers and discounted books are not its specialty. Get a taste by going to the store's website, which is really its blog: www.bridgestreetbooks.com. 2814 Pennsylvania Ave. NW (next to the Four Seasons Hotel). © **202/965-5200.** Metro: Foggy Bottom, then take the D.C. Circulator.

Kramerbooks & Afterwords Café ★★★ Opened in 1976, Kramer's was the first bookstore/cafe in Washington, maybe in this country, and has launched countless romances. It's jammed, is often noisy, stages live music Wednesday through Saturday evenings, and is open all night weekends. Paperback fiction takes up most of its inventory, but the store carries a little of everything. 1517 Connecticut Ave. NW. © **202/387-1400** or 387-3825 for information. www.kramers.com. Metro: Dupont Circle (Q St. exit).

Politics and Prose Bookstore ★★★ Located a few miles north of downtown in a residential area, this much-cherished two-story shop may be worth going out of your way for. It has vast offerings in literary fiction and nonfiction alike and an excellent children's department. The store has expanded again and again over the years to accommodate its clientele's love of books; its most recent enlargement added to the travel and children's sections. The shop hosts author readings nearly every night of the year. A warm, knowledgeable staff will help you find what you need. Downstairs is a cozy coffeehouse. 5015 Connecticut Ave. NW. © **202/364-1919.** www.politics-prose.com. Metro: Van Ness–UDC, and walk, or transfer to an "L" bus to take you the ¾ mile from there.

Reiter's Bookstore ★ Open since 1936, this is D.C.'s oldest independent bookstore. Located in the middle of the George Washington University campus, Reiter's is the go-to place for scientific, technical, medical, and professional books. The store is also known for its intriguing, sometimes amusing, mathematical and scientific toys in the children's section. 1900 G St. NW. (19th St.) © **202/223-3327.** www.reiters.com. Metro: Foggy Bottom.

OLD & USED BOOKS

Second Story Books   If it's old, out of print, custom bound, or a small-press publication, this is where to find it. The store also specializes in used CDs and vinyl and has an interesting collection of campaign posters. 2000 P St. NW. ℂ **202/659-8884.** www.secondstorybooks.com. Metro: Dupont Circle (South/19th St. exit).

7 Cameras & Computers

Apple Store ★   Macs, iPads, iPhones, iPods, iTunes, iTouches. All of them for sale here. Come to hang out and fool around on the floor samples, to check out the merchandise, and to get your questions answered by techy geeks roaming the room. 1229 Wisconsin Ave. NW. ℂ **202/572-1460.** www.apple.com/retail/georgetown. Metro: Foggy Bottom, then take the D.C. Circulator.

Penn Camera Exchange ★★   Penn Camera has been owned and operated by the Zweig family since 1953; its staff is quite knowledgeable, and its inventory wide-ranging. Their specialty is quality equipment and archival paper processing—not cheap, but worth it. 840 E St. NW. ℂ **202/347-5777.** www.penncamera.com. Metro: Gallery Place (9th and G sts. exit). Also at 1015 18th St. NW (ℂ **202/785-7366**).

Crafts

A Mano ★★★   Owner Adam Mahr frequently forages in Europe and returns with the unique handmade French and Italian ceramics, linens, and other decorative accessories for home and garden that you'll covet here. 1677 Wisconsin Ave. NW. ℂ **202/298-7200.** www.amano.bz. Metro: Foggy Bottom, then take the D.C. Circulator

Appalachian Spring ★   Country comes to Georgetown. This store sells pottery, jewelry, newly made pieced and appliqué quilts, stuffed dolls and animals, candles, rag rugs, handblown glassware, an incredible collection of kaleidoscopes, glorious weavings, and wooden kitchenware. Everything is made by hand in the United States. 1415 Wisconsin Ave. NW (at P St.). ℂ **202/337-5780.** www.appalachianspring.com. Metro: Foggy Bottom, then take the D.C. Circulator. There's another branch in Union Station (ℂ **202/682-0505**).

Indian Craft Shop ★★   The Indian Craft Shop has represented authentic Native American artisans since 1938, selling their handwoven rugs and handcrafted baskets, jewelry, figurines, pottery, and other items. Since the shop is situated inside a federal government building, you must pass through security and show a photo ID to enter. Use the C Street entrance, which is the only one open to the public. The shop is open weekdays and the third Saturday of each month. Department of the Interior, 1849 C St. NW, Room 1023. ℂ **202/208-4056**. www.indiancraftshop.com. Metro: Farragut West (17th St. exit), with a bit of a walk from the station.

The Phoenix ★   Around since 1955, the Phoenix sells high-end Mexican folk and fine art; handcrafted sterling silver jewelry from Mexico and all over the world; clothing in natural fibers from Mexican and American designers like Eileen Fisher and Flax; collectors' quality masks; and decorative doodads in tin, brass, copper, and wood. Oaxaca folk and fine art are a specialty. 1514 Wisconsin Ave. NW. ℂ **202/338-4404.** www.thephoenixdc.com. Metro: Foggy Bottom, then take the D.C. Circulator.

Torpedo Factory Art Center ★★★   Once a munitions factory, this three-story building built in 1918 now houses more than 82 working studios and the works of about 165 artists, who tend to their crafts before your very eyes, pausing to explain their techniques or to sell their pieces. Artworks include paintings, sculpture, ceramics, glasswork, and textiles. 105 N. Union St., Alexandria, VA. ℂ **703/838-4565.** www.torpedo

factory.org. Metro: King St., then take the free King Street Trolley or the DASH bus (AT2, AT5) eastbound to the waterfront.

Farmers' & Flea Markets

Alexandria Farmers' Market ★ The oldest continuously operating farmers' market in the country (since 1752), this market offers locally grown fruits and vegetables, along with delectable baked goods, cut flowers, and plants. Open year-round, Saturday mornings from 5:30 to 11am. 301 King St. (at Market Square in front of the city hall), in Alexandria, VA. ✆ **703/746-3200.** www.alexandriava.gov/market. Metro: King St., then take the free King Street Trolley or the DASH bus (AT2, AT5) eastbound to Market Sq.

Dupont Circle FreshFarm Market ★ At least 30 local farmers sell their flowers, produce, eggs, and cheeses here. The market also features kids' activities and guest appearances by chefs and owners of some of Washington's best restaurants: Vidalia, Zaytinya, Bis, and 1789. Held Sundays rain or shine, year-round, from 10am to 1pm January through March and 9am to 1pm the rest of the year. The FreshFarm Market organization stages other farmers' markets on other days around town; go to the website for locations, dates, and times. On 20th St. NW (btw. Q St. and Massachusetts Ave.) and in the adjacent PNC Bank parking lot. ✆ **202/362-8889.** www.freshfarmmarkets.org. Metro: Dupont Circle (Q St. exit).

Eastern Market ★★★ Finally reopened in July 2009 after a devastating fire in April 2007 gutted this Capitol Hill institution, historic Eastern Market can still claim that it has been in continuous operation since 1873: The indoor vendors set up stands across the street in temporary quarters and the outdoor farmers' market stalls remained open throughout, selling fresh produce and other goods on Saturdays and flea market items on Sundays. Today Eastern Market's restored South Hall is once again a bustling bazaar, where area farmers, greengrocers, bakers, butchers, and others sell their wares Tuesday through Sunday, joined by a second line of farmers outside on the weekend, as well as 100 or so local artisans hawking jewelry, paintings, pottery, woodwork, and other handmade items. Best of all is the Saturday morning ritual of breakfasting on blueberry pancakes at the Market Lunch counter. The market is open 7am to 6pm, Sunday 9am to 5pm (call for other days and times of operations). 225 7th St. SE (North Carolina Ave.). ✆ **202/698-5253.** www.easternmarket-dc.org. Metro: Eastern Market.

Montgomery County Farm Woman's Cooperative Market ★ Vendors set up inside every Wednesday, Friday, and Saturday year-round from 8am to about 4pm to sell preserves, homegrown veggies, cut flowers, slabs of bacon and sausages, and mouthwatering pies, cookies, and breads; there's an abbreviated version on Wednesday. Outside, on Saturday, Sunday, Wednesday, and Friday, from 8am to 4pm you'll find flea market vendors selling everything from rugs to tablecloths to furniture to sunglasses. 7155 Wisconsin Ave., in Bethesda, MD. ✆ **301/652-2291.** Metro: Bethesda.

Union Market ★★★ Worth a detour from sightseeing is this year-round, indoor market, whose vendors are called artisans and whose offerings include pop-up marketers hawking their particular specialty, like small-batch pickles. Since it debuted in September 2012, Washingtonians have been turning up in droves. Open Wednesday to Friday 11am-8pm, Saturday and Sunday 8am to 8pm, the market promotes itself as a "one-stop shopping" experience. At least 40 vendors set up in stalls or at counters selling fresh produce, flowers, cheeses, artworks—everything from olive oil to oysters. Stop by Salt & Sundry for lovely handcrafted gifts; visit on the first Saturday of the month to enjoy a gospel choir brunch. 1309 Fifth St. NE. www.unionmarketdc.com. Metro: NoMA-Gallaudet-U St.

Fashion

See also "Shoes," later in this section.

MEN'S CLOTHING

Local branches of **Banana Republic** are at Wisconsin and M streets in Georgetown (✆ 202/333-2554) and F and 13th streets NW (✆ 202/638-2724); **Gap** has several locations in Washington, including 1120 Connecticut Ave. NW (✆ 202/429-0691) and 1258 Wisconsin Ave. NW (✆ 202/333-2657). Also see "Vintage Shops" category.

Brooks Brothers   Brooks sells traditional men's clothes, as well as the fine line of Peal & Company Collection shoes. It also sells an extensive line of women's clothes. A Brooks Brothers store is expected to open in Georgetown at 3077 M St. NW, but call one of these other locations first to confirm. 1201 Connecticut Ave. NW. ✆ **202/659-4650.** www.brooksbrothers.com. Metro: Dupont Circle (19th St./Q St. exit) or Farragut North (L St. exit). Other locations are at National Airport (✆ **703/417-1071**), at 3077 M. St. NW (✆ **202/298-8797**) and at 5504 Wisconsin Ave. in Chevy Chase, MD (✆ **301/654-8202**).

Burberry's   Here you'll find those plaid-lined trench coats, of course, along with well-tailored English clothing for men and women. Hot items include cashmere sweaters and camel's hair duffel coats for men. 1155 Connecticut Ave. NW. ✆ **202/463-3000.** www.burberry.com. Metro: Farragut North (L St. exit).

Jos. A. Bank Clothiers   If you admire the Brooks Brothers line, but only wish it were more affordable, look here. This century-old clothier sells suits, corporate casual, weekend casual, and formal attire at great prices (lots of "buy one, get one free" offers). Union Station. ✆ **202/289-9087.** www.josbank.com. Metro: Union Station. Four other locations: Lincoln Square, 555 11th St. NW (✆ **202/393-5590**), 1200 19th St. NW (✆ **202/466-2282**), 1401 I St. NW (✆ **202/898-0372**), and at National Airport (✆ **703/418-8180**).

Sherman Pickey   This store is prep to the max, but also a little fey: Think red corduroys. Both men's and women's clothes are on sale here, including Bill's Khakis and Barbour Outerwear for men, embroidered capris and ribbon belts for women. 1647 Wisconsin Ave. NW. ✆ **202/333-4212.** www.shermanpickey.com. Metro: Foggy Bottom, then take the D.C. Circulator.

Thomas Pink   A 2011 expansion inside the Mayflower Hotel means that this branch of the London-based high-end establishment has even more beautifully made, bright-colored shirts on offer, along with ties, boxer shorts, women's shirts, cuff links, and other accessories. 1127 Connecticut Ave. NW (inside the Mayflower Hotel). ✆ **202/223-5390.** www.thomaspink.com. Metro: Farragut North (L St. exit).

Urban Outfitters   For the latest in casual attire, from fatigue pants to tube tops. The shop has a floor of women's clothes and a floor of men's clothes, as well as apartment wares, travel books, and accessories, cards, and candles. 3111 M St. NW. ✆ **202/342-1012.** www.urbanoutfitters.com. Metro: Foggy Bottom, then take the D.C. Circulator. 2nd location: Gallery Place, 737 7th St. NW. ✆ **202/737-0259.** Metro: Gallery Place (7th and H sts. exit).

VINTAGE SHOPS

Meeps Vintage Fashionette   This pioneer shop opened on U Street, but has since moved around the corner to lower Adams Morgan; its clientele and inventory remain the same: men and women urbanistas attracted to local designer ware and vintage clothes, from 1930s gabardine suits to 1950s cocktail dresses to satiny lingerie. 2104 18th St. NW (℅ **202/265-6546**. www.meepsdc.com. Metro: U St./Cardozo (13th St. exit) or Woodley Park–Zoo, with a bit of a walk from either station.

Secondhand Rose This upscale second-floor consignment shop has been around for 30 years, specializing in designer merchandise. Creations by Chanel, Armani, Donna Karan, Calvin Klein, Yves Saint-Laurent, Ungaro, Ralph Lauren, and others are sold at about a third of the original price. Everything is in style, in season, and in excellent condition. Secondhand Rose is also a great place to shop for gorgeous furs, designer shoes and bags, and costume jewelry. 1516 Wisconsin Ave. NW (btw. P St. and Volta Place). (℅ **202/337-3378.** no website. Metro: Foggy Bottom, then take the D.C. Circulator.

Secondi Inc. ★ On the second floor of a building right above Starbucks is this high-style consignment shop that sells women's clothing and accessories, including designer suits, evening wear, and more casual items—everything from Kate Spade to Chanel. 1702 Connecticut Ave. NW (btw. R St. and Florida Ave.). (℅ **202/667-1122.** www.secondi. com. Metro: Dupont Circle (Q St. exit).

WOMEN'S CLOTHING

Washington women have many more clothing stores to choose from than men. Stores selling classic designs include **Ann Taylor**, at Union Station ((℅ 202/371-8010), 1140 Connecticut Ave. NW ((℅ 202/659-0120), and 600 13th St. NW ((℅ 202/737-0325). Racy **Victoria's Secret** lingerie stores are located at Union Station ((℅ 202/682-0686), as well as at Connecticut and L streets NW ((℅ 202/293-7530).

See "Men's Clothing," above, for locations of Banana Republic, Gap, Sherman Pickey, Brooks Brothers, and Urban Outfitters, all of which also sell women's clothes. See "Vintage Shops," above, for bargain shopping.

Hip boutiques and upscale shops proliferate as well:

Anthropologie It's a chain, but the fashions seem so individual. Dresses, blouses, sweaters, even accessories, are ultrafeminine, their labels bearing names like "Maeve," "Guinevere," and "Left of Center." The Georgetown store also carries whimsical housewares. You either love it or you don't. I love it. All of it. 950 F St. NW. www. anthropologie.com. Metro: Gallery Place/Verizon Center (9th St. exit). Locations in Georgetown, 3222 M St. NW ((℅ **202/337-1363**), and in Chevy Chase, MD, at the Shops at Wisconsin Place ((℅ **301/654-1481**).

Betsy Fisher ★ A walk past the store is all it takes to know that this shop is a tad different. Its windows and racks show off whimsically feminine fashions by new American, French, and Italian designers. Access the website to find out about upcoming events; Betsy Fisher often hosts an evening cocktail hour to introduce a new line or inventory. 1224 Connecticut Ave. NW. (℅ **202/785-1975.** www.betsyfisher.com. Metro: Dupont Circle (South/19th St. exit).

H&M This Swedish-based store sells trendy clothes for the whole family at reasonable prices. 1025 F St. NW. (℅ **202/347-3306.** www.hm.com/us. Metro: Metro Center (11th St. exit). A 2nd location, in the Shops at Georgetown Park Mall, 3222 M St. NW ((℅ **202/298-6792**).

Nana's Owner Jackie Flanagan left the world of advertising and publishing to open this store in 2003, naming it after her fashion-wise grandmother. The shop sells new creations from independent U.S. and Canadian designers, and a small rack of vintage styles of work and play clothes, the idea being to mix old and new for a fresh look. Handbags, gifts, and bath products also on sale. The shop moved in 2011 from its longtime U Street address to a larger location in the Mount Pleasant part of town, north of the old neighborhood. 3068 Mount Pleasant St. NW. ☎ **202/596-9303**. www.nanadc.com. Metro: Columbia Heights, or take the D.C. Circulator.

Proper Topper   For the longest time, I thought this store was just a hat boutique. Then my husband came home satisfied at Christmas time, delighted at finding this "one-stop shop" for stocking presents and bigger gifts for his girls, me included. I totally approve: lovely designs by Velvet and Nanette Lepore, pretty jewelry, adorable clothes for children, stationery, all sorts of gifty things, and yes, hats. A new Georgetown location may have opened by the time you read this. 1350 Connecticut Ave. NW . ☎ **202/842-3055**. www.propertopper.com. Metro: Dupont Circle (19th St. exit).

Rizik Brothers   The year 2008 marked Rizik's centennial anniversary. This downtown high-fashion store sells bridal dresses and other high-toned fashions by European and American designers such as Carolina Herrera, Sylvia Heisel, and Lourdes Chavez. 1100 Connecticut Ave. NW. ☎ **202/223-4050**. www.riziks.com. Metro: Farragut North (L St. exit).

Rue 14   If you like the latest looks in fashion but not the prices that usually go with them, shop here. Owners Andrew Nguyen and Jiwon Paik-Nguyen fill their second-story boutique with the affordable designs of Free People, BB Dakota, Plastic Island, and other trendsetters. 1803A 14th St. NW. ☎ **202/462-6200**. www.rue14.com. Metro: U St./ Cardozo (13th St. exit).

Wink   Look for Wink beneath the Steve Madden store, and you'll discover Seven jeans and clothes by Diane von Furstenberg, Mystique, and Free People, and happy women of all ages sorting through the mix. 3109 M St. NW. Lower level. ☎ **202/338-9465**. www.shopwinkdc.com. Metro: Foggy Bottom, then take the D.C. Circulator.

Zara   This cheery store is an outpost of a popular chain started in Spain. Clothes are both dressy and casual, but all trendy. A sprinkling of coats is also found here, when the season calls for it. 1238 Wisconsin Ave. NW. ☎ **202/944-9797**. www.zara.com. Metro: Foggy Bottom, then take the D.C. Circulator. Also at 1025 F St. NE. ☎ **202/393-2810**.

Gifts/Souvenirs

See also "Crafts," earlier in this chapter. Museum gift shops (see chapter 6). are another good source. Also check out the White House Historical Association Gift Shop at Decatur House (1610 H St. NW, www.decaturhouse.org) and the White House Gift Shop operated by the U.S. Secret Service Uniformed Division Benefit Fund, at the National Press Building, 529 14th St. NW, and online (www.whitehousegiftshop.com). Both shops sell interesting memorabilia, like the White House Christmas tree ornament newly designed each year, and sundry items, from sweatshirts to mugs, stamped with White House or Armed Forces logos.

America!   Stop here if you want to pick up a baseball cap with COMMANDER IN CHIEF printed across its bill, a T-shirt proclaiming I LOVE MY COUNTRY, IT'S THE GOVERNMENT I'M AFRAID OF, White House guest towels, Obama coasters, or other impress-the-folks-back-home items. Union Station. ☎ **202/842-0540**. www.americastore. com. Metro: Union Station. Or save your shopping for the airport; America! has at least 3 locations at National, 2 at BWI, and 6 at Dulles.

Chocolate Moose   Its website welcomes browsers with the words "Serving weirdly sophisticated Washingtonians since 1978, but now attempting to reach out to the rest of you." I guess my family qualifies as weirdly sophisticated, since we're longtime fans. My husband endears himself to me and our daughters when he brings home gifts from this shop: a Wonder Woman daybook; chunky, transparent, red heart-shaped earrings; wacky cards; paperweight snow globes with figurines inside; candies; eccentric clothing; and other funny presents. 1743 L St. NW. ✆ **202/463-0992.** www.chocolatemoosedc.com. Metro: Farragut North (L St. exit).

Pulp Gifts You'll find must-have items here that you never even knew existed: a deck of slang flashcards, "Dancin' in the Streets" T-shirts, and crazy greeting cards. 1803 14th St. NW. ✆ **202/462-7857.** www.pulpdc.com. Metro: U St./Cardozo (13th St. exit).

Gourmet Goodies to Go

Demanding jobs and hectic schedules leave Washingtonians less and less time to prepare their own meals. Or so they say. At any rate, a number of fine-food shops and bakeries are happy to come to the rescue. Even the busiest bureaucrat can find the time to pop into one of these gourmet shops for a movable feast.

See also "Farmers' & Flea Markets," above.

Bread Line Bread Line attracts the White House crowd for lunch, with favorite sandwiches like the roast pork bun or the muffuletta; tasty soups; and desserts such as bread puddings, pear tarts, and delicious cookies. Seating is available, but most people buy carryout. The shop also sells freshly baked loaves of wheat bread, flatbreads, baguettes, and more. Open weekdays 7:30am to 5:30pm. 1751 Pennsylvania Ave. NW. ✆ **202/822-8900.** www.breadline.com. Metro: Farragut West or Farragut North.

Cowgirl Creamery I don't know how D.C. got so lucky as to have the only Cowgirl Creamery outside of California, but we can all be grateful. The creamery sells its own seven artisanal cheeses as well as those of the best 200 American and European cheese producers. Taste the brie here and you'll never be happy again with your local grocery store's brand. The creamery also sells freshly made sandwiches, salads, and soups, plus beer and wine. Open Monday through Saturday. 919 F St. NW. ✆ **202/393-6880.** www.cowgirlcreamery.com. Metro: Gallery Place/Verizon Center (9th St. exit).

Dean & Deluca This famed New York emporium operates in a historic Georgetown building that was once an open-air market. Though it is now closed in, this huge space still feels airy, with its high ceiling and windows on all sides. You'll pay top prices, but the quality is impressive—charcuterie, fresh fish, produce, cheeses, prepared sandwiches and cold pasta salads, hot-ticket desserts, like crème brûlée and tiramisu, and California wines. Also on sale are housewares; on-site is an espresso bar/cafe. 3276 M St. NW. ✆ **202/342-2500.** www.deandeluca.com. Metro: Foggy Bottom, then take the D.C. Circulator.

Firehook Bakery Known for its sourdough baguettes, apple-walnut bread, fresh fruit tarts, red-iced elephant and blue-iced donkey cookies, and sandwiches like smoked chicken on sesame semolina bread, Firehook also runs the cafe at the National Building Museum (see "Museums of Special Interest," chapter 6). 1909 Q St. NW. ✆ **202/588-2253.** www.firehook.com. Metro: Dupont Circle (Q St. exit). Also at 912 17th St. NW, 3411 Connecticut Ave. NW, 215 Pennsylvania Ave. SE (✆ **202/544-7003**), 555 13th St. NW, 441 4th St. and at 2 locations in Alexandria, VA.

Marvelous Market First there were the breads: sourdough, baguettes, croissants, scones. Now, there are things to spread on the bread, including smoked salmon mousse and tapenade; pastries to die for, from gingerbread to flourless chocolate cake; and prepared foods, such as soups, empanadas, and pasta salads. The breakfast spread on Sunday mornings is sinful, and individual items, like the croissants, are tastier and less expensive here than at other bakeries. The location is grand, with 18th-century chandeliers, an antique cedar bar, and a small number of tables. 1511 Connecticut Ave. NW. ℰ 202/332-3690. www.marvelousmarket.com. Metro: Dupont Circle (Q St. exit). Other locations include 3217 P St. NW (ℰ 202/333-2591) and 1800 K St. NW (ℰ 202/828-0944).

Home Furnishings

You may not have come to Washington to shop for housewares or furnishings, but step inside the shops of Cady's Alley or Home Rule and you may change your mind. Also refer to the listing of antiques stores earlier in this chapter.

Cady's Alley ★   Cady's Alley refers not to a single store, but to the southwest pocket of Georgetown, where about 20 stores reside, in and around said alley, which dangles south of M Street. Look for tony, big-name places, like Waterworks, Thos. Moser Cabinetmakers, and Baker Furniture; European outposts, like the hip kitchen furnishings of Bulthaup; and high-concept design stores, like Contemporaria. 3318 M St. NW (btw. 33rd and 34th sts.). www.cadysalley.com. Metro: Foggy Bottom, then take the D.C. Circulator.

Hill's Kitchen   This gourmet kitchenware store occupies an 1884 town house adjacent to the Eastern Market Metro station on Capitol Hill. Precious take-homes are cookie cutters shaped like the Washington Monument and the Capitol dome, as well as significant shapes for every state in the Union; topflight stovetop dishes, bakeware, cooking utensils and tools; colorful aprons and towels; water bottles that filter as you drink; and specialty foods. Cooking classes and demonstrations are also on offer. 713 D St. SE. ℰ 202/543-1997. www.hillskitchen.com. Metro: Eastern Market.

Home Rule   Unique housewares; bath, kitchen, and office supplies; and gifts cram this tiny store. You'll see everything from French milled soap to martini glasses. 1807 14th St. NW (at S St.). ℰ 202/797-5544. www.homerule.com. Metro: U St./Cardozo (13th St. exit; check the website or call for specific directions from the station).

Jewelry

Beadazzled   The friendly staff demonstrates to you how to assemble your own affordable jewelry from an eye-boggling array of beads and artifacts. The store also sells textiles, woodcarvings, and other crafts from around the world. There are also classes offered to those who prefer a more hands-on experience. 1507 Connecticut Ave. NW. ℰ 202/265-BEAD (2323). www.beadazzled.net. Metro: Dupont Circle (Q St. exit).

Chas Schwartz & Son   In business since 1888, Chas Schwartz specializes in diamonds and sapphires, rubies and emeralds, and is one of the few distributors of Hidalgo jewelry (enameled rings and bracelets). The professional staff also repairs watches and jewelry. 1400 F St. NW, or enter through the Willard Hotel, at 1401 Pennsylvania Ave. NW. ℰ 202/737-4757. www.chasschwartzjewelers.com. Metro: Metro Center (13th St. exit). There's another branch at the Mazza Gallerie (ℰ 202/363-5432); Metro: Friendship Heights.

Keith Lipert Gallery   This decorative-arts gallery sells Venetian glassware, high-end costume jewelry by designers such as Oscar de la Renta, and cute little old things, like Art Deco–style handbags. The owner shops in Europe for fashion jewelry and for exquisite gifts suitable for giving to diplomats and international business executives. 2922 M St. NW. ℰ 202/965-9736. www.keithlipertgallery.com. Metro: Foggy Bottom, then take the D.C. Circulator.

Mia Gemma ★ This pretty boutique sells the original designs of American and European artists, including Judy Bettencourt, Sarah Richardson, and Randi Chervitz. All pieces are handcrafted, either of limited edition or one of a kind. If you'd like a customized design, Mia Gemma can do that, too. 933 F St. NW. ℂ **202/393-4367.** www. miagemma.com. Metro: Gallery Place/Verizon Center (9th St. exit).

Tiffany & Co. Tiffany is known for exquisite diamonds and other jewelry that can cost hundreds of thousands of dollars. But you may not know that the store carries less expensive items as well, like $35 candlesticks. Tiffany will engrave, too. Other items include tabletop gifts and fancy glitz: china, crystal, flatware, and a bridal registry service. 5481 Wisconsin Ave., Chevy Chase, MD. ℂ **301/657-8777.** www.tiffany.com. Metro: Friendship Heights.

Tiny Jewel Box The first place Washingtonians go for estate and antique jewelry, but this six-story store next to the Mayflower Hotel also sells the pieces of many designers, from Links of London to Christian Tse, as well as crystal and other house gifts. In the month leading up to Mother's Day, the Tiny Jewel Box holds its Top-to-Bottom Sale, where you can save anywhere from 10 to 75 percent on most merchandise, including jewelry, handbags, and home accessories. 1147 Connecticut Ave. NW. ℂ **202/393-2747.** www.tinyjewelbox.com. Metro: Farragut North (L St. exit).

Malls

If malls are your thing, the D.C. area has plenty for you to choose from: Chevy Chase Pavilion, 5335 Wisconsin Ave. NW (ℂ 202/686-5335; www.ccpavilion.com), Metro: Friendship Heights; The Shops at Wisconsin Place, Wisconsin Avenue at Western Avenue, in Chevy Chase, Maryland (ℂ 301/841-4000; www.shopwisconsinplace. com), Metro: Friendship Heights; Mazza Gallerie, 5300 Wisconsin Ave. NW (ℂ 202/966-6114; www.mazzagallerie.com), Metro: Friendship Heights; and the Shops at Georgetown Park, 3222 M St. NW (ℂ 202/342-8190; www.shopsatgeorge-townpark.com), Metro: Foggy Bottom, then take the D.C. Circulator. Ronald Reagan Washington National Airport, Arlington, Virginia (ℂ 703/417-8600; www.mwaa.com/reagan), has 100 stores to choose from, too, if you want to do some souvenir shopping on your way out of town.

Even if you aren't a mall rat, you might want to check out the following two establishments, which do double duty as both shopping centers and attractions:

Pavilion at the Old Post Office Not so much a mall as a tourist trap with souvenir shops and a food court. The Pavilion is noteworthy for two reasons: Bike and Roll and Segway tours operate at this location (see p. 244) and the Clock Tower at the top of the Post Office Pavilion offers a stunning 360-degree view of the city. You take 2 elevators to reach the top, but the experience is free and is available daily. For more information, call 202/606-8691 or go online. 1100 Pennsylvania Ave. NW. ℂ **202/289-4224.** www.oldpostofficedc.com. Metro: Federal Triangle.

Union Station One of the most popular tourist stops in Washington, Union Station boasts magnificent architecture and more than 100 shops, including Pendleton's and Appalachian Spring (p. 168). Among the places to eat are America, B. Smith, and an impressive food court. 50 Massachusetts Ave. NE. ℂ **202/289-1908.** www.unionstationdc.com. Metro: Union Station.

emergency SHOPPING

You've just arrived in town, but your luggage hasn't—the airline lost it. Or you're about to depart for home or another destination and you notice that the zipper to your suitcase is broken. Or you've arrived at your hotel all in one piece, only to discover you've forgotten something essential: underwear, allergy medicine, an umbrella. What's a lonesome traveler to do? One of these suggestions might prove your salvation.

CVS: This is Washington's main pharmacy and essentials chain. Among the items sold at CVS stores are pantyhose, over-the-counter and prescription medicines, toys, greeting cards, wrapping paper and ribbon, magazines, film and 1-hour photo developing, and batteries. Two conveniently located 24-hour branches are at 2240 M St. NW (23rd St., near the Ritz-Carlton Hotel; (*℃* **202/296-9876;** Metro: Foggy Bottom) and at 6 Dupont Circle NW ((*℃* **202/785-1466;** Metro: Dupont Circle; www.cvs.com).

Cobbler's Bench Shoe Repair: This shop on the lower (food court) level of Union Station is open daily, Monday to Friday from 7am to 8pm, Saturday 9am to 8pm, and Sunday 10am to 6pm, to come to the rescue of travelers whose shoes or luggage need mending. The cobbler also cuts keys and sells repair items. Union Station, lower level ((*℃* **202/898-9009;** www. cobblersbenchshoerepair.com). Metro: Union Station. Check the website for the shop's four other D.C. locations.

Macy's: This former Hecht's remains an old reliable and the only department store located downtown. But though it's been around a while, the store continually updates its merchandise to keep up with the times. Run here if you need cosmetics, clothes (for men, women, and children), shoes (but not for children), electronics, appliances, lingerie, luggage, raincoats, and countless other need-immediately goods. Open daily: noon to 6pm Sunday, 10am to 8pm Monday through Saturday. 1201 G St. NW ((*℃* **202/628-6661;** www.macys.com). Metro: Metro Center.

Metro Stations: If it starts raining and you're scrambling to find an umbrella, look no further than your closest Metro station, where vendors are at the ready selling umbrellas and other handy things.

Miscellaneous

Ginza, "for Things Japanese"   In business since 1955, Ginza sells everything Japanese, from Hello Kitty merchandise to kimonos to futons to Zen rock gardens. 1717 Connecticut Ave. NW. (*℃* **202/332-7000.** no website. Metro: Dupont Circle (Q St. exit).

Paper Source   If you're a stationery freak like I am, you'll have to stop here to revel in the beautiful writing and wrapping papers, supplies of notebooks, journals, albums, ribbons, folders, containers, and other essentials. I believe it's the best stationery store in D.C. 3019 M St. NW. (*℃* **202/298-5545.** www.paper-source.com. Metro: Foggy Bottom, with a 25-min. walk, or ride the D.C. Circulator.

Shoes

For men's dress shoes, try **Brooks Brothers** (p. 170). For women, try the local outlets of **Nine West,** including locations at 1029 Connecticut Ave. NW ((*℃* 202/331-3243;

www.ninewest.com) and in Georgetown at 1227 Wisconsin Ave. NW (℃ 202/337-7256).

Comfort One Shoes This locally owned, family business was founded in Old Town Alexandria in 1993. Its six D.C. stores (of more than 20 in the area) sell a great selection of popular styles for both men and women, including Doc Martens, Birkenstocks, and Ecco. You can always find something that looks good and actually feels comfortable. 1630 Connecticut Ave. NW. ℃ **202/328-3141.** www.comfortoneshoes.com. Metro: Dupont Circle. Also at 1607 Connecticut Ave. NW (℃ **202/667-5300**), 3222 M St. NW (℃ **202/333-4246**), and many other locations.

Fleet Feet Though part of a national chain, this store feels decidedly part of the community, an Adams Morgan neighborhood fixture since 1984. The Fenty family, as in the family that includes former D.C. Mayor Adrian Fenty, owns the shop. You might see the ex-mayor himself, or his brothers, racing next to you during the weekly Sunday morning 5-mile fun run that Fleet Feet launches from its doorstep at 9am. (Just show up, if you're interested.) Merchandise-wise, the store sells sports and running shoes, apparel, and accessories, and is known for its friendly staff. 1841 Columbia Rd. NW. ℃ **202/387-3888.** www.fleetfeetdc.com. Metro: U St./Cardozo (13th St. exit) or Woodley Park–Zoo, with a bit of a walk from either station.

Hu's Shoes Fashion models in every D.C. photo shoot wear Hu's shoes, it seems. The Georgetown shop sells designer ready-to-wear footwear, handbags, and accessories. Owner Marlene Hu Aldaba travels to New York, Paris, and Milan in search of elegant specimens to suit her discriminating eye. Across the street, at 2906 M St. NW, is Hu's Wear, a two-level store selling designer outfits to accompany the darling shoes. 3005 M St. NW. ℃ **202/342-0202.** www.husonline.com. Metro: Foggy Bottom, then walk or take the D.C. Circulator.

Wine & Spirits

Barmy Wine and Liquor Located near the White House, this store sells it all, but with special emphasis on fine wines and rare cordials. 1912 L St. NW. ℃ **202/833-8730.** www.barmywines.com. Metro: Farragut North (L St. exit).

Central Liquors This store, which opened in 1934, is like a clearinghouse for liquor: Its great volume allows the store to offer the best prices in town on wines and liquor. The store carries more than 250 single-malt scotches. 625 E St. NW. ℃ **202/737-2800.** Metro: Gallery Place (9th and F sts. exit).

Schneider's of Capitol Hill Two blocks south of Union Station is this family-run liquor store, in business for more than 60 years. With a knowledgeable and enthusiastic staff, a 12,000-bottle inventory of wine, and a fine selection of spirits and beer, this shop is a find on Capitol Hill. 300 Massachusetts Ave. NE. ℃ **202/543-9300.** www.cellar.com. Metro: Union Station.

ENTERTAINMENT & NIGHTLIFE

8

Nightlife in the capital is rollicking and diverse. You can play bocce at **Black Jack**, on 14th St. (p. 183), head to U Street to dance your heart out at **Marvin** (p. 184), take a turn at karaoke at **Hill Country** (p. 183) in the Penn Quarter, or settle in for top-notch jazz at **Blues Alley** (p. 186) in Georgetown. Internationally renowned performing-arts venues like the **Kennedy Center** (p. 179) host performances by top theater and dance companies, while smaller theaters such as **Studio Theatre** (p. 182) stage bold new productions. Washington's nightlife scene offers something for everyone.

The truth is that D.C. nightlife is not only vigorous but also competitive. One third of the city's population is between 20 and 35; thanks to the capital's strong economy, most people have jobs and are ready to party. And then there is everyone else, from Hill staffers to expense-account attorneys, many of whom seek entertainment after a long day at the desk. Whether you're trying to score tickets to *Henry IV* at the **Shakespeare Theatre** (p. 181) or nab a seat at the bar at hotspot **The Observatory** (p. 184), success requires a get-there-first strategy.

The best neighborhoods for nightlife are **Adams Morgan;** the **U and 14th streets NW crossroads** (U St. between 16th and 9th sts., and 14th St. btw. P and V sts.); north and south of **Dupont Circle** along Connecticut Avenue; the **Penn Quarter,** notably 7th and 8th streets NW and from Pennsylvania Avenue north as far as I Street; **Georgetown;** the **Atlas District;** and **Columbia Heights,** an area east of Adams Morgan and north of the U Street district.

Most of D.C.'s clubs and bars stay open until 1 or 2am Monday through Thursday and until 3am Friday and Saturday; what time they open varies. It's best to call ahead or check the website.

For current concert and club offerings, check the *Washington Post's* online "Going Out Guide" (www.washingtonpost.com/gog), which covers all entertainment options, including nightlife, reported minute by minute, venue by venue, by the paper's "Going Out Gurus." If you're here on a weekend, try to pick up a copy of the *Post's* Friday "Weekend" section. *Washington City Paper,* available free at restaurants, bookstores, and other places around town, and online at **www.washingtoncitypaper.com,** is another excellent resource. Finally, check out the blog **www.dcist.com** for an irreverent inside look at what's going on around town.

THE PERFORMING ARTS

Washington's performing-arts scene has an international reputation. We have not just one but two Shakespeare theaters. Our **Arena Stage** is renowned for its innovative productions of American masters and new voices. The **Kennedy Center** reigns over all, staging something for everyone in every genre. Don't assume that these three theaters present only classic renditions from a performing-arts hit list; no, they are each wildly creative in their choices and their presentations. On the other hand, for truly avant-garde theater, seek out smaller stages, like **Woolly Mammoth** and **Studio** theaters.

Theater seasons generally span the months of September through May, with the Shakespeare Theatre's calendar often extending into July. The Kennedy Center's season is year-round, though it is certainly less busy in July and August. Performance times at all theaters are usually at 7:30pm or 8pm nightly, with Saturday and Sunday matinee performances at 2pm and occasional Wednesday noon matinee performances on the schedule, especially at Arena Stage and the Shakespeare Theatre.

The bad news is that, as popular as theater-going is in the capital, **ticket prices** have gone through the roof in the past couple of years. A lot of locals subscribe to the big three (Kennedy Center, Shakespeare, Arena), which leaves fewer one-off tickets available. Expect to pay $75 to $100-plus for a ticket—unless you're able to obtain a discounted ticket directly from the theater or from a discounted ticket service; see the "Getting Tickets," below.

Major Theaters & Companies

Arena Stage ★★★ Arena Stage is located in southwest D.C., near the waterfront, away from the downtown area. One day, this part of town will be a happenin' place, but until then, Arena Stage is the neighborhood's main attraction. And an attraction it is, drawing 300,000 people annually to its productions dedicated to "putting the American spirit in the spotlight." A major expansion in 2010 made Arena Stage D.C.'s second largest theater space after the Kennedy Center. Officially called "The Mead Center for American Theater," the venue's three staging areas are the theater-in-the-round Fichandler, the fan-shaped Kreeger, and the intimate (200-seat), oval-shaped Kogod Cradle. Founded in 1950, Arena Stage was a pioneer and remains a leader in the regional theater movement.

Arena's 2013-2014 season highlights include world premiere productions of *The Tallest Tree in the Forest*, by Daniel Beaty, about the life of actor Paul Robeson, and *Camp David*, by Pulitzer Prize winning author Lawrence Wright; a presentation of Bertolt Brecht's *Mother Courage and Her Children*, starring Kathleen Turner; and a pre-Broadway engagement of *The Velocity of Autumn*, starring Estelle Parsons.

1101 6th St. SW (at Maine Ave.). www.arenastage.org. ℂ **202/488-3300 for tickets,** or **202/554-9066 for general information.** Tickets $55–$90; discounts available for students, people with disabilities, groups, and seniors. Metro: Southwest/Waterfront.

John F. Kennedy Center for the Performing Arts ★★★ The capital's most renowned theater covers the entire realm of performing arts: Ballet, opera, plays, musicals, modern dance, classical and chamber music, and children's theater all take the stage at this magnificent complex overlooking the Potomac River. As a living memorial to Pres. John F. Kennedy, the Center considers itself the nation's theater and is committed to fulfilling the president's mission to make the performing arts available to everyone.

GETTING tickets

Most performing-arts and live-music venues mentioned in this chapter require tickets, which you can purchase online at the venue's website, in person at the venue's box office, or through one of the ticket vendors listed below.

The best deals in town might be those posted on the website **www.goldstar.com**. It costs nothing to subscribe, and you'll immediately start receiving e-mail notices of hefty discounts on admission prices to performances and venues, including museums, all over the city.

Washington's discount-ticket outlet, **TICKETPLACE,** sells half-price tickets online at **www.ticketplace.org** until 4pm for that day's performances. TICKETPLACE is a program of the Cultural Alliance of Washington.

Ticket sellers **Live Nation** (www.livenation.com**)** and **Ticketmaster** (www.ticketmaster.com; ✆ **800/745-3000)**

merged in January 2010, which means that you can buy full-price tickets for many performances in town from either operation. Expect to pay taxes plus a service charge, an order-processing fee, and a facility fee (if a particular venue tacks on that charge). Or you can visit the Ticketmaster sales booth at the Verizon Center, at 601 F St. NW (Metro: Gallery Place/Verizon Center). For the same kinds of performances, also check out **www.ticketfly.com** (✆ 877/435-9849). Finally, check out **www.instantseats.com**, which bills itself as the place to go for "online ticketing for the performing arts." (The site also sells tickets for river cruises on the Potomac, so perhaps the company defines "performing arts" to cover a multitude of entertainment.) This is the site that handles sales of tickets to embassy events (see "The Best of D.C.'s International Scene," later in this chapter, for more information).

Within this 17-acre arts facility lie six different theaters: the Opera House, the Concert Hall, the Terrace Theater, the Eisenhower Theater, the Theater Lab, and the Family Theater. And on their stages you can expect to see world-class performances across the cultural and entertainment spectrum. Highlights from the 2013-2014 season give you a hint: Wagner's *Tristan and Isolde*, hip-hop performances, the Bolshoi Ballet's *Giselle*, a jazz tribute to Nat King Cole, an International Theater Festival featuring puppetry to fresh takes on Shakespeare's classics, and Disney's *The Lion King* musical.

Visit the KenCen to attend a performance, for sure, but also consider stopping by for a free guided tour, which take place throughout the day. Finish the visit by attending the free "Millennium Stage" concert staged every single evening at 6pm in the Grand Foyer, each night featuring a different act, local artists mostly, but nationally known performers from time to time, too.

Otherwise, expect to pay ticket prices that range from $15 for a family concert to $300 for a night at the opera; most tickets cost between $45 and $100.

Whatever performance you attend, make sure you head out to the terrace for a grand view of the Potomac.

2700 F St. NW (at New Hampshire Ave. NW and Rock Creek Pkwy.). www.kennedy-center.org. ✆ **800/444-1324** or 202/467-4600. 50 percent discounts are offered (for select performances) to students, seniors 65 and over, people with permanent disabilities, enlisted military personnel, and persons with fixed low incomes (✆ **202/416-8340** for details). Garage parking $22. Metro: Foggy Bottom (though it's a fairly short walk, there's a free shuttle btw. the station and the Kennedy Center, departing every 15 min. 9:45am–midnight Mon–Fri, 10am–midnight Sat, and noon–midnight Sun). Bus: 80 from Metro Center.

Most Kennedy Center performances take place in theaters that lie off the Grand Foyer. But even if the one you're attending is on the Roof Terrace level, one floor up, make sure you visit the foyer anyway. The Grand Foyer is one of the largest rooms in the world. Measuring 630 feet long, 40 feet wide, and 60 feet high, the foyer is longer than the Washington Monument is tall (555⅝ ft.). Millennium Stage hosts free performances here nightly at 6pm, the famous Robert Berks sculpture of President John F. Kennedy is here, and just beyond the foyer's glass doors is the expansive terrace, which runs the length of the building and overlooks the Potomac River.

National Theatre ★ Open since 1835, the National is the capital's oldest continuously operating theater and the country's third oldest. In earlier days, the like of Sarah Bernhardt, Helen Hayes, and John Barrymore took the stage, and Presidents Lincoln and Fillmore and others were among those in the audience. These days, the National is almost entirely about Broadway musicals. So popular has its programming become, that the National's 2013-2014 season offers the theater's first Broadway subscription series in more than a decade. Coming our way are *Porgy and Bess, Stomp, Green Day's American Idiot,* and *West Side Story.* The 1,672-seat National continues its free, family-oriented, public-service programs: Saturday-morning children's theater (puppets, clowns, magicians, dancers, and singers), and free screenings of classic films shown on select Monday nights throughout the year. 1321 Pennsylvania Ave. NW (at 13th and E sts.). www.thenationaldc.com. (© 202/628-6161 for general information, 202/783-3372 for info about free programs, and call 800/514-3849, or go to www.etix.com to charge tickets. Tickets $48–$153 (most are in the $70–$90 range); discounts available for students, seniors, military personnel, and people with disabilities. Metro: Metro Center (13th and G sts. exit).

Shakespeare Theatre Company: at the Lansburgh Theatre and Sidney Harman Hall ★★★ So popular are the Shakespeare Theatre Company's productions that the company has two downtown locations (literally within a stone's throw of each other, the 451-seat **Lansburgh Theatre,** at 450 7th Street NW, and the 775-seat **Sidney Harman Hall,** at 610 F St. NW, across the street from the Verizon Center), and both houses frequently sell out. Critics laud these performances, as well, as the company's 2012 Regional Theatre Tony Award indicates. You can count on imaginative and superb performances, though not all of them are Shakespeare's works. Take a look at the 2013-2014 season whose plays include *Henry IV,* parts I and II, and *Measure for Measure,* but also Oscar Wilde's *The Importance of Being Earnest* and Stephen Sondheim's version of *A Funny Thing Happened on the Way to the Forum.* The Shakespeare Theater also screens live performances of London's National Theatre productions of Shakespeare plays.

An annual plum presentation is the "Free For All," which stages free performances of a Shakespeare play for 2 weeks in late August into mid-September; *Much Ado About Nothing* was the feature in 2013.

Also check out **Happenings at the Harman,** which stages free acts by comedy troupes, avant-garde dance companies, and community organizations, targeting the 20- to 30-somethings. Another great deal for the under-35s is the sale of $15 tickets available after 10am every Tuesday, for performances taking place through the following Sunday. Lansburgh Theatre: 450 7th St. NW (btw. D and E sts.). Sidney Harman Hall: 610 F St. NW. www.shakespearetheatre.org. ✆ 202/547-1122. Tickets $20–$110; discounts available for students, military, patrons 21–35, seniors, and groups. Metro: Archives–Navy Memorial or Gallery Place/Verizon Center (7th St./Arena exit).

Smaller Theaters

Smaller but no less compelling, these theaters stage productions that are consistently professional and often more contemporary and daring than those you'll find in the better-known theaters. These more intimate theaters have their own strong followings, which means their performances often sell out.

Studio Theatre ★★ 1501 14th St. NW, at P Street (www.studiotheatre.org; ✆ **202/332-3300**), since its founding in 1978, has grown in leaps and bounds into a four-theater complex, helping to revitalize this downtown neighborhood in the process. Productions are provocative and the season jam-packed, with 11 plays on tap for the 2013–2014 calendar. Former artistic director Joy Zinoman, who retired in 2010, helped to create buzz for Washington's theater scene as well as for the U Street/14th Street neighborhood in which Studio resides. Her legacy lives in Studio's continuing success in showcasing contemporary plays and in nurturing Washington acting talent.

The **Woolly Mammoth Theatre Company** ★★ (www.woollymammoth.net; ✆ **202/393-3939**) offers as many as six productions every year, specializing in new, offbeat, and quirky plays, often world premieres. The Woolly resides in a 265-seat, state-of-the-art facility at 641 D St. NW (at 7th St. NW), in the heart of the Penn Quarter.

In addition, I highly recommend productions staged at the **Folger Shakespeare Library** ★★ 201 E. Capitol St. SE, at 2nd Street (www.folger.edu; ✆ **202/544-7077**), which celebrates its 82nd anniversary in 2014. Plays take place in the library's Elizabethan Theatre, which is styled after the inn-yard theater of Shakespeare's time. The theater is intimate and charming, the theater company is remarkably good, and an evening spent here guarantees an absolutely marvelous experience. The Elizabethan Theatre is also the setting for musical performances, lectures, readings, and other events.

Headliner Concert Venues

When Lady Gaga, Bruce Springsteen, or Beyoncé come to town, they play at the 20,600-seat **Verizon Center,** 601 F St. NW, at 7th Street (✆ www.verizoncenter.com; **202/628-3200**). Situated in the center of downtown, the Verizon Center hosts plenty of concerts and is also Washington's premier indoor sports arena (see "Spectator Sports," later in this chapter).

DAR Constitution Hall ★★ on 18th Street NW, between C and D streets (www. dar.org; ✆ **202/628-4780**), is housed within a beautiful turn-of-the-20th-century Beaux Arts building and seats 3,746. Its excellent acoustics have supported an eclectic group of performers, from John Legend to John Fogerty.

In summer 2013, the 9:30 Club (see p. 188) took over the operation of the historic **Lincoln Theatre** ★ 1215 U St. NW, at 13th Street (www.thelincolntheatre.org; ✆ **202/328-6000**), and thankfully has breathed new life into it. Look for indie favorites like Neko Case and Fiona Apple in the lineup. Once a movie theater, vaudeville house, and nightclub featuring black stars like Louis Armstrong and Cab Calloway, the theater closed in the 1970s, then reopened in 1994 after a renovation restored it to its former

ENTERTAINMENT & NIGHTLIFE | The Performing Arts

elegance. But somehow the theater's appeal just never took off. Looks like this latest manoeuver by the 9:30 Club may finally have saved the Lincoln from obscurity.

The **Warner Theatre ★**, 513 13th St. NW, between E and F streets (www.warner theatredc.com; ✆ **202/783-4000**), opened in 1924 as the Earle Theatre (a movie/vaudeville palace) and was restored to its original, neoclassical-style appearance in 1992. It's worth coming by just to see its ornately detailed interior. The 2,000-seat auditorium offers year-round entertainment, alternating dance performances, like the Washington Ballet's Christmas performance of the *Nutcracker,* with comedy acts, like those of Russell Brand, Margaret Cho, or John Oliver, and headliner musicians like Jeff Beck.

THE BAR SCENE

Washington has a thriving and varied bar scene. But just when you think you know all the hot spots, a fresh batch pops up. Lately it's the rooftop bars that draw the largest crowds. Here's a smattering of some favorites, old and new.

Black Jack ★★★ Downstairs is the super popular **Pearl Dive Oyster Palace** (p. 76) restaurant, and upstairs is its super-cool bar. Red velvet curtains part to reveal the fully stocked bar, and old movies project black-and-white images on the brick walls. Other bars may have pool tables and DJs; Black Jack has two full-size bocce courts, with 19 stadium seats for spectators. Lots of comfortable red vinyl seating, crafty cocktails, and "really good house-made pies," as in pizzas, make Black Jack everyone's favorite new hangout. 1612 14th St. NW (at Corcoran St.). www.blackjackdc.com. ✆ **202/319-1612.** Metro: U St./Cardozo (U and 13th sts. exit).

ChurchKey This mellow hangout draws a diverse mix, boomers to their 20-something children, all sprawled upon loungey banquettes or perched upon stools at the long bar. This is a haven for beer lovers, especially, with its 50 drafts, 500 bottles, and five cask ales on tap. ChurchKey's downstairs sibling, Birch & Barley, is a popular restaurant. 1337 14th St. NW (at Rhode Island Ave.). www.churchkeydc.com. ✆ **202/567-2576.** Metro: McPherson Sq. (14th St. exit) or U St./Cardozo (U and 13th sts. exit).

The Dubliner ★ Joe Scarborough and Mika Brzezinski from MSNBC's Morning Joe show set up shop here to cover the 2013 presidential inauguration, but on ordinary days, you'll see Capitol Hill regulars hanging here for no other reason but that the atmosphere's Irish and the bar's got Guinness on tap. Open from breakfast through last call, the Dubliner features live Irish music nightly. In the Phoenix Park Hotel, 520 N. Capitol St. NW (separate entrance on F St. NW). www.dublinerdc.com. ✆ **202/737-3773.** Metro: Union Station.

The Gibson ★★ If the word "mixologist" is in your vocabulary, then you'll like The Gibson, where expert drink-makers will concoct a libation just for you, based on your taste preferences. You can throw anything at them: smoky and tequila or citrusy and sweet, or cinnamon and scotchy, and presto! A cocktail answering to those very whims is placed before you. It's clear that they are having fun, and so will you. You'll need to know that the speakeasy is small, dark, and requires a reservation for entry. On busy nights, you're only allowed 2 hours here, but that ought to do it. 2009 14th St. NW (at U St.). www.thegibsondc.com. ✆ **202/232-2156.** Metro: U St./Cardozo (13th St. exit).

Hill Country Barbecue ★★ Everybody knows to go to this Penn Quarter restaurant for awesome barbecue, strong drinks, and, downstairs, live music nearly nightly. The music tends toward outlaw country and honkytonk. But one of the most

CHEAP EATS: happy hours TO WRITE HOME ABOUT

Good-value promotions are often available at area bars and nightclubs, like Lucky Bar's half-price burgers every Wednesday night and 50¢ tacos on Mondays. A step above these are certain restaurants around town that set out tasty bites during happy hour, either free or for an astonishingly low price. Here are several you might like:

In the bar and lounge of **Ceiba,** 701 14th St. NW, at the corner of G Street NW (© **202/393-3983**), not far from the White House, signature cocktails like margaritas and mojitos are $5 each, Monday to Saturday from 3 to 6pm and again from 9:30pm (Fri–Sat from 10pm) to close. Bar-food items that range from a $9 pork pupusa to a $12 fish taco are offered at half those prices.

In Georgetown, **Morton's Steakhouse,** 3251 Prospect St. NW, just off Wisconsin Ave. NW (© **202/342-6258**), serves up "Power Hour" bar bites in its bar, Sunday to Friday 5 to 6:30pm and 9 to 11pm. Drinks are specially priced—$5 for beer, $6.50 for wine, and $7.50 for certain cocktails—and the bar-bites menu features a variety: cheeseburger trio, four petite filet mignon sandwiches, blue cheese french fries, and so on, each priced at $6 or $7 per plate.

On Capitol Hill, **Johnny's Half Shell,** 400 N. Capitol St. NW (© **202/737-0400**), pulls in young Hill staffers Monday through Friday 4:30 to 7:30pm, not for its deals on drinks—$5.50 drafts, $7 to $9 cocktails—but for its delicious bites of miniburgers, shrimp and grits, and the like, priced from $3 to $14.

Finally, in the Penn Quarter's **Oyamel,** at 401 7th St. NW, happy-hour specials 4 to 6pm every weeknight feature $5 margaritas, Dos Equis, or the Mexican *ponche* (tequila, white wine, Cointreau, agave nectar, and fresh fruit), and, for another $4, two of Oyamel's superb tacos.

popular acts in town is one that patrons themselves deliver here every Wednesday night (usually after tossing back a couple of tequilas). The HariKaraoke Band provides live backup as a singer takes the microphone and "rocks 'n twangs" her heart out. 410 7th St. NW (at D St.). www.hillcountrywdc.com. © **202/556-2050.** Metro: Gallery Place/Chinatown (7th and F sts. exit) or Archives–Navy Memorial.

Lucky Bar ★ You looking for a good old-fashioned bar with booths, couches, a pool table, a juke box, and cheap beer? Lucky Bar's the place. It's also Soccer Central, with TV screens broadcasting soccer matches from around the globe. Monday through Wednesday and Friday, Lucky Bar's happy hour runs from 3pm to 8pm. And there are nightly specials, like 50-cent tacos on Monday nights and half-price burgers on Wednesdays. 1221 Connecticut Ave. NW (at N St.). www.luckybardc.com. © **202/331-3733.** Metro: Dupont Circle (South/19th St. exit) or Farragut North (L St. exit).

Marvin ★★ Downstairs is a Belgian bistro, upstairs is the bar, which includes a lounge, rooftop beer garden, and DJ space. Washington's 20-somethings come here to dance and it's always crowded after 10pm. 2007 14th St. NW (at U St.). www.marvindc.com. © **202/797-7171.** Metro: U St./Cardozo (13th St. exit).

The Observatory ★★ Crowning Georgetown's The Graham hotel, is this rooftop bar, which wraps around the entire building, so you're able to view Georgetown and the city, including the Washington Monument, from various angles. The fact that the bar is

Not everyone in Washington, D.C., goes out at night to imbibe at bars. Some imbibe at bookstores.

Bookstore nightlife? Oh yes, and only in the capital, which a 2012 Gallup Poll reported as being the most literate city in the country, based on number of bookstores and other factors. So we like to hang out at bookstores; it's only natural. Only, it isn't completely about the books these days. **Politics and Prose** (5015 Connecticut Ave. NW; www.politics-prose.com; Ⓒ 202/364-1919) serves beer and wine at book signings and hosts trivia nights. **KramerBooks** (1517 Connecticut Ave. NW; www.kramers.com; Ⓒ 202/387-1400), in addition to its bookshop, has a restaurant and bar, stages concerts Wed-Sat nights, stays open all weekend, and is famous for launching romances. Salon/bookstore/restaurant **Busboys and Poets** (2021 14th St. NW; www.busboysandpoets.com; Ⓒ 202/387-7638) has it all going on; spoken word performances and poetry slams, lounge lingering, and political debates. Busboys has other locations at 1025 5th St. NW; Ⓒ **202/789-2227**), and in Arlington, Virginia (4251 Campbell Ave.; Ⓒ **703/379-9756**). Even traditional stores, like **Barnes and Noble** (555 12th St. NW; www.bn.com; Ⓒ 202/347-0176) and **Books-A-Million** (11 Dupont Circle; www.booksamillion.com; Ⓒ 202/319-1374), host nighttime events. So do what the reading locals do while you're here, and stop by one of D.C.'s bookstores of an evening. Hey, and while you're at it: Buy a book!

open not just to hotel guests but to Washington's rowdy drinking crowd means you must reserve a spot. It's a comfortable place to lounge, too, with pretty teal colored cushions and a partially protected bar area. You're here to drink only; no food is served. At The Graham Hotel, 1075 Thomas Jefferson St. NW (just below M St.). www.thegrahamgeorgetown.com. Ⓒ 202/337-0900. Metro: Foggy Bottom, with a 20-minute walk.

Quill ★★★ A pianist plays Tues–Sat starting at 9pm, perfect accompaniment to that Kentucky Salty Dog cocktail you're sipping and plate of charcuterie you're nibbling, at this chicest of lounges, inside the city's chicest hotel. In the Jefferson Hotel, 1200 16th St. NW (at M St.). www.jeffersondc.com. Ⓒ **202/448-2300.** Metro: Dupont Circle (19th St./ South exit) or Farragut North (L St. exit).

Tune Inn ★ Open since 1955, this Capitol Hill is a veritable institution. So when a serious fire engulfed the place in 2011, the community was devastated. Five months later, the Tune Inn reopened, and now it's business as usual. The divey Tune Inn is open from early morning til late at night serving policeman, Hill staffers and their bosses, and folks from the neighborhood. Sometimes they eat here, too: burgers, fries, and crabcakes. 331½ Pennsylvania Ave. SE (at 4th St.). www.tuneinndc.com. Ⓒ **202/543-2725.** Metro: Capitol South.

THE CLUB & MUSIC SCENE

Live Music

If you're looking for a tuneful night on the town, Washington offers everything from hip jazz clubs to DJ-driven dance halls—both places where you sit back and listen and places where you can get up and rock out. Here are some of the best live-music venues.

JAZZ & BLUES

If you're a jazz fan and are planning a trip to D.C. in early to mid-June, check out **www.dcjazzfest.org** for exact dates of the fabulous, 2-week-long **DC Jazz Festival,** which showcases the talents of at least 100 musicians in various venues around town, including free blowout concerts on the National Mall. And if you're a jazz or blues fan, and you're coming to town at some other time of the year, check out the following venues.

The Birchmere Music Hall and Bandstand ★★★ This place started out 40 years or so ago showcasing bluegrass and country acts primarily. Take a look at the calendar now and you'll see the range stretches from French crooner (and France's former first lady) Carla Bruni to John Hiatt. Located in Alexandria, 6 miles and a $12 cab fare from downtown D.C., the Birchmere is well worth the trip. The hall seats 500 and serves food. Purchase tickets at the box office or online from www.ticketmaster. com. 3701 Mt. Vernon Ave. (off S. Glebe Rd.), Alexandria, VA. www.birchmere.com. ⓒ **703/549-7500.** Tickets $17–$60. Take a taxi or drive.

Blues Alley ★★★ An inconspicuous alley off of busy Wisconsin Avenue in Georgetown delivers you to the door of Blues Alley and another world entirely. Jazz greats like Wynton Marsalis and Ahmad Jamal and lesser-known artists play here nightly, usually two sets a night, at 8 and 10pm, with the occasional midnight show thrown in on weekends. Blues Alley is a tiny joint filled with small, candlelit tables, so reservations are a must for the first-come-first served seating. The supper club has been around since 1965 and looks it, but that's part of its charm. Its Creole menu features dishes named after stars (try Dizzy Gillespie's Shrimp Creole). 1073 Wisconsin Ave. NW (in an alley below M St.). www.bluesalley.com. ⓒ **202/337-4141.** Tickets $16–$75 (most $20–$40), plus a $12-per-person food or drink minimum, plus $4.50 per-person ticket surcharge. Metro: Foggy Bottom, then walk or take the D.C. Circulator.

Bohemian Caverns ★ Despite increasing competition from nearby Howard Theatre (see below) and other venues, the Caverns remains a player, hosting both its own orchestra and international jazz artists like Federico Pena. Decades ago, the likes of Duke Ellington and Billie Holiday performed here. The supper club usually presents two performances a night, 5 to 7 nights a week. 2001 11th St. NW (at U St.). www.bohemian caverns.com. ⓒ **202/299-0800.** Cover $7–$22. Metro: U St./Cardozo (U and 13th sts. exit).

Howard Theatre ★★ A $29-million renovation of this historic arts landmark theater, built in 1910, has helped restore not just the building but also a piece of history. The Howard Theatre of old was the Black Broadway showcase for musicians like Duke Ellington and Ella Fitzgerald, and later hosted performances by Marvin Gaye and the Supremes. The theater reopened in April 2012, with a lineup of stars, from the Roots to Mos Def. With its 1,200 seats arranged at tables, the venue is both supper club and concert venue. Cuisine is American with a soul influence, naturally, and food and drink are served throughout the show. A gospel brunch takes place every Sunday. 620 T St. NW (at 7th St.). www.thehowardtheatre.com or www.howardtheatre.org. ⓒ **202/588-5595.** Tickets $15–$95 (most $25–$55). Metro: Shaw/Howard University (7th and S sts. exit.)

The Hamilton ★★ Located on the subterranean level of a large restaurant is this live music venue, with blues, rock, jazz, R&B, and folk performances staged nightly. You sit at communal tables and dine from the upstairs menus. Located in the heart of

ENTERTAINMENT & NIGHTLIFE | The Club & Music Scene

the Penn Quarter, the Hamilton debuted December 2011, and everybody's still talking about it. 600 14th St. (at F St.). www.thehamiltondc.com. © **202/787-1000.** Live music acts $15–$50; most main courses under $20. Metro: Metro Center (13th St. exit).

HR-57 ★   Amidst the Atlas District's of-the-moment hipster bars, restaurants, and alternative music clubs, HR-57 stands out for being the sole jazz club. Its name derives from the 1987 House Resolution that designated jazz "a rare and valuable national American treasure." The club is also the Center for the Preservation of Jazz and Blues. Jam sessions take place Wednesday and Thursday evenings, seasoned artists perform on weekends. 816 H St. NE (at 9th St.). www.hr57.org. © **202/253-0044.** Cover $8 Wed–Thurs; $15 Fri–Sat. Drive or take a taxi.

Madam's Organ Restaurant and Bar ★★★   Everyone stops by the legendary Madam's at some point or another. There's a lot going on throughout its eclectically decorated three levels and it's all fun: live music nightly on the first floor, from funk/jazz/blues on Sunday and Monday to regional blues bands on weekends; the second floor Big Daddy's Love Lounge & Pick-Up Joint (it is what it is); and the year-round rooftop deck, for mingling, playing darts, and taking in the fine view. 2461 18th St. NW (at Columbia Rd.). www.madamsorgan.com. © **202/667-5370.** Cover $3–$7. Metro: U St./Cardozo or Woodley Park–Zoo, then catch the D.C. Circulator.

Twins Jazz ★   Lots of people discover Twins simply by walking by and hearing the sounds of great jazz emanating from within, and following it to this second floor club, which hosts live music every night except Monday. Local artists tend to play weeknights, bigger names on weekends. 1344 U St. NW (at 14th St.). www.twinsjazz.com. © **202/234-0072.** Cover $10–$30, with a $10 per-person minimum on food/drink/merchandise. Metro: U St./Cardozo (13th St. exit).

ROCK, HIP-HOP & DJS

Below are primarily live-music clubs but also a sprinkling of nightclubs known for their DJs and dance floors.

Black Cat ★★★   This club is D.C.'s flagship venue for alternative music. When it opened on 14th Street in 1993, the neighborhood was a red-light district and D.C. was not a major player when it came to a vibrant live-music scene. So hats off to the Black Cat, who played a part in the changes that have happened since. Local, national, and international groups play here, everyone from The Arcade Fire to Black Lips. The Black Cat has two stages: its main concert hall, which holds more than 600 people, and Backstage, the place for soloists, smaller bands, DJs, film screenings, and poetry readings. The Red Room Bar features pinball machines, a pool table, and a jukebox. Concerts are nightly, sometimes twice in a single night, on different stages. 1811 14th St. NW (btw. S and T sts.). www.blackcatdc.com. © **202/667-4490.** Cover $5–$25 for concerts; no cover in the Red Room Bar. Metro: U St./Cardozo (13th and U sts. exit).

Eighteenth Street Lounge ★★   Ever the hotspot, ESL is the place to go for dressing sexy and dancing to live music and DJ-spun tunes, a range of acid jazz, hip-hop, reggae, Latin jazz, soul, and party sounds. The setting is somewhat surprising: a restored, century-old mansion, once the home of Teddy Roosevelt, with fireplaces, high ceilings, and an outside deck. It's open Tuesday through Friday from 5:30pm, Saturday and Sunday from 9:30pm. 1212 18th St. NW (at Jefferson Place and Connecticut Ave.). www.eighteenthstreetlounge.com. © **202/466-3922.** No cover Tues–Thurs and Sun; cover $5–$15 after 10pm Wed and Fri–Sat. Metro: Dupont Circle (South/19th St. exit) or Farragut North (L St. exit).

9:30 Club ★★★ The 9:30 rules over the live music scene. It's a 1,200 capacity concert hall with excellent sightlines, state-of-the-art sound system, four bars, and of course most important, a nightly concert schedule that features every possible star, rising or arrived, in today's varied rock world, from Passenger to Adele. The 9:30 Club is always winning awards, the latest being Third Place in Rolling Stone Magazine's 2013 America's Best Music Venues listing. 815 V St. NW (at 9th St.). www.930.com. ℭ **202/265-0930.** Metro: U St./Cardozo (10th St. exit).

Rock and Roll Hotel ★ Located in the Atlas District, this club features a second-floor pool hall, 400-person concert hall, and a separate, comfy bar for hanging out. Nightly acts range from local garage bands to national groups on tour. *FYI:* Don't expect to stay overnight; despite its name, the hotel is just a club. 1353 H St. NE (at 14th St.). www.rockandrollhoteldc.com. ℭ **202/388-7625.** Cover $8–$15. Drive here or take a taxi.

Comedy Clubs

In addition to these two comedy venues, the **Warner Theatre** (see "Headliner Concert Venues," above) and **Harmon Hall** at the Shakespeare Theatre (see above) also occasionally feature big-name comedians or troupes.

The Capitol Steps ★ *Fiscal Shades of Gray* is the name of the latest album released by this musical political satire troupe, following fast on the heels of *Liberal Shop of Horrors* and *Barackin' Around the Christmas Tree*—just three out of the more than 30 albums the troupe has produced since it debuted in 1981. But really, it's best to see them perform their songs and skits in person, which you can do nearly every weekend at the Ronald Reagan Building and International Trade Center. The performers are former congressional staffers, and so well equipped to satirize politicians and government. In the Ronald Reagan Building, 1300 Pennsylvania Ave. NW (at 13th St.). www.capsteps.com. ℭ **202/312-1555.** Tickets $40. Metro: Federal Triangle.

The Improv ★ The Improv features headliners on the national comedy-club circuit as well as comic plays and one-person shows. Shows are about 1½ hours long and include three comics (an emcee, a feature act, and a headliner). Showtimes are 8pm Tuesday through Sunday, with a second show at 10:30pm on Friday and Saturday. You must be 18 to enter. 1140 Connecticut Ave. NW (btw. L and M sts.). www.dcimprov.com. ℭ **202/296-7008.** Tickets $15–$35, plus a 2-item minimum per person. Metro: Farragut North (L St. exit).

THE GAY & LESBIAN SCENE

Dupont Circle is the gay and lesbian hub of Washington, D.C., with at least 10 gay or lesbian bars within easy walking distance of one another. Here are two from that neighborhood, plus another with two locations, the original on Capitol Hill and the second—you guessed it—in Dupont Circle.

Cobalt This is "D.C's premier gay bar and nightspot." So says Cobalt's owners, but so does everyone else, too. Cobalt is actually the name of the club's third-floor dance space, the first floor holding the club's Level One restaurant and the second floor its 30 Degrees lounge. The clubs hosts themed parties, like karaoke on Wednesdays, and annual events, such as the wildly popular Bare White Party ladies night. 1639 R St. NW (at 17th St.). www.cobaltdc.com. ℭ 202/232-4416. Cover $6–$10, usually Fri–Sat only. Metro: Dupont Circle (Q St. exit).

Washington is home to more than 180 embassies and international culture centers, which greatly contribute to the city's cosmopolitan flavor. There are a number of ways to soak up this international scene. First go to the website **www.embassy.org**, mouse over "Embassies," and click on "Embassy Row Tour" for a detailed tour that leads you past embassies along Massachusetts and New Hampshire avenues NW and includes information about the neighborhoods, the embassies, and all that you see along the way.

The website contains specialized information about individual embassies. Lots of embassies host events that are open to the public—sometimes for free, sometimes at minimal cost. In my opinion, the **French Embassy's Maison Française** (www.la-maison-francaise.org) and the Swedish Embassy's **House of Sweden** (www.houseofsweden.com) offer the most interesting events. A highlight is Nordic Jazz Week, cosponsored by the embassies of Sweden, Denmark, Norway, Finland, and Iceland every June, with the best performances staged on the roof of the House of Sweden building on the Georgetown waterfront overlooking the Potomac River. The cost is usually $25 per person per concert; the experience is priceless.

Finally, you can buy tickets for **Embassy Series** (www.embassyseries.com; Ⓒ **202/625-2361**) program events. These are world-class, mostly classical-music performances hosted by individual embassies, held at the embassy or at the ambassador's residence. Admission tends to be pricier for these events than for those staged separately by the embassy. For instance, on March 7, 2014, the Embassy of Austria hosts a string quartet concert; a ticket cost $65 per person, which also covered a wine, cheese, appetizers, and sweets. Totally worth it!

8

ENTERTAINMENT & NIGHTLIFE

Spectator Sports

J.R.'s Bar and Grill ★ This friendly place is always packed, whether it's during the nightly happy hour or Thursday night at midnight when patrons get free shots. The all-male Dupont Circle club attracts an attractive crowd, here to play pool, participate in sing-alongs, or simply hang out and drink. 1519 17th St. NW (btw. P and Q sts.). www.jrsbardc.com. Ⓒ **202/328-0090.** Metro: Dupont Circle (Q St. exit).

Phase One ★ Open since 1970, Phase One is the oldest continuously operating lesbian bar in the country. Part of its secret must be the no-pressure vibe here. During the week, you might see a mix of persuasions in this neighborly joint; come the weekends, the place is packed with women. A pool table, a tiny dance floor, and televisions are mere distractions. Phase One now has Phase One at Dupont ("the East Coast's largest lesbian bar"), at 1415 22nd St. NW (at P St.). 525 8th St. SE (at G St.). www.phase1dc.com. Ⓒ **202/544-6831.** Metro: Eastern Market.

SPECTATOR SPORTS

Washington, D.C. has professional football, basketball, baseball, ice hockey, and soccer teams, and of those five, it's the Capitals, the ice hockey team, whose fans are the most passionate. And visible: In season you'll see the red-jersey'd devotees swarming the downtown before and after the match at the Verizon Center. Tickets to the Caps games are attainable but not cheap. It's the tickets to the Redskins football matches that remain most elusive, thanks to a loyal subscription base. Here's all you need to know about the major spectator sports events and venues in the city.

Annual Sporting Events

Marine Corps Marathon Thirty thousand runners compete in this 26.2-mile race (the fifth-largest marathon in the United States), which begins at the Marine Corps Memorial (the Iwo Jima statue) and passes major memorials. The race takes place the last Sunday in October; 2014 marks its 39th year. www.marinemarathon.com. ℂ 800/786-8762.

Citi Open (formerly know as the Legg Mason Tennis Classic This U.S. Open series event attracts more than 72,000 people to watch tennis pros compete for big bucks. The classic benefits a good cause: the Washington Tennis and Education Foundation. The tournament takes place for about 9 days, from late July into early August, at the Fitzgerald Tennis Center in Rock Creek Park. www.citiopentennis.com. ℂ 202/721-9500.

General Spectator Sports

Baseball Washington, D.C.'s Major League Baseball team, the **Nationals,** play at the finely designed **Nationals Ballpark** (www.nationals.com; ℂ **202/675-6287**), which opened on March 30, 2008. Located in southeast Washington, the 41,000-seat stadium is helping to spark development in this old neighborhood, which now goes by the name "Capitol Riverfront."

Basketball The 20,600-seat **Verizon Center,** 601 F St. NW, where it meets 7th Street (www.verizoncenter.com; ℂ **202/628-3200**), in the center of downtown, is Washington's premier indoor sports arena, where the **Wizards** (NBA), the **Mystics** (WNBA), and the **Georgetown University Hoyas** basketball teams play.

Football The **Redskins** National Football League team plays at the 85,000-seat stadium **FedEx Field,** outside of Washington, in Landover, Maryland. Obtaining tickets is difficult thanks to season ticket holders, but if you want to try, visit www. redskins.com/fedexfield.

Ice Hockey The **Capitals** of the National Hockey League are beloved in this city. The team rink is inside the 20,600-seat **Verizon Center,** 601 F St. NW (www.verizon center.com; ℂ **202/628-3200**), in the center of downtown.

Soccer D.C.'s men's soccer team, **D.C. United** (www.dcunited.com), has been around since 1994 but continues to play its matches at the creaky 55,000-seat **Robert F. Kennedy Memorial Stadium,** 2400 E. Capitol St. SE (ℂ **202/547-9077**).

Tennis World Team Tennis franchise team, the Washington Kastles (www. washingtonkastles.com), plays at the beautiful, 2,600-seat, waterfront Kastles Stadium at the Wharf, within view of the Washington Monument, Jefferson Memorial, and the Potomac River. WTT is a co-ed professional tennis league; the Kastles team includes Martina Hingus and Leander Paes. **Kastles Stadium at the Wharf,** 800 Water St. SW (ℂ **202/483-6647**).

DAY TRIPS FROM WASHINGTON, D.C.

You've come as far as Washington, D.C.—why not travel just a bit farther to visit Mount Vernon, the home of the man for whom the capital is named? "Washington slept here" is a claim bandied about by many a town. "Washington lived here for 45 years" is a claim only Mount Vernon can make. Located 16 miles south of Washington, D.C., the estate was George Washington's home from 1754 until his death in 1799 (as much as the American Revolution and Washington's stints as the new republic's first president would allow). And where did Washington go to kick up his heels or to worship? In nearby Old Town Alexandria, whose cobblestone streets and historic churches and houses still stand, surrounded now by of-the-moment eateries and chic boutiques. Make time, if you can, for visits to both Old Town and Mount Vernon.

MOUNT VERNON

Only 16 miles south of the capital, George Washington's Southern plantation dates from a 1674 land grant to the president's great-grandfather.

Essentials

GETTING THERE   If you're going by car, take any of the bridges over the Potomac River into Virginia and follow the signs pointing the way to National Airport/Mount Vernon/George Washington Memorial Parkway. Travel south on the George Washington Memorial Parkway, the river always to your left, and pass by National Airport on your right. Continue through Old Town Alexandria, where the parkway is renamed "Washington Street," and head 8 miles farther, until you reach the large circle that fronts Mount Vernon.

You might also take a bus or boat to Mount Vernon. These are narrated bus and boat tours, and their prices **include the price of admission to Mount Vernon.**

Gray Line Buses (www.graylinedc.com; ✆ **301/386-8300,** or 202/289-1995 for the ticket kiosk at Union Station) offers one tour daily to Mount Vernon (except on Christmas, Thanksgiving, and New Year's Day). The 4-hour tour departs from the bus terminal at Union Station at 8am, travels past Old Town Alexandria to Mount Vernon, and returns to Union Station by 12:30. The ticket kiosk is on the first level of the parking garage. The

Though few people realize it, the George Washington Memorial Parkway is actually a national park. The first section was completed in 1932 to honor the bicentennial of George Washington's birth. The parkway follows the Potomac River, running from Mount Vernon, past Old Town and the nation's capital, and ending at Great Falls, Virginia. Today the parkway is a major commuter route leading into and out of the city. Even the most impatient driver, however, can't help but notice the beautiful scenery and views of the Jefferson and Lincoln memorials and the Washington Monument that you pass along the way.

cost is $55 per adult (ages 12 and older), $20 per child (3-11), free for children 2 and under. Gray Line offers several other tours, so call for further information or see "Guided Tours," in chapter 11.

The **Spirit of Washington Cruises'** (www.cruisetomountvernon.com; © **866/835-8851**) *Spirit of Mount Vernon* is a seasonal operation, cruising to Mount Vernon March through October (call or check online for daily schedules, which can vary). The vessel leaves from Pier 4 (6th and Water sts. SW; 3 blocks from the Green Line Metro's Waterfront station) at 8:30am, returning by 3pm. The cost is approximately $49 per adult, $43 per child (ages 6–11; free for younger children), including taxes and surcharges.

Miss Christin, run by the **Potomac Riverboat Company** (www.potomacriverboatco.com; © **877/511-2628** or 703/684-0580), operates Tuesday through Sunday April through August, Friday to Sunday September to mid-October, and Saturday and Sunday mid-October until late October. It departs at 10:30am for Mount Vernon from the pier adjacent to the Torpedo Factory, where Union and Cameron streets intersect, at Old Town Alexandria's waterfront. The rate is $40 per adult, $20 per child (ages 6–11; free for children 5 and under). Arrive 30 minutes ahead of time at the pier to secure a place on the boat. The narrated trip takes 90 minutes each way, stopping at Gaylord's National Harbor to pick up and discharge passengers. The boat departs Mount Vernon at 4pm to return to Old Town by 5:30pm, via Gaylord's.

And here's a clever way to travel to and from Mount Vernon: The Potomac Riverboat Company and **Bike & Roll** (p. 244) have teamed up to offer **Bike & Boat,** which includes bike rental from Bike & Roll's Old Town Alexandria location at the waterfront, admission to Mount Vernon, and a narrated return trip back to Old Town aboard the *Miss Christin.* You pedal your own way along the Mount Vernon Trail (p. 199) to reach the estate. The package costs $63 for ages 13 and older, $40 ages 6 to 12, and $20 ages 2 to 5.

If you're up for it, you can rent a bike and pedal the 18-mile round-trip distance at your own pace any time of year. See p. 158 for bike rental information.

Finally, it is possible to take **public transportation** to Mount Vernon by riding the Metro to the Yellow Line's Huntington station and proceeding to the lower level, where you catch the Fairfax Connector bus (no. 101) to Mount Vernon. The connector bus departs hourly on weekends, every 30 minutes weekdays; it's a 25-minute ride and costs $1.80. Call © **703/339-7200** or check www.fairfaxconnector.com for schedule information.

Touring the Estate

Mount Vernon Estate and Gardens ★★★   If it's beautiful out and you have the time, you could easily spend half a day or more soaking in the life and times of George Washington at Mount Vernon. The centerpiece of a visit to this 500-acre estate is a tour through 14 rooms of the mansion, whose oldest part dates from the 1740s. The plantation was passed down from Washington's great-grandfather, who acquired the land in 1674, to George's half-brother, and eventually to George himself in 1754. Washington proceeded over the next 45 years to expand and fashion the home to his liking, though the American Revolution and his years as president kept Washington away from his beloved estate much of the time.

Start your tour by visiting the estate's modern **Ford Orientation Center** and the **Donald W. Reynolds Museum and Education Center,** located just inside the main gate. Much of the complex is built underground so as not to take away from the estate's pastoral setting. A 15-minute film in the orientation center fills you in on the life and character of George Washington. The education center's 25 galleries and theater presentations, and display of 500 original artifacts, inform you further about Washington's military and presidential careers, rounding out the whole story of this heroic, larger-than-life man. It's especially helpful to absorb this information and gain some context for the life and times of Washington before setting off for the mansion, where tours are self-guided. Attendants stationed throughout the house and grounds do provide brief orientations and answer questions; when there's no line, a walk-through takes about 20 minutes. What you see today is a remarkable restoration of the mansion, displaying many original furnishings and objects used by the Washington family. The rooms have been repainted in the original colors chosen by George and Martha.

After leaving the house, you can tour the **outbuildings:** the kitchen, slave quarters, storeroom, smokehouse, overseer's quarters, coach house, and stables. A 4-acre exhibit area called **"George Washington Pioneer Farmer"** includes a replica of Washington's 16-sided barn and fields of crops that he grew (corn, wheat, oats, and so forth). Docents in period costumes demonstrate 18th-century farming methods. At its peak, Mount Vernon was an 8,000-acre working farm, which reminds us that Washington considered himself first and foremost a farmer.

You'll want to walk around the grounds (especially in nice weather) and see the wharf (and take a 45-min. narrated excursion on the Potomac, offered several times a day Tues–Sun Apr–Oct and weekends only in Mar; $10 per adult, $6 per child 2–11), the slave burial ground, the greenhouse, the lawns and gardens, and the tomb containing George and Martha Washington's sarcophagi (24 other family members are also interred here). Three miles south of Mount Vernon are the restored distillery and gristmill. Costumed staff members demonstrate 18th-century techniques as they operate the gristmill and distillery, which is open April through October. Admission to the distillery and gristmill is included in your ticket to Mount Vernon. If you're not visiting Mount Vernon, the admission here is $5 per adult and $2 per child; kids 5 and under enter free. You'll have to get to the gristmill on your own or take the Fairfax Connector bus no. 152 (www.fairfaxconnector.com; ✆ **703/339-7200**).

Celebrations are held at the estate every year on the third Monday in February, the date commemorating Washington's birthday; admission is free.

Mount Vernon belongs to the Mount Vernon Ladies' Association, which purchased the estate for $200,000 in 1858 from John Augustine Washington, great-grandnephew

Events at Mount Vernon, especially in the summer, include tours on 18th-century gardens, slave life, Colonial crafts, or archaeology, and, for children, hands- on history programs and treasure hunts. Call or check the website for schedule details.

of the first president. Without the group's purchase, the estate might have crumbled and disappeared, for neither the federal government nor the Commonwealth of Virginia wanted to buy the property when it was earlier offered for sale.

Today more than a million people tour the property annually. The best time to visit is off-season; during the heavy tourist months (especially in spring, when schoolchildren descend in droves), it's best to arrive in the afternoon, whether on a weekday or weekend, since student groups will have departed by then.

Note: On September 27, 2103, the Fred W. Smith National Library for the Study of George Washington opened at Mount Vernon as a think tank, repository of documents, and scholars residence, for the purpose of studying all things Washington.

3200 Mount Vernon Memorial Hwy. (mailing address: P.O. Box 110, Mount Vernon, VA 22121). www. mountvernon.org. ℂ **703/780-2000.** Admission $17 adults, $16 seniors, $8 children 6–11, free for children 5 and under. Apr–Aug daily 8am–5pm; Mar and Sept–Oct daily 9am–5pm; Nov–Feb daily 9am–4pm.

Dining & Shopping

Mount Vernon's comprehensive **gift shop** offers a wide range of books, children's toys, holiday items, Mount Vernon private-label food and wine, and Mount Vernon licensed furnishings. A **food court** features indoor and outdoor seating and a menu of baked goods, deli sandwiches, coffee, grilled items, pizza, and cookies. Although you can't **picnic** on the grounds of Mount Vernon, you can drive a mile north on the parkway to Riverside Park, where there are tables and a lawn overlooking the Potomac. However, I recommend the Mount Vernon Inn restaurant.

Mount Vernon Inn ★ AMERICAN TRADITIONAL   Lunch or dinner at the inn is an intrinsic part of the Mount Vernon experience. It's a quaint and charming Colonial-style restaurant, complete with period furnishings and three working fireplaces. The waiters are all in 18th-century costumes. Lunch entrees range from Colonial turkey "pye" (a sort of early American stew served in a crock with garden vegetables and a biscuit pastry top) to a pulled-pork barbecue sandwich. There's a full bar, and premium wines are offered by the glass. At dinner tablecloths and candlelight make this a more elegant setting. Choose from soups, perhaps the homemade peanut and chestnut; entrees such as roasted duck served with George Washington's favorite apricot sauce, or Colonial game pye with venison and rabbit. By the way, Mount Vernon has joined the happy hour trend, and now serves discounted beer, wine, and spirits, along with very un-Colonial appetizers, like duck fat truffle fries, from 4-7pm, Monday through Friday, in the bar.

Near the entrance to Mount Vernon Estate and Gardens. www.mountvernon.org. ℂ **703/780-0011.** Reservations recommended for dinner. Main courses lunch $9–$13, dinner $18–$26. Daily 11am–3:30pm (11:30am–2:30pm weekdays in winter); Mon–Thurs 5–8:30pm; Fri–Sat 5–9pm.

ALEXANDRIA

Old Town Alexandria is about 8 miles S of Washington.

The city of Washington may be named for our first president, but he never lived there. No, he called this other side of the Potomac home from the age of 11, when he joined his half-brother Lawrence, who owned Mount Vernon. Washington came to Alexandria often, helping to map out the 60-acre town's boundaries and roads when he was a lad of 17, training his militia in Market Square, worshiping at Christ Church, and dining and dancing at Gadsby's Tavern.

The town of Alexandria is actually named after John Alexander, the Scot who purchased the land of the present-day town from an English ship captain for "six thousand pounds of Tobacco and Cask." Incorporated in 1749, the town soon grew into a major trading center and port, known for its handsome houses.

Today, thanks to a multimillion-dollar urban renewal effort, some 200 structures from Alexandria's early days survive in Old Town's historic district. (Four thousand structures, in all, are deemed historic.) Market Square is the site of the oldest continuously operating farmers' market in the country. (Catch it on Sat btw. 7am and noon, and you'll be participating in a 261-year-old tradition.) Christ Church and Gadsby's Tavern are still open and operating. Many Alexandria streets still bear their original Colonial names (King, Queen, Prince, Princess, Royal), while others, like Jefferson, Franklin, Lee, Patrick, and Henry, are obviously post-Revolutionary.

Twenty-first-century America thrives in Old Town's many shops, boutiques, art galleries, bars, and restaurants. But it's still easy to imagine yourself in Colonial times as you listen for the rumbling of horse-drawn vehicles over cobblestone (portions of Prince and Oronoco sts. are still paved with cobblestone), dine on Sally Lunn bread and other 18th-century grub in the centuries-old Gadsby's Tavern, and learn about the lives of the nation's forefathers during walking tours that take you in and out of their houses.

Essentials

GETTING THERE If you're driving from the District, take the Arlington Memorial Bridge or the 14th Street Bridge to the George Washington Memorial Parkway south, which becomes Washington Street in Old Town Alexandria. Washington Street intersects with King Street, Alexandria's main thoroughfare. Turn left from Washington Street onto one of the streets before or after King Street (southbound left turns are not permitted from Washington St. onto King St.), and you'll be heading toward the waterfront and the heart of Old Town. If you turn right from Washington Street onto King Street, you'll still be in Old Town, with King Street's long avenue of shops and restaurants awaiting you. Parking is inexpensive at nearby garages and at street meters, but if you want to pay nothing, just drive a couple of blocks to streets off King St., north of Cameron St. or south of Duke St., where you can park for 2 or 3 hours for free. The town is compact, so you should be able to get around on foot, no problem.

The easiest way to make the trip is by Metro (www.wmata.com); Yellow and Blue Line trains travel to the King Street station. From the station, you can catch the free King Street Trolley, which operates daily 11:30am to 10:15pm, making frequent stops between the Metro station and the Potomac River. The eastbound AT2 or AT5 blue-and-gold DASH bus (www.dashbus.com; © **703/370-3274**) marked OLD TOWN or BRADDOCK METRO will also take you up King Street. Ask to be dropped at the corner

Old Town Alexandria

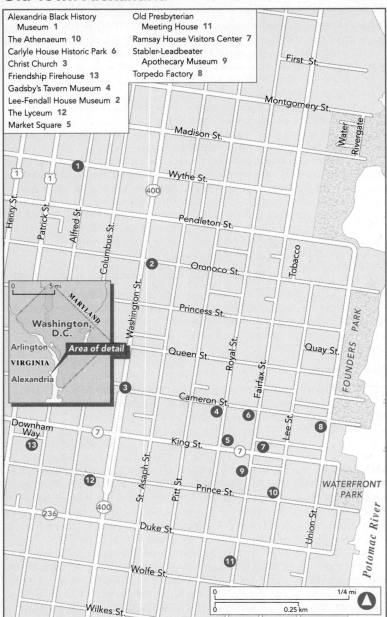

Alexandria Black History
  Museum **1**
The Athenaeum **10**
Carlyle House Historic Park **6**
Christ Church **3**
Friendship Firehouse **13**
Gadsby's Tavern Museum **4**
Lee-Fendall House Museum **2**
The Lyceum **12**
Market Square **5**

Old Presbyterian
  Meeting House **11**
Ramsay House Visitors Center **7**
Stabler-Leadbeater
  Apothecary Museum **9**
Torpedo Factory **8**

First St.

Montgomery St.

Madison St.

Wythe St.

Pendleton St.

Oronoco St.

Princess St.

Queen St.

Cameron St.

King St.

Prince St.

Duke St.

Wolfe St.

Wilkes St.

Henry St.

Patrick St.

Alfred St.

Columbus St.

Washington St.

St. Asaph St.

Pitt St.

Royal St.

Fairfax St.

Lee St.

Union St.

Quay St.

Tobacco

Water
Rivergate

FOUNDERS PARK

WATERFRONT
PARK

Potomac River

Downham
Way

13

12

1

2

3

4

5

6

7

8

9

10

11

7

7

400

400

1

1

236

0   5 mi

MARYLAND

**Washington,
D.C.**

Arlington

VIRGINIA

Alexandria

Area of detail

0   1/4 mi
0   0.25 km

of Fairfax and King streets, across the street from Alexandria Visitors Center at Ramsay House. The fare is $1.60. Or you can walk, and shop, the 1½ miles from the station into the center of Old Town.

VISITOR INFORMATION The **Alexandria Convention and Visitors Association's Visitors Center at Ramsay House,** 221 King St., at Fairfax Street (www. visitalexandriava.com; ℂ **800/388-9119** or 703/746-3301), is open daily April through December from 10am to 8pm (closed Thanksgiving, Dec 25, and Jan 1), and 10am to 5pm January through March. Here you can obtain a map/self-guided walking tour and brochures about the area, learn about special events that might be scheduled during your visit and get tickets for them, and receive answers to any questions you might have about accommodations, restaurants, sights, or shopping. The center supplies materials in five languages. You can also call ahead or go on the website to order a visitors guide and other information. Consider purchasing in advance online, or at the visitors center, a $9 per person "Key to the City" pass which covers admission to nine historic sites, and discounts at many attractions, shops, and restaurants. Valued at $26, the pass saves you $16 per person on admission prices alone, and more if you take advantage of the special offers.

ORGANIZED TOURS Though it's easy to see Alexandria on your own and with the help of Colonial-attired guides at individual attractions, you might consider taking a comprehensive walking tour of the town. Architecture and history tours leave from the visitors center garden March through mid-November, at least once a day, weather permitting. Tours depart at 10:30am Monday through Saturday and at 2pm on Sunday, with additional tours during busy seasons. These walk-up tours (no reservations needed) take 1½ hours and cost $15 per person (free for ages 6 and under). You pay the guide when you arrive.

As you'll see from reading about tours on the visitors center's website or from visiting the center once you're here, a slew of other organized tours is available, each focused on a particular subject. Ghosts tours may be the most popular. Check out **Alexandria Colonial Tours'** (www.alexcolonialtours.com; ℂ **703/519-1749**) **Ghosts and Graveyard Tour,** which is offered March through November (weather permitting) at various times and days—best to call for exact schedule. This 1-hour tour departs from Ramsay House and costs $13 for adults, $7 for children ages 7 to 17; it's free for children 6 and under. Reservations are recommended, though not required, for these tours; or you can purchase tickets from the guide, who will be dressed in Colonial attire and standing in front of the visitors center.

CITY LAYOUT Old Town is very small and laid out in an easy grid. At the center is the intersection of Washington Street and King Street. Streets change from north to south when they cross King Street; for example, North Alfred Street is the part of Alfred north of King Street (closest to Washington, in other words). Guess where South Alfred Street is.

Alexandria Calendar of Events

The **Alexandria Convention and Visitors Association** (www.visitalexandriava.com; ℂ **800/388-9119** or 703/746-3301) posts its calendar of events online and in its visitors guide, which you can order by phone or on its website. Event highlights include:

FEBRUARY

George Washington's Birthday is celebrated over the course of several days, including Presidents' Weekend, which precedes the federal holiday (the third Mon in Feb). Festivities typically include a Colonial-costume or black-tie banquet, followed by a ball at Gadsby's Tavern, a 10km race, special tours, a Revolutionary War encampment at Fort Ward Park (complete with uniformed troops engaging in skirmishes), the nation's largest George Washington Birthday Parade (50,000–75,000 people attend every year), and 18th-century comic opera performances. Most events, such as the parade and historical reenactments, are free. The Birthnight Ball at Gadsby's Tavern requires tickets for both the banquet and the ball.

MARCH

St. Patrick's Day Parade takes place on King Street on the first Saturday in March.

APRIL

Historic Garden Week in Virginia is celebrated with tours of privately owned local historic homes and gardens the third Saturday of the month. Call the visitor center (☎ **703/746-3301**) in early 2013 for more information about tickets and admission prices for the tour.

JULY

Alexandria's birthday (its 265th in 2013) is celebrated with a concert performance by the Alexandria Symphony Orchestra, fireworks, birthday cake, and other festivities. The Saturday following the Fourth of July. All events are free.

SEPTEMBER

Alexandria Festival of the Arts features the ceramics, sculpture, photography, and other works of more than 200 juried artists. On a

Saturday and Sunday in early September. Free.

OCTOBER

Ghost tours take place year-round but pick up around **Halloween.** A lantern-carrying guide in 18th-century costume describes Alexandria's ghosts, graveyards, legends, myths, and folklore as you tour the town and graveyards. Call the visitor center for information.

NOVEMBER

Christmas Tree Lighting is in Market Square, usually the Saturday after Thanksgiving. The ceremony, which includes choir singing, puppet shows, dance performances, and an appearance by Santa and his elves, begins at 7pm. The night the tree is lit, thousands of tiny lights adorning King Street trees also go on.

DECEMBER

The Annual Scottish Christmas Walk takes place on the first Saturday in December. Activities include kilted bagpipers, Highland dancers, a parade of Scottish clans (with horses and dogs), caroling, fashion shows, storytelling, booths (selling crafts, antiques, food, hot mulled punch, heather, fresh wreaths, and holly), and children's games. Admission is charged for some events. Call the Alexandria Convention and Visitors Association at ☎ **800/388-9119** for details.

The Historic Alexandria Candlelight Tour, the second week in December, visits seasonally decorated historic Alexandria homes and an 18th-century tavern. Colonial dancing, string quartets, madrigal and opera singers, and refreshments are part of the celebration. Purchase tickets at the Ramsay House Visitors Center.

What to See & Do

Colonial and post-Revolutionary buildings are Old Town Alexandria's main attractions. My favorites are the Carlyle House and Gadsby's Tavern Museum, but they're all worth a visit.

These sites are most easily accessible via the King Street Metro station, combined with a ride on the free King Street Trolley to the center of Old Town. The exceptions

biking TO OLD TOWN ALEXANDRIA & MOUNT VERNON

One of the nicest ways to view the Washington skyline is from across the river while biking in Virginia. You'll have a breathtaking view of the Potomac and of Washington's grand landmarks: the Kennedy Center, Washington Monument, Lincoln Memorial, Jefferson Memorial, and National Cathedral off in one direction, and the Capitol off in the other. Rent a bike at one of Bike & Roll's locations or at Thompson Boat Center, across from the Kennedy Center and right on the bike path (p. 244). Hop on the pathway that runs along the Potomac River and head toward the monuments and the Arlington Memorial Bridge. In Washington this is the Rock Creek Park Trail; when you cross Memorial Bridge (near the Lincoln Memorial)

into Virginia, the name changes to the Mount Vernon Trail, which leads, not surprisingly, straight to Mount Vernon.

Of course, this mode of transportation is also a great way to see Old Town Alexandria and Mount Vernon. The trail carries you past Reagan National Airport via two pedestrian bridges that take you safely through the airport's roadway system. Continue on to Old Town, where you should lock up your bike, walk around, tour some of the historic properties listed in this chapter, and take in some refreshment from one of the many excellent restaurants before you proceed to Mount Vernon. The section from Memorial Bridge to Mount Vernon is about 19 miles in all.

are the Alexandria Black History and Resource Center, whose closest Metro stop is the Braddock Street station, and Fort Ward, to which you should drive or take a taxi.

Old Town is also known for its fine shopping opportunities. Brand-name stores, charming boutiques, antiques shops, art galleries, and gift shops sell everything you might desire. The visitor center offers brochures for specific stores as well as a general guide to shopping. Notable local favorite shops include **Bellacara,** 1000 King St. (www.bellacara.com; ✆ **703/299-9652**) for fragrant soaps and more than 50 brands of luxe skin- and haircare products; **Society Fair,** 277 S. Washington St. (www.society fair.net; ✆ **703/683-3247**), Cathal Armstrong's (of Restaurant Eve; p. 204) latest venture, part bakery/market/butchery/wine bar/demo kitchen; **An American in Paris,** 1225 King St., Ste. 1 (www.anamericaninparisoldtown.com; ✆ **703/519-8234**), where one must knock on the door to enter and sort through the beautiful, one-of-a-kind cocktail dresses and evening gowns for sale; and **Why Not?,** 200 King St. (✆ **703/548-4420**), around for nearly 50 years selling children's clothes, books, and toys.

Alexandria Black History Museum ★   In 1939, African Americans in Alexandria staged a sit-in to protest the segregation of blacks from Alexandria's main library. The black community built its own public library, and it is this 1940s building that now serves as the Black History Resource Museum. The center exhibits historical objects, photographs, documents, and memorabilia relating to black citizens of Alexandria from the 18th century forward. In addition to the permanent collection, the museum presents rotating exhibits, genealogy workshops, book signings, and other activities. If you're interested in further studies, check out the center's Watson Reading Room. A half-hour may be enough time to spend at the center.

The museum is actually on the outskirts of Old Town. Once you've explored the museum, it makes sense to walk into Old Town, rather than taking the Metro or even a taxi. Have a staff person point you in the direction of Washington Street, east of the center; if you choose, you can turn right (or south) at Washington Street and walk 2 blocks or so to the **Lee-Fendall House** (p. 202) at Oronoco and Washington streets.

902 Wythe St. (at N. Alfred St.). www.alexblackhistory.org. ⓒ **703/746-4356.** Admission $2. Tues–Sat 10am–4pm. Metro: Braddock Road; from the station, walk across the parking lot and bear right until you reach the corner of West and Wythe sts., where you'll proceed 5 blocks east along Wythe until you reach the center.

The Athenaeum ★ This grand building, with its Greek Revival architectural style, stands out among the narrow Old Town houses on the cobblestone street. Built in 1851, the Athenaeum has been many things: the Bank of the Old Dominion, where Robert E. Lee kept his money prior to the Civil War; a commissary for the Union Army during the Civil War; a church; a triage center where wounded Union soldiers were treated; and a medicine warehouse. Now the hall serves as an art gallery and performance space for the Northern Virginia Fine Arts Association. Pop by to admire the Athenaeum's imposing exterior, including the four soaring Doric columns and its interior hall: 24-foot-high ceilings, enormous windows, and whatever contemporary art is on display. This won't take you more than 20 minutes.

201 Prince St. (at S. Lee St.). www.nvfaa.org. ⓒ **703/548-0035.** Free admission (donations accepted). Thurs–Fri and Sun noon–4pm; Sat 1–4pm. Closed major holidays.

Carlyle House Historic Park ★★ One of Virginia's most architecturally impressive 18th-century homes, Carlyle House also figured prominently in American history. A social and political center, the house was visited by the great men of the day, including George Washington. But its most important moment in history occurred in April 1755, when Major General Edward Braddock, commander-in-chief of His Majesty's forces in North America, met with five Colonial governors here and asked them to tax colonists to finance a campaign against the French and Indians. Colonial legislatures refused to comply, one of the first instances of serious friction between America and Britain.

When it was built, Carlyle House was a waterfront property with its own wharf. In 1753, Scottish merchant John Carlyle completed the mansion for his bride, Sarah Fairfax of Belvoir, a daughter of one of Virginia's most prominent families. It was designed in the style of a Scottish/English manor house and is lavishly furnished; Carlyle, a successful merchant, had the means to import the best furnishings and appointments available abroad for his new Alexandria home.

Tours are given on the hour and half-hour and take about 45 minutes; allow another 10 or 15 minutes if you plan to tour the tiered garden of brick walks and boxed parterres. Two of the original rooms, the large parlor and the dining room, have survived intact; the former, where Braddock met the governors, still retains its original fine woodwork, paneling, and pediments. The house is furnished in period pieces; however, only a few of Carlyle's possessions remain. In an upstairs room, an architecture exhibit depicts 18th-century construction methods.

121 N. Fairfax St. (btw. Cameron and King sts.). www.carlylehouse.org. ⓒ **703/549-2997.** Admission $5 adults, $3 children 5–12, free for children 4 and under. Tues–Sat 10am–4pm; Sun noon–4pm.

Christ Church ★★ This sturdy red-brick Georgian-style church would be an important national landmark even if its two most distinguished members had not been

Washington and Lee. It has been in continuous use since 1773; the town of Alexandria grew up around this building—it was once known as the "Church in the Woods." Over the years, the church has undergone many changes, adding the bell tower, church bell, galleries, and organ by the early 1800s, and the "wine-glass" pulpit in 1891. For the most part, the original structure remains, including the hand-blown glass in the windows.

Christ Church has had its historic moments. Washington and other early church members fomented revolution in the churchyard, and Robert E. Lee met here with Richmond representatives to discuss Lee's taking command of Virginia's military forces at the beginning of the Civil War. You can sit in the pew where George and Martha sat with her two Custis grandchildren, or in the Lee family pew. You might also want to walk through the graveyard and note how old the tombstones are, some dating from the mid to late 1700s.

World dignitaries and U.S. presidents have visited the church over the years. One of the most memorable of these visits took place shortly after Pearl Harbor, when Franklin Delano Roosevelt attended services with Winston Churchill on the World Day of Prayer for Peace, January 1, 1942.

Of course, you're invited to attend a service (Sun at 8, 9, and 11:15am and 5pm; Wed at 7:15am and 12:05pm). There's no admission charge, but donations are appreciated. A guide gives brief lectures to visitors. A gift shop is open Tuesday through Saturday 10am to 4pm, and Sunday 8:45am to noon. Twenty minutes should do it here. Be sure to check out the website before you visit, since it offers a wealth of information about the history of the church and town.

118 N. Washington St. (at Cameron St.). www.historicchristchurch.org. © **703/549-1450.** Donations appreciated. Mon–Sat 9am–4pm; Sun 2–4pm. Closed all federal holidays.

Fort Ward Museum & Historic Site ★   A short drive from Old Town is a 45-acre museum and park that transports you to Alexandria during the Civil War. The action here centers, as it did in the early 1860s, on an actual Union fort that Lincoln ordered erected. It was part of a system of Civil War forts called the "Defenses of Washington." About 90% of the fort's earthwork walls are preserved, and the Northwest Bastion has been restored with six mounted guns (originally there were 36). A model of 19th-century military engineering, the fort was never attacked by Confederate forces. Self-guided tours begin at the Fort Ward ceremonial gate.

Visitors can explore the fort and replicas of the ceremonial entrance gate and an officer's hut. A museum of Civil War artifacts on the premises features changing exhibits that focus on subjects such as Union arms and equipment, medical care of the wounded, and local war history.

There are picnic areas with barbecue grills in the park surrounding the fort. Living-history presentations take place throughout the year. This is a good stop if you have young children, in which case you could spend an hour or two here (especially if you bring a picnic).

4301 W. Braddock Rd. (btw. Rte. 7 and N. Van Dorn St.). www.fortward.org. © **703/746-4848.** Free admission (donations welcome). Park daily 9am–sunset. Museum Tues–Sat 10am–5pm; Sun noon–5pm. Call for information regarding special holiday closings. From Old Town, follow King St. west, go right on Kenwood Ave., then left on W. Braddock Rd.; continue for a mile to the entrance on the right.

Friendship Firehouse ★   Alexandria's first firefighting organization, the Friendship Fire Company, was established in 1774. In the early days, the company met in taverns and kept its firefighting equipment in a member's barn. Its present Italianate-style brick building dates from 1855; it was erected after an earlier building was, ironically, destroyed by fire. Local tradition holds that George Washington was involved with the firehouse as a founding member, active firefighter, and purchaser of its first fire engine, although research does not confirm these stories. The museum displays an 1851 fire engine, old hoses, buckets, and other firefighting apparatus. This is a tiny place that you can easily visit in 20 minutes.

107 S. Alfred St. (btw. King and Prince sts.). www.alexandriava.gov/friendshipfirehouse.℃ **703/746-3891.** Admission $2. Sat–Sun 1–4pm.

Gadsby's Tavern Museum ★★   Alexandria commanded center stage in 18th-century America, and Gadsby's Tavern the spotlight. The tavern consisted of two buildings—one Georgian, one Federal, dating from around 1785 and 1792, respectively. Innkeeper John Gadsby combined them to create "a gentleman's tavern," which he operated from 1796 to 1808; it was considered one of the finest in the country. George Washington was a frequent dinner guest; he and Martha danced in the second-floor ballroom, and it was here that Washington celebrated his last birthday. The tavern also welcomed Thomas Jefferson, James Madison, and the Marquis de Lafayette (the French soldier and statesman who served in the American army under Washington during the Revolutionary War and remained close to Washington). It was the setting of lavish parties, theatrical performances, small circuses, government meetings, and concerts. Itinerant merchants used the tavern to display their wares, and traveling doctors treated a hapless clientele (these were rudimentary professions in the 18th c.) on the premises.

The rooms have been restored to their 18th-century appearance. On the 30-minute tour, you'll get a good look at the Tap Room, a small dining room; the Assembly Room, the ballroom; typical bedrooms; and the underground icehouse, which was filled each winter from the icy river. Tours depart 15 minutes before and after the hour. Cap off the experience with a meal right next door, at the restored Colonial-style restaurant, **Gadsby's Tavern,** 138 N. Royal St., at Cameron Street (www.gadsbystavern restaurant.com; ℃ **703/548-1288**).

134 N. Royal St. (at Cameron St.). www.gadsbystavern.org.℃ **703/746-4242.** Admission $5 adults, $3 children 5–12, free for children 4 and under. Tours Apr–Oct Tues–Sat 10am–5pm, Sun–Mon 1–5pm; Nov–Mar Wed–Sat 11am–4pm, Sun 1–4pm. Closed most federal holidays.

Lee-Fendall House Museum ★★   This handsome Greek Revival–style house is a veritable Lee family museum of furniture, heirlooms, and documents. "Light Horse Harry" Lee never actually lived here, though he was a frequent visitor, as was his good friend George Washington. He did own the original lot but sold it to Philip Richard Fendall (himself a Lee on his mother's side), who built the house in 1785.

Thirty-seven Lees occupied the house over a period of 118 years (1785–1903), and it was in this house that Harry wrote Alexandria's farewell address to George Washington, delivered when he passed through town on his way to assume the presidency. (Harry also wrote and delivered the famous funeral oration to Washington that contained the words, "First in war, first in peace, and first in the hearts of his countrymen.") During the Civil War, the house was seized and used as a Union hospital.

Thirty-minute guided tours interpret the 1850s era of the home and provide insight into Victorian family life. You'll also see the Colonial garden, with its magnolia and chestnut trees, roses, and boxwood-lined paths. Much of the interior woodwork and glass is original.

614 Oronoco St. (at Washington St.). www.leefendallhouse.org. (C) **703/548-1789.** Admission $5 adults, $3 children 11–17, free for children 10 and under. Wed–Sat 10am–4pm; Sun 1–4pm. Call ahead to make sure the museum is open, since it often closes for special events. Tours on the hour 10am–3pm. Closed Jan and Thanksgiving.

The Lyceum ★   This Greek Revival building houses a museum depicting Alexandria's history from the 17th to the 20th century. It features changing exhibits and an ongoing series of lectures, concerts, and educational programs. You can obtain maps and brochures about Virginia state attractions, especially Alexandria attractions. The knowledgeable staff will be happy to answer questions.

The striking brick-and-stucco Lyceum also merits a visit. Built in 1839, it was designed in the Doric temple style to serve as a lecture, meeting, and concert hall. It was an important center of Alexandria's cultural life until the Civil War, when Union forces appropriated it for use as a hospital. After the war it became a private residence, and still later it was subdivided for office space. In 1969, however, the city council's use of eminent domain prevented the Lyceum from being demolished in favor of a parking lot. Allow about 20 minutes here.

201 S. Washington St. (off Prince St.). www.alexandriahistory.org. (C) **703/746-4994.** Admission $2. Mon–Sat 10am–5pm; Sun 1–5pm. Closed Jan 1, Thanksgiving, and Dec 25.

Old Presbyterian Meeting House ★   Presbyterian congregations have worshiped in Virginia since the Rev. Alexander Whittaker converted Pocahontas in Jamestown in 1614. The original version of this Presbyterian Meeting House was built in 1775. Although it wasn't George Washington's church, the Meeting House bell tolled continuously for 4 days after his death in December 1799, and memorial services were preached from the pulpit here by Presbyterian, Episcopal, and Methodist ministers. According to the Alexandria paper of the day, "The walking being bad to the Episcopal church the funeral sermon of George Washington will be preached at the Presbyterian Meeting House." Two months later, on Washington's birthday, Alexandria citizens marched from Market Square to the church to pay their respects.

Many famous Alexandrians are buried in the church graveyard, including John and Sarah Carlyle; Dr. James Craik (the surgeon who treated—some say killed—Washington, dressed Lafayette's wounds at Brandywine, and ministered to the dying Braddock at Monongahela); and William Hunter, Jr., founder of the St. Andrew's Society of Scottish descendants, to whom bagpipers pay homage on the first Saturday of December. It is also the site of a Tomb of an Unknown Revolutionary War Soldier. Dr. James Muir, minister between 1789 and 1820, lies beneath the sanctuary in his gown and bands. The cemetery has a larger burial ground located nearby that has been used since 1809.

When lightning struck and set afire most of the original Meeting House in 1835, parishioners rebuilt the church in 1837, incorporating as much as they could from the earlier structure. This is the church you see today. The present bell, said to be recast from the metal of the old one, was hung in a newly constructed belfry in 1843, and a new organ was installed in 1849. The Meeting House closed its doors in 1889 and for 60 years was used sporadically. But in 1949 it was reborn as a living Presbyterian U.S.A. church, and today the Old Meeting House looks much as it did following its first restoration. The original parsonage, or manse, is still intact. There's no guided tour. Allow 20 minutes to look around.

9

DAY TRIPS FROM WASHINGTON, D.C.

Alexandria

323 S. Fairfax St. (btw. Duke and Wolfe sts.). www.opmh.org. © **703/549-6670.** Free admission, but you must obtain a key from the office to tour the church. Sun services 8:30 and 11am (only 10am in summer).

Stabler-Leadbeater Apothecary Museum ★★   When its doors closed in 1933, this landmark drugstore was the second oldest in continuous operation in America. Run for five generations by the same Quaker family (beginning in 1792), the store counted Robert E. Lee (who purchased the paint for Arlington House here), George Mason, Henry Clay, John C. Calhoun, and George Washington among its famous patrons. Gothic Revival decorative elements and Victorian-style doors were added in the 1840s. Today the apothecary looks much as it did in Colonial times, its shelves lined with original handblown gold-leaf-labeled bottles (the most valuable collection of antique medicinal bottles in the country), old scales stamped with the royal crown, patent medicines, and equipment for bloodletting. The clock on the rear wall, the porcelain-handled mahogany drawers, and two mortars and pestles all date from about 1790. Among the shop's documentary records is this 1802 order from Mount Vernon: "Mrs. Washington desires Mr. Stabler to send by the bearer a quart bottle of his best Castor Oil and the bill for it." The museum is open for guided tours only, which take place 15 minutes before and after the hour, and last 30 minutes.

105–107 S. Fairfax St. (near King St.). www.apothecarymuseum.org. © **703/746-3852.** Admission $5 adults, $3 children 5–12, free for children 4 and under. Apr–Oct Tues–Sat 10am–5pm, Sun–Mon 1–5pm; Nov–Mar Wed–Sat 11am–4pm, Sun 1–4pm. Closed major holidays.

Torpedo Factory ★   This block-long, three-story building was built in 1918 as a torpedo shell-case factory but now accommodates some 82 artists' studios, where 165 professional artists and craftspeople create and sell their own works. Here you can see artists at work in their studios: from potters to painters, as well as those who create stained-glass windows and fiber art.

On permanent display are exhibits on Alexandria history provided by Alexandria Archaeology (www.alexandriaarchaeology.org; © **703/746-4399**), which is headquartered here and engages in extensive city research. A volunteer or staff member is on hand to answer questions. Art lovers may end up browsing for an hour or two.

105 N. Union St. (btw. King and Cameron sts., on the waterfront). www.torpedofactory.org. © **703/838-4565.** Free admission. Daily 10am–6pm (Thurs until 9pm). Archaeology exhibit area Tues–Fri 10am–3pm; Sat 10am–5pm; Sun 1–5pm. Closed Jan 1, Easter, July 4, Thanksgiving, and Dec 25.

Where to Eat

There are a number of Alexandria restaurants that are so well liked that Washingtonians often drive over just to dine here. The following are among the best to suit assorted budgets, tastes, and styles; all are easily accessible via the King Street Metro station, combined with a ride on the free King Street Trolley to the center of Old Town.

EXPENSIVE

Restaurant Eve ★★★ NEW AMERICAN   Named for the first child of owners Cathal (the chef) and Meshelle Armstrong, Eve is nationally recognized and locally beloved, which means it can be hard—really hard—to score a reservation. You have two options: the casual bistro with an a la carte menu, and the elegant tasting room where only prix-fixe menus are offered. I recommend the bistro, where the atmosphere is convivial and the cuisine as excellent as you'll find in the tasting room, only the portions are of normal size. (The tasting room's dishes present exquisite morsels, but that's what they are, morsels.) Bistro entrees might include bouillabaisse and sirloin of veal; tasting-menu items range from butter-poached lobster with heirloom carrots to gnocchi with spring garlic and golden beets. Chef Armstrong has long been committed to seasonal cooking, using the fresh produce of local farmers. Don't miss Eve's best dessert: an old-fashioned "birthday cake," which is a mouthwatering slice of white cake layered and iced with pink frosting and sprinkles. And be sure to read over the wine and cocktails list, since sommelier and "liquid savant" Todd Thrasher has gained such renown for his inventive concoctions—"Millions of Peaches" (peach vodka, champagne-vinegar-pickled peaches, and poached peaches), "Jose's Yin and Tonic" (made with house-made tonic)—that he's opened a nearby speakeasy lounge, **PX,** located just above **Eamonn's A Dublin Chipper** (see below), where he dispenses more fun drinks and good times.

110 S. Pitt St. (near King St.). www.restauranteve.com. ℰ **703/706-0450.** Reservations recommended. Jacket advised for men in bistro; jacket and tie advised for men in tasting room. Bistro lunch items $18–$25; dinner main courses $35–$40; tasting room fixed-price 5-course dinner $120, 7-course $135, 9-course $150; lunch menu special (served at the bar weekdays 11:30am–3:30pm) $15 for any two items. Bistro Tues–Fri 11:30am–2:30pm; Tues–Sat 5:30–10pm. Tasting room Tues–Sat 5:30–9:30pm.

MODERATE

Majestic Café ★★ SOUTHERN   A lively bar fronts the narrow restaurant, making a dining experience here a little noisy; that can be either annoying or festive, depending on your mood. I promise, though, that you'll enjoy the grilled calamari salad, soft-shell crabs, artichoke and fontina cheese tart, spoon bread, hush puppies, and, for dessert, German chocolate cake. The Majestic offers a bar lunch special Monday through Friday from 11:30am to 2:30pm—any lunch entree for $12—and a Sunday dinner special: $22 per person and a set menu.

911 King St. (near Alfred St.). www.majesticcafe.com. ℰ **703/837-9117.** Reservations recommended. Main courses lunch $11–$26, dinner $19–$27. Mon–Sat 11:30am–2:30pm; Mon–Thurs 5:30–10pm; Fri–Sat 5:30–10:30pm; Sun 1–9pm.

INEXPENSIVE

Eamonn's A Dublin Chipper ★ FISH & CHIPS   Fish and chips and a few sides (onion rings, coleslaw)—that's what we're talking here. But it's charming. Upstairs is **PX,** an exclusive lounge, where mixologist Todd Thrasher may be on hand to shake the drinks he's created. This is another in the strand of restaurant experiences that Cathal and Meshelle Armstrong are perpetrating on this side of the Potomac. The Chipper is named after their son Eamonn, **Restaurant Eve** (see above) for their first-born daughter. The Armstrongs have a following, so expect a crowd.

728 King St. www.eamonnsdublinchipper.com. ℰ **703/299-8384.** Reservations not accepted. Main courses $5–$9. Mon–Wed 11:30am–10pm; Thurs 11:30am–11pm; Fri 11:30am–midnight; Sat noon–midnight; Sun noon–closing.

La Madeleine ★ FRENCH CAFE   It may be part of a self-service chain, but this place has its charms. Its French-country interior has a beamed ceiling, oak floors, a wood-burning stove, and maple hutches displaying crockery and pewter mugs. The range of affordable menu items here makes this a good choice for families with finicky eaters in tow.

La Madeleine opens early—at 6:30am every day—so come for breakfast to feast on fresh-baked croissants, Danish, scones, muffins, and brioches, or a heartier bacon-and-eggs plate. Throughout the day, there are salads, sandwiches (including a traditional croque monsieur), and hot dishes ranging from quiche and pizza to rotisserie chicken with a Caesar salad. After 5pm additional choices include pastas and specials such as beef tenders *en merlot* or herb-crusted pork tenderloin, both served with garlic mashed potatoes and green beans amandine. Conclude with a fruit tart, or chocolate, vanilla, and praline triple-layer cheesecake with graham-cracker crust. Wine and beer are served.

500 King St. (at S. Pitt St.). www.lamadeleine.com. © **703/739-2854.** Reservations not accepted. Main courses breakfast $5–$9, lunch and dinner $5–$13. Sun–Thurs 6:30am–10pm; Fri–Sat 6:30am–11pm.

Nightlife

Old Town Alexandria's nightlife options center on the bar scene, which is nearly as varied as the one across the Potomac in the District. In fact, a number of popular, in-town restaurant-bars have outposts here, including **Pizzeria Paradiso** (p. 79), at 124 King St. (www.eatyourpizza.com; © **703/837-1245**), whose cozy bar is situated behind a large glass fireplace and serves 14 drafts, one cask ale, American microbrews and Belgian beers. If you're in the mood for raucous singalongs, make your way to **Murphy's Pub,** 713 King St. (www.murphyspub.com; © **703/548-1717**), where live Irish music plays nightly. And for sophisticated ambience, check out **Vermilion,** 1120 King St. (www.vermilionrestaurant.com; © **703/684-9669**), which is both a fine restaurant and upscale cocktail lounge, complete with cushioned benches, specialty drinks, and all the other trappings of a hipster scene. Come here Tuesday or Wednesday nights at 9:30pm and you'll enjoy live performances by established local musicians.

Where to Stay

With a total of 4,200 hotel guest rooms, Alexandria will have no trouble accommodating you should you decide to stay overnight. Hotels run the budget gamut, from **Comfort Inns** (www.comfortinn.com) at the low end to the posh **Lorien Hotel and Spa,** 1600 King St. (www.lorienhotelandspa.com; © **703/894-3434**) at the luxe end. Two properties lie especially close to the heart of historic Old Town. The **Hotel Monaco Alexandria,** at 480 King St. (www.monaco-alexandria.com; © **800/368-5047** or 703/549-6080), is a luxury boutique property with 241 stylish rooms, a pool, a health club, and a chef-driven restaurant. Rates vary by season and date, but expect to pay from $170 to $300 on the weekends, $229 to $370 weekdays, for a standard double room.

Morrison House, 116 S. Alfred St. (www.morrisonhouse.com; © **866/834-6628** or 703/838-8000), is also a standout, often chosen by *Condé Nast Traveler* for its Gold List. Its 45 rooms are appointed with canopied four-poster beds, mahogany armoires, decorative fireplaces, and the like. Rates can start at $129 for the smallest room off-season on the weekend and at $289 for a standard room on a weekday in season. Morrison House is known for its restaurant, the **Grille,** which presents award-winning contemporary American cuisine.

For other recommendations, check the **Alexandria Convention and Visitors Association** website, **www.visitalexandriava.com**, where you can book an online reservation and also read about various promotions that hotels are offering.

SELF-GUIDED WALKING TOURS

One of the greatest pleasures to be had in the nation's capital is walking. You round a corner and spy the Capitol standing proudly at the end of the avenue. You stroll a downtown street and chance to look up and bam, there it is: the tip of the Washington Monument. People brush past you on the sidewalk speaking a pastiche of languages. You decide to walk rather than take the Metro or a taxi back to your hotel and discover a gem of a museum. A limousine pulls up to the curb and discharges—who? A foreign ambassador? The president himself? A famous author or athlete or human rights activist?

Beautiful sights, historic landmarks, unpredictable encounters, and multicultural experiences await you everywhere in Washington. Follow any of these three, self-guided walking tours and see for yourself.

10

WALKING TOUR 1: STROLLING AROUND THE WHITE HOUSE

START:	**White House Visitor Center, 1450 Pennsylvania Ave. NW (Metro: Federal Triangle or Metro Center).**
FINISH:	**The Penn Quarter (Metro: Federal Triangle or Metro Center).**
TIME:	**1½ hours to 2 hours (not including stops). It's about a 1.6-mile trek.**
BEST TIME:	**During the day. If you want to hit all of the museums, stroll on a Thursday of Friday.**
WORST TIME:	**After dark, as some streets can be deserted.**

The White House is the centerpiece of a national park, President's Park, which includes not just the house itself but also its grounds, from the Ellipse to Pennsylvania Avenue to Lafayette Square; the U.S. Treasury Building on 15th Street; and the Eisenhower Executive Office Building on 17th Street. The individual histories of many of the surrounding buildings and sites are entwined with that of the White House. As you wend your way from landmark to landmark, you'll be mingling with White House administration staff, high-powered attorneys, diplomats, and ordinary

Strolling Around the White House

1 U.S. Treasury Building

2 Pennsylvania Avenue

3 Lafayette Square

4 St. John's Episcopal Church on Lafayette Square

5 Decatur House

6 White House

7 Renwick Gallery

8 Eisenhower Executive Office Building

9 Octagon House

10 Todd Gray's Muse at the Corcoran 🍵

11 Corcoran Gallery of Art

12 DAR Museum and Period Rooms

13 Art Museum of the Americas

14 Ellipse

office workers. But all of you are treading the same ground as early American heroes, like Stephen Decatur, whose house you'll see, and every president since George Washington (though the White House was not finished in time for him to live there).

This tour circumnavigates the White House grounds, with stops at historic sites and several noteworthy museums, as well. The White House Visitor Center (see "Midtown," in chapter 6) is a good place to begin and end (for one thing, it's got restrooms!). *Note:* Tours of the White House were suspended in 2013, but should they have resumed by the time you are reading this. If you're interested in a tour, you'll need an advance reservation. A tour of the U.S. Treasury Building requires the same. Go to www.treasury.gov/about/education/pages/tours.aspx to register for a Treasury Building tour; for White House tour info, see p. 128.

From the White House Visitor Center, stroll up 15th Street to your first stop, at 15th and F streets NW.

---

1 U.S. Treasury Building

Poor Alexander Hamilton. His statue outside the south end of the U.S. Treasury Building stands too close to the White House for security's comfort to allow stray tourists a better look, so now you must resign yourself to gazing at him from a distance through the black iron fencing. (Also, Alexander Hamilton was killed in a duel with his political enemy, Vice President Aaron Burr.) Hamilton, who devised our modern financial system, was the first Secretary of the Treasury, established by Congress in 1789. So once you've caught a glimpse of Hamilton's statue, have a look inside the Treasury's headquarters, America's oldest office building, constructed between 1836 and 1869. Its most notable architectural feature is the colonnade you see running the length of the building: 30 columns, each 36 feet tall, carved out of a single piece of granite. In its lifetime, the building has served as Civil War barracks, as a temporary home for President Andrew Johnson following the assassination of President Lincoln in 1865, and as the site of President Ulysses S. Grant's inaugural reception. Today the building houses offices for the U.S. Treasurer, the Secretary of the Treasury, its General Counsel, and their staffs.

Continue north on 15th Street and turn left onto the Pennsylvania Avenue promenade, where you'll notice the statue of Albert Gallatin, the fourth Secretary of the Treasury, standing accessibly on the north side of the Treasury Building. Continue along:

2 Pennsylvania Avenue

Say hello to the President, who resides in that big white house beyond the black iron fencing. Security precautions put in place in 1995 keep this 2-block section of Pennsylvania Avenue closed to traffic. But that's a good thing. You may have to dodge bicyclists, roller skaters, joggers, and random Frisbees, but not cars. Ninety Princeton American elm trees line the 84-foot-wide promenade, which offers plenty of great photo ops as you stroll past the White House. There are benches here, too, in case you'd like to sit and people-watch. L'Enfant's original idea for Pennsylvania Avenue was that it would connect the legislative branch (Congress) at one end of the avenue with the executive branch (the president's house) at the other end.

Turn your back on the White House and walk across the plaza to enter:

3 Lafayette Square

This 7-acre public park is known as a gathering spot for protesters. (In pleasant weather, when the White House keeps its doors and windows open, one can actually hear the protesters from inside the White House, as I discovered during a recent White House tour.) In its early days, the park served as an open-air market and as a military encampment. The park is named after the Marquis de Lafayette, a Frenchman who served under George Washington during the Revolutionary War. But it's General Andrew Jackson's statue that centers the park. Erected in 1853, this was America's first equestrian statue. It's said that sculptor Clark Mills trained a horse to maintain a reared-up pose so that Mills could study how the horse balanced its weight. Other park statues are dedicated to foreign soldiers who fought in the War for Independence, including Lafayette; Tadeusz Kościuszko, from Poland; Prussian Baron von Steuben; and Frenchman Comte de Rochambeau.

Walk through the park and cross H Street to reach 1525 H St. NW, the site of:

4 St. John's Episcopal Church on Lafayette Square

St. John's is known as "the Church of the Presidents" because every president since James Madison has attended at least one service here. If you tour the church, look for pew 54, 8 rows from the front, which is the one traditionally reserved for the current president and first family. Other things to notice in this 1816 church, designed by Benjamin Henry Latrobe, are the steeple bell, which was cast by Paul Revere's son and has been in continuous use since its installation in 1822, and the beautiful stained-glass windows. And be careful not to overlook the Lincoln Pew at the very back of the church, where Lincoln would sit alone for evening services during the Civil War, slipping in after other congregants had arrived and slipping out before they left.

Directly across the street from St. John's is the Hay-Adams Hotel, which turns 86 this year (p. 50). Recross H Street to stand in front of 748 Jackson Place NW, the:

5 Decatur House

In addition to St. John's, Latrobe also designed this Federal-style brick town house in 1818 for Commodore Stephen Decatur, a renowned naval hero in the War of 1812. Decatur and his wife, Susan, established themselves as gracious hosts in the 14 short months they lived here. In March 1820, 2 days after hosting a ball for President James Monroe's daughter, Marie, Decatur was killed in a gentleman's duel by his former mentor, James Barron. Barron blamed Decatur for his 5-year suspension from the Navy, following a court-martial in which Decatur had played an active role. Other distinguished occupants have included Henry Clay and Martin Van Buren, when each was serving as Secretary of State (Clay under Pres. John Quincy Adams, Van Buren under Pres. Andrew Jackson). Decatur House is no longer open for house tours, but do stop in at the White House Historical Association's gift shop, at the entrance to Decatur House, at 1610 H Street.

Walk back through Lafayette Square to return to the Pennsylvania Avenue plaza, where you'll have another chance to admire the:

6 White House

As grand as the White House is, it is at least one-fourth the size that Pierre L'Enfant had in mind when he planned a grand palace to house the President. George Washington and his commission had something else in mind, however, and dismissed L'Enfant, though they kept L'Enfant's site proposal. An Irishman named James Hoban designed the building, having entered his architectural draft in a contest held by George Washington, beating out 52 other entries. Though Washington picked the winner, he was the only president never to live in the White House, or "President's Palace," as it was called before whitewashing brought the name "White House" into use. Construction of the White House took 8 years, beginning in 1792, when its cornerstone was laid. Its facade is made of the same stone as that used to construct the Capitol. See p. 128 for in-depth information about the White House and tours.

Turn around and head toward the northwest corner of the plaza, at 17th Street, to reach the:

7 Renwick Gallery

Its esteemed neighbors are the White House and, right next door, the Blair-Lee House, where the White House sends overnighting foreign dignitaries. The Renwick (p. 126), nevertheless, holds its own. This distinguished redbrick and brownstone structure was the original location for the Corcoran Gallery of Art. James Renwick designed the building (if it reminds you of the Smithsonian Castle on the Mall, it's because Renwick designed that one, too), which opened in 1874. When the collection outgrew its quarters, the Corcoran moved to its current location in 1897 (see below). Decorative arts and American crafts are the focus of the Renwick, which since 1972 has operated as an annex of the Smithsonian American Art Museum, 8 blocks away in the Penn Quarter. Alas, the Renwick is closed until 2016 for a major renovation.

Turn left on 17th Street, where you'll notice on your left the:

8 Eisenhower Executive Office Building

Old-timers still refer to this ornate building as the "OEOB," for "Old Executive Office Building"; as it sounds, the EEOB houses the offices of people who work in or with the Executive Office of the President. Originally, the structure was called the State, War, and Navy Building; when its construction was completed in 1888, it was the largest office building in the world. During the Iran-Contra scandal of the Reagan presidency, the OEOB became famous as the site of document shredding by Colonel Oliver North and his secretary Fawn Hall. Open to the public? Nope.

Cross 17th Street, walk a couple of blocks to New York Avenue, and turn right. Follow it 1 block to 18th Street, where you'll see the unmistakable:

9 Octagon House

Lot of history in this old house. But first, before you enter, admire its unique shape. Count its sides and you'll discover that the Octagon is, in fact, a hexagon. Designed by Dr. William Thornton, first architect of the U.S. Capitol, this 1801 building apparently earned its name from interior features, though experts disagree about that. Enter the Octagon to view the round rooms; the central, oval-shaped staircase that curves gracefully to the third level; the hidden doors; and the triangular chambers. Built originally for the wealthy Tayloe family, the Octagon served as a temporary president's home for James and Dolley Madison after the British torched the White House in 1814. On February 17, 1815, President Madison sat at the circular table in the upstairs circular room and signed the Treaty of Ghent, establishing peace with Great Britain. The house has served as the national headquarters for the American Institute of Architects since 1899. See p. 126 for more info about tours.

Cross New York Avenue and return to 17th Street, where you should turn right and walk to the Corcoran Gallery of Art. Go ahead and enter, but before you start touring, stop for a delicious break at:

10 Todd Gray's Muse at the Corcoran 💭

How wonderful that one of the city's best chefs, Todd Gray, has designed the menu for the Corcoran's in-house cafe (www.toddgraysmuse.com; ℭ 202/639-1786). The setting itself, behind Doric columns and under a lofty skylight ceiling, is lovely and unusual. The menu includes soups, salads, sandwiches, and select desserts. I've ordered the egg salad sandwich on brioche, which, as it turns out, is layered with a wide, thin slice of crisply peppery organic heirloom watermelon radish. The menu is pricey—sandwiches cost around $8.95 and are unaccompanied by the usual chips or fries—but the food is worth it.

After you've satisfied your hunger, start exploring the:

11 Corcoran Gallery of Art

At the Corcoran, you can view historic American art, like Remington sculptures, Albert Bierstadt landscapes, Edward Hopper iconic scenes, and John Singer Sargent portraits. And you can view astonishing European artwork that ranges from an 18th-century period room (the "Salon Doré," or "gilded drawing room"), transported in toto from Paris, to paintings by Picasso, Corot, and Gainsborough. But this gallery, which was the first art museum in Washington and one of the first in the country, has always had a penchant for playing the wild card. In 1851 gallery founder William Corcoran caused a stir when he displayed artist Hiram Powers's *The Greek Slave*, which was the first publicly exhibited, life-size American sculpture depicting a fully nude female figure. Today, provocations might come in the form of a juxtaposition of Civil War photographs and shots of American soldiers in Afghanistan, or of art that engages all of your senses—even smell—as did the recently displayed Mary Early sculpture, which used beeswax and wood to investigate space through the intersection of form, line, light, and shadow.

Exit to 17th Street and turn right, away from the White House. Follow it down to D Street and turn right, following the signs that lead to the entrance of the:

12 DAR Museum and Period Rooms

The National Headquarters of the Daughters of the American Revolution comprises three joined buildings that take up an entire block. The middle building, Memorial Continental Hall, is the one you'll enter. Dedicated to the heroes of the American Revolution, the building's cornerstone was laid in 1902 with the same trowel that George Washington used to lay the cornerstone for the Capitol. At the time, the front of the building faced the White House pasture, where presidential cattle grazed. At any rate, what you're here for is the DAR Museum, which rotates exhibits of items from its 33,000-object collection, and the 31 period rooms, representing decors from the past, as interpreted by different states. The museum's collections veer from folk art to decorative arts and include old rocking chairs, ceramics, needlework samplers, and lots of silver. Quilters from far and wide come to admire a large collection of quilts, many of which are kept in glass sleeves that you can pull out from a case for better viewing. Period rooms are viewable from the doorways, a velvet rope preventing your entry. Highlights include the New Jersey Room, which replicates an English Council chamber of the 17th century, with woodwork and furnishings created from the salvaged oak timbers of the British frigate *Augusta*, which sank during the Revolutionary War; an opulent Victorian Missouri parlor; and New Hampshire's "Children's Attic," filled with 19th-century toys, dolls, and children's furnishings. You can tour the museum and Period Rooms on your own, but you might consider taking a free docent-led tour if you're interested in American decorative arts.

Exit the DAR, turning left and continuing along D Street to 18th Street, where you'll turn left again and follow to 201 18th St. NW, the pretty, Spanish colonial–style building that houses the:

13 Art Museum of the Americas

Off the beaten path, but just slightly—across Constitution Avenue, the World War II Memorial is a short walk to the left, and the Vietnam Veterans Memorial a short walk to the right—the Art Museum of the Americas (AMA) showcases the works of contemporary Latin American and Caribbean artists. For example, a recent exhibit focused on the theme of mobility and migration, as interpreted by Spanish and Latin American artists living in New York City. You'll be on your own; a tour takes 30 minutes, tops. Not to miss: a stunning loggia whose tall beamed ceiling and wall of deep-blue tiles set in patterns modeled after Aztec and Mayan art constitute a work of art on its own. A series of French (and usually locked) doors leads to a terrace and the museum's garden, which separates the museum from the Organization of American States headquarters that owns it. When you leave the museum, you may notice the nearby sculptures of José Artigus, "Father of the Independence of Uruguay," and a large representation of liberator Simón Bolívar on horseback.

From 18th Street, head back in the direction of the White House, turning right on C Street, which takes you past the AMA's garden and the OAS headquarters. Turn left on 17th Street and follow it to E Street. Then cross 17th Street and pick up the section of E Street that takes you between the South Lawn of the White House and the:

14 Ellipse

Sadly, the Ellipse is not the picturesque parkland it once was, thanks to unsightly wire fencing and other barriers that keep you on the circumscribed paths. Should you stray, one of the zillion police officers on duty quickly sets you straight. (I speak from experience.) The Ellipse continues to be the site for the National Christmas Tree Lighting Ceremony every December, and a spot near the Zero Milestone monument remains a favored place for shooting photos against the backdrop of the White House. Rumor has it that a remodeling of the Ellipse is in the works, so perhaps you will arrive to find a welcoming plaza and picnic area with which to end your tour. If not, keep walking a few more steps to return to 15th Street NW in the Penn Quarter, and its many options for an end-of-stroll repast.

START:	**Kafe Leopold's (D.C. Circulator; nearest Metro stop Foggy Bottom).**
FINISH:	**Old Stone House (D.C. Circulator; nearest Metro stop Foggy Bottom).**
TIME:	**2½ to 3 hours (not including stops). The distance is about 3.5 miles.**
BEST TIME:	**Weekday mornings are best to start out. If you want to do the house and museum tours, go Tuesday to Sunday.**
WORST TIME:	**Saturday, when Georgetown's crazy social scene sometimes spills over into the back streets.**

The Georgetown famous for its shops, restaurants, and bars is not the Georgetown you'll see on this walking tour. Instead, the circuit will take you along quiet streets lined with charming houses and stately trees that remind you of the town's age and history. The original George Town, comprising 60 acres and named for the king of England, was officially established in 1751. It assumed new importance in 1790 when President George Washington, with help from his Secretary of State, Thomas Jefferson, determined that America's new capital city would be located on a site nearby on the Potomac River. Georgetown was incorporated into the District of Columbia in 1871.

10

Georgetown

SELF-GUIDED WALKING TOURS

Get your stroll off to a good start by stopping first for pastries or something more substantial at 3315 Cady's Alley NW, no. 213, the charming:

1 Kafe Leopold's ☕

Through a passageway and down a flight of stairs from busy M Street NW lies a cluster of chichi shops and Kafe Leopold's (www.kafeleopolds.com; (✆ 202/965-6005), a cute little Austrian coffeehouse that serves breakfast items until 4pm and assorted other delicious dishes all day. Onion tarts, veal schnitzel, tea sandwiches, endive salad, croque-monsieur sandwiches, apple strudel, smoked fish with caperberries, Viennese coffee, and champagne cocktails are all on the menu. Leopold's opens daily at 8am and stays open until at least 10pm.

Return now to M Street, turn left, and continue to 3350 M St. NW, where you'll find the:

2 Forrest-Marbury House

No one notices this nondescript building on the edge of Georgetown near Key Bridge. But the plaque on its pink-painted brick facade hints at reasons for giving the 1788 building a once-over. Most significant is the fact that on March 29, 1791, Revolutionary War hero Uriah Forrest hosted a dinner here for his old friend George Washington and landowners who were being asked to sell their land for the purpose of creating the federal city of Washington, District of Columbia. The meeting was a success, and America's capital was born. Forrest and his wife lived here until Federalist William Marbury bought the building in 1800. Marbury is the man whose landmark case, *Marbury v. Madison,* resulted in the recognition of the Supreme Court's power to rule on the constitutionality of laws passed by Congress and in the institutionalization of the fundamental right of judicial review. The building has served as the Ukrainian Embassy since December 31, 1992. The interior is not open to the public.

Strolling Around Georgetown

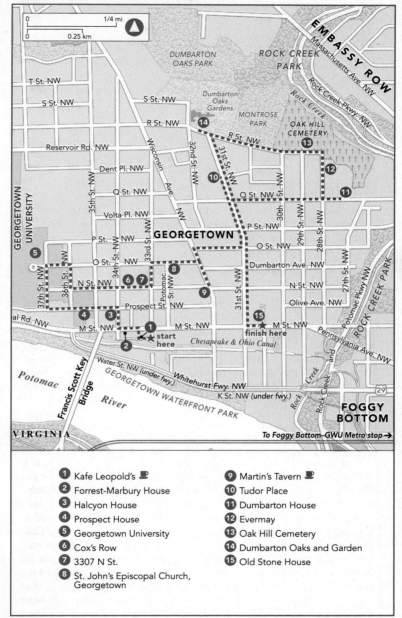

1. Kafe Leopold's ☕
2. Forrest-Marbury House
3. Halcyon House
4. Prospect House
5. Georgetown University
6. Cox's Row
7. 3307 N St.
8. St. John's Episcopal Church, Georgetown
9. Martin's Tavern ☕
10. Tudor Place
11. Dumbarton House
12. Evermay
13. Oak Hill Cemetery
14. Dumbarton Oaks and Garden
15. Old Stone House

Walk to the corner of M and 34th streets, cross M Street, and walk up 34th Street 1 block to Prospect Street, where you'll cross to the other side of 34th Street to view 3400 Prospect St. NW, the:

3 Halcyon House

Benjamin Stoddert, a Revolutionary War cavalry officer and the first Secretary of the Navy, built the smaller, original version of this house in 1789 and named it for a mythical bird said to be an omen of tranquil seas. (Stoddert was also a shipping merchant.) The Georgian mansion, like neighbor Prospect House, is situated upon elevated land, the Potomac River viewable beyond. The river lapped right up to Stoddert's terraced garden—designed by Pierre Charles L'Enfant, no less—220 years ago.

Sometime after 1900, an eccentric named Albert Clemons, a nephew of Mark Twain, bought the property and proceeded to transform it, creating the four-story Palladian facade and a maze of apartments and hallways between the facade and Stoddert's original structure. Clemons is said to have filled the house with religious paraphernalia, and there are numerous stories about the house involving sightings of shadowy figures and sounds of screams and strange noises in the night. Owners of Halcyon House since Clemons's death in 1938 have included Georgetown University and a noted local sculptor, John Dreyfuss. In 2011, Japanese pharmaceutical moguls Dr. Sachiko Kuno and Dr. Ryugi Ueno purchased Halcyon House and Evermay (see below).

Continue along Prospect Street to no. 3508, the site of:

4 Prospect House

This privately-owned house was built in 1788 by James Maccubbin Lingan, a Revolutionary War hero and wealthy tobacco merchant. He is thought to have designed the house himself. Lingan sold the house in the 1790s to a prosperous banker named John Templeman, whose guests included President John Adams and the Marquis de Lafayette. In the late 1940s, James Forrestal, the Secretary of Defense under President Harry Truman, bought the house and offered it to his boss as a place for entertaining visiting heads of state, since the Trumans were living in temporary digs at Blair House while the White House was being renovated. The restored Georgian-style mansion is named for its view of the Potomac River. Note the gabled roof with dormer window and the sun-ray fanlight over the front door; at the rear of the property (not visible from the street) is an octagonal watchtower used by 18th-century ship owners for sightings of ships returning to port.

Keep heading west on Prospect Street until you reach 37th Street. Turn right and follow 37th Street to its intersection with O Street, where you'll see:

5 Georgetown University

Founded in 1789, Georgetown is Washington's oldest university and the nation's first Catholic and first Jesuit-run university. Founder John Carroll, the first Catholic bishop in America and a cousin of a Maryland signer of the Declaration of Independence, opened the university to "students of every religious profession." His close friends included Benjamin Franklin and George Washington, who, along with the Marquis de Lafayette, addressed students from "Old North," which is the campus's oldest building. After the Civil War, students chose the school colors blue (the color used for Union uniforms) and gray (the color used for Confederate uniforms) to celebrate the end of the war and to honor slain students. The 104-acre campus is lovely, beginning with the stunning, spired Romanesque-style stone building on display beyond the university's main entrance on 37th Street. That would be Healy Building, which is named for Patrick Healy, university president from 1873 to 1882 and the first African-American to head a major, predominantly white university.

Turn right on O Street and walk 1 block to 36th Street, where you'll turn right again. Stroll past Holy Trinity Church, built in 1829, and continue to N St., where you should turn left to view Holy Trinity's parish chapel (3519 N St.), the city's oldest standing church. Built in 1794, the chapel has been in continuous use ever since. Continue further on N Street, strolling several blocks until you reach nos. 3327 to 3339, collectively known as:

6 Cox's Row

Built in 1817 and named for their owner and builder, John Cox, these five charming houses exemplify Federal-period architecture, with their dormer windows, decorative facades, and handsome doorways. Besides being a master builder, Cox was also Georgetown's first elected mayor, serving 22 years. He occupied the corner house at no. 3339 and housed the Marquis de Lafayette next door at no. 3337 when he came to town in 1824.

Follow N Street to the end of the block, where you'll see:

7 3307 N St. NW

John and Jacqueline Kennedy lived in this brick town house while Kennedy served as the U.S. senator from Massachusetts. The Kennedys purchased the house shortly after the birth of their daughter Caroline. Across the street at no. 3302 is a plaque on the side wall of the brick town house inscribed by members of the press in gratitude for kindnesses received there in the days before Kennedy's presidential inauguration. Another plaque honors Stephen Bloomer Balch (1747–1833), a Revolutionary War officer who once lived here.

Turn left on 33rd Street and walk 1 block north to O Street. Turn right on O Street and proceed to no. 3240, the site of:

8 St. John's Episcopal Church, Georgetown

Partially designed by Dr. William Thornton—first architect of the Capitol, who also designed the Octagon (see above), and Tudor Place (see below)—the church was begun in 1796 and completed in 1809. Its foundation, walls, roof, and bell tower are all original. Its early congregants were the movers and shakers of their times: President Thomas Jefferson (who contributed $50 toward the building fund), Dolley Madison, Tudor Place's Thomas and Martha Peter, and Francis Scott Key. The beautiful stained-glass windows include one by Tiffany: the sanctuary window to the right of the altar depicting "Easter Lilies Crowned with the Gifts of God." To tour the church, stop by the office, just around the corner on Potomac Street, weekdays between 10am and 4pm, or attend a service on Sunday at 9am or 11am. Visit www.stjohnsgeorgetown.org or call © 202/338-1796 for more info.

Follow O Street to busy Wisconsin Avenue and turn right, walking south to reach this favorite Washington hangout. Too early for a break? Return here or to another choice restaurant later; you're never far from Wisconsin Avenue wherever you are in Georgetown.

Martin's Tavern ☕

At 1264 Wisconsin Ave. NW (www.martins-tavern.com; ☏ 202/333-7370), you'll find this American tavern, run by a string of Billy Martins, the first of whom opened the tavern in 1933. The original Billy's great-grandson is running the show today. So it's a bar, but also very much a restaurant (bring the children—everyone does), with glass-topped white table-cloths, paneled walls, wooden booths, and an all-American menu of burgers, crab cakes, Cobb salad, and pot roast. Martin's is famous as the place where John F. Kennedy proposed to Jacqueline Bouvier in 1953—look for booth no. 3. Open Monday to Thursday 11am to 1:30am, Friday 11am to 2:30am, Saturday 9am to 2:30am, and Sunday 8am to 1:30am.

Back outside, cross Wisconsin Avenue, follow it north to O Street, and turn right. Walk to 31st Street and turn left; follow it until you reach the entrance to the grand estate at 1644 31st St. NW:

10 Tudor Place

Yet another of the architectural gems designed by the first architect of the Capitol, Dr. William Thornton, Tudor Place crowns a hill in Georgetown, set among beautiful gardens first plotted some 200 years ago. The 5.5-acre estate belonged to Martha Washington's granddaughter, Martha Custis Peter, and her husband, Thomas Peter; Martha Custis purchased it in 1805 using an $8,000 legacy left to her by her step-grandfather, George Washington. Custis-Peter descendants lived here until 1983.

Tours of the house ($10) are docent-led only and reveal rooms decorated to reflect various periods of the Peter family tenancy. Exceptional architectural features include a clever floor-to-ceiling windowed wall, whose glass panes appear to curve in the domed portico (an optical illusion: It's the woodwork frame that curves, not the glass itself). On display throughout the first-floor rooms are more than 100 of George Washington's furnishings and other family items from Tudor Place's 8,000-piece collection. Docents reveal the rich history of the estate. From a sitting-room window in this summit location, Martha Peter and Anna Maria Thornton (the architect's wife) watched the Capitol burn in 1814, during the War of 1812. The Peters hosted a reception for the Marquis de Lafayette in the drawing room in 1824. Friend and family relative Robert E. Lee spent his last night in Washington in one of the upstairs bedrooms.

Tours of the gardens ($3) are self-guided, with or without the use of an audio guide; a bowling green and boxwood ellipse are among the plum features. Tudor Place (www.tudorplace.org; ☏ **202/965-0400**) is open Tuesday to Saturday 10am to 4pm and Sunday noon to 4pm, with tours given every hour on the hour. *Note:* Tudor Place is closed for the entire month of January.

From 31st Street, retrace your steps as far back as Q Street, where you'll turn left and walk several blocks to reach 2715 Q St. NW:

11 Dumbarton House

This stately red-brick mansion (www.dumbartonhouse.org; ☏ **202/337-2288**), originally called Bellevue, was built between 1799 and 1805. In 1915 it was moved 100 yards to its current location to accommodate the placement of nearby Dumbarton Bridge over Rock Creek. The house exemplifies Federal-period architecture, which means that its rooms are almost exactly symmetrical on all floors and are centered by a large hall. Federal-period furnishings, decorative arts, and artwork fill the house; admire the dining room's late-18th-century sideboard, silver and ceramic pieces, and paintings by Charles Willson Peale. One of the original owners of Dumbarton House was Joseph Nourse, first Register of the U.S. Treasury, who lived here with his family from 1805 to 1813. Dumbarton House is most famous as the place where Dolley Madison stopped for a cup of tea on August 24, 1814, while escaping the British, who had just set fire to the White House. It is open year-round Tuesday to Sunday from 11am to 3pm. Admission is $5, and tours are self-guided.

Exit Dumbarton House and turn right, retrace your steps along Q Street, and turn right on 28th Street. Climb the hill to reach 1623 28th St. NW, the estate of:

12 Evermay

This is a private residence, purchased in 2011 by Japanese pharmaceutical moguls Dr. Sachiko Kuno and Dr. Ryugi Ueno. And though much of the estate is obscured by brick ramparts and dense foliage, what's on view is impressive. As the plaque on the estate wall tells you, Evermay was built from 1792 to 1794 by Scottish real estate speculator and merchant Samuel Davidson, with the proceeds Davidson made from the sale of lands he owned around the city, including part of the present-day White House and Lafayette Square properties. By all accounts, Davidson was something of an eccentric misanthrope, guarding his privacy by placing menacing advertisements in the daily papers with such headlines as EVERMAY PROCLAIMS, TAKE CARE, ENTER NOT HERE, FOR PUNISHMENT IS NEAR.

Follow the brick sidewalk and iron fence that run alongside:

13 Oak Hill Cemetery

Founded in 1850 by banker/philanthropist/art collector William Wilson Corcoran (see Corcoran Gallery of Art, p. 125), Oak Hill is the final resting place for many of the people you've been reading about, within this chapter and in other chapters of this book. Corcoran is buried here, in a Doric temple of a mausoleum, along with the Peters of Tudor Place (see above) and the son of William Marbury of the Forrest-Marbury House (see above). Corcoran purchased the property from George Corbin Washington, a great-nephew of President Washington. The cemetery consists of 25 beautifully landscaped acres adjacent to Rock Creek Park, with winding paths shaded by ancient oaks. Look for the Gothic-style stone Renwick Chapel, designed by James Renwick, architect of the Renwick Gallery (p. 126), the Smithsonian Castle (p. 118), and New York's St. Patrick's Cathedral. The Victorian landscaping, in the Romantic tradition of its era, strives for a natural look: Iron benches have a twig motif, and many of the graves are symbolically embellished with inverted torches, draped obelisks, angels, and broken columns. Even the gatehouse is worth noting; designed in 1850 by George de la Roche, it's a beautiful brick-and-sandstone Italianate structure. Want to go for a stroll here? Download a cemetery map from the website, www.oakhillcemeterydc.org, or stop by the gatehouse (© 202/337-2835) to pick one up. The grounds and gatehouse are open weekdays from 9am to 4:30pm; the grounds are also open on Sunday from 1 to 4pm.

Exit Oak Hill through the main entrance, and continue on the brick pathway to your right, strolling along R Street past Montrose Park until you reach the garden entrance to Dumbarton Oaks, on 31st Street. Or, if you'd prefer to visit the historic house and museum, continue around the corner to enter at 1703 32nd St. NW.

14 Dumbarton Oaks and Garden

In the mood for love? Head straight to the walled gardens, whose tiered park includes masses of roses, a Mexican tile-bordered pebble garden, a wisteria-covered arbor, cherry-tree groves, overlooks, and lots of romantic winding paths. The oldest part of Dumbarton Oaks mansion dates from 1801; since then the house has undergone considerable change, notably at the hands of a couple named Robert and Mildred Bliss, who purchased the property in 1920. As Robert was in the Foreign Service, the Blisses lived a nomadic life, amassing collections of Byzantine and Pre-Columbian art, books relating to these studies, and volumes on the history of landscape architecture. After purchasing Dumbarton Oaks, the Blisses inaugurated a grand re-landscaping of the grounds and remodeling of the mansion to accommodate their collections and the library, which now occupy the entire building. In 1940 the Blisses conveyed the house, gardens, and art collections to Harvard University, Robert's alma mater. In the summer of 1944, at the height of the Second World War, Dumbarton Oaks served as the location for a series of diplomatic meetings that would cement the principles later incorporated into the United Nations charter. The conferences took place in the Music Room, which you should visit to admire the immense 16th-century stone chimney piece, 18th-century parquet floor, and antique Spanish, French, and Italian furniture. (See p. 148 for more information about the museum and gardens.) Dumbarton Oaks Museum (www.doaks.org; ℂ **202/339-6401**) is open year-round Tuesday to Sunday 2 to 5pm, with free admission. The garden is open Tuesday to Sunday 2 to 6pm from March 15 to October 31, for an admission fee of $8; and Tuesday to Sunday 2 to 5pm from November 1 to March 14, with free admission.

From the intersection of R and 31st streets, follow 31st Street downhill all the way to M Street and turn left to find your final destination at 3051 M St. NW:

15 Old Stone House

Located on one of the busiest streets in Washington, the unobtrusive Old Stone House offers a quiet look back at life in early America, starting in 1765, when the Layman family built this home. Originally, the structure was simply one room made of thick stone walls, oak ceiling beams, and packed dirt floors. In 1800 a man named John Suter bought the building and used it as his clock-maker's shop. The grandfather clock you see on the second floor is the only original piece remaining in the house. Acquired by the National Park Service in the 1950s, the Old Stone House today shows small rooms furnished as they would have been in the late 18th century, during the period when Georgetown was a significant tobacco and shipping port. Park rangers provide information and sometimes demonstrate cooking in an open hearth, spinning, and making pomander balls. Adjacent to and behind the house is a terraced lawn and 18th-century English garden, a spot long frequented by Georgetown shop and office workers seeking a respite. Old Stone House (www.nps.gov/olst; ℂ **202/426-6851**) is open daily noon to 5pm; the garden is open daily dawn to dusk.

You're in the middle of Georgetown, surrounded by shops, restaurants, and bars. Go crazy! See chapters 5 and 7 for recommendations.

DUPONT CIRCLE/EMBASSY ROW

START:	**Dupont Circle**
FINISH:	**Vice President's Residence/U.S. Naval Observatory**
TIME:	**2½ to 3 hours (not including stops). The distance is about 3.5 miles.**
BEST TIME:	**Weekday mornings are best to start out. If you want to do the house and museum tours, go Tuesday to Sunday.**
WORST TIME:	**Saturday, when Georgetown's crazy social scene sometimes spills over into the back streets.**

This is a rather lengthy walk. It's worthwhile, we think, especially because you'll see nearly the whole world—or at least its embassies—on this route. (To see more look for the national flags of other embassies located on side streets a few steps to the left or right.)

If you feel yourself tiring, you can catch the N2 Metrobus at a number of stops along this route and it will take you back to Dupont Circle. Some of the walk is uphill, which is why I'm suggesting this precaution. You can do the walk in reverse, taking the bus to your starting point as well, though the more interesting Gilded Age sites are closer to Dupont Circle, and we want you to see those while you're still fresh.

Embassies are not normally open to visitors. Some do organize art shows and concerts featuring homeland artists. The *City Paper,* a free tabloid newspaper, lists embassy shows in its Thursday "Galleries" column. Take advantage of these shows to step inside for a look at the embassy itself.

As for food, you won't find much of it as you wander along. Better to pick up a picnic at Teaism and stop in one of the garden areas along the way to nosh.

1 Dupont Circle

We'll start right in the center of the traffic circle so you can get a good look around. Dupont Circle is one of the most famous place names in DC, at one and the same time a historic district, a traffic circle and a progressive neighborhood that's been home, since the mid-70's, to the city's gay and lesbian community. In fact, every year, on the Tuesday before Halloween, they stage the "High Heel Race" during which two dozen or so drag queens, in outrageous regalia, dash around the circle.

Named for Civil War Naval hero Samuel Francis du Pont, the circle is placed exactly where Washington's famed architect Charles Pierre L'Enfant envisioned it, though construction didn't begin until 1871, long after L'Enfant's death. For its center, Congress commissioned a small bronze statue of the Admiral, but the proud du Pont family would have none of it. Without asking permission, they commissioned the two men behind the Lincoln Memorial—sculptor Daniel Chester French and architect Henry Bacon—to create the fountain you see in front of you. It replaced the bronze statue in 1921; on its shaft are allegorical figures representing the elements a sea captain needs to navigate and propel the boat forward. See if you can figure out which is "the stars", which "the sea" and which "the wind".

Cross Massachusetts Avenue to New Hampshire Avenue until you come to Sunderland Place and see at 1307 New Hampshire Ave.:

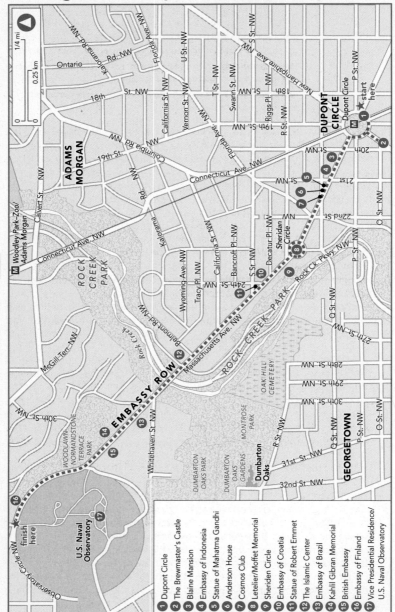

1 Dupont Circle
2 The Brewmaster's Castle
3 Blaine Mansion
4 Embassy of Indonesia
5 Statue of Mahatma Gandhi
6 Anderson House
7 Cosmos Club
8 Letelier/Moffet Memorial
9 Sheriden Circle
10 Embassy of Croatia
11 Statue of Robert Emmet
12 The Islamic Center
13 Embassy of Brazil
14 Kahlil Gibran Memorial
15 British Embassy
16 Embassy of Finland
17 Vice Presidential Residence/
U.S. Naval Observatory

2 The Brewmaster's Castle (The Christian Heurich House Museum)

Known in less polite circles as "burp castle", this is the house beer built. Christian Heurich was a highly successful brewer, who was the largest landowner in Washington, DC after the Federal Government. He loved his work so much that he never retired, continuing to manage his brewery until his death at the age of 102 in 1945. That wasn't just a work ethic—the man had murals celebrating the joys of beer in his breakfast room and used as the slogan for his company "Beer recommended for family use by Physicians in General". Yup, those were the days. You can see the interior on **tours** (Thurs-Sat at 11:30am and 1pm, Sat 11:30, 1pm, 2:30pm; $5 requested donation; www.brewmasterscastle.com).

And if you can tour it, do so—the house is notable not just for the colorful history of its owner but for its importance architecturally. Built between 1892 and 1894, it is likely the first domestic structure framed with steel and poured concrete, an effort to make it fireproof. (The salamander symbol, at the top of the tower, was used as a superstitious shield against fire). Many consider this Romanesque-style, 31-room structure to be one of the most intact late Victorian structures in the country. But we really like spotting the gargoyles.

Walk towards 20th Street, turn right and continue north two blocks to Massachusetts Ave. Turn left and on the corner you'll find 2000 Massachusetts Ave which is:

3 Blaine Mansion

The last standing Mansion from the early days of Dupont Circle, this imposing brick and terracotta structure retains the name of its first owner: James G. Blain. Had it not been for the Mugwumps—and don't you love it that we used to have political parties with such colorful names—he might well have become President instead of Grover Cleveland. As it was, charges of corruption involving illicit dealings with the railroads, ahem, derailed his campaign. This, despite the fact that Blaine, had a longer and more distinguished career than most, having served as Secretary of State twice, Speaker of the House, Congressman and Senator from Maine. The vertical sweep of the house surely impresses as much as the man, though to be honest, he barely lived here. Once the home was built, he decided it would be too costly to maintain and he leased it, first to Levi Leiter (an early co-owner of Marshall Field) and then to George Westinghouse. Yes, that Westinghouse. The latter bought it in 1901 and lived here until his death in 1914.

Continue in the same direction on Massachusetts Avenue to our first embassy at 2020 Massachusetts Ave.:

4 Embassy of Indonesia

The ornate structure occupied today by the Embassy of Indonesia is said to have cost $835,000 when it was built in 1903--the city's most expensive house at the time. Sadly, by the time the house was purchased by the Indonesians in 1951, the family fortune was so depleted, they let it go for a mere $350,000. A reminder that housing bubbles have been around for quite some time.

The man who commissioned its construction, Thomas Walsh, came to the United States from Ireland in 1869 at the age of 19. He headed west, and in 1876 struck it rich not once but twice, finding what is widely thought to be the one of the richest veins of gold in the world. Suddenly a modern-day Midas, he moved his family to Washington, figuring a grand 60-room mansion was the way to make a splash in society. And remembering his roots, he's said to have embedded a nugget of gold ore in the porch. You'll notice that this neo-Baroque mansion is unusually curvaceous. That's because it's meant to evoke the look of an ocean liner. A grand staircase in the home itself is a direct copy of one on the White Star ocean liner.

The fortune depleter, daughter Evalyn Walsh McLean was notable for the tragic turn her life took. Despite the jaunty title of her autobiography, *Father Struck It Rich!*, not much else went right in her life. Her son was killed at the age of 9 in a car crash and her daughter o'ded as a young women. Husband Edward Beale McLeane, an heir to the Post fortune, turned out to ban an alcoholic and together they burned through some $100 million dollars. A large chunk of it went to the purchase of the famed Hope Diamond. Those who believe the diamond is cursed, claim that her misfortunes started with that purchase. She died nearly penniless at the age of 58. The Diamond is now on display at the Smithsonian (see p. 116).

Keep walking in the same direction to a small triangular park where you'll find the:

5 Statue of Mahatma Gandhi

Striding purposefully, the man who led India to freedom from British rule in 1947 seems to be headed (aptly) for the **Embassy of India** (2107), just across the adjacent side street. His walking stick, simple bowl, dress and age in the sculpture suggest that this is a portrait of him on the famed protest march when he and a number of followers walked 200 miles to the Arabian Sea to collect salt (and evade the British tax on that condiment). A turning point in the non-violent fight for Indian freedom, it's an apt subject for this striking portrait.

Keep walking in the same direction to 2118 Massachusetts Ave., the:

6 Anderson House

Larz Anderson, an American diplomat, and his wife Isabel Weld Perkins, author and Red Cross volunteer, took advantage of their immense Boston wealth and built not just a home but a palace. Their intent? To create a space, large enough to serve as a headquarters of the Society of the Cincinnati, of which Larz was a member (and to which they bequeathed the home upon their death). Guided tours to this museum of the gilded age and clubhouse, are available (see full write up on p. 141) The membership of the society, founded in 1783, is composed of male descendants of officers in George Washington's Continental Army.

The building itself, sporting a cavernous two-story ballroom, a dining room seating 50, grand staircase, massive wall murals, acres of marble, and 23-karat gold trim, is more palatial than Hillwood, Washington's other palace museum. But the Andersons couldn't match Marjorie Merriweather Post's astute and energetic collecting of European treasures. The Andersons bought lots of nice objects on their world travels, but they are of only slight interest. If you have time for only one palace, make it Hillwood (p. 145).

Head across the street to 2121 Massachusetts Ave., the:

7 Cosmos Club

A prestigious private social club, it was founded in 1878 as a gathering place for scientists and public policy intellectuals. The National Geographic Society spun off from the Cosmos ten years later. The Cosmos Club's first meeting was held in the home of John Wesley Powell, the soldier and explorer who first navigated the Colorado River through the Grand Canyon in a dory. Since then, three presidents, two vice presidents, a dozen Supreme Court justices, 32 Nobel Prize winners, 56 Pulitzer Prize winners, and 45 recipients of the Presidential Medal of Freedom have numbered among its ranks. But none of them were women, until 1998, that is, when the Washington, DC Human Rights ruled that the Club's men only policy was illegal and discriminatory. A similar racial

The club is the latest occupant of a French-inspired chateau built in 1901 with the railroad wealth of Richard and Mary Scott Townsend. His fortune came from the Erie Line; hers from the Pennsylvania Railroad (no joke). They hired the famed New York architectural firm of Carrere & Hastings, which created the New York Public Library, to build a chateau built to resemble the Petit Trianon—the royal hideaway at Versailles. Somewhat superstitious, the couple had the structure built around an older one. Apparently, a gypsy had once predicted that Mrs. Townsend would die "under a new roof." Despite these precautions, Mrs. Townsend did eventually pass away (darn!).

As you head towards Sheridan Square, look for the Romanian Chancery and the **Embassy of Ireland** (2234). In front of these two is the:

8 Letelier/Moffitt Memorial

On Sept 21, 1976 Orlando Letelier, the former foreign minister of ousted President Salvador Allende offered his colleague Ronni Karpen Moffitt a ride home. A car bomb killed them both; this small cylindrical monument, honors their memory. Thousands showed up later that week for a hastily organized protest funeral march. Eventually, five men were prosecuted for the crime. One, who led police to the others, was given just 2 years of prison before being taken into the witness protection program. For years, rumors circulated that the American government was also in some way involved.

Turn away from the Memorial and look at:

9 Sheridan Circle

The Civil War officer mounted on his muscular horse is General Philip H. Sheridan, commander of the Union cavalry and the Army of the Shenandoah. His horse Rienzi, who carried him through 85 battles and skirmishes, became almost as famous during the war as "the steed that saved the day."

Sculpted by Gutzon Borglum, who carved the presidential faces on South Dakota's Mount Rushmore, the statue depicts Sheridan rallying his men at the Battle of Cedar Creek in Northern Virginia on October 19, 1864. Sheridan was 15 miles north in the town of Winchester when a Confederate force under General Jubal A. Early surprised and drove back his army. Racing to the battle site on stout-hearted Rienzi, Sheridan led his men in a victorious counterattack.

Sheridan's wife is said to have chosen the site for the statue, which is flanked by two hidden pools. His son, Second Lieutenant Philip H. Sheridan, Jr., served as a model for the statue. He was present at the unveiling in 1908, as was President Theodore Roosevelt. I suggest crossing (carefully) into the circle to get a close-up look.

Carefully cross the Circle again, back to Massachusetts Avenue and continue going north-west to 2343 Massachusetts Ave., the:

embassy row: SOME EXPLANATIONS

Today, about 75 embassies, chanceries, or ambassadorial residences are located on or near the 2-mile stretch of Massachusetts Avenue between Dupont Circle and Wisconsin Avenue NW. As a result, it was dubbed Embassy Row.

A word on those distinctions: An embassy is the official office or residence of the ambassador. Some ambassadors live and work in the embassy; others maintain separate residences, commuting to their job like the rest of us. A chancery is the embassy's office; this is where you might apply for a visitor's visa. It could be located within the embassy or not. Some countries also provide separate offices for special missions, such as the military attaché's office. In all, about 180 countries maintain a diplomatic presence in Washington.

10 Embassy of Croatia

Outside the building the muscular figure of St. Jerome the Priest (A.D. 341–420) sits hunched over a book, his head in his hand. Jerome, the pedestal of the statue informs us, was "the greatest Doctor of the Church." This is a reference to his work in translating the Bible from Hebrew into Latin, a version called the Vulgate because it was in the language of the common people of the day. Historically, it is considered the most important vernacular edition of the Bible. At times in his younger years, Jerome's religious faith declined; he became involved in numerous theological disputes, and he spent several years in the desert leading an ascetical life while fighting temptations. We get the feeling this glum statue is commemorating those troubled times. The statue initially sat on the grounds of the Franciscan Abbey near Catholic University; it was moved here when the nation of Croatia was created at the breakup of Yugoslavia.

Continue walking to the 2400 block of Massachusetts Avenue where, in a triangular park, you'll see the:

11 Statue of Robert Emmet

Though somewhat obscured by foliage, the Irish revolutionary stands in a pose that he reportedly struck in Dublin in 1803 when a British court sentenced him to death by hanging. He appears to be gazing toward the Embassy of Ireland 2 blocks away. Born in 1778, Emmet led a failed uprising in Dublin on July 23, 1803. The statue was presented to the Smithsonian Institution in 1917 as a gift to the American public from a group of American citizens of Irish ancestry. It was moved to its present site in 1966, marking the 50th anniversary of Irish independence.

Note the numerous embassies en route to the next stop. Two marble elephants guard the **India Supply Mission** (2536). Above them, a strip of blue squares across the front of the building serve as a backdrop to a white water lily, symbolizing peace and tranquility, and a wheel, which represents the continuous cycle of life. Its neighbor is the **Embassy of Japan** (2516). The structure set back behind the cobblestone courtyard dates to 1932. Georgian revival in style, it suggests the Far East with a subtle "rising sun" above the balcony over the door.

On the right is the new **Embassy of Turkey** (2525). The statue in front is of Mustafa Kemel Ataturk, the founder of modern Turkey.

Just before the bridge, head to 2551 Massachusetts Ave.:

12 The Islamic Center

The 160-foot tall white limestone minaret, soaring above Embassy Row, makes the Islamic Center impossible to miss. From it, a loudspeaker intones the call to prayer five times daily. Built in 1949, the center does not line up directly with the street, instead it faces Mecca. On Friday afternoons, throngs of the faithful pour into the mosque for prayer services, many of them embassy employees attired in their native dress. At times, prayer rugs are spread in the courtyard or even on the sidewalk outside the iron railing fence. This is when Embassy Row takes on its most dramatic multicultural look.

Visitors are welcome inside (daily 10am–5pm), so don't be shy about stepping through the open gates. But be sure to remove your shoes before entering the mosque itself; leave them in one of the slots provided on the entrance wall. Men should dress neatly; no shorts. Women are not allowed to wear sleeveless clothes or short dresses and must cover their hair. The interior, filled with colorful Arabic art, is well worth these preliminaries. Persian rugs drape the floor, overlapping one another; 7,000 blue tiles cover the lower walls in mosaic patterns; eight ornate pillars soar overhead, ringing a huge copper chandelier. The carved pulpit is inlaid with ivory, and stained-glass windows add more color.

Cross the bridge. Take a look down: 75 feet below is Rock Creek Parkway as well as the 1,700-acre Rock Creek Park (see p. 154). At the other end of the bridge, walk on and take the time to look at the embassies you'll be passing until you get to 3000 Massachusetts Ave., the:

13 Embassy of Brazil

This stately, palacelike building next to the big, black boxlike building (the chancery) is the ambassador's residence. The older building, derived from an Italian Renaissance palazzo, was designed in 1931 by John Russell Pope, a leader of the city's early 20th-century neoclassicist movement. The Jefferson Memorial, National Gallery of Art, and National Archives are among Pope's other local works.

Keep walking in the same direction and look to the right side to find the:

14 Kahlil Gibran Memorial

An elaborate 2-acre garden, eight-sided star fountain, circular walkway, shaded benches, and bronze bust celebrate the life and achievements of the Lebanese-American philosopher. Dedicated on May 24, 1991, it is a gift "to the people of the United States" from the Kahlil Gibran Centennial Foundation. Born in 1883 in a village near the Biblical Cedars of Lebanon, Gibran arrived in Boston as a child. Building a successful career as artist and author, he published widely-quoted books in English and Arabic. He died in New York City in 1931. Excerpts from his writings are etched into the memorial's circular wall, among them: "We live only to discover beauty. All else is a form of waiting." If you need to rest your feet for a few moments, this lovely garden is the perfect place to do so in.

Continue your stroll to 3100 Massachusetts Ave., the:

15 British Embassy

Out in front and instantly recognizable in a familiar pose, **Sir Winston Churchill** stands in bronze. One foot rests on Embassy property, thus British soil; the other

"An embassy in Washington D.C. is different from embassies in most other capitals, where people visit them only if they have to; that is, to get a visa or to conduct official business. In Washington D.C., embassies are expected to be much more. They need to be able to open windows on the life and culture of the countries they represent, not only for the select few, but for all Washingtonians and visitors to the capital who want to know. Many do, because Americans are curious by nature."

—Jukka Valtasaari, Finnish ambassador, 1988–1996 and 2001–2005

is planted on American soil. Anglo-American unity is the symbolism, but the placement also reflects Churchill's heritage as the child of a British father and American mother. And, of course, his right hand is raised in the iconic familiar V for Victory sign he displayed in World War II. His other hand often sports a small bouquet of fresh flowers, left by admirers. The English-Speaking Union of the United States commissioned the statue, which was erected in 1966. The statue stands on a granite plinth; beneath it are blended soils from Blenheim Palace, his birthplace; from the rose garden at Chartwell, his home; and from his mother's home in Brooklyn, N.Y.

The U-shaped, red-brick structure rising behind the World War II prime minister is the main chancery, built in 1931. Sir Edwin Lutyens, one of Great Britain's leading architects of the day, designed both it and the ambassador's residence, located out of sight behind the chancery. The American Institute of Architects describes the pair as a "triumph," noting that Lutyens rejected the prevailing passion for neoclassical structures and instead created a colonial American design. Others suggest it looks like an 18th-century English country house. Whatever, it makes an impressive show. Too bad the concrete box on the right, an office building dedicated by Queen Elizabeth II in 1957, failed to match the architectural standard Lutyens set. The round glass structure, another unfortunately bland modern addition, is used for conferences.

On your right as you continue around Observatory Circle (a wide curve in Embassy Row) is a steep, heavily wooded slope that drops into a slender canyon. It is Rock Creek Trail, and if you wish you could take a little nature detour. It's amazing how quickly, within 60-seconds really, you leave the hubbub of the city and find yourself in nature. Okay, enough greenery. Continue walking to 3301 Massachusetts Ave., the dramatic:

16 Embassy of Finland

An abstract metal and glass front forms a green wall of climbing plants on a bronze, gridlike trellis. Within, huge windows in the rear look out onto a thickly forested slope, as if—to quote architectural historian William Morgan—"The Finns have brought a bit of the woods to Washington." The architects, Mikko Heikkinen and Markku Komonen, are considered one of Finland's hottest architectural partnerships. Completed in 1994, the embassy was designed to display the life and culture of Finland. To see the interior, attend one of the two annual art shows displaying Finnish artworks. You can get a very limited glimpse by stepping into the all-glass reception—if only to pick up a tourist brochure for Finland. The embassy is open Monday through Friday from 8:30am to 4:45pm.

From the Finnish Embassy, look across the street to the green slope behind the tall iron fence. That white Victorian-style house atop the hill partially visible is the:

17 Vice President's Residence/U.S. Naval Observatory

Number One Observatory Circle is the official residence of the U.S. vice president. As I write this, it is home Joseph and Jill Biden. The wooded estate surrounding the residence is the site of the U.S. Naval Observatory; the large white dome holding its 12-inch refracting telescope is easily seen on the right. Built in 1893, the Veep's house initially was assigned to the observatory's superintendent. But in 1923 the Chief of Naval Operations took a liking to it, booted out the superintendent and made the house his home. In 1974, Congress evicted the Navy and transformed it into the vice president's residence.

Up to that time, vice presidents occupied their own homes, as Supreme Court judges, Cabinet members, and senators still do. But providing full security apparatus for the private homes of each new vice president became expensive. Nelson Rockefeller, vice president in the Gerald Ford administration, was the first potential resident, but he used the house only for entertaining. So Vice President Walter Mondale became the first official occupant, followed by the elder Bush, Quayle, and Gore If you see a big tent on the front lawn, it usually means the vice president is hosting a gala reception. Traffic along Massachusetts Avenue is brought to a halt many mornings and afternoons when the vice president's security motorcade races past carrying him to or from his offices at the White House or U.S. Capitol.

The observatory moved from Foggy Bottom to its present location in 1910. At the time, the hilltop site was rural countryside. One of the oldest scientific agencies in the country, it was established in 1830. Its primary mission was to oversee the Navy's chronometers, charts, and other navigational equipment. Today it remains the preeminent authority on precise time. Scientists take observations of the sun, moon, planets, and selected stars; determine the precise time, and publish astronomical data needed for accurate navigation.

And with that, we'll allow you to navigate on to wherever else your travels may take you today in D.C. We hope you enjoyed these walking tours.

PLANNING YOUR TRIP TO WASHINGTON, D.C.

A s with any trip, a little preparation is essential before you travel to Washington, D.C. This chapter provides a variety of planning tools, including information on getting to D.C., tips on transportation within the city, and additional on-the-ground resources.

GETTING THERE

By Plane

Three airports serve the Washington, D.C. area. General information follows that should help you determine which airport is your best bet.

Ronald Reagan Washington National Airport (DCA) lies 4 miles south of D.C., across the Potomac River in Virginia, about a 10-minute trip by car in non-rush-hour traffic, and 15 to 20 minutes by Metro anytime. Its proximity to the District and its direct access to the Metro rail system are reasons why you might want to fly into National. Another reason: A climate-controlled pedestrian bridges connects the terminal directly to a Metro station; Blue and Yellow lines stop here and will whisk you inexpensively into the heart of the city. The Metropolitan Washington Airports Authority oversees both National and Dulles airports, so the website is the same for the two facilities: **www.mwaa.com.** Check there for airport information, or call © **703/417-8000.** For Metro information, go online at **www.wmata.com** or call © **202/637-7000.**

Washington Dulles International Airport (IAD) is 26 miles outside the capital, in Chantilly, Virginia, a 35- to 45-minute ride to downtown in non-rush-hour traffic. Of the three airports, Dulles handles more daily flights, with more than 33 airlines flying nonstop to 129 destinations, including 48 foreign cities. The airport is not as convenient to the heart of Washington as National, but it's more convenient than BWI, thanks to an uncongested airport access road that travels half the distance toward Washington. The airport's website is **www.mwaa.com** and its information line is © **703/572-2700.**

Last but not least is **Baltimore–Washington International Thurgood Marshall Airport (BWI),** which is located about 45 minutes from downtown, a few miles outside of Baltimore. A vast expansion has added 11 gates to a newly improved concourse and skywalks from parking garages to terminals, and the number of parking spaces has tripled. One factor especially accounts for this tremendous growth, the same that recommends BWI to travelers: the major presence of **Southwest Airlines,** whose bargain fares and flights to about 50 cities seem to offer something for everyone. (Southwest also serves Dulles and National airports, but in a much smaller capacity.) Call ✆ **800/859-7111** for airport information, or point your browser to **www.bwiairport.com.**

GETTING INTO TOWN FROM THE AIRPORT

Each of the three airports offers similar options for getting into the city. All three airports could really use better signage, especially because their ground transportation desks always seem to be located quite a distance from the gate at which you arrive. Keep trudging, and follow baggage claim signs, too, since ground transportation operations are always situated near baggage carousels.

TAXI SERVICE   For a trip to downtown D.C., you can expect a taxi to cost close to $15 for the 10- to 20-minute ride from National Airport, $57 to $60 for the 30- to 45-minute ride from Dulles Airport, and about $90 for the 45-minute ride from BWI.

SUPERSHUTTLE   These vans offer shared-ride, door-to-door service between the airport and your destination, whether in the District or in a suburban location. You make a reservation by phone or online (www.supershuttle.com; ✆ **800/258-3826**) and then proceed to the SuperShuttle desk in your airport to check in. The only drawback to this service is the roundabout way the driver must follow, as he or she drops off or picks up other passengers en route. If you arrive after the SuperShuttle desk has closed, you can summon a van by calling customer service at the above number. The 24-hour service bases its fares on zip code, so to reach downtown, expect to pay about $14, plus $10 for each additional person, from National; $29, plus $10 per additional person, from Dulles; and $37 plus $12 per additional person, from BWI. SuperShuttle also tacks on a $1 to $2 fuel charge in certain vicinities, Maryland being one.

Transportation Options by Airport
FROM RONALD REAGAN WASHINGTON NATIONAL AIRPORT   If you are not too encumbered with luggage, you should take **Metrorail** into the city. Metro's Yellow and Blue lines stop at the airport and connect via an enclosed walkway to level two, the concourse level, of the main terminal, adjacent to terminals B and C. If yours is one of the airlines that still uses the "old" terminal A (Sun Country, AirTran, JetBlue, Air Canada, Frontier), you will have a longer walk to reach the Metro station. Signs pointing the way can be confusing, so ask an airport employee if you're headed in the right direction; or, better yet, head out to the curb and hop a shuttle bus to the station, but be sure to ask the driver to let you know when you've reached the enclosed bridge that leads to the Metro (it may not be obvious, and drivers don't always announce the stops). **Metrobuses** also serve the area, should you be going somewhere off the Metro route. But Metrorail is fastest, a 15- to 20-minute non-rush-hour ride to downtown. It is safe, convenient, and cheap; the base fare is $2.70 for a paper fare card, $1.70 if you use a SmarTrip card (see box on SmarTrips, p. 236), and goes up from there depending on when (fares increase during rush hours) and where you're going.

If you're renting a car from an on-site **car rental agency—Alamo** (✆ 800/462-5266), **Avis** (✆ 703/419-5815), **Budget** (✆ 703/419-1021), **Enterprise** (✆ 703/414-8310), **Hertz** (✆ 703/419-6300), or **National** (✆ 703/414-8310)—go to level two, the concourse level, follow the pedestrian walkway to the parking garage, find garage A, and descend one flight. You can also take the complimentary Airport Shuttle (look for the sign posted at the curb outside the terminal) to parking garage A. If you've rented from off-premises agencies **Dollar** (📞 866/434-2226) or **Advantage** (📞 703/838-1666), head outside the baggage claim area of your terminal, and catch the Dollar or Thrifty shuttle bus.

To get downtown by car, follow the signs out of the airport for the George Washington Parkway, headed north toward Washington. Stay on the parkway until you see signs for I-395 north to Washington. Take the I-395 north exit, which takes you across the 14th Street Bridge. Stay in the left lane crossing the bridge and follow the signs for Route 1, which will put you on 14th Street NW. (You'll see the Washington Monument off to your left.) Ask your hotel for directions from 14th Street and Constitution Avenue NW. Or take the more scenic route, always staying to the left on the GW Parkway as you follow the signs for Memorial Bridge. You'll be driving alongside the Potomac River, with the Capitol and memorials in view across the river; then, as you cross over Memorial Bridge, you're greeted by the Lincoln Memorial. Stay left coming over the bridge, swoop around to the left of the Memorial, take a left on 23rd Street NW, a right on Constitution Avenue, and then, if you want to be in the heart of downtown, left again on 15th Street NW (the Washington Monument will be to your right).

FROM WASHINGTON DULLES INTERNATIONAL AIRPORT The **Washington Flyer Express Bus** (www.washfly.com; 📞 **888/927-4359**) runs between Dulles and Metro's Orange Line station at West Falls Church, where you can purchase a Metro farecard to board an Orange Line train bound for New Carrollton, which heads into D.C. In the airport, look for signs for the Washington Flyer Coach, which leaves from Door 4 on the Arrivals level (follow the ramp up to the ticket counter, where you can buy a ticket). Buses to the West Falls Church Metro station run daily, every 30 minutes, and cost $10 one-way.

More convenient is the **Metrobus** service (no. 5A) that runs between Dulles (buses depart from curb 2E, outside the Ground Transportation area) and the L'Enfant Plaza Metro station, located across from the National Mall and the Smithsonian museums, and downhill from nearby Capitol Hill. The bus departs every 30 to 40 minutes weekdays, hourly on weekends. It costs $6 (you must use a SmarTrip card—see box, this chapter—or have exact change) and takes 45 minutes to an hour.

If you are renting a car at Dulles, head down the ramp near your baggage claim area and walk outside to the curb to look for your rental car's shuttle-bus stop. The buses come by every 5 minutes or so en route to nearby rental lots. Almost all the major companies are represented (see above for their phone numbers).

To reach downtown Washington from Dulles by car, exit the airport and stay on the Dulles Access Road, which leads right into I-66 east. Follow I-66 east, which takes you across the Theodore Roosevelt Memorial Bridge; be sure to stay in the center lane as you cross the bridge, and this will put you on Constitution Avenue (Rte. 29). Ask your hotel for directions from this point.

FROM BALTIMORE–WASHINGTON INTERNATIONAL AIRPORT Washington's Metro service runs an Express Metro Bus ("B30") between its Metrorail Green Line Greenbelt station and BWI Airport. The airport has two bus stops on its lower level, one in the International Concourse, the other in Concourse A/B. Look for PUBLIC TRANSIT signs to find the bus, which operates daily, departs every 40 minutes, takes about 30 minutes to reach the station, and costs $6. At the Greenbelt Metro station, you purchase a Metro farecard and board a Metro train bound for Branch Avenue, which will take you into the city. Depending on where you want to go, you can either stay on the Green Line train to your designated stop or get off at the Fort Totten station to transfer to a Red Line train, whose stops include Union Station (near Capitol Hill) and various downtown locations.

You also have the choice of taking either an **Amtrak** (www.amtrak.com; ✆ 800/872-7245) or the Penn line of the **Maryland Rural Commuter** train, or MARC (http://mta.maryland.gov/marc-train; ✆ **800/325-7245**), into the city. Both trains travel between the BWI Railway Station (✆ **410/672-6169**) and Washington's Union Station (✆ **202/906-3104** for MARC info, **202/906-3260** for Amtrak info), about a 30-minute ride. Amtrak's service is daily ($15–$45 per person, one-way, depending on time and train type), while MARC's is weekdays only ($6 per person, one-way). A courtesy shuttle runs every 12 minutes or so between the airport and the train station; stop at the desk near the baggage-claim area to check for the next departure time of both the shuttle bus and the train. Trains depart about once per hour.

BWI operates a large off-site car rental facility. From the ground transportation area, board a shuttle bus to the lot.

Here's how you reach Washington: Look for signs for I-195 and follow the highway west until you see signs for Washington and the Baltimore–Washington Parkway (I-295); head south on I-295. Get off when you see the signs for Rte. 50/New York Avenue, which leads into the District, via New York Avenue NE. Ask your hotel for specific directions from New York Avenue NE.

By Car

More than one third of visitors to Washington arrive by plane, and if that's you, don't worry about renting a car. In fact, it's better if you don't, since the traffic in the city and throughout the region is absolutely abysmal, parking spaces are hard to find, garage and lot charges are exorbitant, and hotel overnight rates are even worse. Furthermore, Washington is amazingly easy to traverse on foot—so easy, in fact, that assorted sources, from *Prevention* magazine to the Brookings Institution, name D.C. among the most walkable cities in the country. Our public transportation and taxi systems are accessible and comprehensive, as well.

But if you are like most visitors, you're planning on driving here. No matter which road you take, there's a good chance you will have to navigate some portion of the **Capital Beltway** (I-495 and I-95) to gain entry to D.C. The Beltway girds the city, its approximately 66-mile route passing through Maryland and Virginia, with some 56 interchanges or exits leading off from it. The Beltway is nearly always congested, but especially during weekday morning and evening rush hours (roughly 5:30–9:30am and 3–7pm). Drivers can get a little crazy, weaving in and out of traffic.

The District is 240 miles from New York City, 40 miles from Baltimore, 700 miles from Chicago, 500 miles from Boston, and about 630 miles from Atlanta.

By Train

Amtrak (www.amtrak.com; ✆ **800/USA-RAIL** [872-7245]) offers daily service to Washington from New York, Boston, and Chicago. Amtrak also travels daily between Washington and points south, including Raleigh, Charlotte, Atlanta, cities in Florida, and New Orleans. Amtrak's **Acela Express** trains offer the quickest service along the "Northeast Corridor," linking Boston, New York, Philadelphia, and Washington. The trains travel as fast as 150 mph, making the trip between New York and Washington in times that range from less than 3 hours to 3 hours and 45 minutes, depending on the number of stops in the schedule. Likewise, Acela Express's Boston-Washington trip takes anywhere from 6½ hours to more than 8 hours, depending on station stops.

Amtrak runs fewer Acela trains on weekends, and honors passenger discounts, such as those for seniors and AAA members, only on weekend Acela travel.

Amtrak offers a smorgasbord of good-deal rail passes and discounted fares; although not all are based on advance purchase, you may have more discount options by reserving early. Tickets for up to two children ages 2 to 15 cost half the price of the lowest available adult fare when the children are accompanied by a fare-paying adult. For more information, go to **www.amtrak.com** and click on the website's "Deals" section, where you'll find assorted discount possibilities. *Note:* Most Amtrak travel requires a reservation, which means that every traveler is guaranteed, but not assigned, a seat.

Amtrak trains arrive at historic **Union Station,** 50 Massachusetts Ave. NE (www.unionstationdc.com; (C) **202/371-9441**), a short walk from the Capitol, across the circle from several hotels, and a short cab or Metro ride from downtown. The station connects with Metro service and taxis are almost always available. (For more on Union Station, see chapter 6.)

By Bus

Bus travel is now in vogue, thanks to the rise of fabulously priced, comfortable, clean, and fast bus services. Quite a number of buses travel between Washington, D.C. and New York City, and a growing number travel between D.C. and cities scattered up and down the East Coast.

Check out one of these fleets: **BoltBus** (www.boltbus.com; (C) **877/265-8287**) travels multiple times a day between D.C.'s Union Station and NYC for $1 to $25 each way. **Megabus** (www.megabus.com; (C) **877/462-6342**) travels between Washington, D.C.'s Union Station and NYC (also many times a day), for as little as $1 and as much as $43, one-way (most fares run in the $13 to $25 range); and travels between D.C. and 17 other locations, including Boston, Toronto, and Knoxville, Tennessee, for similarly low fares.

Vamoose Bus (www.vamoosebus.com; (C) **212/695-6766**) travels between Rosslyn, Virginia's stop near the Rosslyn Metro station and Bethesda, Maryland's stop near the Bethesda Metro station, and NYC's Penn Station, for $30 each way, with a coupon given at the end of each trip: Collect four and ride one-way for free.

Greyhound (www.greyhound.com; (C) **800/231-2222**) is actually the company behind BoltBus, but oddly, it's often more expensive and slower on its routes (many of which are doubled by BoltBus). The D.C. Greyhound bus depot is at Union Station.

GETTING AROUND

Washington is one of the easiest U.S. cities to navigate, thanks to its comprehensive public transportation system of trains and buses. Ours is the second-busiest rail transit network and the sixth-largest bus network in the country. But because Washington is of manageable size and marvelous beauty, you may find yourself shunning transportation and choosing to walk. A truly excellent source for considering all of your transportation options is the website **www.godcgo.com**, an initiative of the D.C. government's Department of Transportation, which continually updates the information.

City Layout

Washington's appearance today pays homage to the 1791 vision of French engineer Pierre Charles L'Enfant, who created the capital's grand design of sweeping avenues intersected by spacious circles, directed that the Capitol and the White House be placed on prominent hilltops at either end of a wide stretch of avenue, and superimposed this overall plan upon a traditional street grid. The city's quadrants, grand avenues named after states, alphabetically ordered streets crossed by numerically ordered streets, and parks integrated with urban features are all ideas that started with L'Enfant. President George Washington, who had hired L'Enfant, was forced to dismiss the temperamental genius after L'Enfant apparently offended quite a number of people. But Washington recognized the brilliance of the city plan and hired surveyors Benjamin Banneker and Andrew Ellicott, who had worked with L'Enfant, to continue to implement L'Enfant's design. (For further background, see chapter 2.)

The U.S. Capitol marks the center of the city, which is divided into **northwest (NW), northeast (NE), southwest (SW), and southeast (SE) quadrants.** Most, but not all, areas of interest to tourists are in the northwest. The boundary demarcations are often seamless; for instance, you are in the northwest quadrant when you visit the National Museum of Natural History, but by crossing the National Mall to the other side to visit the Freer Gallery, you put yourself in the southwest quadrant. Pay attention to the quadrant's geographic suffix; as you'll notice when you look on a map, some addresses appear in multiple quadrants (for instance, the corner of G and 7th sts. appears in all four).

MAIN ARTERIES & STREETS   From the Capitol, North Capitol Street and South Capitol Street run north and south, respectively. East Capitol Street divides the city north and south. The area west of the Capitol is not a street at all, but the National Mall, which is bounded on the north by Constitution Avenue and on the south by Independence Avenue.

The primary artery of Washington is **Pennsylvania Avenue,** which is the scene of parades, inaugurations, and other splashy events. Pennsylvania runs northwest in a direct line between the Capitol and the White House—if it weren't for the Treasury Building, the president would have a clear view of the Capitol—before continuing on a northwest angle to Georgetown, where it becomes M Street.

Constitution Avenue, paralleled to the south most of the way by Independence Avenue, runs east-west, flanking the Capitol and the Mall. Washington's longest avenue, **Massachusetts Avenue,** runs parallel to Pennsylvania (a few avenues north). Along the way, you'll find Union Station and then Dupont Circle, which is central to the area known as Embassy Row. Farther out are the Naval Observatory (the vice president's residence is on the premises), Washington National Cathedral, American University, and, eventually, Maryland.

Connecticut Avenue, which runs more directly north (the other avenues run southeast to northwest), starts at Lafayette Square, intersects Dupont Circle, and eventually takes you to the National Zoo, on to the charming residential neighborhood known as Cleveland Park, and into Chevy Chase, Maryland, where you can pick up the Beltway to head out of town. Connecticut Avenue, with its chic-to-funky array of shops and clusters of top-dollar to good-value restaurants, is an interesting street to stroll.

Wisconsin Avenue originates in Georgetown; its intersection with M Street forms Georgetown's hub. Wisconsin Avenue basically parallels Connecticut Avenue; one of the few irritating things about the city's transportation system is that the Metro does not connect these two major arteries in the heart of the city. (Buses do, and, of course, you can always walk or take a taxi from one avenue to the other; read about the supplemental bus system, the D.C. Circulator, below.) Metrorail's first stop on Wisconsin

Be Smart: Buy a SmarTrip Card

Whether you plan to use D.C.'s Metro-rail and bus service once or many times while you're here, I absolutely recommend that you purchase a **SmarTrip** card, which is a permanent, recharge-able farecard that's way faster to use than a regular farecard—you just touch it to the target on a faregate inside a Metro station or farebox inside a Metro-bus. Not only is it quicker, but it's cheaper, since you pay $1 less per Metrorail trip, 20¢ less per Metrobus trip, every time you use it. SmarTrip cards are also usable on other area tran-sit systems, including D.C. Circulator buses and DASH buses in Old Town Alexandria. You can purchase SmarTrip cards online at www.wmata.com; at vending machines in certain Metro sta-tions; and at WMATA headquarters (weekdays only), 600 5th St. NW; its sales office at Metro Center (weekdays only), 12th and F streets NW; or at one of many retail stores, like Giant or Safe-way grocery stores. The initial cost of a SmarTrip card is $5, but you get $3 back by rebate when you purchase the card online. You can add value and special value passes (see below) as needed online and at the passes/farecard vend-ing machines in every Metro station, or even on a Metrobus, using the farebox. For more information, contact Metro (www.wmata.com; ✆ **888/762-7874**). *One other tip:* Do try to order the card in advance online, so you'll have it with you when you arrive in D.C. That will be one less hassle to deal with at the Metro stations, where first-time use of the vending machines can be confusing.

Avenue is in Tenleytown, a residential area. Follow the avenue north and you land in the affluent Maryland cities of Chevy Chase and Bethesda.

FINDING AN ADDRESS   If you understand the city's layout, it's easy to find your way around. As you read this, have a map handy.

Each of the four corners of the District of Columbia is exactly the same distance from the Capitol dome. The White House and most government buildings and impor-tant monuments are west of the Capitol (in the northwest and southwest quadrants), as are major hotels and tourist facilities.

Numbered streets run north-south, beginning on either side of the Capitol with 1st Street. Lettered streets run east-west and are named alphabetically, beginning with A Street. (Don't look for J, X, Y, or Z streets, however—they don't exist.) After W Street, street names of two syllables continue in alphabetical order, followed by street names of three syllables; the more syllables in a name, the farther the street is from the Capitol.

Avenues, named for U.S. states, run at angles across the grid pattern and often intersect at traffic circles. For example, New Hampshire, Connecticut, and Massachu-setts avenues intersect at Dupont Circle.

With this in mind, you can easily find an address. On lettered streets, the address tells you exactly where to go. For instance, 1776 K St. NW is between 17th and 18th streets (the first two digits of 1776 tell you that) in the northwest quadrant (NW). *Note:* I Street is often written as "Eye" Street to prevent confusion with 1st Street.

To find an address on numbered streets, you'll probably have to use your fingers. For instance, 623 8th St. SE is between F and G streets (the sixth and seventh letters of the alphabet; the first digit of 623 tells you that) in the southeast quadrant (SE). One thing to remember: You count B as the second letter of the alphabet even though B

To avoid risking the ire of commuters, be sure to follow these guidelines: Stand to the right on the escalator so that people in a hurry can get past you on the left. And when you reach the train level, don't puddle at the bottom of the escalator, blocking the path of those coming behind you; move down the platform. Eating, drinking, and smoking are strictly prohibited on the Metro and in stations.

Street North and B Street South are now Constitution and Independence avenues, respectively, but because there's no J Street, K becomes the 10th letter, L the 11th, and so on.

By Public Transportation
METRORAIL

The **Metrorail** system continues to be the best way to get around the city, in spite of the fact that it's showing its age: 38 years old. In fact, a $5 billion rehabilitation project is underway now and will continue for many years on the Metro system.

You should expect delays on weekends especially, throughout the long period of repair and maintenance, as trains travel at reduced speeds and schedules are disrupted to allow for service. For more information, contact **Washington Metropolitan Area Transit Authority** (WMATA; www.wmata.com; © 202/637-7000). If you have concerns, you can always ride the buses (see information below), which will always be slower than the train system, but will get you wherever you want to go.

If you do ride Metrorail, try to avoid traveling during rush hour (Mon–Fri 5–9:30am and 3–7pm), since delays can be frequent, lines at farecard machines long, trains overcrowded, and Washingtonians at their rudest. You can expect to get a seat during off-peak hours (weekdays 10am–3pm, weeknights after 7pm, and weekends). All cars are air-conditioned and fitted with comfortable upholstered seats.

Metrorail's system of 86 stations and 106 miles of track includes locations at or near almost every sightseeing attraction; it also extends to suburban Maryland and northern Virginia. There are five lines in operation—**Red, Blue, Orange, Yellow**, and **Green**. The lines connect at several central points, making transfers relatively easy. All but Yellow and Green line trains stop at Metro Center; all except Red Line trains stop at L'Enfant Plaza; all but Blue and Orange line trains stop at Gallery Place–Chinatown. See the map inside the back cover of this book.

Metro stations are indicated by discreet brown columns bearing the station's name and topped by the letter M. Below the M is a colored stripe or stripes indicating the line or lines that stop there. To enter a Metro station, you need a computerized **SmarTrip** card (see above) or a paper **farecard. SmarTrip** card dispenser machines and farecard vending machines are located inside the vestibule areas of the Metro stations. SmarTrip card dispensers sell SmarTrip cards for $10 ($5 for the card and $5 in trip value) and accept debit and credit cards, as well as $1, $5, and $10 bills. The black Farecard vending machines sell paper farecards and accept cash only, up to $20, with change up to $10 returned in coins(!). The blue Passes/Farecards vending machines sell paper farecards as well as special value passes, and accept debit and credit cards, as well as cash up to $20, with change up to $10 returned in coins.

Metrorail doesn't go to Georgetown, and though Metro buses do (nos. 31, 32, 36, 38B, D1, D2, D3, D5, D6, and G2), the public transportation I'd recommend is that provided by the **D.C. Circulator** (p. 240), which travels two Georgetown routes: one that runs between the Rosslyn, Virginia and Dupont Circle Metro stations, stopping at designated points in Georgetown along the way, and a second one that runs between Georgetown and Union Station. The buses come by every 10 minutes from 7am to midnight Sunday through Thursday, 7am to 2am Friday and Saturday. One-way fares cost $1, or 50¢ with a SmarTrip card.

Metrorail fares are calculated on distance traveled, time of day, and whether you're using a SmarTrip card or a paper farecard. **Base fare** using a SmarTrip card during non-peak hours (Mon–Fri 9:30am–3pm and 7pm–midnight; all day Saturday until midnight; and all day Sunday) ranges from a **minimum of $1.70** to a **maximum of $3.50**. During **peak hours** (Mon–Fri 5–9:30am and 3–7pm; Fri and Sat midnight–3am), the fare would range from a **minimum of $2.10** to a **maximum of $5.75**. If you are using a paper farecard, simply add $1 to each of those fares, for example, off-peak travel fares would range from $2.70 to $4.50.

For best value, consider buying a $14 **1-Day**, $35 **7-Day**, or $57.50 **28-Day** pass for unlimited travel on Metrorail. You can buy these online, adding the value to the SmarTrip card you're purchasing, or at Passes/Farecards machines in the stations. See Metro's website for details, www.wmata.comfares/purchase/passes.cfm.

Up to two children ages 4 and under can ride free with a paying passenger. Seniors (65 and older) and people with disabilities (with valid proof) ride Metrorail and Metrobus for a reduced fare.

To get to the train platforms, you enter the station through the faregates, touching your SmarTrip card to the SmarTrip logo-marked target on top of the regular faregates or on the inside of the wide faregates. If you're using a paper farecard, you insert your card in the entrance gate, which records the time and location, then spits out your card. Don't forget to snatch it up and keep it handy; *you have to reinsert your paper farecard in the exit gate at your destination,* where the fare will automatically be deducted. The farecard will be returned if there's any value left on it. If you're using a SmarTrip card, you simply touch your card again to the SmarTrip logo-marked target on the faregate at your destination. If you arrive at a destination and your farecard doesn't have enough value, add what's necessary at the Exitfare machines (which only accept cash).

Most Metro stations have more than one exit. To save yourself time and confusion, try to figure out ahead of time which exit gets you closer to where you're going. In this book, I include the specific exit you should use for every venue mentioned, including hotels, restaurants, and attractions.

Metrorail opens at 5am weekdays and 7am Saturday and Sunday, operating until midnight Sunday through Thursday, and until 3am Friday and Saturday. *Note:* Call ✆ **202/637-7000** or visit www.wmata.com for holiday hours and for information on Metro routes.

Washington, D.C., is bringing back the streetcar. An eight-line system covering 37 miles eventually will be in place, transporting people to pockets of the city where the subway and buses don't go. The first line opened in late 2013, connecting Union Station with points along H St., in the Atlas District. This is good news for residents of the neigh-borhood and for locals and visitors interested in checking out H Street's popular restaurants, bars, and live music venues. (See the dining and nightlife chapters for suggestions.) Instead of cabbing it, all you have to do is ride Metro to Union Station, and transfer to the streetcar from there. For more infor-mation, go to www.dcstreetcar.com.

METROBUS

The Transit Authority is in the process of improving its bus system, a comprehensive operation that encompasses 1,500 buses traveling 325 routes, making about 12,000 stops, operating within a 1,500-square-mile area that includes major arteries in D.C. and the Virginia and Maryland suburbs. The system is gradually phasing in the new, sleekly designed, red and silver buses that run on a combination of diesel and electric hybrid fuel.

The Transit Authority is also working to improve design elements and placement of bus stop signs. For now look for red, white, and blue signs that tell you which buses stop at that location. Eventually, signage should tell you the routes and schedules for the buses that stop there. In the meantime, the Transit Authority has inaugurated a cool new alert system to find out when the next bus is due to arrive. You simply call Metro's main number, ② 202/637-7000, and then type in the seven-digit bus stop identifier that's posted on the bus stop sign to find out when the next bus is expected to arrive.

Base fare in the District, using a SmarTrip card, is $1.60, or $3.65 for the faster express buses, which make fewer stops. If you pay with cash, the base fare is $1.80, or $4 for the express bus. There may be additional charges for travel into the Maryland and Virginia suburbs. Bus drivers are not equipped to make change, so if you have not purchased a SmarTrip card (see box) or a pass, be sure to carry exact change.

If you'll be in Washington for a while and plan to use the buses a lot, consider buy-ing a 1-week pass ($16), which must be loaded onto a SmarTrip card (see above).

Most buses operate daily around-the-clock. Service is quite frequent on weekdays, especially during peak hours, and less frequent on weekends and late at night.

Up to two children 4 and under ride free with a paying passenger on Metrobus, and there are reduced fares for seniors (② 202/637-7000) and people with disabilities (② 202/962-1245 or 962-1100; see "Disabled Travelers," later in this chapter, for transit information). If you leave something on a bus, on a train, or in a station, call Lost and Found Tuesday through Friday 11am to 5pm at ② 202/962-1195.

By Car

If you must drive, be aware that traffic is always thick during the week, parking spaces are hard to find, and parking lots are ruinously expensive. You can expect to pay over-night rates of $25 to $50 at hotels, hourly rates starting at $8 at downtown parking lots and garages, and flat rates starting at $20 in the most popular parts of town, like Georgetown and in the Penn Quarter when there is an event at the Verizon Center. If

Meet D.C. fantastic supplemental bus system. It's efficient, inexpensive, and convenient, traveling five circumscribed routes in the city. These red-and-gray busses travel:

o The **Southeast D.C. route** between the Potomac Metro Station and points in Anacostia (weekdays 6am–7pm Oct–Mar, weekdays 6am–9pm and Sat 7am–9pm Apr–Sept)

o **The East-West route** between upper Georgetown and Union Station (7am–9pm daily, with a special service added between upper Georgetown and the intersection of 14th and K sts. NW, from 9pm–midnight Sun–Thurs, 9pm–2am Fri–Sat);

o **A second Georgetown route** that travels between the Rosslyn Metro station in Virginia and the Dupont Circle Metro station in the District, via Georgetown (Sun–Thurs 7am–midnight, Fri–Sat 7am–2am)

o **The Union Station–to–Washington**

Navy Yard track (located near Nationals Park, the service operates 6am–7pm weekdays Oct–March, 6am–9pm weekdays and 7am–9pm Sat Apr–Sept, with extended hours on Nationals game days).

o The route between the Woodley Park–Zoo Metro station and the McPherson Square Metro station (7am–midnight Sun–Thurs; 7am–3:30am Fri–Sat).

Buses stop at designated points on their routes (look for the distinctive red-and-gold sign, often topping a regular Metro bus stop sign) every 10 minutes. The fare at all times is $1, and you can order passes online at www.commuter-direct.com, or pay upon boarding with the exact fare or the use of a SmarTrip Metro card, or with a D.C. Circulator pass purchased at a street meter near the bus stop. For easy and fast transportation in the busiest parts of town, you can't beat it. Call ℂ **202/962-1423** or go to www.dccirculator.com.

you're hoping to snag a parking space on the street, you may or may not be happy to know that the D.C. government makes it as easy as possible for you to pay for that spot: Although the city still has many traditional parking meters that take coins, all 17,000 on-street metered spaces now accept allow you to use your cell phone to pay for parking. Sign up online at www.parkmobile.com to register your license plate number and credit card or debit card number. Once you arrive in D.C. and park on a street that requires payment for parking, you simply call the phone number marked on the meter or nearby kiosk and follow the prompts to enter the location ID marked on the meter and the amount of time you're paying for. Some kiosks allow you to use cash or a credit card to pay for parking time, in which case, you print a receipt and place it against the windshield inside your car, so that it's visible to the officer checking on expired parking coverage.

For a listing of other D.C. stations selling the cheapest gas, access the local AAA website, www.aaamidatlantic.com, and go to the Fuel Price Finder function.

Sections of certain streets in Washington become **one-way** during rush hour: Rock Creek Parkway, Canal Road, and 17th Street NW are three examples. Other streets change the direction of some of their traffic lanes during rush hour. Connecticut Avenue NW is the main one: In the morning, traffic in four of its six lanes travels south to downtown, and in late afternoon/early evening, downtown traffic in four of its six lanes heads north; between the hours of 9am and 3:30pm, traffic in both directions keeps to the normally correct side of the yellow line. Lit-up traffic signs alert you to what's going on, but pay attention. Unless a sign is posted prohibiting it, a right-on-red law is in effect. The **speed limit** within city boundaries is usually 25 mph, up to 30 mph on some streets.

To keep up with street closings and construction information, go online to the *Washington Post's* home page, www.washingtonpost.com, and click on "Local," then "Traffic" to learn about current traffic and routing problems in the District and suburban Maryland and Virginia.

CAR RENTALS

If you need to rent a car while you're here, you have several options.

Residents and tourists alike seem to be turning to car sharing, rather than ownership, for flexible car-use arrangements, whether to cover the needs of an hour or for a month, with parking and other services included. Three such companies exist in D.C. **Zipcar** (www.zipcar.com; ✆ **866/494-7227**) has a downtown D.C. office at 403 8th St. NW, entrance on 8th Street (✆ **202/737-4900**) and **Daimler's Car2Go** has a downtown office at 1710 Rhode Island Ave. NW, Suite 100 (email WashingtonDC@car2go.com). **Hertz 24/7®** (www.hertzondemand.com; ✆ **877/654-4400**) does not have a central office for handling its car sharing operation. All three are rental clubs that require membership signup and driver's license validation before allowing you access to a car. Hertz 24/7® does not charge a membership fee and does allow for more spontaneity in that you can rent a car by going in person to one of Hertz's participating 24/7® locations, of which there are scores in Washington. For further information, visit the individual car rental websites.

Or you can rent a car the usual way from one of the major car rental companies. Car rental rates can vary even more than airfares. Check out **BreezeNet.com**, which offers domestic car-rental discounts with some of the most competitive rates around.

By Taxi

The D.C. taxicab system charges passengers according to time- and distance-based meters. Fares may increase, but at press time, fares began at $3, plus $2.16 per each additional mile, $1 per additional passenger, and 50¢ per piece of luggage that the driver places in the trunk. Other charges might apply (for instance, if you telephone for a cab, rather than hail one in the street). *Note:* The big news about D.C. taxis is that they now accept credit cards. You'll pay an extra fifty cents for the service.

Try **Diamond Cab Company** (✆ **202/387-4011**) or **Yellow Cab** (✆ **202/546-7900**).

For more information, call ✆ **202/645-6018** or check out the D.C. Taxicab Commission's website, www.dctaxi.dc.gov. Also refer to **www.godcgo.com** for a full listing of D.C. cab companies.

By Bike

Thanks to a robust bike-share program (**Capital BikeShare**, www.capitalbikeshare. com, is the nation's largest, with more than 1,500 bikes and close to 200 bike stations), Washington, D.C. is increasingly a city where locals themselves get around by bike. The flat terrain of the National Mall and many neighborhoods make the city conducive to two wheels. Fifty-seven miles of bike lanes throughout D.C., and bike paths through Rock Creek Park, the C&O Canal in Georgetown, and around the National Mall encourage the practice, too. Interested? Visit the www.godcgo.com website and click on the "Bicycling" link for more information and to download a map that shows bike lanes and Capital Bikeshare stations, which are all over, including at the National Mall and in Georgetown. The Capital BikeShare program might be a better option economically for members who use the bikes for short commutes, but be sure to consider that option, along with traditional bike rental companies (p. 158), which are also plentiful.

GUIDED TOURS

D.C. offers a slew of guided tours, from themed jaunts that take you to sites at which famous scandals occurred to Segway tours of Capitol Hill. Beyond the ones in this chapter, will be several listed at the **Cultural Tourism D.C.** website, **www. culturaltourismdc.org** (click on "Things to Do and See" for info on guided options as well self-guided neighborhood heritage walking trails).

On Foot

DC by Foot: These tours are free (though tips are expected)! DC by Foot (www. dcbyfoot.com; ✆ **202/370-1830**) guides like to spin humor with history as they shepherd participants around the National Mall, narrating all the way. History is the emphasis on the popular More Than Just Monuments tour, but other offerings cover such topics as spies and scandals or Lincoln's assassination. Unlike other guided tours, DC by Foot operates year-round, although on a restricted schedule during the winter.

Washington Walks: Excellent guides and dynamite in-depth tours of neighborhoods off the National Mall make Washington Walks (www.washingtonwalks.com; ✆ **202/484-1565**) the guide service most frequently mentioned by reviewers. The "Get Local Saturdays" series of tours is especially popular, traveling to a different locale weekly and revealing surprising facts. Public walks take place April through October; private and group tours are year-round. Tours, usually $15 per person, are free during an annual 10-day event in September known as WalkingtownDC.

DC Metro Food Tours: DC Metro (www.dcmetrofoodtours.com; ✆ **202/683-8847**) conducts participants on 3½-hour-long gastronomic adventures within a particular neighborhood, serving side dishes of historical and cultural references. For example, a Georgetown tour might include a walk along the C&O Canal; a sampling of in-house-made pasta at a decades-old restaurant; tales of the neighborhood's famous residents, like Pres. and Jacqueline Kennedy; finishing with dessert at one of the city's best bakeries. Inquire about pub crawls, which include behind the scenes tours of neighborhoods and stops at 3 to 6 bars. Rates vary by tour, from about $30 to $65 per person.

The Guild of Professional Tour Guides of Washington, D.C.: Would you like your tour conducted in French? How about a tour tailored to your interest in women's history? The Guild (www.washingtondctourguides.com; ✆ **202/966-4935**), which is a membership organization for licensed, professional tour guides and companies, operates a guide-for-hire service on its website. You simply enter your dates, interests, and other details, and individual guides respond to your query. You choose from among the responders, but the price is always the same: $40 per hour for a minimum of 4 hours. These guides are the best of the best, with many members doubling as docents at places like the Capitol Visitor Center.

Spies of Washington Walking Tours (www.spiesofwashingtontour.com; ✆ **703/569-1875**) offers four walking tours that focus on espionage-related sites in Georgetown and around the White House, Pennsylvania Avenue, Capitol Hill, and the

Russian Embassy areas. Carol Bessette, a retired Air Force intelligence officer, conducts the tours, which cost $15 per person. Private tours and bus tours are also available.

Segway Tours (www.dc.citysegwaytours.com; © **877/734-8687**) offers a 3-hour tour year-round daily at 10am and 2pm, with an additional tour at 6pm March to December, as well as a 2-hour version available daily March through December at 11am and 3pm. Though technically they aren't "on foot," Segways are self-propelling scooters that operate based on "dynamic stabilization" technology, which uses your body movements. The 2-hour tours cost $65 per person; the 3-hour tours cost $75 per person. The cost includes training. Ages 16 and up.

By Bus

Martz Gray Line of Washington, D.C. (www.graylinedc.com; © **800/862-1400** or 301/386-8300) operates quite a number of good sightseeing tours. Narrated motor coach tours include an After Dark tour, D.C. in a Day, and D.C. in 2 Days. Most popular are its excursions aboard the red, double-decker, Open Top sightseeing buses, also known as Big Buses (www.bigbustours.com), which provide hop-on/hop-off narrated tours of the sites, in various combinations of time and circuits. The 24 hour Red and Blue "Patriot" tour is the one that takes you around the National Mall and across the Potomac River to Arlington Cemetery; the price is $35 per adult, $20 per child, which reflected a 10 percent discount for online purchase. Gray Line is the only company allowed by the National Park Service to provide interpretive tours of Arlington Cemetery (p. 150). Gray Line also operates an un-narrated express shuttle service between Arlington Cemetery and Union Station, with a few stops en route. See "Express Bus Service Around the National Mall and Memorial Parks," p. 99.

Old Town Trolley tours (www.trolleytours.com; © **888/910-8687** or 202/832-9800) offer fixed-price, on-off narrated service as you travel in three loops around the city, with a transfer point at the Lincoln Memorial stop to go on to Arlington Cemetery, and a second transfer point near Ford's Theatre to get to Georgetown and to Washington National Cathedral. The vehicles are trolleys, not buses; although enclosed and heated in winter, the trolleys in summer open their windows, meaning that most of the trolleys are not air-conditioned. Many hotels sell tickets; otherwise you can purchase tickets online or at the Old Town Trolley Tour booths at Union Station and Georgetown Park (spring and summer only). Trolleys operate daily from 9am to 5:30pm. You can buy tickets online in advance and at a discount ($35.10 for adults, $26.10 for children 4 to 12, free for children 3 and under) and use those e-tickets to board at any of the stops on the route. The full narrated tour takes 2 hours (if you don't get off and tour the sites, obviously), and trolleys come by every 30 minutes or so.

By Boat

Since Washington is a river city, why not see it by boat? Potomac cruises allow sweeping vistas of the monuments and memorials, Georgetown, the Kennedy Center, and other Washington sights. Read the information below carefully, since not all boat cruises offer guided tours. Some of the following boats leave from the Washington waterfront and some from Old Town Alexandria.

Spirit of Washington Cruises, Pier 4 at 6th and Water streets SW (www.spiritof washington.com; © **866/302-2469;** Metro: Waterfront), offers a variety of trips daily, including evening dinner, lunch, brunch, and moonlight dance cruises, as well as a half-day excursion to Mount Vernon and back. Lunch and dinner cruises include DJ entertainment.

The *Spirit of Washington* is a luxury climate-controlled harbor cruise ship with carpeted decks and huge panoramic windows designed for sightseeing. There are three well-stocked bars onboard.

Dandy Restaurant Cruises (www.dandydinnerboat.com; ✆ **703/683-6076**) operates *Nina's Dandy,* a climate-controlled, all-weather, glassed-in floating restaurant that runs year-round. You board the vessel in Old Town Alexandria, at the Prince Street pier, between Duke and King streets. Trips range from a 2½-hour weekday lunch cruise to a 3-hour Saturday dinner cruise.

Odyssey (www.odysseycruises.com; ✆ **866/306-2469**) was designed specifically to glide under the bridges that cross the Potomac. The boat looks like a glass bullet, its wraparound, see-through walls and ceiling allowing for great views. You board the *Odyssey* at the Gangplank Marina, on Washington's waterfront at 6th and Water streets SW (Metro: Waterfront). Cruises available include lunch, Sunday brunch, and dinner excursions, with live entertainment provided during each cruise.

From April through October, the **Potomac Riverboat Company** ★ (www.potomacriverboatco.com; ✆ **877/511-2628** or 703/684-0580) offers several 90-minute round-trip, narrated tours aboard sightseeing vessels that take you past Washington landmarks or along Old Town Alexandria's waterfront; certain cruises also travel to Mount Vernon, where you hop off and re-board after you've toured the estate. You board the boats at the pier behind the Torpedo Factory in Old Town Alexandria at the foot of King Street, or, for the Washington monuments and memorials tour, at Georgetown's Washington Harbour. A concession stand sells light refreshments onboard.

The **Capitol River Cruise's** *Nightingales* (www.capitolrivercruises.com; ✆ **800/405-5511** or 301/460-7447) are historic 65-foot steel riverboats that can accommodate 90 people. The *Nightingales'* narrated jaunts depart Georgetown's Washington Harbour every hour on the hour, from noon to 9pm, April through October (the 9pm outing is offered in summer months only). The 45-minute narrated tour travels past the monuments and memorials to National Airport and back. Bring a picnic or eat from the snack bar. To get here, take the Metro to Foggy Bottom and then walk into Georgetown, following Pennsylvania Avenue, which becomes M Street. Turn left on 31st Street NW and follow to the Washington Harbour complex on the water.

Old Town Trolley also operates **DC Ducks** (www.dcducks.com; ✆ **202/832-9800**), which feature unique land and water tours of Washington aboard the *DUKW,* an amphibious army vehicle (boat with wheels) from World War II that accommodates 30 passengers. Ninety-minute guided tours aboard the open-air canopied craft include a land portion taking in major sights—the Capitol, Lincoln Memorial, Washington Monument, White House, and Smithsonian museums—and a 30-minute Potomac cruise. Purchase tickets online or inside Union Station at the information desk; board the vehicle just outside the main entrance to Union Station. Hours vary, but departures usually follow a daily schedule mid-March through October: 10am to 4pm, every hour on the hour.

By Bike

Bike and Roll/Bike the Sites, Inc. ★ (www.bikethesites.com; ✆ **202/842-2453**) offers a more active way to see Washington, from March to December. The company has designed several different biking tours of the city, including the popular Capital Sites Ride, which takes you past museums, memorials, the White House, the Capitol, and the Supreme Court. The ride takes 3 hours, covers 7 to 8 miles, and costs $40 per adult, $30 per child 12 and under. Bike the Sites provides you with a comfortable mountain bicycle fitted to your size, a bike helmet, a water bottle, a light snack, and two guides to lead the ride. Tours depart from three locations: the rear plaza (12th St. NW side) of the Old Post Office Pavilion, which is located at 1100 Pennsylvania Ave. NW (Metro: Federal Triangle, on the Blue and Orange line); Union Station (© **202/962-0206**); or Old Town Alexandria (© **703/548-7655**). Guides impart historical and anecdotal information as you go. The company rents bikes to those who want to go their own, unnarrated way; rates vary depending on the bike you choose but always include helmet, bike, lock, and pump; there's a 2-hour minimum. Another option: customized guided bike rides to suit your tour specifications.

[FastFACTS] WASHINGTON, D.C.

Area Codes Within the District of Columbia, the area code is 202. In Northern Virginia it's 703, and in D.C.'s Maryland suburbs, the area code is 301. You must use the area code when dialing a phone number, whether it's a local 202, 703, or 301 phone number.

Business Hours Most museums are open daily 10:30am to 5:30pm; some, including several of the Smithsonians, stay open later in spring and summer. Most banks are open from 9am to 3pm Monday through Thursday, with some staying open until 5pm on Friday and some open for business on Saturday mornings. Stores typically open between 9 and 10am and close between 5 and 6pm from Monday to Saturday.

Customs For customs information, consult your nearest U.S. embassy or consulate, or the U.S. Customs website, www.cbp. gov. In Washington, D.C. the U.S. Customs and Border Protection agency has

an office at 1300 Pennsylvania Ave. NW, Washington, DC 20229 (www.cbp.gov; © **877/227-5511**).

Disabled Travelers Although Washington, D.C. is one of the most accessible cities in the world for travelers with disabilities, it is not perfect—especially when it comes to historic buildings, as well as some restaurants and shops. Theaters, museums, and government buildings are generally well equipped. Still, for least hassle call ahead to places you hope to visit to find out specific accessibility features. In the case of restaurants and bars, I'm afraid you'll have to work to pin them down—no one wants to discourage a potential customer. Several sources might help. Destination: D.C.'s website offers some helpful, though hardly comprehensive, information, http://washington. org/DC-information/washington-dc-disability-information, including links to the **Washington Metropolitan Transit Authority,** which

publishes accessibility information on its website, www. wmata.com.

Doctors Most hotels are prepared for medical emergencies and work with local doctors who are able to see ill or injured hotel guests. Also see "Hospitals," below.

Drinking Laws The legal age for purchase and consumption of alcoholic beverages is 21; proof of age is required and often requested at bars, nightclubs, and restaurants, so it's always a good idea to bring ID when you go out. Do not carry open containers of alcohol in your car or any public area that isn't zoned for alcohol consumption. The police can fine you on the spot. Don't even think about driving while intoxicated.

Liquor stores are closed on Sunday. District gourmet grocery stores, mom-and-pop grocery stores, and 7-Eleven convenience stores often sell beer and wine, even on Sunday. Bars and nightclubs serve liquor until 2am Sunday through

Thursday and until 3am Friday and Saturday.

Electricity   Like Canada, the United States uses 110–120 volts AC (60 cycles), compared to 220–240 volts AC (50 cycles) in most of Europe, Australia, and New Zealand. Downward converters that change 220–240 volts to 110–120 volts are difficult to find in the United States, so bring one with you.

Embassies & Consulates   All embassies are located here in the nation's capital. If your country isn't listed below, call for directory information in Washington, D.C. (© 202/555-1212) or check www.embassy.org/embassies.

The embassy of **Australia** is at 1601 Massachusetts Ave. NW, Washington, DC 20036 (www.usa.embassy. gov.au; © 202/797-3000). Consulates are in Honolulu, Houston, Los Angeles, New York, and San Francisco.

The embassy of **Canada** is at 501 Pennsylvania Ave. NW, Washington, DC 20001 (http://can-am.gc.ca/washington/menu.aspx; © 202/682-1740). Other Canadian consulates are in Buffalo, New York; Detroit; Los Angeles; New York; and Seattle.

The embassy of **Ireland** is at 2234 Massachusetts Ave. NW, Washington, DC 20008 (www.embassyofireland.org; © 202/462-3939). Irish consulates are in Boston, Chicago, New York, San Francisco, and other cities. See website for complete listing.

The Embassy of **New Zealand** is at 37 Observatory Circle NW, Washington, DC 20008 (www.nzembassy. com/usa; © 202/328-4800). New Zealand consulates are in Los Angeles, Salt Lake City, San Francisco, and Seattle.

The embassy of the **United Kingdom** is at 3100 Massachusetts Ave. NW, Washington, DC 20008 (www.gov.uk/government/world/usa; © 202/588-6500). Other British consulates are in Atlanta, Boston, Chicago, Cleveland, Houston, Los Angeles, New York, San Francisco, and Seattle.

Emergencies   Call © **911** for police, fire, and medical emergencies. This is a toll-free call. (No coins are required at public telephones.)

If you encounter serious problems, contact the **Travelers Aid Society International** (www.travelersaid. org; © **202/546-1127**), a nationwide, nonprofit, social-service organization geared to helping travelers in difficult straits, from reuniting families separated while traveling, to providing food and/or shelter to people stranded without cash, to offering emotional counseling. Travelers Aid operates help desks at Washington Dulles International Airport (© **703/572-7350**), Ronald Reagan Washington National Airport (© **703/417-3975**), and Union Station (© **202/371-1937**). At Baltimore–Washington International Thurgood Marshall Airport,

a volunteer agency called **Pathfinders** (© **410/859-7826**) mans the customer service desks throughout the airport.

Family Travel   Field trips during the school year and family vacations during the summer keep Washington, D.C. crawling with kids all year long. More than any other city, perhaps, Washington is crammed with historic buildings, arts and science museums, parks, and recreational sites to interest young and old alike. The fact that so many attractions are free is a boon to the family budget.

Look for boxes on family-friendly hotels, restaurants, and attractions in their appropriate chapters.

Hospitals   If you don't require immediate ambulance transportation but still need emergency-room treatment, call one of the following hospitals (and be sure to get directions): Children's Hospital National Medical Center, 111 Michigan Ave. NW (© **202/476-5000**); George Washington University Hospital, 900 23rd St. NW, at Washington Circle (© **202/715-4000**); Georgetown University Medical Center, 3800 Reservoir Rd. NW (© **202/342-2400**); or Howard University Hospital, 2041 Georgia Ave. NW (© **202/865-6100**).

Insurance   As a rule, check your health insurance policies to make sure you're covered should you get sick away from home. If you require additional medical insurance, try Travel Assistance International (© **800/821-2828** or 410/987-6233; www.travel assistanceinternational. com). Also consider buying travel insurance that covers costs incurred due to trip cancellation or interruption. You can get estimates from various providers through **InsureMyTrip.com**, or try one of these recommended insurers: **Travel Guard International** (© **800/826-4919**; www.travelguard. com) or **Access America** (© **800/419-8016**; www. accessamerica.com).

Internet & Wi-Fi   More and more hotels, resorts, airports, cafes, and retailers are going Wi-Fi (wireless fidelity), becoming "hotspots" that offer free Wi-Fi access or charge a small fee for usage. To find public Wi-Fi hotspots in Washington, go to **http:// v4.jiwire.com/search-hotspot-locations.htm**; its Hotspot Finder holds the world's largest directory of public wireless hotspots (1,171 within the city of Washington, last time I checked). Or you could just head to your corner Starbucks, which has offered Wi-Fi service with its lattes for quite some time.

Likewise, all three D.C. airports offer complimentary Wi-Fi.

All of the D.C. hotels listed in chapter 4 offer Internet access, and nearly all of the hotels offer it for free.

Legal Aid   While driving, if you are pulled over for a minor infraction (such as

speeding), never attempt to pay the fine directly to a police officer; this could be construed as attempted bribery, a much more serious crime. Pay fines by mail or directly into the hands of the clerk of the court. If accused of a more serious offense, say and do nothing before consulting a lawyer. In the U.S., the burden is on the state to prove a person's guilt beyond a reasonable doubt, and everyone has the right to remain silent, whether he or she is suspected of a crime or is actually arrested. Once arrested, a person can make one telephone call to a party of his or her choice. The international visitor should call his or her embassy or consulate.

LGBT Travelers   The nation's capital is most welcoming to the gay and lesbian community. In fact, as of March 9, 2010, same-sex couples can now legally marry each other in the nation's capital. Even if you're not planning to get married here, you should know that D.C.'s LGBT population is one of the largest in the country, with 10 percent of residents identifying themselves as such. The capital's annual, week-long Capital Pride celebration is held in June, complete with a street fair and a parade.

Dupont Circle is the unofficial headquarters for gay life, site of the annual 17th Street High Heel Drag race on the Tuesday preceding Halloween, and home to long-established

gay bars and dance clubs (see chapter 8 for some suggestions), but the whole city is pretty much LGBT-friendly.

Mail   At press time, domestic postage rates were 33¢ for a postcard and 46¢ for a letter. For international mail, a first-class letter of up to 1 ounce costs $1.10; a first-class postcard costs the same as a letter. For more information, go to **www.usps.com**.

Medical Requirements   Unless you're arriving from an area known to be suffering from an epidemic (particularly cholera or yellow fever), inoculations or vaccinations are not required for entry into the United States.

Mobile Phones   If you are American and own a **cellphone**, bring your phone with you to D.C., making sure first, of course, that your cellphone service does not charge excessively—or at all—for long-distance calls. In fact, if you are from outside the country and own an international cellphone with service that covers the Washington area, bring that phone along. The point is that hotels often charge outrageous fees for each long-distance or local call you make using the phone in your hotel room.

AT&T, Verizon, Sprint Nextel, and T-Mobile are among the cellphone networks operating in Washington, D.C., so there's a good chance you'll have full and excellent coverage anywhere in the city.

WHAT THINGS COST IN WASHINGTON, D.C.

	US$
Taxi from National Airport to downtown	15.00
Double room, moderate	250.00
Double room, inexpensive	150.00
Three-course dinner for one without wine, moderate	40.00
Glass of wine	8.00
Cup of coffee	2.00
1 gallon regular unleaded gas	4.10
Admission to most museums	Free
1-day Metrorail pass	14.00
Dinner for one, without wine, at Cosmo (moderate)	29.99

International visitors should check their **GSM (Global System for Mobile Communications) wireless network** to see where GSM phones and text messaging work in the U.S.; go to the website www.t-mobile.com/coverage.

In any case, take a look at your wireless company's coverage map on its website before heading out. If you know your phone won't work here, or if you don't have a cellphone, you have several options:

You can **rent** a phone before you leave home from **InTouch USA** (www.intouchusa.us; ✆ **800/872-7626** in the U.S., or 703/222-7161 outside the U.S.).

You can **buy** a phone once you arrive. All three Washington-area airports sell cellphones and SIM cards. Look for the **Airport Wireless** shops at Dulles International Airport (✆ **703/661-0411**), at National Airport (✆ **703/417-3983**), and at BWI Airport (✆ **410/691-0262**).

You can purchase a pay-as-you-go phone from all sorts of places, from Amazon.com to any Verizon Wireless store. In D.C., Verizon has a store at Union Station (✆ **202/682-9475**) and another at 1314 F St. NW (✆ **202/624-0072**), to name just two convenient locations.

Money & Costs If you are traveling to Washington, D.C., from outside the United States, you should consult a currency exchange website such as http://www.xe.com/currency converter/to check up-to-the-minute exchange rates before your departure.

Anyone who travels to the nation's capital expecting bargains is in for a rude awakening, especially when it comes to lodging. Less expensive than New York and London, Washington, D.C.'s daily hotel rate nevertheless reflects the city's popularity as a top destination among U.S. travelers, averaging $204 (according to most recent statistics). D.C.'s restaurant scene is

rather more egalitarian: heavy on the fine, top-dollar establishments, where you can easily spend $100 per person, but with plenty of excellent bistros and small restaurants offering great eats at lower prices. When it comes to attractions, though, the nation's capital has the rest of the world beat, since most of its museums and tourist sites offer free admission.

In Washington, D.C., ATMs are ubiquitous, in locations ranging from the National Gallery of Art's gift shop, to Union Station, to grocery stores. **MasterCard's** (www.mastercard.com; ✆ **800/424-7787**) Maestro and Cirrus, and **Visa's** (www.visa.com; ✆ **800/336-3386**) PLUS networks operate in D.C., as they do across the country. Go to your bank-card's website or call one of your branches to find ATM locations in Washington. Be sure you know your personal identification number (PIN) and daily withdrawal limit before you depart. If your

PIN is five or six digits, you should obtain a four-digit PIN from your local bank before you leave home, since four-digit PINs are what most ATMs in Washington accept.

Note: Many banks impose a fee every time you use a card at another bank's ATM, and that fee is often higher for international transactions (up to $5 or more) than for domestic ones (where they're rarely more than $2).

In addition to debit cards, credit cards are the most widely used form of payment in the United States: **Visa** (Barclaycard in Britain), **MasterCard** (Eurocard in Europe, Access in Britain, Chargex in Canada), **American Express, Diners Club,** and **Discover.** Beware of hidden credit card fees while traveling. Check with your credit or debit card issuer to see what fees, if any, will be charged for overseas transactions. Fees can amount to 3% or more of the purchase price. Check with your bank before departing to avoid any surprise charges on your statement.

Newspapers & Magazines Washington's preeminent newspaper is the *Washington Post,* available online and sold in bookstores, train and subway stations, drugstores, and sidewalk kiosks all over town. These are also the places to buy other newspapers, like the *New York Times,* and *Washingtonian* magazine, the city's popular

monthly full of penetrating features, restaurant reviews, and nightlife calendars. The websites of these publications are: www.washingtonpost.com, www.nytimes.com, and www.washingtonian.com.

Also be sure to pick up a copy of *Washington Flyer* magazine, available free at the airport or online at www.washingtonflyer.com, to find out about airport and airline news and interesting Washington happenings.

Passports Virtually every air traveler entering the U.S. is required to show a passport. All persons, including U.S. citizens, traveling by air between the United States and Canada, Mexico, Central and South America, the Caribbean, and Bermuda are required to present a valid passport. **Note:** U.S. and Canadian citizens entering the U.S. at land and sea ports of entry from within the Western Hemisphere must now also present a passport or other documents compliant with the Western Hemisphere Travel Initiative (WHTI; see www.getyouhome.gov for details). Children 15 and under may continue entering with only a U.S. birth certificate, or other proof of U.S. citizenship.

Police The number of different police agencies in Washington is quite staggering. They include the city's own Metropolitan Police Department, the National Park Service police, the U.S. Capitol

police, the Secret Service, the FBI, and the Metro Transit police. The only thing you need to know is: In an emergency, dial ✆ **911.**

Safety In the years following the September 11, 2001, terrorist attack on the Pentagon, the federal and D.C. governments, along with agencies such as the National Park Service, have continued to work together to increase security, not just at airports, but also around the city, including at government buildings and tourist attractions, and in the subway. The most noticeable and, honestly, most irksome aspect of increased security at tourist attractions can be summed up in three little words: **waiting in line.** Although visitors have always had to queue to enter the Capitol, the Supreme Court, and other federal buildings, now it can take more time to get through because of more intense scrutiny when you finally reach the door.

Besides lines, you will notice the intense amount of security in place around the White House and the Capitol, as well as a profusion of vehicle barriers. A tightly secured underground visitor center at the Capitol, which opened in late 2008, was built in great part to safeguard members of Congress as well as all who work for them. Greater numbers of police and security officers are on duty around and inside government buildings, the monuments, and the Metro.

Just because so many police are around, you shouldn't let your guard down. Washington, like any urban area, has a criminal element, so it's important to stay alert and take normal safety precautions.

Ask your hotel front-desk staff or the city's tourist office if you're in doubt about which neighborhoods are safe. See "The Neighborhoods in Brief," in chapter 2, to get a better idea of where you might feel most comfortable.

Avoid deserted areas, especially at night, and don't go into public parks at night unless there's a concert or a similar occasion that will attract a crowd.

Avoid carrying valuables with you on the street, and don't display expensive cameras or electronic equipment. If you're using a map, consult it inconspicuously—or better yet, try to study it before you leave your room. In general the more you look like a tourist, the more likely someone will try to take advantage of you. If you're walking, pay attention to who is near you as you walk. If you're attending a convention or event where you wear a name tag, remove it before venturing outside. Hold on to your purse, and place your wallet in an inside pocket. In theaters, restaurants, and other public places, keep your possessions in sight. Also remember that hotels are open to the public, and in a large hotel, security may not be able to screen everyone

entering. Always lock your room door.

Senior Travel Members of **AARP,** 601 E St. NW, Washington, DC 20049 (www.aarp.org; 🕽 **888/687-2277**), get discounts on hotels, airfares, and car rentals. AARP offers members a wide range of benefits, including *AARP The Magazine* and a monthly newsletter. Anyone over 50 can join.

With or without AARP membership, seniors often find that discounts are available to them at hotels, so be sure to inquire when you book your reservation.

Venues in Washington that grant discounts to seniors include the Metro; certain theaters, such as the Shakespeare Theatre; and those few museums, like the Phillips Collection, that charge for entry. Each place has its own eligibility rules, including designated "senior" ages: The Shakespeare Theatre's is 60 and over, the Phillips Collection's is 62 and over, and the Metro discounts seniors 65 and over.

Smoking The District is smoke free, meaning that the city bans smoking in restaurants, bars, and other public buildings. Smoking is permitted outdoors, unless otherwise noted.

Taxes The United States has no value-added tax (VAT) or other indirect tax at the national level. Every state, county, and city may levy its own local tax on all purchases, including hotel and restaurant checks, and

airline tickets. These taxes will not appear on price tags. The sales tax on merchandise is 5.75% in the District, 6% in Maryland, and 5.3% in Virginia (6% in Northern Virginia). Restaurant tax is 10% in the District, 6% in Maryland, and varied in Virginia, depending on the city and county. Hotel tax is 14.5% in the District, from 5% to 8% in Maryland, and an average of 9.75% in Virginia.

Telephones Most long-distance and international calls can be dialed directly from any phone. **To make calls within the United States and to Canada,** dial 1 followed by the area code and the seven-digit number. **For other international calls,** dial 011 followed by the country code, the city code, and the number you are calling.

Calls to area codes **800, 888, 877,** and **866** are toll free. However, calls to area codes **700** and **900** (chat lines, bulletin boards, "dating" services, and so on) can be expensive—charges of 95¢ to $3 or more per minute. Some numbers have minimum charges that can run $15 or more.

For **reversed-charge or collect calls,** and for person-to-person calls, dial the number 0 then the area code and number; an operator will come on the line, and you should specify whether you are calling collect, person-to-person, or both. If your operator-assisted call is international, ask for the overseas operator.

For **directory assistance** ("Information"), dial 411 for local numbers and national numbers in the U.S. and Canada. For dedicated long-distance information, dial 1 then the appropriate area code, plus 555-1212.

Time The continental United States is divided into **four time zones:** Eastern Standard Time (EST)—this is Washington, D.C.'s time zone—Central Standard Time (CST), Mountain Standard Time (MST), and Pacific Standard Time (PST). Alaska and Hawaii have their own zones. For example, when it's 9am in Los Angeles (PST), it's 7am in Honolulu (HST),10am in Denver (MST), 11am in Chicago (CST), noon in Washington, D.C. (EST), 5pm in London (GMT), and 2am the next day in Sydney.

Daylight saving time (summer time) is in effect from 1am on the second Sunday in March to 1am on the first Sunday in November, except in Arizona, Hawaii, the U.S. Virgin Islands, and Puerto Rico. Daylight saving time moves the clock 1 hour ahead of standard time.

Tipping In hotels, tip **bellhops** at least $1 per bag ($2–$3 if you have a lot of luggage) and tip the **chamber staff** $1 to $2 per day (more if you've left a big mess for him or her to clean up). Tip the **doorman** or **concierge** only if he or she has provided you with some specific service (for example, calling a cab for you or obtaining difficult-

to-get theater tickets). Tip the **valet-parking attendant** $1 every time you get your car.

In restaurants, bars, and nightclubs, tip **service staff** and **bartenders** 15% to 20% of the check, tip **checkroom attendants** $1 per garment, and tip **valet-parking attendants** $1 per vehicle.

As for other service personnel, tip **cab drivers** 15% of the fare; tip **skycaps** at airports at least $1 per bag ($2–$3 if you have a lot of luggage); and tip **hairdressers** and **barbers** 15% to 20%.

Toilets You won't find public toilets or "restrooms" on the streets of D.C., but they can be found in hotel lobbies, bars, restaurants, museums, and service stations, and at many sightseeing attractions. Starbucks and fast-food restaurants abound in D.C., and these might be your most reliable option. Restaurants and bars in resorts or heavily visited areas may reserve their restrooms for patrons.

Visas The U.S. State Department has a Visa Waiver Program (VWP) allowing citizens of the following countries to enter the United States without a visa for stays of up to 90 days: Andorra, Australia, Austria, Belgium, Brunei, Czech Republic, Denmark, Estonia, Finland, France, Germany, Greece, Hungary, Iceland, Ireland, Italy, Japan, Latvia, Liechtenstein, Lithuania, Luxembourg, Malta, Monaco, the Netherlands,

New Zealand, Norway, Portugal, San Marino, Singapore, Slovakia, Slovenia, South Korea, Spain, Sweden, Switzerland, Taiwan, and the United Kingdom. (**Note:** This list was accurate at press time; for the most up-to-date list of countries in the VWP, consult www. travel.state.gov/visa.) Even though a visa isn't necessary, in an effort to help U.S. officials check travelers against terror watch lists before they arrive at U.S. borders, visitors from VWP countries must register online through the Electronic System for Travel Authorization (ESTA) before boarding a plane or a boat to the U.S. Travelers must complete an electronic application providing basic personal and travel eligibility information. The Department of Homeland Security recommends filling out the form at least 3 days before traveling. Authorizations will be valid for up to 2 years or until the traveler's passport expires, whichever comes first. Currently, there is one $14 fee for the online application. Existing ESTA registrations remain valid through their expiration dates. **Note:** Any passport issued on or after October 26, 2006, by a VWP country must be an e-Passport for VWP travelers to be eligible to enter the U.S. without a visa. Citizens of these nations also need to present a round-trip air or cruise ticket upon arrival. E-Passports contain computer chips capable of storing biometric information, such as the required digital photograph of the holder. If your passport doesn't have this feature, you can still travel without a visa if the valid passport was issued before October 26, 2005, and includes a machine-readable zone; or if the valid passport was issued between October 26, 2005, and October 25, 2006, and includes a digital photograph. For more information, go to www.travel.state.gov/visa. Canadian citizens may enter the United States without visas but will need to show passports and proof of residence.

Citizens of all other countries must have (1) a valid passport that expires at least 6 months later than the scheduled end of their visit to the U.S. and (2) a tourist visa.

For information about U.S. visas, go to **www.travel.state.gov** and click on "Visas."

Visitor Information

Destination D.C. is the official tourism and convention corporation for Washington, D.C., 901 7th St. NW, 4th Floor, Washington, DC 20001-3719 (www.washington.org; ℃ **202/789-7000**). Before you leave home, order (or download) a free copy of the bureau's *Washington, D.C. Visitors Guide*, which covers hotels, restaurants, attractions, shops, and more and is updated twice yearly. Call ℃ **202/789-7000** to speak directly to a staff "visitor services specialist" and

get answers to your specific questions about the city.

Besides using Destination D.C.'s website to obtain a copy of the visitors guide, you can read about the latest travel information, including upcoming exhibits at the museums and anticipated closings of tourist attractions. The website is also a source for maps, which you can download and print from the site or order for delivery by mail.

Once you've arrived, stop by Destination D.C.'s offices on 7th Street NW (Metro: Gallery Place–Chinatown, H St. exit), to pick up the visitors guide and maps, and to talk to visitors services specialists. Office hours are Monday to Friday 8:30am to 5pm.

If you're arriving by plane or train, you can think of your airport or the train station as visitor information centers; all three Washington-area airports and Union Station offer all sorts of visitor services. See "Getting There," earlier in this chapter.

National Park Service information kiosks are located inside or near the Jefferson, Lincoln, FDR, Vietnam Veterans, Korean War, and World War II memorials, and at the Washington Monument (www.nps.gov/nama for National Mall and Memorial Parks sites; ℃ **202/426-6841** or 619-7222).

The **White House Visitor Center,** on the first floor of the Herbert Hoover Building, Department of Commerce, 1450

Pennsylvania Ave. NW (btw. 14th and 15th sts.; ℃ **202/208-1631,** or 202/456-7041 for recorded information), is open daily (except for New Year's Day, Christmas Day, and Thanksgiving) from 7:30am to 4pm.

The **Smithsonian Information Center,** in the Castle, 1000 Jefferson Dr. SW (www.si.edu; ℃ **202/633-1000,** or TTY [text telephone] 633-5285), is open every day but Christmas from 8:30am to 5:30pm; knowledgeable staff answer questions and dispense maps and brochures.

Visit the D.C. government's website, **www.dc.gov,** and that of the nonprofit organization Cultural Tourism D.C., **www.culturaltourismdc.org,** for more information about the city. The latter site in particular provides helpful and interesting background knowledge of D.C.'s historic and cultural landmarks, especially in neighborhoods or parts of neighborhoods not usually visited by tourists.

Check out **www.washingtonpost.com, www.washingtonian.com, www.dcist.com,** and one of my favorite websites, **www.welovedc.com,** for the latest commentary and information about Washington happenings.

Wi-Fi See "Internet & Wi-Fi," earlier in this chapter.